D1259740

Compromise

A Political and Philosophical History

This book offers for the first time a conceptual history of compromise. Alin Fumurescu combines contextual historical analysis of daily parlance and a survey of the usage of the word from the end of the sixteenth century to the beginning of the eighteenth century in both French and English with an analysis of canonical texts in the history of political thought. This work fills a significant gap in the literature about compromise and demonstrates the connection between different understandings of compromise and corresponding differences in understandings of political representation. In addition, Fumurescu addresses two controversial contemporary debates about when compromise is beneficial and when it should be avoided at all costs. A better understanding of the genealogy of compromise offers new venues for rethinking basic assumptions regarding political representation and the relationship between individuals and politics.

Alin Fumurescu is visiting assistant professor in the Department of Political Science at Tulane University.

Compromise

A Political and Philosophical History

ALIN FUMURESCU

Tulane University

CAMBRIDGE
UNIVERSITY PRESS

32 Avenue of the Americas, New York NY 10013-2473, USA

Cambridge University Press is part of the University of Cambridge.

It furthers the University's mission by disseminating knowledge in the pursuit of
education, learning and research at the highest international levels of excellence.

www.cambridge.org
Information on this title: www.cambridge.org/9781107448544

First published 2013
First paperback edition 2014

A catalogue record for this publication is available from the British Library

Library of Congress Cataloguing in Publication data
Fumurescu, Alin, 1967– author.
  Compromise : a political and philosophical history / Alin Fumurescu,
  Tulane University.
     pages   cm
  Includes bibliographical references and index.
  ISBN 978-1-107-02943-9 (hardback)
  1. Political science – Philosophy.   2. Compromise (Ethics)   I. Title.
  JA71.F85   2013
  302.3–dc23   2012021022

ISBN 978-1-107-02943-9 Hardback
ISBN 978-1-107-44854-4 Paperback

Contents

Acknowledgments

For many (too many) years I was convinced that the 'acknowledgments' page found in so many books is merely a polite convention – until I wrote one. It is now clear to me – and, I am convinced, to others as well – that this work would not have been possible absent the support of many who deserve my unconditional gratitude.

It would probably be neater to organize my thanks under different categories – people I have benefited from scholarly, financially, emotionally, and the like. However, it would be a futile enterprise, first and foremost because support does not come in neatly organized packages, each with its own label. As a matter of fact, what makes it so great is precisely its boundless generosity: it is not just provided, it is offered; it is not just the display of a rational calculation (although many times it has to be one as well), it is also a 'habit of the heart.'

Allow me therefore to compromise without compromising. I would like first to thank the members of my doctoral committee at Indiana University, Bloomington: Jeffrey Isaac, Russell Hanson, and William Scheuerman. Without their advice and relentless support there would have been no doctoral dissertation, and thus no book. Aurelian Craiutu has demonstrated over and over again that it is entirely possible to combine criticism with encouragement, and to be a hard-to-please committee chair and a true friend at the same time.

Among many other scholars from whose expertise I have benefited these past years, I am also indebted to Quentin Skinner, Nancy Rosenblum, Nannerl Keohane, and Cary Nederman for comments and suggestions that proved crucial at various stages of this process. I can only hope that their enthusiasm for ideas remains as contagious as I feel it was. Michael Zuckert's help in particular was by far more important that he would care to accept, while the final review of the manuscript during my first year at Tulane University was made possible by the support and – shall I dare to say it? – friendship of Martyn Thompson.

Last but not least, I have to acknowledge the evidence: regardless of all of the above, this work could not have been completed without the unconditional love and patience of my wife, Anca. After all these years, I could not compromise on this point. To her, therefore, I dedicate this book with all my love.

Introduction

"In Politics We Have an Art..."

> Since human beings are not merely political animals but also language-using animals, their behavior is shaped by their ideas. What they do and how they do it depends upon how they see themselves and their world, and this in turn depends upon the concepts through which they see.
>
> Hanna Pitkin

In December 2010, during a press conference, President Barack Obama made headlines declaring that "this country was founded on compromise." In July 2011, he noticed with surprise that "compromise has become a dirty word," despite the fact that "America, after all, has always been a grand experiment in compromise." In 2012, he was echoed, surprisingly for many, by Barbara Bush, during a March conference on First Ladies: "I hate the fact that people think compromise is a dirty word. It is not!" Their words were fiercely debated by pundits and in the blogosphere, yet from a scholarly perspective there was nothing extraordinary in his observation. In the English-speaking world at least, most politicians and theorists would agree that "politics is the art of compromise" and that the Americans are particularly good at it.[1]

In 1957, for example, Francis Biddle, Attorney General during World War II and primary American judge during the Nuremberg trials, wrote: "Of course, it is obvious to any American that our whole national life is built on compromise, and that the great institution, the American Constitution, from which we suck the strength of our public life, is in itself a series of compromises, great and

---

[1] Despite prolonged efforts, I was unable to track down the original author of this widely used saying. The quote is sometimes mistakenly attributed to Bismarck, who is known for saying in effect that "politics is the art of possible." Also, John Morley claimed in his book *On Compromise* that "in politics we have an art..." yet failed to complete the quote. See further.

small...."[2] Decades later, Peter B. Knupferstill agreed: "It has become a truism among political scientists, historians, and informal observers of American political history that compromise is the hallmark of liberal polity." After briefly reviewing the historians and political scientists who have "celebrated the framing and the substance of the American Constitution as a microcosm of American political thought and process ... [p]roceeding from an understanding of compromise based on pluralistic democratic theory," Knupfer goes on to assert: "Federalists not only explained the Constitution's compromises as the product of mutual affections that transcended the advancement of narrow interests, but they also provided future generations of compromisers with a battery of arguments with which to defend similar types of agreements."[3] In support of his thesis, he cites among other Founders the private confession of Nicholas Gilman that the new Constitution "was done by bargain and Compromise,"[4] and Alexander Hamilton's public declaration before the New York ratifying convention: "In our state legislatures, a compromise is frequently necessary between the interests of counties; ... the same must happen, in the general government, between states."[5]

Yet this American devotion to compromise as a central political method has an earlier inspiration – the British. Lord Macaulay ("A life of action, if it is to be useful, must be a life of compromise")[6] and Edmund Burke ("All government, indeed every benefit and enjoyment, every virtue, and every prudent act, is founded on compromise and barter")[7] have probably long been the most quoted politicians on both sides of the Atlantic when it comes to justifying the necessity of compromise in politics.

This apparent agreement remains, however, far from universal. In the United States, some of the most vocal supporters of the Tea Party movement, for example, brag openly about their unwillingness to compromise, while in continental European politics, 'compromise' was and still seems to remain, more often than not, "a dirty word." Decisions that in the English-speaking world would

---

[2] Francis Biddle (1957), "Necessity of Compromise," in *Integrity and Compromise: Problems of Public and Private Conscience*, ed. R.M. MacIver (New York: Harper & Brothers), 1.

[3] Peter B. Knupfer (1991), "The Rhetoric of Conciliation: American Civic Culture and the Federalist Defense of Compromise," *Journal of the Early Republic* 11, no. 3: 315–317.

[4] Gilman to Joseph Gilman, Sept. 18, 1787, in Max Farrand, ed. (1937), *The Records of the Federal Convention of 1787* (New Haven), 111, 82.

[5] Remarks of Alexander Hamilton, New York Convention, June 25, 1788, in Jonathan Elliot, ed. (1888), *The Debates in the Several State Conventions on the Adoption of the Federal Constitution...* (Philadelphia), 11, 318.

[6] Thomas Babington, Lord Macaulay (1833), "War of the Succession in Spain" in *Critical and Historical Essays Contributed to the Edinburgh Review,* 5th ed. (London: Longman, Brown, Green and Longmans), vol. 2, p. 91.

[7] Edmund Burke (1999), "Speech of Edmund Burke, Esq., On Moving His Resolutions for Conciliation with the Colonies" in *Select Works of Edmund Burke*, A New Imprint of the Payne Edition, foreword and biographical note by Francis Canavan (Indianapolis: Liberty Fund), vol. 1, p. 223.

be proudly presented as successful compromises are in Europe repacked and reframed as something totally different.[8]

Obviously, then, 'compromise' is not just another word in the vocabulary of politics. It has been argued "that every political system can be classified ... on the basis of its prevalent attitude toward compromise"[9] or that "democracy and compromise are somehow, perhaps intimately, related to one another."[10] Yet despite its purported centrality to politics the concept draws much less attention from political philosophers than other related ones, such as representation, toleration, election, and the like.[11] In more than a century, barely a dozen of books and articles have more or less seriously dealt with this concept, and they did so mostly from a normatively objective perspective, making the *theme* of political compromise one of the most neglected by political theorists.[12]

---

[8] A recent exception would be the 'financial compact' between the EU states, presented by the Commission President, Jose Manuel Barosso, as an "attempt to compromise" at the European Summit held on December 8–9, 2011. However, even this exception can be seen in a new light, considering the connection between 'compromise,' 'contract,' and 'compact.' See further.

[9] Marvin Rintala (1969), "The Two Faces of Compromise," *Western Political Quarterly* 22, no. 2: 326.

[10] Arthur Kuflik (1979), "Morality and Compromise," in *Compromise in Ethics, Law, and Politics*, ed. J. Roland Pennock and John W. Chapman (New York: New York University Press), 41.

[11] Terence Ball, James Farr, and Russel L. Hanson, eds. (1988), *Political Innovation and Conceptual Change* (Cambridge: Cambridge University Press), ix.

[12] **Books:** John Morley (1906) [1886], *On Compromise* (London: Macmillan and Co.); T.V. Smith (1956), *The Ethics of Compromise and the Art of Containment* (Boston: Starr King Press); R.M. MacIver, ed. (1957), *Integrity and Compromise: Problems of Public and Private Conscience* (New York: Institute for Religious and Social Studies); J. Rolland Pennock and John W. Chapman, eds. (1979), *Compromise in Ethics, Law, and Politics* (New York: New York University Press); Barry Jay Seltser (1984), *The Principles and Practice of Political Compromise: A Case Study of the United State Senate*, vol. 12 (New York and Toronto: Edwin Mellen Press); Martin Benjamin (1990), *Splitting the Difference: Compromise and Integrity in Ethics and Politics* (Lawrence: University Press of Kansas); Patrick J. Dobel (1990), *Compromise and Political Action* (Savage, Md.: Rowman and Littlefield Publishers); Richard Bellamy (1999), *Liberalism and Pluralism: Towards a Politics of Compromise* (London and New York: Routledge); Avishai Margalit (2009), *On Compromise and Rotten Compromises* (Princeton: Princeton University Press); Amy Gutmann and Dennis Thompson (2012), *The Spirit of Compromise: Why Governing Demands It and Campaigning Undermines It* (Princeton and Oxford: Princeton University Press). **Articles:** T.V. Smith (1942), "Compromise: Its Context and Limits," *Ethics: An International Journal of Social, Political, and Legal Philosophy* 53, no. 1; John H. Hallowell (1944), "Compromise as Political Ideal," *Ethics* 54, no. 3; Oliver Martin (1948), "Beyond Compromise," *Ethics* 58, no. 2; John Livingston (1956), "Liberalism, Conservatism, and the Role of Reason," *Western Political Quarterly* 9, no. 3: 641–657; Marvin Rintala (1969), "The Two Faces of Compromise," *Western Political Quarterly* 22, no. 2; Francis Edward Devine (1972), "Hobbes: The Theoretical Basis of Political Compromise," *Polity* 5, no. 1: 57–76; Frank R. Ankersmit (2002), "Representational Democracy: An Aesthetic Approach to Conflict and Compromise," *Common Knowledge* 8, no. 1: 24–46; Avishai Margalit (2005), "Indecent Compromise, Decent Peace," *Tanner Lectures on Human Values*, delivered at Stanford University, May 4–5, 2012; Chiara Lepora, "On Compromise and Being Compromised," *Journal of Political Philosophy* 20, no. 1: 1–22.

However, even within such a scarce literature, a compromise about the proper role of compromise in politics appears impossible. There are several explanations for this lack of agreement. First, the semantic field covered by the concept makes it difficult to manage. 'Bargain,' 'accommodation,' 'trade-off,' 'contract,' even 'consensus' but also 'sellout' are but a few of the accepted meanings of compromise. Second, what makes compromise such a 'boo–hur-ray' concept besides its built-in ambiguity is a difference of visions about what politics is or should be.[13] Evidently, once one embraces the economic picture of politics everything is potentially subject to compromise. If, on the contrary, one embraces a value-laden perspective nothing can ever be compromised.[14] Last but not least, concepts are difficult to fully grasp in the absence of their genealogy – an enterprise never undertaken so far in the case of compromise.

It is precisely this gap that I seek to address with the hope that in the process I might be able to clarify not only where this ambivalent attitude toward com-promise comes from, but also its relationship with other key concepts, such as representation and self-representation. For, as I will try to demonstrate, the willingness or unwillingness to compromise in politics is related not only with particular understandings of political representation but with peculiar repre-sentations of the self as well. These overlooked connections, however uncon-scious, may help illuminate many of the political conundrums, old and new.

If, what, and when a politician is willing to compromise depends not only on her or his understanding of what political representation stands for, but also on her or his representation of the self. Furthermore, it depends on how her or his supporters understand what she or he is representing. The stake could not be higher. The dangers of an uncompromising stance in politics need no exemplifications, but neither does the unqualified embrace of compromise as the political method par excellence. The worrisome loss of trust of citizens in 'their' representatives might be a misstated problem whose roots are to be found in the split genealogy of compromise. The Occupy Wall Street movement and the Tea Party supporters might have more history to share that they would dare to admit.

I.I. THE OPPORTUNITY

Compromise is a word of Roman origin, designating a reciprocal promise (a co-promise) to solve a dispute by abiding by the decision of an impartial third party, a *compromissarius*. It was a verbal contract meant primarily to avoid the hassle of a formalized court of justice, and for this reason it was rather popular especially during the early Middle Ages. It later acquired a second, mostly for-gotten, meaning as a method of election, mainly but not exclusively inside the Church. In both cases, the selected *compromissarius* served as a representative

---

[13] Margalit, "Indecent Compromise."
[14] Ibid., 195.

for the parties or the communities involved. These basic facts are rather well known, at least by specialists. However, the overlooked history of compromise also reveals a dazzling discrepancy between the usages of the word in England compared with continental Europe, notably France, starting with the sixteenth century and lasting all the way to the late eighteenth century. Despite the increased intellectual exchanges of that time, during that period virtually all French authors used 'compromise' in negative contexts with an astonishing consistency, while their English counterparts embraced it as a virtue in a display of consistency turned upside-down. The first British and French dictionaries from the seventeenth century confirm this discrepancy. Even today, after a long process of homogenization, these differences are still discernible, both across the English Channel and across the Atlantic, but at the beginning of the modern period such discrepancies were indeed striking.

Literally tens of British writers, from Heywood and Shakespeare to Swift and Burnet, used 'compromise' in a positive or at least a neutral context – and they did so with remarkable concordance. For them, 'to compromise' meant mainly to bargain, to give and take for the sake of reaching an agreement otherwise impossible. In other words, compromise remained the only alternative to open violence. At that time, even Christ was described as a compromiser because he was a peacemaker, and many authors talked openly about 'the virtues of compromise.' Furthermore, by the beginning of the seventeenth century, the classical sense of arbitration by an impartial third party had started to fade away, being replaced with the sense of mutual agreement between two parties, a contract, a covenant, or a voluntary association of a multitude. I suspect that this assimilation of compromise with contract and covenant explains why the British enthusiasm for compromise coincides with the explosion of contractarian language and the practice of covenant.

Across the Channel, on the contrary, by the second half of the sixteenth century Coquille, Montaigne, and Charron were already concerned about 'compromise' and 'compromising' – a concern shared by later writers as distant in time and style as Corneille, Descartes, and even Rousseau and Guizot. Author after author worried about compromising 'his conscience,' 'his virtue,' 'himself,' and so on. For Frenchmen, 'compromise' was (and has remained) a dangerous word, hence the later distinction between *compromis* (used mainly but not exclusively in a positive context) and *compromission* (marked exclusively by negative connotations).

For now, one can only make note of the obvious and look for an explanation: by the end of the sixteenth century the French had started to be increasingly *méfiants* about compromise, while their British counterparts, far for manifesting such worries, became increasingly enthusiastic about it. Why? How did it come about that the neutral Latin term *compromissum*, initially confined to a particular, delimited meaning, came to signify so many different things – a virtue, a bargain, a contract, a mutual adjustment of otherwise irreconcilable positions, a method of election, but also 'endangerment,' 'jeopardy' or 'putting one's own reputation to hazard'?[15] If linguistic disagreements are also disagreements about our social world, one can hardly find a concept with a more contested meaning, and therefore one more able to shed light on otherwise less obvious disagreements.[16] More often than not, conceptual change signals important political changes when located in particular historical contexts.[17]

If so, such a salient discrepancy between commendable and condemnable compromise presents us not only with a challenge but with a rare opportunity as well. What we have to deal with is a case in which the split in the meaning of an ambiguous concept and the linguistic disagreements that followed can be relatively easily circumscribed (almost pinpointed) both in time (between the end of the sixteenth century and the beginning of the eighteenth) and space: Britain and France.

A methodological clarification is in order. While I am focusing almost exclusively on the French–English differences in the usages of compromise, I also suspect – following Spanish, Italian, and German dictionaries and the general occurrences of compromise in these countries – that the French caution about compromise was typical for the rest of continental Europe as well. However, much more research in this direction is needed before reaching a definitive conclusion.[18]

I.2. THE CHALLENGES

Obviously, this is not an easy enterprise for several reasons. To begin with, a conceptual history of compromise presupposes exploring a remarkably virgin territory. As I will show in the next chapter, until the second half of the nineteenth century there was no substantive effort to seriously consider the ambiguity of compromise and/or its theoretical and practical usefulness for politics, let alone its history. There are therefore no previous bibliographical reference points to guide the enterprise. Second, unlike with other concepts, determining the nature and range of the criteria in virtue of which a word is used is further complicated precisely by its intrinsic commendable or condemnable connotations.[19] To call a particular action or state of affairs a "compromise" means more than to describe it: it also means praising or condemning it.

---

[15] See, e.g., *The Barnhart Dictionary of Etymology* (1988), ed. Robert K. Barnhart.

[16] Quentin Skinner (1988), "Language and Political Change," in Ball, Farr, and Hanson, *Political Innovation*, 11.

[17] See James Farr (1988), "Understanding Conceptual Change Politically," in Ball, Farr, and Hanson, *Political Innovation*, 37.

[18] See the next chapter for further clarification on this English peculiarity.

[19] I am following here the three main requirements of conceptual history, as described by Quentin Skinner in "Language and Political Change."

Such an enterprise requires thus "the comparison of texts to contexts as well as of texts to other texts."[20] The methodological challenge, therefore, most of the time concerns the proper balance between the analysis of everyday language as disclosed in rather obscure or even nonpolitical writings and the more or less conscious usage of certain concepts by authors belonging to the 'canon' of political theory. Both are sides of the same coin. Any societal and political event "in its manifold connections is based on advanced communicative work and on the work of linguistic mediation."[21] If Wittgenstein is right in asserting that concepts are tools and "to understand a concept, it is necessary to know the full range of things that can be done with it,"[22] then a conceptual history should neglect neither everyday utterances of the concept nor its more elaborate usages.[23]

The multitude of labels for such an enterprise – *Begriffgeschichte,* history of ideas, intellectual history, philosophical history of ideas, conceptual history, and so on – indicate, I suspect, a bit of scholarly vanity at work. I find the label of 'conceptual genealogy' not only simple and accurate but also most likely to be met with wide approval from all parties involved in this kind of dispute.[24] I share with the *Begriffgeschichte* school the focus on both the continuities and the shift in the meaning of the concept of compromise, trying to contextualize them, being convinced that precisely because, as Koselleck put it, "social history

[20] Cary J. Nederman (2009), *Lineages of European Political Thought: Explorations along the Medieval/Modern Divide from John of Salisbury to Hegel* (Washington, D.C.: Catholic University of America Press), xxi.

[21] Reinhart Koselleck (2002), *The Practice of Conceptual History*, trans. Todd Samuel Presner et al., foreword by Hayden White (Stanford, Calif.: Stanford University Press), 24.

[22] Melvin Richter (1995), *The History of Political and Social Concepts: A Critical Introduction* (New York and Oxford: Oxford University Press), 133.

[23] To discover the foundations of modern political thought, e.g., Quentin Skinner – emphatically a historian of ideologies (to be distinguished from one 'of ideas') – "tried not to concentrate ... exclusively on the leading theorists, and ha[s] focused instead on the more general social and intellectual matrix out of which these works arose," helping thus "to illuminate some of the connections between political theory and practice." Quentin Skinner (1978), *The Foundations of Modern Political Thought* (Cambridge: Cambridge University Press), x–xi. To properly analyze the meaning of representation, Hanna Pitkin too combined a careful analysis of "the way in which we are ordinarily using words when we are not philosophizing or wondering about their meaning" with "a study in the history of political thought, tracing the treatment of representation by major political theorists." And Pierre Rosanvallon – supporter of a philosophical history of the political – agrees that such history "cannot be limited to the analysis of and commentary of the great works, even though these can often justifiably be considered 'moments' crystallizing the questions that an era poses and the responses that it attempts to these questions." Pierre Rosanvallon (2006), "The Study of Politics in History," in *Democracy Past and Future*, ed. Samuel Moyn (New York: Columbia University Press), 46.

[24] I tend to favor the term 'genealogy' to 'history' for, following Foucault, 'genealogy' suggests a more accidental and less linear development than 'history.' For a similar argument, see J. Peter Euben (1988), "Corruption," in Ball, Farr, and Hanson, *Political Innovation*, 221. This being said, I will not shy from sometimes using the two terms indiscriminately. If more clarification will be required it will be made in due course.

and conceptual history stand in a reciprocal, historical tension that can never be canceled out," their relationship cannot be ignored.[25] Yet I also believe that "the achievements ... of analogous Anglophone work on the philosophy and history of political languages are compatible with *Begriffgeschichte* ... and indeed offer means for coping with some of its inadequacies."[26] As a matter of fact, it might very well be the case that "there is no right way to construct a conceptual history"[27] and "no recipes that can be mechanically applied."[28] The subject at hand and the structure of the argument impose, more or less, the choice between focusing on the "great texts," secondary sources, and historical context.

It is easy to see why, from a methodological perspective, this book makes no great claims to originality. It too combines contextual historical analysis of compromise in daily parlance and an almost quantitative survey of the usage of compromise in both French and English between the end of the sixteenth century and the beginning of the eighteenth, with an analysis of some well-known texts in the history of political thought. Obviously, by 'daily parlance' I understand here the ordinary use of compromise in texts that are focused neither on compromise nor necessarily on its political virtues or lack thereof. But the fact that in one particular context one finds repeatedly the same concept used with the same connotation, even unconsciously, should be enough to indicate that at the conscious level things are no different, both for the individual and for her or his audience. Thanks to the new digitalized libraries, I was able to peruse some hundreds of instances of 'compromise' used in texts during that period, both in English and in French, making use of the ones that I find emblematic not only in terms of common usage, but also in connection with my working hypothesis. While I am not claiming that I have covered every single such instance, I believe that I was able to gather sufficient evidence to prove a radical split in the understanding of compromise on either side of the Channel.

As far as the selection of philosophical texts is concerned, a somewhat different rationale applies. Since I am trying to demonstrate the connection between different usages of compromise and different understandings of self-representation and contractarianism, I choose to focus on the authors who directly addressed these issues from different perspectives. Even so, any selection of this kind will be partially subjective and any thorough treatment of these thinkers, whether Bodin, Hobbes, Hotmann, Locke, Burnet, or Jurieu, is beyond the scope of this enterprise. What I have tried to consider is the hypothesis that despite more obvious similarities and differences, a closer look shows the same divide that holds for compromise also holds on either side of the Channel on issues related to basic underlying assumptions about contractarianism and (self-) representation.

[25] Reinhart Koselleck, *The Practice of Conceptual History*, 23.
[26] Melvin Richter, *The History of Political and Social Concepts*, 5.
[27] Ball, Farr, and Hanson, *Political Innovation*, ix.
[28] Pierre Rosanvallon, "The Study of Politics in History," 76.

Yet in the specific case of this conceptual genealogy, things are further complicated by the span of time required by such an endeavor – from medieval time to early modernity – a period about whose proper interpretation academic debates are still ongoing. On the one hand we have, roughly speaking, the partisans of the 'continuity thesis' (such as J.H. Burns, Brian Tierney, and Francis Oakley), for whom the importance of the unbroken connections between medieval times and early modernity cannot and ought not to be overlooked. On the other hand, we find the supporters of the 'rupture thesis' (among them J.G.A. Pocock, Constantin Fasolt, and Sverre Bagge), for whom the real focus should be on the departures of early modern thinking from the medieval frame of thought.[29] But, however challenging, the choice of the period, although partially subjective, is by no means arbitrary. As the structure of the argument determines the appropriate methodology, it also imposes, at least to a certain extent, the time limits.

The end of the sixteenth century marks the time when the first French negative connotations of compromise arose, but also the years when, as Allen observes, "the lines on which political thought proceeded in the two countries rapidly diverges"[30]; the beginning of the seventeenth century is the time when, in England, compromise came to signify a peaceful agreement that did not necessarily imply the presence of an impartial arbitrator, but also the time when cross-Channel political realities started to differ substantially; as a whole, the entire seventeenth century witnessed in France the raise of administrative centralization and political absolutism, but also in England the final victory of Parliament and the increasing popularity of the social contract theory in different versions; finally, the end of the period, that is, the beginning of the eighteenth century, marks a time when, thanks mainly to the popular translations of Barbeyrac and Burlamaqui, the French became accustomed with a theory of social contract based upon individual wills, but also the time when one can safely assume that a particular representation and self-representation of the French individual was already so deeply embedded in the collective imagination that it could hardly be affected (at least for a long time) by any new 'imports.'

Hopefully, by the conclusion of the book, both the supporters of the continuity between medieval and early modern times and the partisans of the 'rupture thesis' will have been in part vindicated.

1.3. COMPROMISE AND SELF-REPRESENTATION

The tip of the iceberg has a bad reputation. It is deceitful, we are told, since it fails to signal the huge mass of ice underneath the surface of the ocean. Only one-seventh to one-tenth of an iceberg's total mass is above water. Yet in

---

[29] For a survey of the literature surrounding this dispute, see, e.g., Nederman, *Lineages of European Political Thought*, esp. the introduction and part 1.

[30] J.W. Allen (1957), *A History of Political Thought in Sixteenth Century* (London: Methuen), xv.

condemning the tip we tend to forget the most important thing: it might not warn us about the true size or shape of the iceberg, but it does something else – it signals its very existence. It reveals, so to speak, its own concealment. When it comes to political philosophy, the ignored history of compromise might very well be the top of an iceberg: in itself it might not seem much – just another tortuous history among many others that in the past few decades have stirred the interests of political philosophers and historians of ideas. Yet such a perception is as deceitful and revealing as the tip of an iceberg, like which the conceptual history of compromise signals much more – concealed differences in the underlying assumptions we make about individuals and their relationships with the political sphere.

Thus, if not methodological requirements then common sense pushes the research further back. Before even asking why differences in the usages of compromise are there, one must clarify what the common significance was to begin with. Furthermore, one has to move behind the objective consideration of compromise into the subjective realm, regardless of how uncomfortable this move might feel to the scientist. Considering how morally charged are both the sympathy and the antipathy toward compromise, one cannot avoid the elusive question of self-apprehension for the person facing the possibility of compromise. One is willing or not to compromise depending on how one represents oneself and what one thinks is at stake in the process of compromising.

So how did the medieval man apprehend himself and how was he apprehended by his fellows *before* the split in the meaning of the compromise took place? How did he perceive himself before being afraid to compromise or, on the contrary, before he came to embrace it as a virtue? The quest for this medieval man reveals the now forgotten dialectic between *forum internum* and *forum externum*, formalized already at the beginning of the twelfth century, a dialectic that, despite today's oblivion, for more than a thousand years provided the foundation for individualism across the Western world. *Forum internum* was the forum of conscience, authenticity, and freedom, subject to no one and punishable by no one except God. *Forum externum*, on the other hand, was the forum in which the individual identified himself and was identified through belonging to one or several communities, or a combination thereof. Only from this perspective was he liable to judgment and punishment by the community.[31]

I claim therefore that, far from being just a small wheel in a huge mechanism turned by social forces beyond his control, medieval man was more sophisticated than we moderns might care to admit and this sophistication was reflected in his attitude toward compromise. As all the words that we associate today with individuality indicate, he was apprehended and apprehended

---

[31] For more details, see Alin Fumurescu (2011), "Lost in Translation: Centripetal Individualism and the Classical Concept of Descending Representation," *European Journal of Political Theory* 10, no. 2.

himself both as a member of one or more *universitates* and as a distinct and unique individual. He managed, most of the time that is, to strike a balance between his *forum internum* and his *forum externum* – a balance that was reflected in the workings of the entire society.

However, it would be a mistake to consider these two constitutive poles separately without regard for their interdependency. While distinct, they also constitute each other through their very difference. One was an 'I' because one was a member of a larger community. And one could be a member only because one was a unique 'I.' One had an identity because one was identical with everyone else, and one was identical because one had a distinctive identity. Uniqueness was not the exclusive characteristic of the *forum internum*, nor did sameness belong only to the *forum externum*.

Thanks to the Christian Weltanschauung, medieval man saw no problem in handling what appears straightforwardly illogical to his modern descendant. Fully accepting the idea of a God one-in-three, and the idea that Christ was both fully God and fully human, he also accepted that he was both unique and identical to others in both fora. In *forum internum* he was unique in the eyes of God and yet created like everyone else after God's image. In *forum externum* he shared membership in the *universitas* yet remained a unique member fulfilling a unique role. He was at once a public and a private person, belonging yet independent. Thus, since compromise involved only his *forum externum*, he was not afraid to compromise when no other choice was available – for he perceived no direct threat to his *forum internum* – but neither did he embrace compromise as a virtue, political or otherwise. For him, it was just a tool among others.

The split in the usage of compromise on either side of the Channel starting in the second half of the sixteenth century offers new insights into the medieval/modern divide. I claim that during this period we are witnessing an upset of the dialectic of the individual, with long-lasting political consequences. Not accidentally, this period contains some of the most important stepping-stones in the differentiation of French and English representations of the political individual *and* in the usage of 'compromise.' This should come at little surprise considering that the series of crises – religious, intellectual, social, and political – that dominated the period from the end of the sixteenth century all the way through the seventeenth served as a catalyst.

I argue that these challenges were differently addressed in England and France. Faced with the increased pressure toward conformity on his *forum externum*, the French individual tried to compensate by almost obsessively protecting his *forum internum*. If Montaigne and Charron, for example, were afraid of compromising their consciences, it was because they were afraid of compromising their *forum internum*. If this required sacrificing one's *forum externum* for the sake of public peace, so be it. The inner self remained the only 'true self' while *forum externum* was reduced to a mere costume. If *raison d'état* has such good grip on the French psyche, at least one of the causes is to be found in the fact that everyone was able to resonate with the requirements of an abstract and all-encompassing *universitas* – the modern State.[32] The stoicism and skepticism that helped frame this centripetal brand of individualism (which still baffles scholars by its lack of civil involvement) are to be understood in this context. However, the sacrifice was greater than imagined. By trying to preserve the integrity of *forum internum*, the dialectic between the two fora was sacrificed in the process. *Forum externum* became the sole repository of sameness, while *forum internum* remained the protector of authenticity and uniqueness. With this centripetal form of individualism, focused almost exclusively on *forum internum*, the sophisticated interplay of uniqueness and sameness inside and between the two fora was lost and the fear to compromise became something close to an obsession.

On the other hand, in England the same dialectic was affected by a collapse in the distance between the two poles. Many theorists have observed the peculiar English version of atomic individualism, advancing as possible explanations either the prevalence of the common law, the differences between the British version of the 'ancient constitution' and its continental counterparts, the balance of the political forces in the Parliament, and so forth. While I do not deny the impact of such factors, the explanation, I shall argue, is easier to understand once one considers the centrifugal version of individualism due to the effacement of the distinction between the two constitutive fora and their inherent dialectic. The Englishman was the first to enjoy rights, but he enjoyed them at the expense of this dialectic. He became, differently put, one-dimensional. Under these circumstances, contractarianism became the basis of politics and compromise was raised from the status of method to one of principle, as John Morley will observe by the nineteenth century. If he was not afraid to compromise, it was because he had nothing left to be compromised. His self was apprehended mainly if not solely through his *forum externum*. The costume *became* the man.

From this perspective, as I will show, Hobbes becomes a key figure not only in the history of the social contract, but also in several other, interrelated histories: the history of compromise and the development of the centrifugal individualism in which the distance between *forum internum* and *forum externum* was effaced in favor of the latter. In *De cive*, his first claim to fame, Hobbes makes specific references to the two fora, when discussing the obligations raised by the laws of nature in the internal court (*"in Foro interno"*) and in the external court (*"in Foro externo"*) respectively.[33] He will replay almost verbatim the same distinction in chapter 15 of the *Leviathan*, using the Latin labels

---

[32] For the development of the modern state in France, see, e.g., Howell A. Lloyd (1983), *The State, France and the Sixteenth Century* (London: George Allen & Unwin). For the increasing popularity of the concept of *raison d'état* in continental Europe, see Richard Tuck (1993), *Philosophy and Government, 1572–1651* (Cambridge: Cambridge University Press).

[33] Thomas Hobbes (1998) [1647], *De cive/On the Citizen*, ed. and trans. Richard Tuck and Michael Silverthorne (Cambridge: Cambridge University Press), 54.

even in the English version. Revealing for how deeply forgotten this dialectic of the individual remains nowadays is the fact that, following in the footsteps of Carl Schmitt, contemporary scholars still credit Hobbes with the 'invention' of the two fora, while in effect, with Hobbes, this dialectic was about to be irremediably affected and in the end forgotten.[34] As David Runciman observes, the main aim of Hobbes's political writings was to make *forum internum* irrelevant, "to reconfigure how people understand the language of 'conscience,' so that they might come to accept that conscientious action simply means acting in accordance with the will of the sovereign."[35]

As I will argue, if Hobbes's contract theory can be – and was – understood as a generalized compromise meant to *create* a political society it is because at that time, as in the classical period, compromise came once again to be apprehended as a contract, only now one of a peculiar kind. I suspect that this is not mere coincidence if the embrace of compromise as virtue coincides with the widespread popularity of different versions of contract theory – a popularity that bewildered even its contemporaries – for it was able to overcome most if not all rational criticisms. For the first time, the authority of the arbitrator, the *compromissarius*, was undisputable since it was the very result of compromise. One would no longer *accept* or *select* an arbitrator; one would *create* one. In turn, the very existence of a *compromissarius* ensured the existence of the willingly created *ab nihilo* political society. The fact that several Englishmen, including Gilbert Burnet, a contemporary of Locke, explicitly used 'compromise' as the equivalent of 'covenant,' 'contract,' and even 'social contract' proves that, at that time, the two concepts were interchangeable.

Yet the most important political event of the seventeenth century, the Glorious Revolution, also bears undisputable witness to the newly acquired centrality of compromise for British political life. Many scholars from various perspectives have discussed the revolution of 1689 as a compromise. Some have pointed toward William's intentionally ambiguous *Declaration of Reasons* (of which Gilbert Burnet was at least partially the author), meant to find a compromise between Whigs and Tories; others emphasized that all parties agreed to put aside ideological differences in search of a practical compromise. The Bill of Rights was considered a compromise, and even the entire outcome was defined as 'the compromise of 1689.'[36] At various levels, these scholars are

---

[34] Carl Schmitt (1996), *The Leviathan in the State Theory of Thomas Hobbes – Meaning and Failure of a Political Symbol*, foreword and introduction by George Schwab, trans. George Schwab and Erna Hilfstein (Westport: Greenwood Press), especially ch. 5. For a recent emphasis of Hobbes's "innovation," see David Ragazzoni (2011), "Identity vs. Representation: What Makes 'the People'? Rethinking Democratic Citizenship through (and Beyond) Carl Schmitt and Hans Kelsen," *Perspectives on Federalism* 3, no. 2.

[35] David Runciman (2008), *Political Hypocrisy: The Mask of Power, from Hobbes to Orwell and Beyond* (Princeton and Oxford: Princeton University Press), 22.

[36] For a sample of the body of literature on compromise and the Glorious Revolution, refer to Chapter 6, esp. "The Revolution of Compromise." For the Bill of Rights as compromise and for

undoubtedly right, yet they are even more correct than they would care to admit. The Glorious Revolution was the proof that in politics even seemingly abstract ideas find ways of materializing and/or institutionalizing themselves.

At that time, many perceived this political compromise, understood as mutual contract, as the only way of avoiding open violence and civil war. There was no party placed in a clearly superior position, and (what is even more important) all traditional legitimacy had been called into question. Therefore, the only rational solution out of this conundrum was to create a new form of legitimacy – not only through voluntary consent upon a *compromissarius*, but also through the creation of such an arbitrator by a delegation of individual rights.

1.4. COMPROMISE AND POLITICAL REPRESENTATION

Throughout most of the last century at least, the tendency of political philosophers has been to concentrate on the meaning of political representation rather than its justification.... What these discussions have lacked, however, is an attempt to pose questions about the philosophical foundations of political representation, that is, to defend or attack the conceptual underpinnings of the idea of representative government. At the dawn of the twenty-first century, however, the situation has changed noticeably. Among contemporary democratic theorists, a debate has simmered.... Recent efforts to evaluate political representation have remained largely ahistorical in bearing, however.[37]

It is precisely this lack of historical contextualization that I shall try to address. Since compromise and representation were, from the very beginning, so tightly connected, for accepting a *compromissarius* meant accepting a representative, the genealogy of the former can illuminate the latter. If for the medieval man's compromise involved only one's *forum externum*, it was because one could have been represented only insofar as one's *forum externum* was concerned. One's *forum internum* was off limits. Thus, no one could have been represented without a rest. If one was, say, a king or a pope sending representatives (ambassadors), one did so in one's public capacity as occupant of the office. If, on the contrary, one was a yeoman, one was represented exclusively as member of the *universitas* one belonged to – as a member of the Church, of a certain guild, village, or of the people – and therefore representation involved once more only one's *forum externum*. *Forum internum* could never be represented, nor compromised, and therefore the uniqueness of each individual was safe. In all cases, as I shall demonstrate, the representative was always of a lower status than the represented, so naturally representation preserved its descending character.

"the compromise of 1689," see Denis Baranger (1999), *Parlamentarisme des origines – Essai sur les conditions de formation d'un exécutive responsable en Angleterre (des années 1740 au début de l'âge victorien)* (Presses Universitaires de France), especially the introduction and ch. 1.

[37] Nederman, *Lineages of European Political Thought*, 119–120.

Thus, absent this dialectic of *self*-representation one cannot properly grasp another overlooked distinction, namely the one between *descending* and *ascending* political *representation*. Considering the amount of recent scholarship on the problem of representation one is surprised by two things: on the one hand, by how the distinction between ascending and descending representation has been misconstrued; on the other, by how the scholarly shaming finger points either toward the representatives or the process itself, but almost never toward us, the representees, namely toward how we represent ourselves. Because of the widespread understanding of representation as ascending, when it comes to the problems of political representation we, the representees, appear to enjoy a free ride.

Following in the footsteps of Walter Ullmann, most of the authors in the past decades who have seriously considered the challenges posed by the idea of political representation (from Hanna Pitkin to Edward S. Morgan and F.R. Ankersmit to Nadia Urbinatti) have taken it as a matter of fact: once the descending theory of representation was discarded altogether with the divine rights of kings, it was replaced once and for all by its long-time competitor, the ascending version – the representation of the people.[38]

Even early critics of Ullmann's distinction, such as Francis Oakley, misdirected their attacks. Oakley argues that the ascending/descending framework proposed by Ullmann does not sustain close scrutiny.[39] And yet if Oakley's criticism scores some excellent points, he too fails to observe the evidence: only the representation of people qua individuals properly qualifies as the ascending theory of representation, and this radically new understanding appears only in England by the second half of the sixteenth century. Among other consequences, here, for the first time, the individual felt that he could have been represented without a rest.

---

[38] In fact, rather than preceding the contractualist theory, the theory of the divine right of kings is better understood as a reaction to the latter, as Gordon Schochet has persuasively argued: Gordon J. Schochet (1975), *Patriarchalism in Political Thought: The Authoritarian Family and Political Speculation and Attitudes Especially in Seventeenth-Century England* (New York: Basic Books). For a somewhat different perspective, but one that argues also in favor of the modernity of this theory, see Daniel Engster (2001), *Divine Sovereignty: The Origins of Modern State Power* (Dekalb: Northern Illinois University Press). For the ascending versus descending theories of representation see, e.g., Walter Ullmann (1966), *The Individual and Society in the Middle Ages* (Baltimore: Johns Hopkins University Press); Hanna Fenichel Pitkin (1967), *The Concept of Representation* (Berkeley and Los Angeles: University of California Press); Edmund S. Morgan (1988), *Inventing the People: The Rise of Popular Sovereignty in England and America* (New York: W.W. Norton); F.R. Ankersmit (1996), *Aesthetic Politics: Political Philosophy Beyond Fact and Value* (Stanford, Calif.: Stanford University Press); Nadia Urbinati (2006), *Representative Democracy: Principles and Genealogy* (Chicago: University of Chicago Press); Philip Petit (2008), *Made with Words: Hobbes on Language, Mind, and Politics* (Princeton and Oxford: Princeton University Press); Jane Mansbridge (2003), "Rethinking Representation," *American Political Science Review* 97, no. 4: 515–528. Obviously, this list is far from exhaustive.

[39] Francis Oakley (1973), "Celestial Hierarchies Revisited: Walter Ullmann's Vision of Medieval Politics," *Past and Present* 60: 3–48.

On continental Europe and especially in France the representation of people was understood for a longer period in the classical sense as descending (sometimes circular, as I will show) representation. To consider such "populist" theories of representation ascending, as both Ullmann and Oakley do, is a serious misapprehension. The whole, be it the body of the Church or the body of the people (or any type of *universitas* for that matter), was always apprehended as above its parts, including its head – pope, emperor, or king. Thus, whenever we encounter in medieval or early modern writings mentions of 'the people' one must carefully consider what kind of people they are referring to: people understood as a collection of individuals or people understood as a conceptual, organic whole, that is, a *universitas*. In the second case, all the "populist" theories of representation remain in effect descending ones.

The distinction and its importance were seized upon even by seventeenth century Englishmen. It is no mere accident that a Tory, Roger L'Estrange, pinpointed them in a 1683 dialogue between the Observator (a Tory) and the Trimmer (a Whig). Unlike the descending, corporatist understanding of the people, the ascending, individualistic one is prone to favor compromise, to be "couched in a trimming, middling way" for individual wills take over the public good and, as we shall see, political representatives become professional *compromissores*.

The people are the nation; and the nation is the people: *but do we speak of the multitude, or of the community?* If of the community, why do ye not rather call it the government? If of the multitude; they have no right of acting, judging, or interposing otherwise than in obedience and submission to the rules of order and society. So that your telling of people that they may do this or that; is the same thing with telling them, that if they don't like their laws and their governors, they may provide better, and shift for themselves: now here's sedition, not only licensed, but encouraged; for being couched in this trimming, middling way; it speaks plain English to the rabble; though the law will scare lay hold on it. 'Tis the very *Veni, Vidi, Vici* of the cause; first, that the people are the source of power. Secondly, that upon maladministration they may recall their power. And thirdly, to tell 'em, gentlemen, you are most damnably abused, up and be doing. To pass over your engrossing the intent of people and nation, to yourselves; as if all the royalists and conformists were no more than vagabonds and outlaws.[40]

Considering this early awareness of what it is at stake, it is surprising to see that even the most recent studies to have acknowledged the crucial importance of corporatist thinking for the understanding of representation in medieval and early modern times fail to capture this rather obvious distinction and its consequences. Nederman, for example, who talks at length about the distinctive corporatist understanding of representation, has nothing to say about its descending character and what it means for the individual. The ascending theory, while empowering the individual, making him the source of any political

---

40 Robert L'Estrange (February 10, 1683), *Observator in Dialogue*, quoted in Steven C.A. Pincus (2006), *England's Glorious Revolution, 1688–1689: A Brief History with Documents* (New York: Palgrave Macmillan), 143.

power, also has a major drawback. As some scholars have observed, the individual acquires rights only to hand them over to his representatives, and even more disturbing, in the process he loses the uniqueness that he formally cherishes so much. By being equally represented with many other fellow-citizens, he becomes more of a number. Furthermore, if political societies are based upon voluntary contracts and these contracts are assimilated with compromises, there is little wonder that compromise will come to be embraced as a virtue.

In his more recent writings Skinner sees Hobbes as a particular turning point between corporatism and individualism. On the one hand, he argues, Hobbes opposed the classical, descending, and corporatist understanding of representation, as exemplified, for example, by Henry Parker. "Any king, as Parker had declared, 'though he be *singulis Major*, yet he is *universis minor*,' always lesser in standing than the *universitas* or 'politique corporation' from which his rights and powers are derived."[41] Yet in the *Leviathan*, Hobbes explicitly scorns such position, arguing that there is no such thing as a body of people awaiting representation. On the other hand, despite his individualistic premises, Hobbes (unlike other individualists) was not ready to entirely abolish the idea of a corporation. His answer, 'an epoch-making' one, as Skinner put it, was to conceive of the corporation as the end of a covenant (a contract or a compromise, as I will try to demonstrate) between otherwise independent and equal individuals. The state, or Leviathan, is such an artificially created corporation. Yet, as I will argue in Chapter 8, the difference between the two corporatist theories becomes significant once one takes into consideration the difference between, on the one hand, the ascending and descending views of representation, and on the other hand, the classical assumption of an internal dialectic of the individual versus the modern presupposition of a one-dimensional man.

David Runciman holds a somewhat similar position, yet he acknowledges that "Hobbes is not entirely consistent here, and this reading, which emphasizes the corporate character of representation in Leviathan, is hard to square with some other passages, where he suggests that representation is indeed the representation of the sovereign's individual subjects."[42] Thus, the contemporary problem for any democratic theory of representation is "to strike a balance between the need to give the state a collective identity and the wish to avoid giving the state priority over the judgment of the individuals."[43] While the space

[41] Quentin Skinner (2007) "Hobbes on Persons, Authors and Representatives," in *The Cambridge Companion to Hobbes's Leviathan*, ed. Patricia Springborg (Cambridge: Cambridge University Press), 164. Skinner quotes Henry Parker (1642), *Observations upon some of his Majesties late Answers and Expresses* (London), 1, 2.

[42] David Runciman (2009), "Hobbes's Theory of Representation: Anti-democratic or Proto-democratic?" in *Political Representation*, ed. Ian Shapiro et al. (Cambridge: Cambridge University Press), 20. See also David Runciman (1997), *Pluralism and the Personality of the State* (Cambridge: Cambridge University Press), or David Runciman (2000), "What Kind of Person Is Hobbes's State? A Reply to Skinner," *Journal of Political Philosophy* 8: 268–278.

[43] Runciman, "Hobbes's Theory of Representation."

of this introduction does not allow for a full discussion of Runciman's solution, I hope that the genealogy of compromise that I am about to present will help clarify some of the problems that Skinner and Runciman skillfully raise.

Two more caveats are in order here. First, more often than not the differences in the usages of compromise, the understandings of representation, or recourse to the idea of the two fora were rather unconscious. Yet, as suggested before, "[i]n many cases the most revealing are semi-conscious or even altogether unwitting utterances that disclose habits of formulation shared in a particular milieu at a particular moment."[44] Secondly, it goes almost without saying that the perspective that I argue for is rather overstated for explanatory purposes. Obviously, for a long period of time, languages remained mixed and competing, both when one considers the similarities and the differences between medieval and modern times and within each of the two countries. Even when one understanding decisively won the confrontation with another, the loser did not vanish overnight. The fact that, for example, individual contractariansim took an undisputable firm grip on the British psyche by the seventeenth century did not prevent more classical understandings of the origins of governmental authority to linger.

I.5. THE STRUCTURE OF THE ARGUMENT

Since this work primarily centers on the rediscovery of the forgotten genealogy of compromise, it seems natural to start digging from the contemporary surface of confused and confusing understandings and keep going down through history. Thus, the next chapter starts from the same place where this personal inquiry did, namely with the question of where disagreement about the usefulness of compromise in politics comes from. To find an answer I will review the literature pertaining more or less directly to the theme of political compromise, beginning at the end of the nineteenth century, when John Morley published his undeservedly forgotten book *On Compromise*, and continuing to the most recent arguments, at the turn of the twenty-first century, except for the discussion of Avishai Margalit's work, which will be postponed until the concluding chapter. For most other political concepts of interest for theorists this would have been an almost impossible task due to the amount of scholarly literature – but not for compromise.

As mentioned in the beginning of this introduction, the literature on compromise is (surprisingly and revealingly) scarce. It is surprising, given the centrality of the concept for Anglo-American politics. But the lack of interest is also revealing for what is perceived by the majority as an undisputable concept. Why spend too much time discussing the meaning and the utility of compromise in politics when there is so little disagreement about both? If there is

---

44 Dror Wahrman (1995), *Imagining the Middle Class: The Political Representation of Class in Britain, c. 1780–1840* (Cambridge: Cambridge University Press), 15.

still some debate about compromise, it is due mainly to the effort to protect its positive meaning from pejorative continental importations. Although it is difficult to pinpoint the precise moment when both the commendable and the condemnable meanings became familiar to the greater public on both sides of the English Channel, based on the evidence I was able to gather so far it is safe to assume that it happened some time before the end of the eighteenth century. Since then, a handful of Anglo-American theorists have struggled to safeguard the first meaning while somehow taking the second into account as well, both on a theoretical and a more practical level.

Schematically, except for the scholars who simply deny the negative connotations of compromise altogether by severing the political aspect from the moral, the most common answers to this challenge can be divided among (a) those who make a distinction between compromising interests and compromising principles (thus suggesting a gap between the theory and the practice of compromise), and (b) those who, along with their praise of compromise, agree that its beneficial role can properly work only within certain limits. Unfortunately, both strategies appear easier to proclaim than to defend. To distinguish between interests and principles proves an almost impossible endeavor, since a question as 'practical' as dividing a budget between defense and education can be framed either in terms of interests or in terms of principles. And at least as difficult are several attempts to impose artificial limits on the domains on which compromise is not only acceptable, but beneficial as well. The final part of the chapter discusses the works of the few authors to have realized that the special popularity enjoyed by compromise in the English-speaking world is rather a peculiarity and who have tried to offer some explanations. Obviously, such attempts can hardly go too far in the absence of a conceptual history of compromise.

The aim of Chapter 3 is precisely to provide this missing history. The line of argumentation presented above is expanded and backed by a substantial body of evidence gathered from Roman and medieval times, when compromise was understood as verbal contract, both as *arbitratio* and *electio*, followed by exemplification of the split in the usage of compromise in France and England. Using dozens of examples from each side, it shows how consistent the positive usage of compromise in England was at that time, and how sharply it contrasts with the negative context in which compromise was placed in French writings from the end of sixteenth century until the beginning of the nineteenth. While this material has been gathered from a wide variety of sources ranging from well-known to rather obscure figures of the time, representing an entirely original enterprise, the same cannot be said about the historical background against which the two opposite usages of compromise appeared on the two sides of the Channel.

However, before focusing on early modern France and England, the quest for an explanation starts in medieval times, with a chapter dedicated to the explanation of the dialectic of the individual between *forum internum* and *forum externum.* The chapter analyzes the ambivalence brought forward by Christianity in the understanding of individualism and indicates the moment when the distinction between the two fora was formally accepted as a matter of fact by the Church, at the beginning of the twelfth century. It shows how this dialectic was at work inside the Church, where the debate between the partisans of the preeminence of the *forum internum* and the supporters of the *forum externum* culminated yet did not end with the Reformation, but also how powerfully the same dialectic was echoed in the political realm. The end of Chapter 4 points out the ways in which the interplay between *forum internum* and *forum externum* directly relates to the descending directionality of representation, involving exclusively just one side of the individual, namely his *forum externum*, and how this understanding relates to the attitude toward compromise.

The next two chapters take a closer look at the historical particularities – political, social, and institutional – of France and England, respectively, during the sixteenth and seventeenth centuries in order to find an explanation for the divergent trajectories in the understanding of the individual suggested by the different usages of compromise. The purpose of this book not being to rewrite from scratch the history of the two countries, I rely here heavily on historians and historians of ideas in order to discover how these historical changes affected the use of language and how they were in turn affected by it – how they 'legitimate' each other. At this point, the personal contribution is mainly restricted to putting together the scrambled pieces of the puzzle. The aim is to show that, despite appearing counterintuitive for some, the conceptual history of compromise that I argue for is backed up by (and helps illuminate in turn) a multitude of other, much better known 'histories.'

What I am trying to bring new in this dialogue of intertwined histories is a different perspective and, as a result, a different emphasis. Most authors writing about seventeenth century France and England focused on one or the other, and the ones that dealt with both did so on the assumption that the intellectual exchange between the two was little affected by differences in political realities. Without trying to downplay the continuous dialogue that went on across the Channel, the strikingly different usages of compromise require not just an explanation but also a switch in emphasis that points toward much different assumptions than we have cared so far to admit. Much like the relationship between the two fora, the histories of France and England are better understood as opposite yet interrelated. Chapter 5 analyzes the development of centripetal individualism in France and its consequences, not only from a theoretical but also from a practical, institutional perspective. It shows how the emergence of the state as another conceptual community, that is, *universitas*, offers an overview of both the theoretical claims and the practices of the French institutions claiming to represent the people. It explains why under those circumstances compromise was not an option, either theoretically or practically. Chapter 6 does the same for the emergence of the British version of centrifugal individualism, pointing out not only the unique centrality of the British Parliament, but also the explosion of contractualist parlance, the practice of oaths of allegiances, and the increased electoral franchise, followed by disputed elections. Under these circumstances, it is no surprise that compromise became so central to British politics, not only in theory but in practice as well.

The next two chapters turn once again to the theoretical aspects, dealing with the most elaborate and most self-conscious theories of the time involving the self-apprehension of the individual and his political representation, namely contractarian theories in France and England respectively. While this time the focus will be mostly though not exclusively on some well-known texts from the time dealing with this topic, the intention is not to provide yet another exhaustive account of this impressive body of literature but to check a hypothesis. The premises are straightforward: (a) if the proposed account of the conceptual history of compromise is correct, then the French contract theories should differ from their English counterparts at least in one important respect – the political role reserved to the individual; (b) if these different understandings of the 'political individual' were at that time as widespread as the different usage of compromise seems to indicate, then they ought to be identifiable not only in the works of authors supporting various versions of contract, but also in the works of their opponents. Therefore, the survey of the literature in both countries is a sectional one, checking whether this particular aspect is shared by both the partisans of the contract theory and by their opponents. It is, with astonishing consistency.

Chapter 7 challenges the underlying common assumption of an ideal contract theory against which all versions are measured as more or less 'evolved' and argues for two distinctive lines of evolution. Although similar in outlook, contract theories in France and England differ in their basic assumptions about what political representation stands for and the relationship between individuals and the political sphere. Not only the French versions of contractarianism, whether of Protestant or Catholic origin, from the sixteenth and seventeenth centuries, but also other continental versions (those of Alhusius, Pufendorf, Grotius, and Spinoza) display the same communitarian outlook. They remain first and foremost 'contracts of reason,' not 'contracts of will.'

Chapter 8 demonstrates the British assimilation of the social contract with compromise. The impact of contractarianism, I will argue, was so great at the time that even rival theories, such as patriarchalism and republicanism, could not avoid taking it into consideration. The well-known theories of Hobbes and Locke are interpreted from this perspective. The aim is to show that the interpretation of Hobbes's contract as a compromise meant to create the authority of an arbitrator able and enabled to solve all political disputes is not very different in essence from Locke's version. Despite their obvious differences, they both start from individual wills in order to create both civil society and government. That this assimilation of contract with a generalized compromise is more than a mere speculation is proven, among others, by the work of Gilbert Burnet who, apparently following Locke, explicitly stated: "the true and original notion of civil society and government is that is a compromise." Such a 'contract of wills' creates, among other unintended consequences, the dependency of civil society on the political sphere. While supposedly the first creates the latter, it also depends for its very survival on its creation.

1.6. PRELIMINARY CONCLUSIONS

Where do these findings lead us? More will be said in the concluding chapter. For now, though, let us make some preliminary remarks. While this genealogy is today largely forgotten, it does not follow that it lost entirely its ability to influence our contemporary outlook on political compromise and, therefore, both politicians' willingness to compromise and the willingness of their supporters to accept and eventually praise it. Quite the opposite: in many respects, the fact that we are unaware of this genealogy makes compromise's influence even more persuasive. When it comes to haunting, dead histories can be more effective than the living ones.

Obviously, this oblivion will subject the attitude toward compromise to other factors, completely independent of its origins, first and foremost to how it resonates with the electoral body. Today, no one thinks about compromise in terms of arbitration, election, or contract. Yet a couple of underlying features remain surprisingly constant across time. First, one is still willing to compromise in politics if and only if one considers the other party as equal, at least as far as the disputed matter is concerned. Second, one refuses to do so if the compromise is perceived as potentially threatening one's uniqueness, that is, identity, or the identity of the group one is supposed to represent.

For example, if Barbara Bush was shocked by the unwillingness of the contenders in the Republican primaries to compromise, it was because she perceived them all as first and foremost Republicans. Under these circumstances, to refuse to compromise for the benefit of the party is unacceptable. From the contenders' point of view, however, things looked differently. They all struggled to differentiate themselves 'from the pack.' Thus, to compromise was threatening for their identities. Furthermore, to compromise for a candidate such as Rick Santorum, standing tall for socially conservative values, would have meant to threaten not only his own authenticity but also the identity of the entire group that he felt he represented – the Christian Evangelical.

An excellent exemplification of the stubborn survival of these old lessons is to be found in the American Founding. We have already seen that the short answer to President Obama's question, "Since when has compromise become a dirty word?" is, at least as France is concerned, "since the second half of the sixteenth century." But when it comes specifically to American politics, the answer could be "at least to a certain extent, from the very beginning." Thanks to its peculiar history, the American case offers an early opportunity to survey the intertwining – and sometimes the clashing – of the British and French understandings of compromise, contractarianism, and representation. But this will have to be the subject of a different book.

Thus, the modern ambiguity 'enjoyed' today by political compromise, not only on the part of political theorists or politicians, but above all on the citizenry at large can be disambiguated at least to a certain extent. As I will exemplify in the concluding chapter with plenty of concrete examples, most if not all of the disputes surrounding 'necessary' or 'wicked' compromise may be solved once one takes into consideration several key factors: (1) Are the parties involved in the compromise equal, and, if 'yes,' from what perspective? (2) Does the compromise threaten the identity of one of the parties? (3) What is the (self-) perceived defining *universitas* for each of the parties as far as their *forum externum* is concerned? Using this analysis on a handful of cases I shall argue that the main mistake in trying to decide if a political compromise is suitable or damaging is the use of an exclusively external, objective perspective. Game theorists and ethicists alike use this approach, trying to judge each case of political compromise from a third-party perspective, the first by denying any personal involvement, the others by considering this involvement exclusively from an 'objective' ethical point of view, disregarding its subjective, moral dimension.[45] In other words, they have tried to duplicate the position of the *compromissarius*.

One cannot but observe the irony at work here: the parties involved in a classical compromise were in search of a trustworthy – because objective – third party; their modern descendants thought they solved the problem once and for all by artificially creating one; and contemporary theorists try to judge compromise yet again from a pretended impartial perspective. Obviously, according to the classical meaning of compromise this is a futile attempt. The parties are the ones who have to agree on what is at stake in a compromise, not some objective observer who fails to take into consideration the involvement of the two fora. A political compromise involves first and foremost the perceived and self-perceived identity of the politician qua person and qua representative of some *universitas*. Without restoring the dialectic of the individual and the interplay between uniqueness and sameness, we are condemned to run in the same ruts over and over again.

It goes without saying that, even if this analysis is accurate, it will not offer a straightforward solution to 'the crisis of representation,' the excess of compromise or its lack thereof. No scholarly work in itself will be able to change by fiat the ways in which the individuals apprehend themselves, and I suspect that some old Latin names would not make the perspective more popular either. However, I hypothesize that, in a paradoxical and somewhat twisted way, some postmodern developments might very well have a similar effect. The concomitant movements of globalization and localization (the fancy glocalization, if you prefer), the extraordinary multiplication of virtual social networks and the

---

[45] Needless to say, in differentiating between 'ethics' and 'morality' I follow here in the footsteps of Hegel's distinction as presented in his *Philosophy of Right*.

success, even if temporary, of political mobilization through nonconventional venues and in nonconventional settings may all indicate and contribute to a change in the self-representation of the postmodern individual. I tentatively label it here a process of neo-medievalization, despite the obvious risk of unintentional negative connotations.

It is a twisted process, in that the self-identification of the individual with multiple communities is as unstable and as fugitive as it can be, at least when compared with the stability and the rather given character of the medieval *universitas*. Yet in a paradoxical way, it is precisely this fugitive and freely chosen (or renounced) belonging to several communities that helps in opening new venues of rethinking the representation and self-representation of the individual. In effect, it becomes increasingly evident that the postmodern individual enjoys the uniqueness conferred by a particular combination of allegiances to different groups – a tendency already identified by Georg Simmel almost a century ago.[46]

All the contemporary debates about what political representation is or ought to be and what benefits or damages it can bring to politics can be rethought in the light of this forgotten dialectic. Group representation, minority representation, descriptive versus aesthetic representation, and the entire variety of labels created by political scientists during the past two decades alone could be reinterpreted using this medieval dialectic and the distinction between ascending and descending representation. If today most people would agree that we have a problem with political compromise, representation, and the loss of trust of people in their representatives, such perspective may offer not only fresh insights but may also indicate possible solutions. If we have a problem with representation it is at least in part because we have a problem with the (self-) representation of the individual.

If we are still struggling with the 'embedded self' or the 'messy self,' it is, at least partly, because the memory of the dialectic between *forum internum* and *externum* has not been entirely lost. And if we are not able to compromise about the proper political function of compromise, it is because both branches resulting from the split understanding of the seventeenth century are still discernible.

We are living in a haunted world.

---

[46] "On the one hand the individual finds a community for each of his inclinations and strivings which makes it easier to satisfy them. This community provides an organizational form for his activities, and it offers in this way all the advantages of group-membership as well as of organizational experience. On the other hand, the specific qualities of the individual are preserved through the combination of groups which can be a different combination in each case. Thus one can say that society arises from the individual and the individual arises out of association. An advanced culture broadens more and more the social groups to which we belong with our whole personality; but at the same time the individual is made to rely on his own resources to a greater extent and he is deprived of many supports and advantages associated with the tightly-knit, primary group." Georg Simmel (1964), *Conflict and The Web of Group-Affiliations*, trans. Kurt H. Wolff and Reinhard Bendix (London: Collier-Macmillan), 162–163.

2

No Compromise about Compromise

> Compromise is odious to passionate natures because it seems a surrender; and to intellectual natures because it seems a confusion.
>
> George Santayana

> To the philosopher's eye the unexamined language ... is not worth speaking.
>
> Philip Petit

As mentioned in the previous chapter, compromise is either no longer a "fashionable" concept or it is so embedded in our discourse that nobody even notices it. Except for Avishai Margalit's, few recent books have bothered to mention it at all, and another exception aside, no articles in recent decades deal with the concept.[1] It is as if 'compromise' has ceased to have any relevance for the field of politics, despite former claims that it "pervades democratic politics"[2] and that it is "indeed the rule and the art of the game of politics."[3] The rare books that consider methodically key concepts in politics do not count 'compromise' as a word worthy of careful consideration.[4]

---

[1] To offer just one example: several recent editions of Edmund Burke's *Reflections on Revolution in France* make no reference to 'compromise' in their indexes, although the concept plays a central role for Burke, especially in this book, in which it is mentioned several times. From their indexes one can easily find how many times and in which contexts Burke used the word 'clown' (once) but not 'compromise.' A very recent article that deals with compromise, yet from the same ahistorical perspective is, as mentioned in Chapter 1, Chiara Lepora (2012), "On Compromise and Being Compromised," *Journal of Political Philosophy* 20, no. 1: 1–22.

[2] Arthur Kuflik (1979), "Morality and Compromise," in *Compromise in Ethics, Law, and Politics*, ed. J. Roland Pennock and John W. Chapman (New York: New York University Press), 41, quoting also Daniel Bell.

[3] Marvin Rintala (1969), "The Two Faces of Compromise," in *Western Political Quarterly* 22, no. 2: 326.

[4] Raymond Williams (1976), *Keywords: A Vocabulary of Culture and Society* (London: Fontana Communication Series/Croom Helm); Terence Ball, James Farr, and Russell L. Hanson, eds.

This is not to deny or even to minimize the relevance of a survey of the literature on compromise. On the contrary, besides recovering some undeniable insights, such an endeavor can be helpful precisely by pointing out deeper disagreements, overlooked connections and severed bridges of communication. Such 'weaknesses' represent in effect very powerful signals about limits that cannot be overcome by maintaining the discussion inside a contemporary frame, with little or no attention to the genealogy of the concept or to the historical contexts in which different usages of compromise arose.

Despite their infrequency, debates about the role of compromise in politics spreading across roughly a century and a half were fiercely and passionately argued, and no resolution is yet in sight. When it comes to compromise, politicians, political scientists, and 'regular' citizens alike seem to be unable to ... compromise. While in the Anglo-American world the majority of politicians and political scientists, from Burke to Bellamy and from T.V. Smith to Senator McCarthy, support the old tradition of praising the benefits of political compromise, there is also an often-disregarded counter-movement, with its own forgotten tradition, going back to the nineteenth century. From John Stuart Mill and John Morley to Oliver Martin and Francis Devine, a handful of people worried about the possible consequences of a political life centered on compromise. The stakes of these arguments are high; they transcend mere academic interest if indeed "political beliefs, actions and practices are partly constituted by the concepts which political actors hold about those beliefs, actions and practices."[5] If so, "conceptual conflict may express political conflict."[6]

As I will try to show in this chapter, a strictly 'conceptual' debate about what should qualify as compromise with no attention paid to its historical genealogy and to its intimate connection with the problem of (self-) representation has little or no chance of being resolved as long as the supporters of a commendatory usage of compromise have a different understanding of politics than that of the fewer partisans of a condemnatory one. Since "politics is inevitably conducted in normative language," such a morally ambiguous concept raises two sets of interrelated challenges.[7] On the one hand, it is impossible to even consider compromise as a political practice as long as there are basic disagreements about *what* should qualify as compromise. On the other hand, if the label of 'compromise' is applied indiscriminately to practices that on closer examination do not qualify as such, one runs the risk of self-confining our understanding of compromise to give-and-take, bargaining, and balancing

---

(1989), *Political Innovation and Conceptual Change* (Cambridge: Cambridge University Press); Richard Bellamy and Andrew Mason, eds. (2003), *Political Concepts* (Manchester and New York: Manchester University Press).

5 James Farr (1989), "Understanding Conceptual Change Politically," in Ball, Farr, and Hanson, *Political Innovation*, 26–27.

6 Ibid., 28.

7 Philip Petit (1997), *Republicanism: A Theory of Freedom and Government* (Oxford: Clarendon Press), 2.

interests between individuals and interest groups, that is, to the modern meaning of compromise.

As Oliver Martin points out, to embrace this modern meaning – give-and-take meant primarily to avoid violence in a pluralist world where no consensus is to be found – comes with a more or less conscious alternative (either democracy, i.e., compromise, or dictatorship, i.e., force). Many contemporary debates about compromise are framed in these terms, yet such an either-or approach presupposes that "persuasion, with its normative use of reason, cannot be depended as workable." It implies, "consciously or unconsciously, that reason cannot serve as a critic of wills, but that its chief function is to find good reasons for defending what is already willed." "In making the method of compromise absolute, a doctrine of human nature and a function of reason are implied that restrict the realm of possibilities."[8] Even a remote possibility that such warnings are right demands a renewed attention to the debate surrounding political compromise.

Between the end of the nineteenth century and the beginning of the twenty-first, disagreement centered on two main issues: (1) what should qualify as a compromise, and (2) how (and whether) one should limit compromise to solve the conundrum of its seemingly inherent moral ambiguity – in other words, "how is it possible for persons to be compromising toward each other without thereby compromising their own moral integrity in the bargain."[9] In retrospect, it is easy to affirm, for example, that Chamberlain should have never agreed to compromise with Hitler or, say, the abolitionists with pro-slavery politicians. But if these two famous compromises had ended, as originally intended, with the avoidance of the Second World War and the Civil War, respectively, would our contemporary judgment be as harsh as it tends to be? If so, why? These are not easy questions and are addressed in more detail in the concluding chapter.

Surprisingly, neither of the two themes has ever been discussed in the context that could shed the most light on such controversial topics – the conceptual history of the word. Consequently, little advancement has been made on both accounts and most scholars have abandoned the debate altogether. So far, few exceptions aside, the twenty-first century has not witnessed any other attempt to restart the debate, either by defending or by challenging the usefulness of political compromise.[10] And as long as the distinction between classical and modern compromise remains obscure, confusions about the subject matter are prone to happen and arguments will end in an unavoidable *cul de sac*.

Turning a blind eye on historical realities to focus exclusively on conceptual reconstructions presents a double trap. One should not, for example, claim a

---

[8] Oliver Martin (1948), "Beyond Compromise," *Ethics* 58, no. 2: 121, 120, 122.
[9] Kuflik, "Morality and Compromise," 38.
[10] Frank R. Ankersmit (2002), "Representational Democracy: An Aesthetic Approach to Conflict and Compromise," *Common Knowledge* 8, no. 1: 24–46, and Avishai Margalit (2009), *Compromise and Rotten Compromise* (Princeton: Princeton University Press). The most recent attempt is Amy Gutmann and Dennis Thompson (2012), *The Spirit of Compromise*.

homogenous practice of embracing compromise where historical realities and actors display an obvious condemnation just for the sake of fitting reality to the Procrustean bed of theory. If a thinker such as Guizot uses the term "compromise" with consistently negative connotations, to present him as a typical example of a skillful compromiser (as Ankersmit does) is to assume a 'rightful' contemporary understanding at odds with the thinker's 'deficient' one.

A rather similar mistake, only this time in reverse, is to overlook common underlying assumptions among supporters of political compromise that cannot be properly understood outside the historical development of the concept. One has therefore to inquire why authors otherwise so different in their explicit claims repeatedly concur *both* in regard to compromise *and* whenever it comes to some less obvious yet essential premises. In the process, connections will become evident that would otherwise remain obscure: such as the one between the praise of compromise as the political method *par excellence* and the development, through representation, of a 'professional' political sphere meant primarily to arbitrate conflicting interests.

It is no accident if, for example, T.V. Smith – for whom "politics is the institutionalized art of compromise" – follows unaware in the footsteps of Hobbes. Since "men are diverse in interest, and they are not always harmonious in principle," the only alternative to open violence is a common settlement that requires the presence of a third party.[11] "Such settlement is politics; such third party is the politician."[12] In this account, the politician replaces Hobbes's Leviathan and becomes the professional compromiser. The "lay" individual can stick with his principles and let the specialists do "the dirty work for him."[13]

By pointing out such connections and contradictions inside the scholarly literature on compromise, this chapter aims to delineate a century-old debate – limits that would be challenged in the chapters to follow. The first part will consider the possibility that the practice of compromise preceded the invention of the term, and for this purpose Aristotle's *mesotes* will serve as an example to illuminate the difference between the classical *mean* and the contemporary understanding of compromise. It will be followed by a detailed analysis of John Morley's largely forgotten book *On Compromise*. Written in the shadow of his mentor, John Stuart Mill, Morley's book is the first to seriously consider the 'proper' place of compromise in the context of politics, setting to a certain extent the terms of the debates that followed in the twentieth century. It therefore deserves particular attention. The next two parts will review the contemporary body of literature, considering the possibility of disentangling the immoral and moral aspects of compromise by either limiting compromise, arguing for its intrinsic morality, or trying to escape the dilemma by assuming an *amoral*

---

[11] T.V. Smith (1942), "Compromise: Its Context and Limits," *Ethics: An International Journal of Social, Political, and Legal Philosophy* 53, no. 1: 2.

[12] Ibid., 6.

[13] Ibid., 13.

perspective. I will conclude with a review of the literature that emphasizes a peculiar Anglo-American propensity for compromise. While the peculiarity in itself is difficult to deny, I found the idea of 'national character' to lack sufficient explanatory power. Hopefully, by the end of this excurse, the necessity for seriously considering the history of the concept will become obvious.

2.1. COMPROMISE BEFORE COMPROMISE?

Defenders of compromise have tried to bolster its status by asserting that *the concept* of compromise was present well before *the word* itself was coined by the Romans and/or acquired its present day meanings. This allegation is to be seriously considered since, as some scholars have pointed out, many historians of ideas fail to consider the possible differences between words and concepts.[14] Theoretically speaking, it is therefore possible that, in politics, compromise was used under a different label. Furthermore, if indeed compromise as concept predated the word, going back all the way to antiquity and with no significant changes occurring since, then the proposed connection between modern compromise and social contract would be seriously challenged.

The safest method to analyze the allegation would be to check if the vocabulary of mixing opposites or of finding the mean between extremes – so common for Greeks and Romans alike – is the precursor of the vocabulary of compromise. After all, in his *Politics*, Aristotle describes "the *mixed* regime" as the best one, an idea shared later on by Polybius (*The Histories*) and Cicero (*The Republic* and *The Laws*). Undoubtedly then, something close to what today is understood as compromise was already present in the ancient world as well. But how close was it? To answer this question we have to consider the ancient idea of *mesotes* more carefully.

For obvious reasons, Aristotle represents the ideal case study for tackling this problem. Many consider him the first theorist of political compromise. More than a century ago, Edmund Burke – himself a defender of compromise – stops short of depicting Aristotle as a compromiser.[15] And yet he mentions him in the same famous paragraph in which he argues for the centrality of compromise, and the context leaves no room for doubting that this was indeed his understanding:

All government, indeed every human benefit and enjoyment, every virtue and every prudent act, is founded on compromise and barter. We balance inconveniencies; we give and take; we remit some rights that we may enjoy others; and we choose rather to be happy citizens than subtle disputants.... Man acts from adequate motives relative to his interest, and not on metaphysical speculations. Aristotle, the great master of reasoning,

---

[14] Quentin Skinner (1989), "Language and Political Change," in Ball, Farr, and Hanson, *Political Innovation*, esp. 7–9.

[15] Despite the fact that many defenders of compromise use Burke in support of their thesis, the only author who cared to analyze the quote in a larger context is John Morley. See further.

cautions us, and with great weight and propriety, against this species of delusive geo-metrical accuracy in moral arguments, as the most fallacious of all sophistry.[16]

Like many English politicians during the eighteenth and nineteenth centu-ries, Burke is well documented and well known as a supporter of compromise as an essential political practice, despite the limits he agrees with – "none will barter away the immediate jewel of his soul."[17] Yet the version he endorses is already a modern one. For Burke, it is "barter," "give and take," done pri-marily for the sake of avoiding greater evils, *not* for the sake of justice. It is a balance of "inconveniencies," as it is made clear in the discussions of rights. "The rights of men in government are their advantages; and these are often in balances between differences of good; in compromises between *good and evil*, and sometimes *between evil and evil*."[18] Clearly, Burke is not the only one to think this way.

In more recent years, David Resnik considers Aristotle one of the chief the-oreticians of political compromise mainly for proposing the "mixed polity" as the best possible constitution and for his praise of the "mean."[19] "A com-promise for Aristotle is a mixture, a resultant that combines elements from each particular to yield a new compound having elements from both."[20] If one adds to this observation Aristotle's definition of virtue as a mean between two extremes, the label of 'compromiser' appears self-evident. This is a common modern-day assumption, namely that all combinations of opposites, means, and/or mixtures represent compromises.[21] Yet not just any 'mixture' or any 'mean' can be equated with a 'compromise,' as even a brief analysis of Aristotle can reveal.

There is an impressive body of literature dealing with the question of the *mesotes*: Is it the same as the middle? Is it different from moderation? The interpretations go on and on.[22] However, the aim of this section is not to engage

---

[16] Edmund Burke (1949) [1775], "Speech on Moving Resolutions for Conciliation with the Colonies," in *Burke's Politics: Selected Writings and Speeches of Edmund Burke on Reform, Revolution, and War*, ed. Ross J.S. Hoffman and Paul Levack (New York: Alfred A. Knopf), 89–90.

[17] Ibid., 100.

[18] Edmund Burke (2003), *Reflections on the Revolution on France*, ed. Franks M. Turner (New York: Yale University Press), 52.

[19] David Resnik (1979), "Justice, Compromise, and Constitutional Rules in Aristotle," in Pennock and Chapman, *Compromise in Ethics*, 69–86. See also Peter B. Knupfer (1991), "The Rhetoric of Conciliation: American Civic Culture and the Federalist Defense of Compromise," *Journal of the Early Republic* 11, no. 3: 318.

[20] Resnick, "Justice, Compromise, and Constitutional Rules," 75.

[21] See, e.g., T.V. Smith (1942; 1956), Benjamin Martin (1990), Oliver Martin (1948).

[22] See, e.g., W.F.R. Hardie (1964), "Aristotle's Doctrine That Virtue Is a Mean," *Proceedings of the Aristotelian Society* 65; L.W. Rosenfeld (1965), "The Doctrine of the Mean in Aristotle's Rhetoric," *Theoria* 31: 191–198; W.W. Forthenbaugh (1968), "Aristotle on the Questionable Mean-Dispositions," *Transactions of the American Philological Association* 99: 23–31; R. Hursthouse (1989), "A False Doctrine of the Mean," *Proceedings of the Aristotelian Society*, 80:

this literature, nor to propose a radical new interpretation of the Aristotelian 'mean,' but just to examine specifically the extent to which it coincides with the present-day understanding of compromise. After all, if – as most scholars agree – *mesotes* is a central concept for Aristotle's ethical *and* political theory, the best place to start is with an inquiry into the history of compromise's moral ambiguity as a political practice.

Although Aristotle defined virtue as "a mean between two vices, one of excess and one of deficiency," he was also eager to add that "not every activity or feeling admits of the mean" (NE, II, 6, 1107a, 1–10).[23] Theft and murder or cowardice and shamelessness can have no mean. This is a first indication that the difference between 'mean' and 'extremes' might be more essential than it is usually considered. "There are many ways to be in error ... but there is only one way to be correct" (NE, II, 6, 1106b, 3–35). As Ioannis D. Evrigenis points out, "Aristotle does not claim universal application of the doctrine [of the mean], since the very nature of certain types of actions and feelings makes them by definition vices, and thus not open to the trichotomy of deficiency, mean and excess."[24] The terms 'mean' or 'intermediate,' as Aristotle put it, can be misleading for suggesting a strict quantitative difference between virtue and vices and therefore a basic common nature. Indeed, "virtue and vice are *about* the same thing" – feelings (pleasures and pains) and actions – but "neither virtues nor vices *are* feelings." Both are *about* the same things yet they *are not* the same thing because they are not *for* the same thing. Eating properly, too much, or too little, are all *about* food, yet only the first is *for* health (NE, II, 3,5,6; V, 1–2, 5). It is the goodness of the end that reveals the nature of virtue.

The observation that "there is no mean of excess or of deficiency, and no excess or deficiency of a mean" (NE, II, 6, 1107a, 25) also indicates that virtue and vices do *not* share a common nature. While there can be an excess of deficiency or a deficiency of an excess, none of the two would qualify as virtue. Although excess and deficiency seem from a quantitative perspective further removed from each other than their mean, they are in fact closest and can easily switch places. "Recourse to quantity carries with it connotations of the middle, which are clearly not a part of Aristotle's concept of *mesotes*."[25] To use a well-known Aristotelian metaphor, the difference between hitting the target

---

57–72; B. Williams (1985), *Ethics and the Limits of Philosophy* (Harvard: Harvard University Press); P. Losin (1987), "Aristotle's Doctrine of the Mean," *History of Philosophy Quarterly* 4, no. 3: 329–341; J.O. Umson (1991), *Introduction to Aristotle's Ethics* (Oxford: Oxford University Press).

[23] Aristotle (2005), "Nicomachean Ethics," in *Classics of Moral and Political Theory*, ed. Michael L. Morgan (Indianapolis and Cambridge: Hackett Publishing), henceforth referred to as NE. Also Aristotle (2007), "Politics," in *The Politics and the Constitution of Athens*, ed. Stephen Everson (Cambridge: Cambridge University Press), henceforth referred to as P.

[24] Ioannis D. Evrigenis (1999), "The Doctrine of the Mean in Aristotle's Ethical and Political Theory," *History of Political Thought* 20, no. 3: 400.

[25] Ibid., 404.

and missing it is not merely a quantitative one, that is, of inches or feet, but also qualitative. As Evrigenis again carefully points out, "the fact that quantification is admissible in certain parameters of certain circumstances ... should not be taken to imply that the doctrine of the mean is a 'quantitative notion' since Aristotle cautions that the determination of the mean should rest on the determination of the circumstances (i.e., at the right time, on the right occasion, toward the right people, for the right reason, and in the right way) (NE II 6, 1106b, 20–24); these parameters, taken together, demonstrate that to attempt to quantify the doctrine of the mean is to miss something about its essence."[26] Furthermore, as Aristotle emphasizes in *Politics*, Book III, things that differ in quality cannot be treated in terms of quantity or regarded as commensurable (P, III, 1283a).

As far as the definition of compromise is concerned, it is important to point out the first major difference between the Aristotelian *mesotes* and modern compromise. This 'mean' is not reached by balancing two extreme positions to meet halfway in a quantitative fashion, as the modern conception of compromise would have it. On the contrary, it is qualitatively different, that is, different in nature from the extremes. In the case of the arrow on target metaphor, missing by aiming either too high or too low is still a miss. Thus, viewed from the 'intermediate' position, the extremes are less different and closer than they may otherwise appear. As shown in the beginning of *Politics*, man himself is 'intermediate' between god and beast, but this does not mean that he shares *nature* with either of the two.[27] On the contrary, he is the only one who is "by nature intended to live in a polis."

> If we adopt as true the statement made in the Ethics – (1) that a truly happy life is a life of goodness lived in freedom from impediments, and (2) that goodness consists in a mean – it follows that the best way of life is one which consists as a mean. Further, the same criteria which determines whether the citizen-body has a good or a bad way of life must also apply to the constitution; for a constitution is the way of life of a citizen body. (P, IV, 11, 1295a, 35–40)

Thus, to better understand whether the Aristotelian virtue (and mixed constitution) is indeed a compromise between extremes, one has to turn to the polis, for man is a *zoon politikon* endowed with speech, and "speech is for making clear what is ... just or unjust" (P, I, 1253a, 15). As a matter of fact, the philosopher himself makes the connection between ethics and politics clear at the very beginning of both the *Nicomachean Ethics* and the *Politics* when he states that there is a supreme good for which all other things are sought (*eudaimonia*), and the science that concerns itself with this supreme good is political science (NE, I, 1–2, 1094a, 19–23, 27; P, I, 1 1252a). Yet *eudaimonia* is "the

---

[26] Ibid., 396–397 (footnote).
[27] Pascal would put it later, "*l'homme n'est ni ange ni bête, et le malheur veut que qui veut faire l'ange fait la bête.*"

activity of the soul in accordance with perfect excellence" (NE, I, 7, 1098a, 16–18) and "the best and most perfect excellence is justice towards others" (NE, V, 1, 1129b, 25–27). The insistence upon the just solution is the second feature that distinguishes the Aristotelian *mesotes* from present-day compromise – meant primarily to avoid the greatest evil, violence.

If Aristotle proposed a combination of oligarchy and democracy, he did so in order to find the best practical solution (P IV, 1, 1288), that is, the *politically just* solution for a 'real world' in which "one part of the political just is natural, and the other part legal" (NE, V, 7, 1134b, 18–20). But what if the parties – say, oligarchs and democrats – cannot agree upon what is just by nature, the law remains silent on that particular aspect, and therefore no political decision can be reached "for [the] parties distrust each other"? Then they "resort to a judge, and an appeal to a judge is an appeal to the just; for the judge is intended to be a sort of *living embodiment of the just*" (NE, V, 1132a, 20; emphasis). Because oligarchs and democrats, the rich and the poor "distrust one another ... the arbitrator is most trusted everywhere, and the man in the middle is an arbitrator" (P, IV, 12, 1297b).

Being the living embodiment of the just, such a judge is by necessity virtuous, for "justice is complete virtue to the highest degree because it is the complete exercise of complete virtue" (NE, V, 1, 1129b, 30). And by being the embodiment of complete virtue, he is also an 'intermediate,' acknowledged as such by parties to a dispute.

[T]hey seek the judge as an intermediary, and in some cities they actually call a judge a 'mediator', assuming that if they are awarded an intermediate amount, the award will be just. If, then, the judge is an intermediary, the just is in some way intermediate. (NE, IV, 4, 1132a, 20)

As Aristotle observes in Books III and IV of the *Politics*, there is a certain sense in which both oligarchs and democrats are justified in the claims they advance, though none of them is absolutely so. "The *mesotes* that serves as the formal rule for the pursuit of excellence (and thus *eudaimonia*) for the individual, is equally important as a tool for the political scientist and the statesman who aim at providing the right environment for a group of individuals with the same ultimate aim."[28] The political scientist and the statesman are therefore the best arbitrators, the best 'intermediaries.' The implication that one of the best-suited intermediaries remains Aristotle himself is obvious. He is the man in the middle *par excellence*.

Aristotle is neither simply not Greek nor not simply Greek. He is at once 'of Greece' by lineage and 'of Macedon' by familial affiliation, yet not readily identified as Greek *or* Macedonian, nor as Greek *and* Macedonian.... [His] birthplace, Stagira, uncannily replicates Aristotle's ambiguous identity. As a place, the town was situated on the border of

---

[28] Evrigennis, "The Doctrine of the Mean," 407. See also *Politics*, Book IV, 1283b, 11–12.

Macedon and Greece; as a political space it occupied "the borderland between city-state and municipality" (Hansen, 1993, 75). Stagira was therefore neither fully *polis* (i.e., an independent city-state in Hellas), nor exactly *kome* (i.e., a dependent entity associated with barbarian habitations, including those in Macedon).... Insofar as Stagira's annihilation in the name of the cause of the empire also robs Aristotle of a home, he is left *apolis* (cityless), a "strange figure" in the Hellenic world.[29]

Envisaging the mixed regime, Aristotle did not 'compromise' anything, because, as philosopher and political scientist, he was – and should have been – between the particular interests of either of the two camps. From this standpoint, he was eventually a '*compromissarius*' yet not a 'compromiser.' In the classical understanding, a *compromissarius* arbitrated a compromise yet was not part of the compromise. He was trusted to be just precisely because he was 'in between' and 'above' the interests of the parties.

From this 'neither-nor,' 'in-between' position, he occupied the best standpoint for understanding various particular interests and therefore for envisaging a mixed regime meant to do justice to all parties. As a matter of fact, Resnick himself agrees, in that "the best strategy for *constructing* a compromise that would be acceptable to both parties is to show that the preferred compromise is in the self-interest of each party ... and furthermore that the solution is a more desirable one from the point of view of *justice*."[30] What he misses is that the one who 'constructs' such 'compromises' is not part of them. In this account, the philosopher proposed mixing extremes not (primarily) for the sake of solving conflicts but *for the sake of justice*. This is neither a give-and-take compromise nor a medium but a radically new solution, not only acceptable to both parties but also just for both the parties and the whole.

Yet the differences between the ancients and the moderns do not stop at philosophy. If politics preceded 'political philosophy,' then politics has no need for independent 'philosophical' arbitration. Politicians, be they oligarchs or democrats, Athenian or Melian ambassadors, can manage their disputes by themselves, even (or even better) in the absence of an 'independent arbitrator.' After all, such a 'face-to-face' disputation without a neutral third party is what modern compromise pretends to be all about. However, for the ancients, the absence of the arbitrator did not prevent each party from acting, thinking, and arguing *as if* it were in the presence of one.

Francis E. Devine, perhaps the subtlest challenger of compromise as a political method, develops this argument even further, making some interesting points worth consideration. He argues that in the Greek understanding of politics, there was no question of compromise as bargaining. On the contrary,

---

[29] Mary G. Dietz, "Between Polis and Empire: Aristotle's Politics," paper prepared for Political Theory Workshop, Department of Political Science, Indiana University, April 25, 2008. See also Mary G. Dietz (2012), "Between Polis and Empire: Aristotle's Politics," *American Political Science Review*, 106, no. 2: 275–293.

[30] Resnick, "Justice, Compromise, and Constitutional Rules," 70.

as each side raised objections to the other side's argument, each party was supposed to adjust its discourse to meet *rational requirements*.

Mutual correction is achieved as each side raises difficulties to the other's argument.
To compromise would truncate the necessary discussion short of reaching *the truest
answer possible*, and thus risk a false or at least an unnecessarily uncertain, answer.
From the point of view of a party to the dispute, *compromise* involves *compromising –*
in the negative sense which we still retain – one's principles or beliefs *without being
convinced of their erroneousness*.[31]

   Devine rightly observes that the total absence of consideration of compromise by ancient writers seems to be "as true of the historians as of the philosophers." "Thucydides, for example, describes in great detail at least six policy
decisions made by four different poleis [and] in none of these decision making
is a process of compromise mentioned or described."[32] In each case the assembly made a decision after a confrontation of 'reasoned opinion.' As Pericles
makes clear in his "Funeral Speech," "we Athenians decide public questions ...
or at least endeavor to arrive at a sound understanding of them, in the belief
that it is not debate that is a hindrance to action, but rather *not to be instructed
by the debate* before the time comes for action."[33] "What is decided is what has
been previously deliberated," "for decision involves reason and thought" and
"decision seems to be most proper to virtue" (NE, III, 2, 111b, 112a).
   Devine's observations point out a huge gap between the ancient and the
modern perspectives on settling political differences: the former emphasizes
'instructed' deliberation, assuming therefore at least the possibility of a dia-
lectical approximation of the 'truth,' qualitatively different from the opposite
positions; the latter is eager to discard this possibility as at best naïve if not
hegemonic, and proposes economical, quantitative bargaining between irreconcilable positions since all hope for reasoned persuasion is given up almost
beforehand. The ancients proposed a 'positive' solution – finding the best
approximations of 'the good' or of 'the truth.' The moderns, convinced that
such 'approximations' are never reachable, proposed a 'negative' one – since
we cannot agree about 'the good,' we can at least flee the evil, that is, the violence of the disagreement.

This is not to assert that the ancients never made what we would describe as a compromise. However, the concept of compromise was not the basis for their understanding
of the process by which disputes, and in particular political disputes, are settled. They
believed instead that given sufficient discussion, free from partisanship, the right solution to a dispute could be discovered.[34]

---

[31] Francis Edward Devine (1972), "Hobbes: The Theoretical Basis of Political Compromise,"
Polity 5, no. 1: 59; emphasis added.
[32] Ibid., 58.
[33] Thucydides (1965), *History of the Peloponnesian War*, trans. C.F. Smith (Cambridge: Loeb
Classical Library edition), 329; emphasis added.
[34] Devine, "Hobbes," 59.

In effect, the ancients knew everything about 'modern' compromise – made essentially for fear of violence, not for the sake of justice. As Glaucon in the *Republic* reveals, at least some ancients shared with Hobbes the same assumption about human evil in the state of nature and, long before Hobbes, some thought that justice is but a mutual contract meant to protect human beings from their own impulses to harm others. According to this interpretation, justice is nothing but a convention – the lesser evil.

By nature, *they* say, to commit injustice is good and to suffer it is an evil, but what the excess of evil in being wronged is greater than the excess of good in doing wrong, so that when men do wrong and are wronged by one another and taste of both, those who lack the power to avoid the one and take the other determine that it is for their profit to *make a compact with one another* neither to commit nor to suffer injustice, and that this is the beginning of legislation and of covenants between men, ... and that *this is the genesis and essential nature of justice* – a '*compromise*' [sic] between the best, which is to do wrong with impunity, and the worst, which is to be wronged and be impotent to get one's revenge. Justice, they tell us ... is accepted and approved *not as a real good*, but as a thing honored in the lack of vigor to do injustice.[35]

Obviously then the ancients too were familiar with the 'theory' of modern compromise. However, as Devine argues and I have tried to demonstrate, they never seriously considered it as a proper basis of political practice. After all, the entire *Republic* is but an attempt to refute this type of argument about justice. As Gauthier observes, "he offers this view to Socrates to refute, not to defend."[36] Once the history of this difference was lost, scholars and politicians alike had trouble pinpointing what, if any, was the problem of political compromise – and the first one to seriously consider its downside was John Morley.

2.2. COMPROMISE: FROM METHOD TO PRINCIPLE

The nineteenth century witnessed the first attempts to conceptualize some of the key political terms of the modern age – such as representation, democracy, liberty, and ... compromise. That the last term has had a much less fortunate trajectory in the field of political philosophy compared to the others cannot obscure the fact that it started off in excellent company. Just a few decades separate François Guizot's *On Representative Government*, Alexis de Tocqueville's seminal discussion of *Democracy in America*, John Stuart Mill's *On Liberty* and *Considerations on Representative Government*, and John Morley's *On*

---

[35] Plato, *The Republic*, II, 359a; emphasis added. Translated by Paul Shorey in *Plato: The Collected Dialogues*, ed. Edith Hamilton and Huntington Cairns (Princeton: Princeton University Press, 1999). Instead of "compromise between" other translations use "in-between," or "midway between." The entire passage will become even more relevant once we start discussing the social contract. See further.

[36] David Gauthier (1986), *Morals by Agreement* (Oxford: Clarendon Press), 10. See further.

Compromise, respectively.[37] The connection between these books goes well beyond the directedness of their titles.[38] From different perspectives, to be sure, they all grapple with the same set of new challenges raised by the rapid spread of political representation: Does political representation create an independent sphere of 'professional politics'? If so, to what extent does this newly discovered 'independence' affect the relationship between ethics and politics? What, if any, is the role left for direct democracy?

To his merit, Morley is the one who most clearly articulates the connection between the steady development of representative government in England, followed by the creation of an easily identifiable political sphere, and the increasing popularity of compromise as the political method *par excellence*. Yet he is also among the first to warn about the dangers involved with these new developments. As I will try to demonstrate in the following pages, his finely crafted distinction between the roles compromise *is* and *ought to be* playing in politics reveals a much more complex political thinker than most commentators would care to admit.

Unfortunately, among the late Victorians, Morley is considered more of a secondary figure.[39] Very few of his books are still in print, and even one of his most recent editors, Peter Stansky, agreed that "for all the variety of his activities and the considerable quality of his accomplishments, in none of them has he proved to be quite distinguished enough – the difference perhaps between being eminent and preeminent – to win an enduring place in the front rank."[40]

One possible explanation may reside in his hard-to-label political stance. In 1885 he wrote about himself: "I am a cautious Whig by temperament, I am a sound Liberal by training, and I am thorough Radical by observation and experience."[41] And yet, despite his professed radicalism, he never approved of anything even closely remote to socialism – quite the contrary. "Whatever his Radical position on certain issues, in general he was an elitist who believed in a democracy that should dedicate itself to ratifying the decisions of sage rulers from the middle and upper classes, rather than bothering to put forward leaders of its own from the multitude."[42] Another explanation, as Stansky tentatively argues, might be found in a focus of modern scholars on Morley's performance as a politician (between 1880 and 1890, and especially his years as Secretary of State for India, from 1905 to 1910) – a time when his essays

---

[37] Guizot published *On Representative Government* in 1816. The two volumes of Tocqueville's *Democracy in America* appeared in 1835 and 1840. John Stuart Mill published *On Liberty* in 1859, while Morley's *On Compromise* was first published in 1874.

[38] There is an evident connection between Guizot and Tocqueville, as well as between Tocqueville and Mill, which connects all these authors by a thread that runs far deeper than the concept of compromise.

[39] For a list of bibliographical studies on John Morley, see Peter Stansky, ed. (1970), *John Morley: Nineteenth-Century Essays* (Chicago and London: University of Chicago Press), xix.

[40] Ibid., xi.

[41] Quoted in ibid., xiv.

[42] Ibid., xiv–xv.

"suffer from diffuseness and prolixity."[43] Fortunately, this is not true of *On Compromise* (1874).

By the nineteenth century, thanks to the works of both politicians and historians, such as Burke and Macaulay, compromise was already a popular concept and accepted practice in the English political milieu. Yet despite this centrality, none of these prominent figures of English politics ever attempted to fully theorize the relationship between compromise, morality, and politics. It was a task undertaken for the first time by Morley, who thus set in many respects the terms of the debates to follow.

When considering John Morley's *On Compromise*, one has to keep in mind that he was John Stuart Mill's disciple and the book was written just a year after Mill's death. Undoubtedly, Morley not only admired in but also shared with Mill "the exceptional degree in which he was alive to the constant tendency of society to lose some excellence of aim, to relapse at some point from the standard of truth and right which had been reached by long previous effort, to fall back in height of moral ideal."[44] Both were equally aware of the advantages and troubled by the challenges brought by what Morley called the "Age of Comfort."

Mill is also among the few Englishmen of the time who criticized his contemporaries' propensity for compromise. About England, Mill observes disdainfully that is "the native country of compromise."[45] According to him, the English mind is "too ready to satisfy itself with any medium, merely because it is a medium, and to acquiesce in a union of the disadvantages of both extremes instead of their advantages."

The age seemed smitten with an incapacity of producing deep or strong feelings.... An age like this, an age without earnestness, was the natural era of compromises and half-convictions.... It is easy to be practical in a society all practical: there is a practicalness which comes by nature, to those who know little and aspire to nothing; exactly this is the sort which the vulgar form of the English mind exemplifies.[46]

If the hypothesis advanced in the introductory chapter holds, it is more than mere coincidence if the same Mill opposed the popular doctrine of social contract as representation of individual wills (for "society is not founded on a contract, and ... no good purpose is answered by inventing a contract in order to deduce social obligation from it")[47] *and* praised the educative role of local representative bodies for offering many citizens a unique opportunity – a direct say in the political process. "In these positions they have to act, for public

---

[43] Ibid., xiii.

[44] John Morley (1970) [1873], "The Death of Mr. Mill," in ibid., 107.

[45] John Stuart Mill (1963) [1840], "Coleridge," in *Autobiography, Collected Works of John Stuart Mill*, ed. John M. Robson (Toronto: University of Toronto Press) (CW) 10, 131.

[46] *Collected Works of John Stuart Mill*, 10, 141–142. CW 20, 173. See also Mill's critique of Macaulay.

[47] John Stuart Mill (1859), *On Liberty*, ch. 4.

interests, *as well as to think and to speak, and the thinking cannot be all done by proxy.*"[48] From this perspective Mill was much closer to republicanism than his liberal interpreters would care to admit.[49]

It is revealing that Morley observes about him that "one of his most remarkable characteristics was *less English than French*; his constant admission of an ideal and imaginative element in social speculation, and a glowing persuasion that the effort and wisdom and ingenuity of men are capable, if free opportunity is given by social arrangements, of raising human destiny to a pitch that it is at present beyond our powers of conception" (emphasis added). However, such "infinite aspiration" and "luminous hope" was united in Mill with a "rigorous sense of what is real and practicable" – a "mixture" that in many ways defines Morley's own perspective.[50] After all, despite his disdainful attitude toward compromise, Mill also acknowledged in his *Autobiography* that after getting involved in politics, "I became practically conversant with the difficulties of moving bodies of men, the necessities of compromise, the art of sacrificing the non-essential to preserve the essential."[51]

As far as the political sphere is concerned, Morley's perspective on compromise *appears* at first glance to follow the British mainstream that held compromise almost as the quintessence of politics – and as such runs against Mill's general disdain for this 'national treat.' He seems more concerned with the expansion of compromise in other domains, such as ethics or religion, but less so as far as the political realm itself was concerned. After all, the young Morley wrote this book after a quarrel with his father over religion, not over politics.[52] According to Morley, in the political sphere, the practical domain *par excellence*, "the right kind" of compromise is not only unavoidable but also beneficial. It is "a fashion of compromise ... fully compatible with fervor and hopefulness and devotion to great causes."[53]

He agrees with Burke in that "all government, indeed every benefit and enjoyment, every virtue, and every prudent act, is founded on compromise and barter."[54] Yet the patient reader will soon discover that Morley's

[48] John Stuart Mill (1964) [1861], *Considerations on Representative Government*, introduction by F.A. Hayek (Chicago: Henry Regnery), 287; emphasis added.

[49] For a much more challenging reading of Mill's liberalism, see, e.g., Neil Thornton (1987), *The Problem of Liberalism in the Thought of John Stuart Mill* (New York and London: Garland Publishing).

[50] Stansky, *John Morley*, 103.

[51] John Stuart Mill, "Autobiography," in *Autobiography, The Collected Works*, 87. For a more detailed analysis of Mill's attitude toward compromise, yet one that does not take seriously into consideration his manifest disdain for it, see Rafael Cejudo (2010), "J.S. Mill and the Art of Compromise," *Human Affairs* 20: 300–307.

[52] D.A. Hamer (1968), *John Morley: Liberal Intellectual in Politics* (London: Oxford University Press).

[53] John Morley (1906) [1886], *On Compromise* (London: Macmillan), 86, henceforth referred to as OC.

[54] Quoted in ibid., 228.

conceptualization of compromise is much more complex, pointing in effect in the opposite direction, while at the same time setting up most of the terms of the future debates surrounding this controversial concept.

Burke's words are to be understood with a qualification: "These are the words of wisdom and truth, *if we can be sure that men will interpret them in all the fullness of their meaning*, and not be content to take only that part of the meaning which falls in with the dictates of their own love of ease."[55] So what is, according to Morley, the right interpretation of Burke's words?

> Compromise and barter do not mean the undisputed triumph of one set of principles. Nor, on the other hand, do they mean the mutilation of both sets of principles, with a view to producing a tertium quid that shall involve the disadvantages of each, without securing the advantages of either.[56] What Burke means is that we ought never to press our ideas up to the remotest logical issues, without reference to the conditions in which we are applying them. In politics we have an art.[57]

According to Morley, the English particular propensity for compromise and the development of a vigorous and healthy political sphere are intimately connected. It is no accident if England succeeded in having the most "robust political sense, which has discovered so many of the secrets of good government, which has given ... freedom with order, and popular administration without corruption, and unalterable respect for law along with indelible respect for individual rights."[58]

> Of all societies since the Roman Republic, and not even excepting the Roman Republic, England has been the most emphatically and essentially political. She has passed through military phases and through religious phases, but they have been transitory, and the great central stream of national life has flowed in political channels. The political life has been stronger than any other, deeper, wider, more persistent, more successful.[59]

The political channels he is alluding to are, obviously, channels of representation. "The gradual concentration of power in the hands of a supreme deliberative body..., the kind of dignity that has been lent to parliamentary methods by the great importance of the transactions ... have all helped both to fix our strongest and most constant interests upon politics, and to ingrain the mental habit proper to politics."[60] This tendency, as Mill or Burke had already noticed,

---

[55] Ibid., 228; emphasis added.

[56] Obviously, Morley follows here in the footsteps of Mill. Compare this passage with the following from Mill's preface to *On Representative Government*: "Such a better doctrine [than the contemporary Conservative and Liberal ones] must be possible; not a mere compromise, by splitting the difference between the two, but something wider than either, which, in virtue of its superior comprehensiveness, might be adopted by either Liberal or Conservative without renouncing anything which he really feels to be valuable in his own creed" (v–vi). See further.

[57] OC, 229.

[58] Ibid., 19.

[59] Ibid., 105.

[60] Ibid., 106.

had only been reinforced by the French "premature attempts to convert a crude reality, and to found a new social order on a number of uncompromising deductions from abstract principles of the common weal. They have the natural effect of deepening the English dislike of a general theory."[61] What Englishmen preferred to emphasize all along were "the practical arrangements," not a set of general principles or utopian ends.

The English feeling for compromise is *on its better side* the result of a shrewd and practical, though informal, recognition of a truth which the writer [i.e., John Stuart Mill] has here expressed in terms of Method. The disregard which the political action of France has repeatedly betrayed of a principle really so important has hitherto strengthened our own regard for it.[62]

Morley's wording should not be confusing. If in this passage 'method' appears to be equated with 'principle' it is because in the larger context he talks about "practical principles" that later on will be distinguished from what he calls "principles of political morality."[63] For all that matters, Morley, while acknowledging the distinctiveness of the political sphere, is not yet ready to sever its bonds with the ethical realm. The political sphere cannot subsist by itself, for practical principles are not formative ones. 'Method' then is something that helps you get from point 'A' to point 'B,' regardless of what these points are. 'Method' is essentially neutral toward 'ideologies' and eminently practical. And, of course, compromise represented the method at hand *par excellence* when it comes to politics. Yet a method, Morley argues, can never be exclusive and final since a practical principle cannot account by itself for political life.

The danger comes from mistaking the 'tool' for its 'purpose.' A knife can be used either way: to peel a potato or to kill. It is the purpose that determines if and when it is beneficial. By overemphasizing the centrality of compromise in politics Morley's contemporaries started "not only ... [to] look on its importance as *exclusive and final*, but [had] extended our respect for *the right kind* of compromise to *wrong* and injurious kinds."[64] The proper limits of the method have broken down. The tool has become an end in itself, a principle in its own right. "Thus the political spirit has grown to be ... the dominant force, extending its influence over all our ways of thinking in matters that have least to do with politics, or even nothing at all to do with them."[65]

Compromise has become pernicious by overstepping its boundaries: the reasoning that is perfectly suitable for politics has been insidiously extended "also in spheres of thought away from the political sphere" where it does not belong.[66] According to Morley, such a dangerous development was made

---

[61] Ibid., 23.
[62] Ibid., 25; emphasis added.
[63] Ibid., 27.
[64] Ibid., 25; emphasis added.
[65] Ibid., 107.
[66] Ibid., 100.

possible by a particular historical context. Nineteenth century England offered a unique combination of elements conducive to "a profound distrust of all general principles."[67] There were three main ingredients that reinforced one another. "The most important in the intellectual development of the prevailing forms of thought and sentiment is the growth of the Historic Method," according to which all truths are relative to their time.[68]

Once again, Morley is not against this method per se, especially as far as scientific inquiry is concerned, but against its unwise overuse beyond its proper boundaries. "Though there is no necessary or truly logical association between systematic use of this method *rightly limited*, and a slack and slipshod preference of vague general forms over definite ideas, yet everyone can see its tendency, if uncorrected, to make men shrink from importing anything like absolute quality into their propositions."[69]

Coupled with "the immense increase of material prosperity" and "the immense decline in sincerity of spiritual interest," this moral relativism "lowers men's aims and unstrings their firmness of purpose." Thus, "management and compromise appear among the permitted arts because they tend to comfort, and comfort is the end of ends, comprehending all ends."[70] An all-pervasive rush for comfort, transformation of means into ends, lack of great visions, and weakness of convictions – these are, according to Morley, the characteristics of the new times. "Every age is in some sort an age of transition, but our own is characteristically and cardinally an epoch of transition in the very foundations of beliefs and conduct."[71]

The resulting picture is rather grim, characterized by "weakened aspiration and impoverished moral energy"[72] and debilitating mental tone,[73] "a time of loud disputes and weak convictions."[74] In the end, this "triumph of the political method over the spiritual things" in the nineteenth century affects not only some of the most important domains of the British society, but the political sphere as well.[75] The very success of compromise in politics ended up by undermining the practice of politics, "for the extension of the ways of thinking which are proper in politics, to other than political matter, *means at the same time the depravation of the political sense itself.*"[76]

As a forerunner, Morley manages surprisingly well to identify some of the critical aspects of the relationship between compromise and politics, starting

---

[67] Ibid., 5.
[68] Ibid., 28.
[69] Ibid., 31; emphasis added.
[70] Ibid., 34–35.
[71] Ibid., 36.
[72] Ibid., 28.
[73] Ibid., 22.
[74] Ibid., 129.
[75] Ibid., 40.
[76] Ibid., 19–20; emphasis added.

with the relationship itself: the particular English fondness for this method and its transformation into principle; the connection between compromise, representation, and a 'professional' political sphere; the challenging relationship between compromise, politics, and morality; the rise of instrumental rationality, and so on. A few decades later, each of these aspects would be addressed in its own right by several political thinkers.

2.3. COMPROMISE WITHOUT COMPROMISING?

The core problem raised by the concept of compromise in politics is the normative question – its connection with morality. Here the lack of awareness about the connection between representation and self-representation proves decisive. If compromise is used (as it is in the Anglo-American world) by the majority of politicians and political scientists in a commendatory fashion, how is one to dispel the negative connotations inevitably associated with it? The normative issue is further complicated by the possibility that misinterpretation and consequently a widespread misuse of compromise in practice might dangerously constrain the possibilities open to the political actors involved in the painful process of finding a solution between competing interests, ideologies, and values in a world dominated by pluralism.

This is precisely what Oliver Martin, the first American scholar who "tried to show the necessity of transcending compromise, and to prove the impossibility of identifying completely the democratic way with the method of compromise," was worried about.[77] Although he agrees with T.V. Smith that the best solution for solving disputes is the one that avoids violence, he disagrees that the only alternative to violence remains compromise. The ideal method for him remains instead 'rational persuasion.' To confound persuasion and compromise is a widespread and dangerous mistake. More often than we care to consider, what the term 'compromise' expresses "is the essence of the method of persuasion, for good will and the appeal to reason are presupposed on the part of the disputants."[78]

If, for example, for some reason or other a decision has to be rendered on the question at issue between two disputants before there is time enough to work out the matter in detail through rational discussion, then for one of the disputants to accept the point of view of the other, or both to adopt some third position, is certainly not to compromise.... Referring to the second case – when some third position is accepted by both disputants because, with good will and after sufficient rational discussion, there still remains an honest and sincere difference of opinion – we do not find the essence of compromise here.[79]

Properly distinguishing between the three methods of solving disputes, namely persuasion, compromise, and force, is rendered difficult by the fact that the

---

[77] Oliver Martin (1948), "Beyond Compromise," *Ethics* 58, no. 2: 118.
[78] Ibid., 119.
[79] Ibid., 120.

presuppositions of compromise "are the same as, or similar to, the method of force, but the end it aims at is the same as, or similar to, that of the method of persuasion."[80] As a matter of fact, "the method of compromise is ... itself a compromise between the two methods, that of persuasion, on the one hand, and that of force, on the other."[81]

As persuasion, argues Martin, compromise aims at the avoidance of violence, and yet, as in the case of the use of force, it presupposes a lack of good will. Reason is non-normative and remains merely instrumental – "its chief function is to find good reasons for defending what is already willed."[82] In compromise as we understand it today none of the parties tries to transcend itself, *placing itself in the position of the missing arbitrator* and becoming a critic of its own will, for there is no assumption of an objective truth or a common interest. If the disputants are asked and expected to be 'reasonable,' it is only because they have no expectations of reaching "a new or fuller truth but to alleviate the effects of bad will."[83] "The disputants 'listen to reason' only because they are irrational to begin with, to put it paradoxically."[84]

The normative difficulties became obvious from the first attempt to draw limits between 'proper' and 'improper' compromise made by one of its most enthusiastic supporters – T.V. Smith, by the middle of the twentieth century. The first limit is, for him, "*necessity*": "a man does not have to compromise with himself."[85] Compromise is desirable only when necessary, and "necessary only when somehow desirable."[86] The second limit is "*peace*." Since, as we have seen, compromise is "an alternative to war, it loses its nature if it does not lead to peace."[87] Chamberlain's compromising with Hitler at Munich did not lead to peace but to war. It was, therefore, a "bad compromise." The third limit of compromise is "*progress*": if a compromise does not further the "perfectibility of mankind," but instead breeds further sacrifices at the next stage, it should be avoided altogether.

However, for authors like John H. Hallowell, this account is far from satisfactory: only because compromise is sometimes inevitable, it does not follow that it is also desirable. "The inevitability of the existence of crime will never be an argument for its desirability or for the toleration of criminals."[88] For Hallowell, Smith faces insurmountable logical difficulties in trying to argue both for the centrality of compromise *and* for the moral dangers it possesses

---

[80] Ibid.
[81] Ibid., 121.
[82] Ibid., 120.
[83] Ibid.
[84] Ibid., 121.
[85] As one remembers, the same 'limit' was set forth before by Burke: "a man won't barter away the jewels of his soul."
[86] Smith, "Compromise," 8.
[87] Ibid., 9.
[88] John H. Hallowell (1944), "Compromise as Political Ideal," *Ethics* 54, no. 3: 158.

beyond certain limits. How is one to find, he asks, "some standards with which to measure the limits of what, in specific situations, can be safely conceded" since the "principle of compromise, as a self-sufficient principle, cannot supply the standard"?[89] How is one to determine "the lesser evil" when one is left with no normative way to determine what evil is (or for that matter virtue)? "How can individuals possibly know if they are making progress, whether a compromise will hasten or retard this progress"?[90] None of the three limits proposed by Smith can withstand Hallowell's logical scrutiny. "Since we cannot properly question the legitimacy of the demands, the honesty of the parties to the compromise, or the justice of the substance of the compromise, we cannot anticipate the consequences of making any particular compromise."[91]

Morley's warning against confusing method with principle appears clearer by now. If one elevates the *method* of compromise to the rank of a democratic *principle*, one will be tempted to say with Smith that "democracy is *whatever* can be arrived at democratically, and not another thing."[92] Since there are no commonly-accepted higher principles or values to which democracy is to be kept accountable, "anything goes" so long as it is a democratically taken decision – even, in extremis, a totally undemocratic law. In Hallowell's words, "if democracy is *anything*, it is nothing."[93] As Morley warned some hundred years before, it seems that once accepted as a self-sufficient principle, the inherent logic of compromise refuses 'confinement.'

Despite this warning, Smith's attempt to 'limit' compromise was not the last. For a long time, it has remained the main strategy followed to solve the "air of paradox surrounding the connection between morality and compromise."[94] Several authors have differentiated between compromising interests and compromising principles or rights, between compromise 'as end-state' and compromise 'as process,' between 'decent' and 'indecent' compromise, but also between the contexts in which compromise occurs, between the passive or reflexive ("the code has been compromised" or "Henry compromised himself") and the active form of compromise as verb, on the one hand, and compromise as substantive ("they reached a compromise").[95] Unfortunately, such distinctions are easy to assert but difficult to maintain, and so far none of the authors who have seriously considered this issue have cared about the distinction that could

---

[89] Ibid., 159.
[90] Ibid., 167.
[91] Ibid., 168.
[92] Quoted in ibid., 172.
[93] Ibid.
[94] Kuflik, "Morality and Compromise," 38.
[95] See, e.g., Patrick J. Dobel (1990), *Compromise and Political Action* (Savage: Rowman and Littlefield Publishers); Martin Benjamin (1990), *Splitting the Difference: Compromise and Integrity in Ethics and Politics* (Lawrence: University Press of Kansas); George Armstrong Kelly (1979), "Mediation versus Compromise in Hegel," in Pennock and Chapman, eds., *Compromise in Ethics*; Avishai Margalit (2005), "Indecent Compromise, Decent Peace," Tanner Lectures on Human Values, delivered at Stanford, Calif., May 4–5, 2005.

help illuminate matters – that between the two fora. If 'being compromised' carries a negative connotation it is because it affects one's *forum internum*, that is, one's identity and authenticity. To her merit, in a recent article Chiara Lepora tackles with the problem, yet from the same normative and ahistorical perspective. She concludes by saying that in choosing compromise the feeling of 'being (morally) compromised' is almost unavoidable and should not be taken lightly.[96]

Other distinctions also meant to keep the negative connotations of compromise at bay have proved problematic as well – for example, Martin Benjamin's distinction between compromising interests (which is beneficial) and compromising principles (which may be pernicious). Because the border between the two is subject to rephrasing, translating principles into interests and vice versa appears to be rather a matter of skill, as Benjamin is the first to acknowledge. "Politicians, diplomats, mediators, and others on the front of social conflict are … often inclined to construe disagreements that may have been originally formulated in terms of moral values or principles as conflicts of nonmoral interests."[97]

The genius of American politics – observed Wolff in the same vein – is its ability to treat even matters of principles as though they are conflicts of interest. (It has been remarked that the genius of French politics is its ability to treat even conflicts of interest as matters of principle.)[98]

How is one then to decide what represents a "principle" and what an "interest," especially since one individual's interest may very well constitute another individual's principle? Even a question as technical as budget allocation for education or defense can be construed equally justly in terms of interests or principles. But if the distinction between interests and principles is so difficult, then the difference between "compromising yourself," that is, changing one's self-defining principles or values, and "reaching a compromise" between competing interests is also called into question. Burke's caution that no one will willingly barter away "the jewel of his soul" appears therefore suddenly problematic. Lacking the forgotten dialectic between *forum internum*, which – in the classical understanding – cannot be represented nor compromised, and *forum externum* – the only of the two fora that can be the subject of both – it is extremely difficult to understand why compromising on principles came to be equated by so many authors with 'compromising oneself.'

To solve the conundrum, Martin P. Golding evades altogether the very possibility of compromising principles, since "it is far from clear that conflicts that are rooted in differences of principle or ideology, for example, can be

[96] Chiara Lepora (2012), "On Compromise and Being Compromised," *Journal of Political Philosophy*, 20:1, 1–22.

[97] Benjamin, *Splitting the Difference*, 15.

[98] R.P. Wolff (1965), "Beyond Tolerance," in *A Critique of Pure Tolerance*, ed. Robert Paul Wolff, Barrington Moore, Jr., and Herbert Marcuse (Boston: Beacon Press), 21.

terminated either by direct negotiated compromise or by submission to a third party."[99] "We are reduced, therefore, to conflict of interests and conflicts of rights." Yet the distinction is also a difficult one, as Golding himself acknowledges, for "it is certainly difficult to see how the opponents will come to a compromise if they insist upon standing on their rights." If they are doing so, it is "in terms of the interests these rights are seen to protect."[100]

In an attempt to reconcile the non-normative approach with the normative one, Martin P. Golding distinguishes between compromise *as end-state* and compromise *as process,* and asserts that "a process approach to the phenomenon of compromise requires that we go beyond mathematical game theory and into the disciplines of psychology, sociology, and moral philosophy."[101] Given the intimate connection between morality and compromise – at least in everyday life – any attempt to sever it appears futile and artificial. Furthermore, as Arthur Kuflik observes in the same volume, the fact that we readily use such pairs of expressions as "a compromise has been reached" and "reaching a solution *through* compromise" signals that Golding's distinction is not easy to maintain. "It is often difficult to speak plausibly of compromise unless *both* procedural and end-state criteria have been met."[102]

2.4. THE (A)MORALITY OF COMPROMISE

The difficulty of severing the connection between morality and compromise did not discourage attempts to purge compromise of any moral connotations whatsoever. Once the normative issue is bracketed, it appears the rational choice *par excellence.* No wonder "if philosophers have tended to ignore [this] subject, the same cannot be said of game theorists, economists, and writers on industrial and international relations."[103] If you accept the non-normative assumptions of the formal theory of games in which politics is understood in terms of conflict situations whose payoff matrix is known, compromise becomes the method of choice. "Given certain axioms or criteria of rationality or equity, the utilities of the possible outcomes, and the strategic possibilities available to opponents, the desirable results may be deduced."[104]

Since delimitating moral from immoral compromises proved problematic to say the least, only two other possible ways to tackle this conundrum appear to remain: either one accepts that compromise, properly understood, is *essentially* a *moral* political practice, or one takes the opposite path, arguing that compromise is *neither moral nor immoral, but amoral* and ought to be

[99] Martin P. Golding (1979), "The Nature of Compromise: A Preliminary Inquiry," in Pennock and Chapman, eds., *Compromise in Ethics,* 10–11.
[100] Ibid., 11.
[101] Ibid., 8.
[102] Kuflik, "Morality and Compromise," 40.
[103] Golding, "The Nature of Compromise," 6.
[104] Ibid., 8.

apprehended from an entirely different perspective. Some of the most recent attempts to conceptualize political compromise did exactly that – with mixed results. Obviously, trying to get rid by fiat of some obvious connotations of a concept implies a bit of vanity and a strong dose of naivety. But once again there is much to be learned from such weaknesses. And once again, the intellectual history of the concept will help us understand why and how apparently opposite assumptions about the normative character of compromise end up disputing the relationship between compromise 'properly understood' and 'consensus.'

David Gauthier took the rational choice method a step further. "Morality," he argues, "can be generated as a rational constraint from the non-moral premises of rational choice."[105] As a matter of fact, as Peter Vallentyne observes, he was "engaged in three distinct but closely related projects: (1) defending a contractarian theory of morality, (2) defending a theory of rational choice, and (3) defending the claim that rationality requires that we comply with the dictates of morality."[106]

Although he is not the first to posit a connection between rational choice and justice – John Rawls and John Harsanyi made more or less similar arguments – "neither Rawls nor Harsanyi develops the deep connection between morals and rational choice" that he defends.[107] He claims that his *Morals by Agreement* constitutes no more nor less than "the correct moral theory."[108] Such confidence should come as no surprise, considering that Gauthier's acknowledged inspirer is none other than Hobbes, who claimed in turn that political philosophy was "no older than my own book *De cive.*"[109] Besides Hobbes, Gauthier draws heavily on John Locke, David Hume, and Glaucon's description of justice in Plato, so, as one might expect, his theory is a combination of game theory, rational choice theory, and contractarianism.

What distinguishes his theory from Glaucon's, Hobbes's, or even Locke's and drives him closer to Hume is the assumption that bargaining a collective agreement between self-interested individuals fulfills more than the negative function of protecting each of them from the others' potential evil acts. At least under certain circumstances it betters each one's own interests. Following

---

[105] Gauthier, *Morals by Agreement*, 4.

[106] Peter Vallentyne (1991) "Gauthier's Three Projects," in *Contractarianism and Rational Choice: Essays on David Gauthier's Morals by Agreement*, ed. Peter Vallentyne (New York: Cambridge University Press), 1.

[107] Gauthier, *Morals by Agreement*, 4. See also John Rawls (1971), *A Theory of Justice* (Cambridge, Mass.: Harvard University Press); and John C. Harsanyi (1976), "Advances in Understanding Rational Behavior," in *Essays on Ethics, Social Behavior, and Scientific Explanation* (Dordrecht: Reidel Publishing), and (1982) "Morality and the Theory of Rational Behavior," in *Utilitarianism and Beyond*, ed. A. Sen and B. Williams (Cambridge: Cambridge University Press).

[108] Gauthier, *Morals by Agreement*, vi.

[109] Thomas Hobbes (1839), *English Works*, ix, quoted in Hannah Arendt (1998), *The Human Condition*, introduction by Margaret Canovan (Chicago and London: University of Chicago Press), 249.

Hume, Gauthier assumes that it is in each man's self-interest to partially ... give away his own self-interest.

Glaucon represents justice as a necessary evil because he supposes that it affords us only a second-best means to our ends. But he is mistaken. The co-operation that justice makes possible, considered both in terms of what it brings about, and in terms of the participatory activity that it involves, is not a second-best way of realizing what could, but for some particular obstacles, better be realized in some other way. In co-operating we make the most effective use of our powers to attain ends that could otherwise lie beyond our individual capacities.[110]

Gauthier's bargaining has all the ingredients of the modern compromise: it is an agreement made between parties that "each has her own independent conception of the good"[111] and reason is used instrumentally – "the equal rationality of the bargainers leads to the requirement that the greatest concession ... be as small as possible" (the principle of minimax relative concession).[112] If such agreement is called 'justice' (or 'morality,' for the two terms are used indiscriminately) it is because Gauthier is set to save morality's "foundational crisis" in the face of pluralism through "the only plausible resolution of the crisis" – contractaniarism.[113] If in the process the traditional conception of morality is challenged, so be it. Gauthier is quite clear on this point:

If the reader is tempted to object to some part of this view, on the ground that his moral intuitions are violated, then he should ask what weight such an objection can have, if morality is to fit within the domain of rational choice.[114]

However, it is not the aim of this section to critically engage Gauthier's theory. Several scholars have already done so from a variety of perspectives.[115] What is important to emphasize is the *logical* connection that Gauthier underlines between social contract and modern compromise. True, he prefers talking about 'bargaining' instead of 'compromise' – unlike his commentators, who do not make this distinction[116] – but the explanation is to be found in his peculiar attention to conceptual use (another particular trait shared with Hobbes). If his 'bargain' is not properly speaking a compromise, it is because it does not carry any negative connotations at all. On the contrary, it becomes the very realization of morality.

---

[110] Gauthier, *Morals by Agreement*, 345.

[111] Ibid., 346.

[112] Ibid., 14.

[113] David Gauthier (1991), "Why Contractarianism?" in Vallentyne, *Contractarianism and Rational Choice*, 15–16.

[114] Gauthier, *Morals by Agreement*, 296.

[115] See ibid., esp. the contributions of Christopher W. Morris, Jean Hampton, Peter Danielson, Jan Noverson, Geoffrey Sayre-McCord, and David Copp.

[116] See, e.g., Gauthier, "Why Contractarianism?" 5n: "The agreement of these contractarian theories [Thomas Scanlon's and Jurgen Habermas's] is thus to be understood as that of a consensus rather than a bargain or compromise."

Richard Bellamy chooses a different path. If for Gauthier morals by agreement supposedly captures the understanding of the economic man and the affections of the liberal individual, for Bellamy compromise bridges the gap between the liberal individual and the democratic one. For him, the mistake all along was to confound 'compromise' with 'consensus' or 'general agreement.' In a book published in 1999, Richard Bellamy coined the term 'democratic liberalism' in contradistinction to the classical 'liberal democracy.' Trying to find the proper solution for healing the tension between liberalism and democracy posed by pluralism, Bellamy found it in compromise – "the stuff of both democracy, with its concern that everyone has a stake, and liberalism, defending individual and group freedom."[117] He took position against the 'republic of reasons' in which the most compelling argument is expected to prevail, arguing that "pluralism renders such reasoning problematic, since more than one rationally compelling argument may be in play."[118] According to his reading, most liberal answers to the challenges of pluralism end up with compromise understood as a variety of consensus. Therefore, he started off acknowledging the intractable character of pluralism, "in many respects both a product and a problem for liberalism," and arguing that the three models of democratic compromise that attract contemporary liberals (*traders*, *trimmers*, and *segregationists*) are all to be found wanting, "not least in their exclusion of democratic politics."[119]

For libertarian *traders*, for whom the central figure remains F.A. Hayek, different views and values should be treated as subjective preferences. Agreement through compromise can be reached by trading the resources needed to satisfy them. Politics is kept at a minimum and replaced whenever possible by the market. As already observed, such an approach goes hand in hand with the theory of rational choice and its derivatives.

To underwrite the hope that this is a satisfactory approach, there is the theory of rational choice, extending to the theory of games and bargaining. Generalized to an 'economic' theory of human behaviour, it has been presented as an account of democratic politics. It offers a liberal notion of rationality as the enlightened assessing of advantage, and of neutrality as a refusal to pass moral judgment on the interests included. On this account, 'mutually beneficial compromises' naturally emerge from the 'partisan mutual adjustment' encouraged by democratic bargaining.[120]

However, Bellamy finds this approach to compromise less than satisfactory, because "a rational agent seems bound to reason that it is rational not to contribute [to a non-excludable good], unless forced, whether or not others do." "A theory which makes rational choice a matter of individual self-interest

---

[117] Richard Bellamy (1999), *Liberalism and Pluralism: Towards a Politics of Compromise* (London and New York: Routledge), 94.
[118] Ibid., 138.
[119] Ibid., 13.
[120] Ibid., 96.

gives no reason to think that a sum of rational choices will be in the collective interest." The gap between the good of each and the good of all cannot be bridged unless "the theory of rational choice ... comes up with a contractarian theory of ethics – a speculative territory at best."[121] Even then, the problem of minority/identity groups remains unsolved, for such conflicting values as group identities cannot be "homogenized as preferences in search of a common utility."[122] Not everything can be easily translated into money. "Like Oscar Wilde's cynic, market traders know the price of everything and the value of nothing."[123]

Liberal *trimmers* (a term inspired by George Savile, Marquis de Halifax's *The Character of a Trimmer*), on the other hand, seek compromise as consensus by avoiding altogether any 'hot' issue that is not susceptible to compromise. If the principles are not agreed upon, they are 'trimmed down' and thus kept off the agenda. "Thus, Charles Larmore and John Rawls have characterized what they call a political liberalism as an approach that abstracts as far as possible from controversial comprehensive moral positions."[124] Apparently, such self-restraint is supposed to stop "democracy from tearing itself apart by keeping the rights and liberties that define the democratic sphere clear of political controversy." "In the spirit of Halifax, they contend that such trimming is essential to the long-term stability of a pluralist society, characterized by profound and interminable disagreements over the meaning of life."[125]

Yet, as Bellamy points out, trimmers' search for the 'lowest common denominator' is a search for "stability, rather than justice *tout court*," and as such it might be compatible even with a great wrong so long as this wrong cannot become subject of agreement. "Any attempts to divorce principles of justice from all controversial moral and metaphysical considerations risk vacuity."[126] According to him, "trimmers resemble G.K. Chesterton's man of universal good will, ridiculed for saying, 'Whatever the merits of torturing innocent children to death, and no doubt there is much to be said on both sides, I am sure we all agree that it should be done with sterilized instruments.'" The middle ground is not always "the home of truth and virtue."[127]

Finally, *segregators*, such as Michael Walzer, take pluralism at face value and reach the assessment therefore that "the plurality of goods and principles operating both within and between different communities ... make universal or generalisable rules of justice inappropriate."[128] As a result, segregators "aim at avoiding compromise by preserving the integrity of each value, culture

---

[121] Ibid., 97.
[122] Ibid.
[123] Ibid., 11.
[124] Ibid., 99.
[125] Ibid.
[126] Ibid., 100.
[127] Ibid., 99–100.
[128] Ibid., 67.

or interest within its own domain."[129] However, as in the previous cases, this might be easier said than done. In practice, "setting the boundaries itself entails compromise and the participation of those affected both within and outside them."[130] If one adds to this difficulty that of trying to maintain fixed boundaries between groups in flux and individuals with multiple allegiances, one comes to realize that, in effect, "segregation to avoid all compromises requires all questioning of existing boundaries be suppressed, and so invariably entrenches the domination of hegemonic elites."[131]

The astuteness of most of these criticisms is undermined by Bellamy's own interpretation of compromise – one that pays little or no consideration either to the way some of the authors he mentions clearly distinguished between 'consensus' and 'compromise,' or to the history of the concept. It follows instead its own agenda. As a result, the accuracy of the diagnosis and the solution he proposes are open to question. For example, he imposes the label of 'compromiser' on an author such as Rawls, regardless of the fact that he specifically delimits 'compromise' from 'consensus.' Rawls clearly states that "a balance of reasons as seen within each citizen's comprehensive doctrine, and *not a compromise* compelled by circumstances, is the basis of citizens' respect for the limits of public reason."[132] He is adamant that his 'overlapping consensus' has nothing to do with political compromise and goes to great lengths to elucidate this misunderstanding: "the acceptance of the political conception *is not a compromise* between those holding different views, but rests in the totality of reasons specified within the comprehensive doctrine affirmed by each citizen."[133]

Besides, Bellamy offers as alternative solution a 'fair' and 'negotiated' compromise that on closer examination proves to have little to do with the concept as it is used today, being almost entirely an artificial construction. The roots of this confusion are to be found in yet another – between the classical and the modern versions of compromise. Whenever he attacks 'democratic compromise' in what he labels as its 'liberal' version, Bellamy assumes an Enlightenment understanding of compromise – one in which "rationalism ... treats political questions as a matter for experts in the public good and ... overrides or re-educates people's ideas in their interests in the name of a vision of progress."[134] It is then unsurprising if he finds third-party arbitration unsatisfactory. "Much as the Rawlsean 'method of avoidance' assumes that a line between the 'political' and the 'metaphysical', the 'public' and the 'private' can be drawn a priori, so deference to an allegedly 'neutral' arbitrator presupposes the possibility of an impartial standpoint from outside the debate."[135]

---

[129] Ibid., 100.

[130] Ibid., 100–101.

[131] Ibid., 101.

[132] John Rawls (2005), *Political Liberalism*, expanded ed. (New York: Columbia University Press), 169; emphasis added.

[133] Ibid., 170–171; emphasis added.

[134] Bellamy, *Liberalism and Pluralism*, 95.

[135] Ibid., 102.

For Bellamy, the Aristotelian arbitrator is impossible under the condition of pluralism. On the ground that values are incommensurable, any attempts to discover a just solution for both parties and for the whole are prima facie discarded from the start as either impossible or hegemonic. Since true impartiality cannot be reached it is not only impossible but also dangerous to be sought at all, either by the parties involved in a dispute or by the arbitrator. *The classical understanding of compromise is here turned upside-down.* It is in effect the modern assumption about the classical compromise. According with this modern understanding, rational persuasion is from the start suspicious on two accounts – for being 'rational' and for being 'persuasive.' The 'rationality' assumption is dubious because it assumes an objective and shared rationality that can be discovered providing that the parties are willing to do so. On the contrary, the 'persuasion' part is suspect because it appears to make appeal to some nonrational forms of winning an argument.

Not surprisingly then, when it comes to his solution, Bellamy turns things around once again, labeling as 'fair compromise' a practice that, according with his own description, has nothing to do with the modern understanding, but relies heavily on the classical: rational persuasion for the sake of the common good. The focus is on the process of negotiation hereby understood as rational debate. As a result he ends up endorsing a slightly modified version of republicanism in which parties are not by necessity individuals but also groups with various values, interests, and so on – all getting as much direct involvement in politics as possible. (It goes without saying that he does not endorse a 'professional political sphere' – the prerequisite of modern compromise, as shown before.) Once again, the lack of awareness about the connection between political representation and self-representation proves damaging to the argument. His 'democratic liberalism' aims at restoring democracy to the heart of liberalism. "This model of democracy draws on the pre-liberal notion of a political constitution based around the separation and dispersal of power and the mixing and balancing of social classes."[136] He is in effect, as one can easily see by now, much closer to Aristotle than he would care to admit. "At its heart, this conception of politics has an attachment to civic liberty, the guiding principles of which are non-domination, mutual acceptance and accommodation."[137]

Achieving a fair compromise also entails a *change in the character of politics*, but of a slightly different nature to one oriented towards consensus. It requires *a move from purely individualistic and instrumental politics* to a more interactive and problem-solving model. Rather than viewing other people's interests and values as mere constraints on getting one's own way to which minimal concessions should be made, this approach leads to the search for *solutions that attempt to integrate the various concerns* of the parties involved.[138]

[136] Ibid., 140.
[137] Ibid., 138.
[138] Ibid.

What Bellamy fails to see from lack of attention to the genealogy of the concept is that if this practice qualifies as compromise at all, it is compromise in the classical sense, where the *compromissores* was supposed not to obtain 'consensus,' nor to bargain between various interests, but to find the solution 'just' for both the parties and the whole. It was, as Bellamy's solution, a practice guided essentially by a vision of a common good. "It is doubtful that any process of negotiation would be possible unless people saw the political norms framing the discussion as generating some form of common good."[139] Absent the dialectic between the two fora of the individual, the move from an individualistic understanding of politics to a more communitarian and public-good oriented one remains problematic at best, resembling wishful thinking.

Frank R. Ankersmit took the opposite path to Bellamy's and yet ended up in a similar place through making the same confusion between the classical and modern versions of compromise. He attempts to find a way out of the moral conundrum by discarding ethical considerations altogether.[140] Yet to his merit, he sees the connection between compromise and political representation more clearly than do other scholars. His theory of "aesthetic representation," closely linked to a particular interpretation of compromise and to the distinction between Anglo-American political systems and continental European ones, aims to reduce to "irrelevance" the normative or ethical question.[141] Ankersmit criticizes what he identifies as "the three traditions in mainstream contemporary philosophy – the *liberal* tradition (as exemplified by Rawls or Dworkin), that of *republicanism* (as exemplified by John Pocock), and that of *communitarianism* (as exemplified by Alisdair MacIntyre, Charles Taylor, or Amitai Etzioni)" – by leveling against them the same argument: for all, the individual represents "the basis or 'foundation' of the social and political order; and no clear distinction is made between the social or pre-political, and the political order."[142]

By breaking down the barriers between society and politics on the one hand, and between ethics and politics on the other, "each of these three traditions is therefore, to greater or lesser extent, tainted by (or at least vulnerable to) the seductions of totalitarianism inherent in much pre-nineteenth century political thought."[143] The paradoxical result of this extreme individualization is the "complete politicization of all interhuman relationships." Yet the individual is not the only "victim." The state suffers too, because the distance between

---

[139] Ibid., 139.

[140] In the following pages I chiefly rely on Frank Ankersmit (1996), *Aesthetic Politics: Political Philosophy Beyond Fact and Value* (Stanford, Calif.: Stanford University Press); Frank Ankersmit (2002), "Representational Democracy"; and Frank Ankersmit (2004), "Trust and Value," in *Trust: Cement of Democracy?* ed. Frank R. Ankersmit and Henk Te Velde (Leuven, Paris: Peters).

[141] Ankersmit, *Aesthetic Politics*, 23.

[142] Ibid., 7.

[143] Ibid.

itself and civil society is abolished, resulting in a fragmentation of the political center, a domination of economic discourse over political discourse, and a preeminence of bureaucracy.

Ankersmit's solution is a return of political philosophy from ethics to aesthetics – a third domain able to transcend the gap between facts and values, between *is* and *ought*. Only an aesthetic theory of representation, he argues, can properly account for "the difference between the representative and the person represented, the absence of identity of the representative and the person represented [which] is as unavoidable in political representation as the unavoidable difference between a painted portrait and the person portrayed."[144] This aesthetic representation will recapture the idea of the state as *wholeness* "in terms of which the political consciousness of the citizen preferably and probably even exclusively, articulates itself." As it is now, the contemporary democratic state "has exchanged the *top-down* approach for the *bottom-up* approach to politics and is no longer interested in achieving a coherence in its policies expressing or suggesting a conception of the whole."[145]

Surprisingly, though, after all these criticisms, Ankersmit himself opts for a bottom-up, ascending theory of representation, centered once again on the individual. He too subscribes "to the current opinion that only human beings can be represented and not abstractions such as 'Reason' (Guizot) or a 'transcendent truth' (Voegelin), or, to mention a few more prosaic examples, party manifestos, interests, or political ideals."[146] As a result, his historical narrative, meant to back up the theory, remains equally open to question. However, as will become clear in the following chapters, some of his insights about the inherent connection between compromise, representation, and a certain understanding of the relationship between civil society and politics remain valuable.

In Ankersmit's account, 'true' representative democracy came into being not, as orthodoxy has it, in England, but instead in the Romantic climate of post-Napoleonic Europe. Only then was consensus (as Rawls, among others, understood it) discarded as a viable political solution between competing factions, and representative democracy became "the political system best suited for achieving compromise." Only then was "the very idea of a compromise about basic political principles," "*a principled unprincipledness*," really able to flourish.[147]

The reason for this is to be found for Ankersmit in the different relationships between state and civil society across the English Channel, and, later, across the Atlantic. "In neither England nor the United States did people fight *against* each other over the question of who was to control the state; they fought *together* to keep the power of the executive within acceptable limits."[148]

[144] Ibid., 28.
[145] Ankersmit, "Trust and Value," 46; emphasis added.
[146] Ankersmit, *Aesthetic Politics*, 25.
[147] Ankersmit, "Representational Democracy," 27.
[148] Ibid., 29.

Consequentially, the logics of Anglo-American democracies and the continental ones respectively differ deeply. "Anglo-Saxon democracy is so monistically monarchical that, if it had to deal with large number of smaller parties (none of them possessing close to a majority) that obtain in continental democracies, the result would be as disorienting for the state as if there were an absolute king who wanted several conflicting things at once and was unable to decide among them."[149] Paradoxically, argues Akersmit, by starting with an opposition between civil society as a whole and the state, the English representational system ended by diminishing the distance between the two, thus reducing politics to mere administration, where the "conservative consensus" stands in contrast with the "creative compromise" typical of ideologically fragmented continental democracies.

Although some of Ankersmit's insights concerning compromise, representation, and the relationship between civil society and politics are fascinating and worth consideration, his theory suffers a serious blow when confronted with historical reality. As a survey of multiple sources from the sixteenth and seventeenth centuries demonstrates, the attitude toward compromise across the English Channel refuses to follow his account: as I will show in the following chapter, it is precisely in the Anglo-American world where compromise was most valued, while conversely continental thinkers (and politicians for that matter) tried their best to avoid the pitfalls of the necessity to compromise.

2.5. COMPROMISE AS A NATIONAL FEATURE?

Every political system is characterized by a prevalent attitude toward important political concepts. The sum of these prevalent attitudes may be seen as the national character of politics in these systems. One such fundamental concept is compromise. It could be argued that every political system can be classified by students of comparative politics on the basis of its prevalent attitude toward compromise.[150]

If we are to take Marvin Rintala's observation seriously, the general disregard of political scientists for the peculiar positive usage of compromise in Anglo-American discourse, in contrast to the rest of the world, appears as an oddity. As Peter B. Knupfer observes: "It has become a truism among political scientists, historians, and informal observers of American political history that compromise is the hallmark of the liberal polity."[151] The few authors alluded to before who observed that "such a positive conception of compromise is far from universal" cared more about its implications for real-life politics than about searching for its roots.[152] Rintala himself, after making such a bold

---

[149] Ibid.
[150] Marvin Rintala (1969), "The Two Faces of Compromise," *Western Political Quarterly* 22, no. 2: 326; henceforth referred to as TF.
[151] Knupfer, "The Rhetoric of Conciliation," 315.
[152] TF, 327.

claim, focuses his attention solely "on the widely divergent attitudes toward compromise prevalent in British and German politics."[153]

He quotes, among other key figures of English politics, "the distinguished British political scientist, Sir Ernest Baker," who argued that "in a compromise all ideas are reconciled,"[154] only to observe that "his conception of compromise is typically British, representing a wide variety of political views."[155] It is no wonder then if "in British politics compromise is a virtue imputed *to gentlemen and all other decent persons*" while "in German politics compromise is the weakness of the moral flabby" and "the greatest of all sins."[156]

For virtually all British politicians it is a self-evident truth that "the willingness to compromise is as desirable as it is essential to the working of free institutions."[157] It is, in contrast, the highest mark for a German political leader to appear so courageous as to refuse all compromise with the forces of evil that are all about him in society. A British student of *The Essentials of Parliamentary Democracy*, R. Bassets, holds that compromise, "far from being the source of political immorality, is, from the democratic standpoint one of its cardinal virtues." In German political discussion there are few references to the possible good that a compromise might accomplish; instead, the evils of *Kuhhandel* (literally, "cattle-trading" or "log-rolling" in its American manifestation) are constantly stressed.[158]

George Armstrong Kelly makes an observation that reinforces Rintala's, yet unfortunately he too stops short from tracing back the origins of such discrepancy, focusing instead on whether or not Hegel can be considered a 'compromiser.' Unsurprisingly, he concludes that "there is no hint of compromise in the procedures of the Hegelian dialectics."[159] "In the Anglo-Saxon lexicon, 'compromise' is basically a far more positive word in politics than it could have been for Hegel, or indeed for any writer imbued with rationalist metaphysics or the 'spirit of system.'"[160] It is only in Anglo-Saxon discourse, he remarks, that "compromise is at least on the edge of being a virtue."[161]

"Compromise" in our sense is difficult to render into German. Among the candidates we might cite are *Ubereinkunft*, which has the basic meaning of "agreement" or "accord"; *Vertrag*, which means specifically "contract"; *Mithilfe*, usually rendered as (voluntary) "cooperating"; *Mitbestimmung*, "codetermination"; and *Kompromiss*, a loanword that often means "the state of being compromised." "Mediation" is *Vermittlung*.[162]

---

[153] Ibid., 326.
[154] Ernest Barker (1958), *Reflections on Government* (New York: Oxford University Press), quoted in TF, 326.
[155] Ibid.
[156] Ibid., 327; emphasis added.
[157] The quote is from Henry Fairlie (1967), "The Lives of the Politicians: Ordinary and Extraordinary," *Encounter* 29: 22.
[158] TF, 328.
[159] Kelly, "Mediation versus Compromise in Hegel," 93.
[160] Ibid., 89.
[161] Ibid., 91.
[162] Ibid., 101.

It is, as Rintala put it, a "fundamental dichotomy" between the British and the Germans that" flows "from different conceptions of politics."[163] The paragraph is worth quoting, for it reveals a deeper gap in the understanding of politics than we normally care to consider – that between *governability* and *representativity*, which in turn underlines the debates between the partisans of a majoritarian system of representation versus the supporters of a PR system – an issue heavily disputed in the field of comparative politics whose connection with different understandings of compromise will be discussed later.[164]

> For a Britisher, the primary purpose of politics is to arrive to some agreement as to common action; in other words, to make a decision – to govern. For a German, on the other hand, the primary purpose of politics is to represent the divers forces in society whose interests are assumed to be incompatible.[165]

To the reader already familiar with the modern understanding of compromise, Rintala's praise of it as the only alternative to violence should by now come as no surprise. According to him, "the politics of violence is the logical alternative to the politics of compromise."[166] Hitler ("world views admit of no compromise") and Nietzsche ("compromise is mediocrity, though it be called moderation") are both used as examples to stress the point that "in the final analysis the divergent British and German conceptions of compromise rest upon contradictory assumptions about human nature."

> The positive conception of compromise rests upon the assumption of human *equality*. The rejection of compromise rests upon the assumption that the opinions of all individuals are not of equal *value*. Those who believe in compromise assume that everyone has something valuable to offer, and that all men are fallible, while those who reject compromise believe that only a select group, such a particular nation or class, or even a particular individual, has anything valuable to offer, and that this group or individual is infallible. This latter attitude was exemplified by Adolf Hitler in *Mein Kampf*.[167]

Rintala's article captures extremely well the modern and, shall we say, uncompromising assumptions about compromise as the result of the tension between an abstract equality and an undisputable inequality in terms of aptitudes and therefore competency. The renowned Arab scholar Tarek Heggi would not go so far as his predecessors, although he takes the same down-to-earth approach to the differences he observes in the usage of compromise across the world. By the beginning of the twenty-first century, he too notes with unconcealed surprise the differences between the general Anglo-American meaning and that of the rest of the world and finds the Arab world in dire need of this specific word.

---

[163] TF, 327, 329.
[164] See, e.g., Pippa Norris (2004), *Electoral Engineering: Voting Rules and Political Behavior* (Cambridge: Cambridge University Press).
[165] TF, 329.
[166] Ibid.
[167] Ibid., 331.

A few years ago, I discovered that there is no equivalent in the Arabic language, classical or colloquial, for the English word [sic!] "compromise," which is more commonly translated into Arabic in the form of two words, literally meaning 'halfway solution.' I went through all the old and new dictionaries and lexicons I could lay my hands on in a futile search for an Arabic word corresponding to this common English word, which exists, with minor variations in spelling, in all European languages, whether of the Latin, Germanic, Hellenic or Slavic families.[168]

Since "language is not merely a tool of communication but the depositary of a society's cultural heritage, reflecting its way of thinking and the spirit in which it deals with things and with others, as well as the cultural trends which have shaped it," Heggi realized to his merit that he had come "before a phenomenon with cultural (and, consequently, political, economic and social) implications." Deploring the fact that the Arabic language has no equivalent for 'compromise,' he observes that Latin peoples tend to use 'compromise' less often and with a different connotation than their Anglo-Saxon counterparts. The explanation, according to Heggi, is to be found no earlier than the nineteenth century, when the widespread success of the utilitarian and pragmatist philosophies in the Anglo-American world helped shape a particular mode of thought.

One of the principal influences on the reforming thought of the nineteenth century, English philosopher Jeremy Bentham (1748–1832), believed all systems, laws, institutions and ideas should be based on the principle of utility (utilitarianism). The United States, for its part, produced two renowned philosophers, William James (1842–1910) and John Dewey (1859–1952), whose works reflected Bentham's ideas but with modifications dictated by the passage of time and the unfolding of events and under the different name of pragmatism. The notion of compromise spilled beyond the Anglo-Saxon world into societies belonging to different cultural traditions.[169]

In his narrative, the recent history of the Muslim world "is made up largely of losses which could have been avoided had we had not persistently rejected the notion of compromise as tantamount to submission, retreat, surrender, capitulation and even, as some of our more fiery orators put it, as a form of bondage to the will of others," because "although Islamic scripture is totally compatible with a culture characterized by compromise, Muslim history (especially its Arab chapter) has proceeded in a spirit that is antithetical to the notion of compromise."[170] The solution, according to Heggi, requires "immediate action": "For a start, a team of intellectuals with a cultural formation made up of a synthesis of Arab, Islamic and other humanistic cultures should come together and lay down a charter to instill the rationale of compromise in

---

[168] Tarek Heggi (2002), "The Culture of Compromise" (Arabic: Thaqafet Al-Holoul Al-Wassat), *Al-Ahram*, trans. at http://www.mideastweb.org/compromise.htm. See also http://www.heggy.org.
[169] Ibid.
[170] Ibid.

the minds of the young people of Egypt through educational curricula and by promoting the idea that compromise is the strongest product of nature, life and the march of civilizations and cultures."[171]

Without trying to minimize in any way Heggi's enthusiasm about compromise, one may still wonder if, before undertaking any "immediate action," one should not first inquire into the path by which compromise came to signify so different things for different cultures, for the explanation that he advances is evidently defective. The difference in the usage of compromise across the Channel was already present by the end of the sixteenth century and was fully manifest during the entirety of the seventeenth.

The next chapters aim to demonstrate precisely this and to find an explanation that goes beyond a vague and scientifically unconvincing 'national character.'

[171] Ibid.

3

The Genealogy of Compromise and Its Vagaries

Dès le commencement le peuple a établi les Rois comme par voie de compromis, pour éviter la confusion qui seroit, si en chacune affair d'importance il fallout rechercher l'avis de tous pour délibérer et conclure.

Guy Coquille (ca. 1585)

The said Members being thus setled, addrest themselves immediately to the settlement, &c. making the General Captain General of all the Forces in the three Kingdomes ... and then according to the contract and compromise with the General, on the day of March, dissolved that long and fatal Parliament, having ordered Writs to issue out for a new one to sit down at Westminster the 25th of April next the year 1661.

James Heath (1662)

It is probably more than mere coincidence that usage of the word "compromise" between France and England diverged by the end of the sixteenth century and became fully distinct throughout the seventeenth. These were years of challenge and change. The Reformation, the wars of religion, the increased movement of ideas thanks to the development of printing and traveling, and economic upheavals shook the confidence in the prevailing medieval paradigm of order, 'the great chain of being,' that connected the divine with the mundane order.[1] The poet John Donne (1572–1631) observed in his *Anatomie of the World*:

'Tis all in pieces, all coherence gone;
All just supply, and all relation:
Prince, subject, father, son, are things forgot,

[1] See Arthur Lovejoy (1936), *The Great Chain of Being* (Cambridge: Harvard University Press); Victor Harris (1949), *All Coherence Gone* (Chicago: University of Chicago Press); W.H. Greenleaf (1964), *Order, Empiricism, Politics* (London: Oxford University Press); or more recently Daniel Engster (2001), *Divine Sovereignty: The Origins of Modern State Power* (Dekalb, Ill.: Northern Illinois University Press).

> For every man alone thinks he hath got
> To be a phoenix, and that then can be
> None of that kind of which he is, but he.[2]

New paradigms were needed to address this period of profound, multilayered change, and various solutions were crafted in response to these challenges.[3] By the beginning of the seventeenth century, a rethinking of the individual and her or his relationship with the political sphere was well under way. It will affect not only the understanding of political representation but of self-representation as well, with consequences for the attitude toward compromise. "At a time of such intense cultural ferment about issues of obligation both in the personal and political sphere, it was clear to all that the relationship between the individual and the state needed to be reconceived."[4] It was, in the words of Theodore Rabb, a generalized "crisis of authority."[5] However, as the split in the usage of compromise seems to indicate, this crisis of authority was quite differently addressed on either side of the Channel, with long-lasting consequences. The rethinking of politics went hand-in-hand with new apprehensions of the self and since compromise was already situated at the crossroads between politics and morality it proved a concept that aptly reflected these changes.

Most authors deal with early modern intellectual developments from a pan-European perspective in which the differences between, say, England and France, France and Spain, or Spain and Italy are mere glitches in communication impeded by distance and/or religious, philosophical, or political particularities. As in the long run all such glitches are destined to be smoothed over, one can safely talk from a general perspective about "Foundations of Modern Political Thought," "Contexts of Conscience in Early Modern Europe, 1500–1700," "The Languages of Political Theory in Early Modern Europe," "The Individual in Political Theory and Practice," and "European Political Thought 1450–1700 – Religion, Law, and Philosophy," without paying too much attention to particularities.[6]

---

[2] John Donne (1985), *The Complete English Poems of John Donne*, ed. C.A. Patrides (London: J.M. Dent and Sons), 276.

[3] For a detailed discussion of the social, political, and economical crisis of sixteenth-century France, see the excellent study of J.H.M. Salmon (1975), *Society in Crisis: France in the Sixteenth Century* (London: Ernest Benn Limited). For the same crisis in seventeenth-century England, see Steve Pincus (2009), *1688: The First Modern Revolution* (New Haven and London: Yale University Press).

[4] Victoria Kahn (2004), *Wayward Contracts: The Crisis of Political Obligation in England, 1640–1674* (Princeton and Oxford: Princeton University Press), 8.

[5] Theodor K. Rabb (1975), *The Struggle for Stability in Early Modern Europe* (New York: Oxford University Press). See also Trevor H. Aston, ed. (1967), *Crisis in Europe 1560–1600* (Garden City. N.Y.: Anchor Books).

[6] See Quentin Skinner (1978), *The Foundations of Modern Political Thought*, 2 vols. (Cambridge: Cambridge University Press); but also Annabell Brett, James Tully, and Holly Mailton-Bleakley, eds. (2006), *Rethinking the Foundations of Modern Political Thought* (Cambridge: Cambridge University Press); Harald E. Braun and Edward Wallace, eds. (2004), *Contexts of Conscience in*

It is easy to see the reason for taking such a "holistic perspective." During Early Modernity (a period increasingly hard to circumscribe in the light of new research) the intellectual life of Europeans strived (as today) to overcome the obvious parochialism manifested at a social and political level and to address various challenges from a universalistic perspective. The concept of nation was still being forged while borders were subject to frequent changes. Even before the invention of printing, intellectual exchanges did not stop because of language barriers, let alone provisional political borders. Translations were commonplace. Universities all across Europe lived up to their name (by 1500 there were already some seventy-two universities across Europe, while by 1650 the number had more than doubled), and most intellectuals of the time were fluent in at least three European languages.[7] Students' mobility delivered "the countries on the fringes of Europe from their isolation and made them partners in the development of an entire continent."[8] Such travelers across Europe felt more or less at home, regardless of the changes in décor, and saw the differences as mere curiosities. They all felt members of the 'republic of letters.'[9]

However, I argue that the striking and long-enduring discrepancy in the usage of compromise on the two sides of the Channel suggests that these divergent histories are worth considering in their own right. Instead of assuming, as is commonly done, that they were mere variations of the same underlying change that all across Europe realized a common thrust toward 'modernity' in various guises, let us bracket for the time being this linear, evolutionary perspective.[10] I do not mean to deny the importance of looking at such histories in a larger context, which would deny historical realities and confine oneself to a pernicious parochialism. I would just caution against the assumption of a relatively homogeneous European 'republic of letters' that enables us to safely talk about 'modern political thought' as a whole and instead emphasize the need to focus on different evolutionary lines. After all, parallel discourses and vocabulary can and do coexist and the momentary success of one precludes neither the validity nor the endurance of another.[11] I will push the argument a

---

Early Modern Europe, 1500–1700 (Basingstoke: Palgrave Macmillan); Anthony Pagden, ed. (1987), *The Languages of Political Theory in Early-Modern Europe* (Cambridge: Cambridge University Press); Janet Coleman, ed. (1996), *The Individual in Political Theory and Practice* (Oxford: Clarendon Press); Howell A. Lloyd, Glenn Burgess, and Simon Hodson, eds. (2007), *European Political Thought, 1450–1700: Religion, Law, and Philosophy* (New Haven and London: Yale University Press). Obviously, the list of examples is much longer.

[7] For a detailed description of common cultural background during that period, see Lloyd, Burgess, and Hodson, *European Political Thought*, 9–54.

[8] Hilde de Ridder-Symoens (2003), "Mobility," in *A History of the University in Europe*, vol. 2: *Universities in Early-Modern Europe, 1500–1800*, ed. Hilde de Ridder Symoens (Cambridge: Cambridge University Press), 444.

[9] Lloyd, Burgess, and Hodson, *European Political Thought*, 27.

[10] For a discussion of 'modern' and 'modernity' as a general pattern all across Europe during the seventeenth century, see Pincus, *1688*, esp. the introduction, 8–9.

[11] See, among other works of these authors, J.G.A. Pocock (1985), *Virtue, Commerce and History: Essays on Political Thought and History, Chiefly in the Eighteenth Century*

bit further: such parallel discourses cannot just coexist, but in different places, different discourses will prove more successful than others. Same as the evolution of mankind, the evolution of ideas is far from a straight line.

The period I am interested in, stretching from the second half of the sixteenth century to the end of the seventeenth, offers an excellent example of intertwined discourses. For a while, on both sides of the Channel constitutionalist arguments coexisted with the development of absolutist thought, which in turn paralleled the first contractualist arguments – to name just the most popular types of discourse. In the end, however, some of them proved more persuasive than others and predominated. The main point of this chapter is to prove that for more than a century France and England acknowledged different types of discourse as 'winners' because different basic assumptions took hold of the popular psyche. This was no accident. I argue that, for a variety of historical reasons, two distinct forms of individualism evolved on either side of the Channel. It is the aim of this chapter to make a preliminary sketch of these different lineages to pinpoint as accurately as possible the moment of divergence.

The first part considers the classical roots of compromise as used during the Middle Ages in both secular and religious settings. Here, one finds the first connections between the classical understandings of compromise as contract, authority, and representation. The ways in which the French became increasingly distrustful of compromise by the second half of the sixteenth century are presented in the second part with an abundance of examples, after which I consider the English case during the same era. Here one finds a striking discrepancy. The fact that 'compromise,' a rather common word, was consistently used with opposite connotations during a time of increasing cultural exchanges should be enough to suggest that there is much more here than meets the eye. If the French were constantly worried about compromising themselves (their conscience, honor, virtue, etc.) while their British counterparts considered compromise a perfect method to solve conflicts and even a virtue in itself, the explanation needs to be found in the development of two different kinds of individualism. The next chapters will further check this hypothesis.

3.1. COMPROMISSUM AS ARBITRATIO

As a Latin word, *compromissum* had a paralegal sense that came straight from the Roman jurisprudence and retained most of the original sense:[12] *com-promissum* – promise together, as to abide by an arbiter's decision (*com* = together + *promittere* = promise) – and nothing else.[13] It was a method

---

(Cambridge: Cambridge University Press); and Quentin Skinner (1998), *Liberty Before Liberalism* (Cambridge: Cambridge University Press).

[12] Latin *compromissum*, from neuter of *compromissus*, past participle of *compromittere*.

[13] See *The Barnhart Dictionary of Etymology* (1988), ed. Robert K. Barnhart.

of last resort to solve a disagreement whenever a mutually acceptable solution between two individuals could not be reached otherwise, that is, through informed dialogue and rational persuasion. In other words, *compromissum* was accepted in Roman law as a verbal *contract* or promise (*stipulatio*) to abide by the decision of an arbitrator (*compromissarius* or *compromissor*) accepted as such by all parties.

The arbitrator was the *arbiter ex compromisso* and his agreement to so act was *receptum arbitrii*. "In their *compromissum*, the parties had to appoint the arbiter (it was concluded "*in aliquem arbitrum*"), they had to confer upon him *the full and unrestricted power* to decide their dispute, and they had to indicate *which subject matter* they wished to submit to him. No appeal was possible against the arbiter's decision."[14] The *compromissarius* had even more powers than a formal *judex* (ruler, judge) since he was not required to take into consideration any existing laws and could rule at his own discretion.[15] According to this meaning, the arbitrator's authority was already present at the time of the *compromissum* and was *not* the result of being chosen or designated. As strange as it might sound today, authority was *identified* yet not *created*. Both parties agreed upon the *compromissarius* precisely because both acknowledged his authority in judging the matter at hand and no further.

As such, *compromissum* was not used in political contexts but mainly in judicial ones, as its main role was to remove "the dispute from the ordinary jurisdiction of the courts."[16] *Paulus 2 ad edictum: Compromissum ad similitudinem iudiciorum redigitur et ad finiendas lites pertinet.* ("A compromise is similar to judgments in court, and it establishes the end of a dispute.") It was in essence a *private* system of justice, acknowledged as such by the parties involved. The specification is important because a few centuries later French dictionaries assume that the avoidance of official justice implies a guilty conscience of the parties involved. The first edition of the *Dictionaire de L'Academie Francaise* (1694) mentions that "*on ne met en compromis que les affaires douteuses*" ("one puts to compromise none but dubious affairs"). Yet the avoidance of the courts did not entail a lack of regulations – quite the contrary.

When parties who had a matter to litigate, *had agreed* to refer it to an arbitrator, which reference was called Compromissum, and a person *had accepted* the office of arbitrator (arbitrium receperit), the praetor *would compel him to pronounce a sentence, unless he had some legal excuse*. The Praetor could compel a person of any rank, as a Consularis for instance, to pronounce a sentence after taking upon him the office of arbitrator; but he could not compel a person who held a Magistratus or Potestas, as a Consul or Praetor, for he had no Imperium over them. The parties were bound to submit to the

---

[14] Reinhard Zimmermann (1996), *The Law of Obligations: Roman Foundations of the Civilian Traditions* (Oxford: Oxford University Press), 526; emphasis added.

[15] John H. Pryor (1981), *Business Contracts of Medieval Provence: Selected Notulae from the Cartulary of Giraud Amalric of Marseille: 1248* (Wetteren: Universa), 286–287.

[16] Peter Stein (1961), "Review of *Ricerche in Tema di 'Compromissum'* by Mario Talamanca," *Journal of Roman Studies* 51, parts 1 and 2: 247.

award of the arbitrator; and if either party refused to abide by it, the other had against him a poenae petitio if a poena was agreed on in the compromissum; and if there was no poena in the compromissum, he had an Incert actio. (Dig. 4.8)[17]

To enforce the *compromissum* and make it 'legal,' "the agreement was always accompanied by penal stipulations [*poena*] in which each party bound himself to pay to the other a fixed sum of money if he broke the agreement."[18] The question whether these financial stipulations constituted a central part of *compromissum* or whether "the stipulation was essentially accessory to the *conventio* even though without the stipulation the *conventio* was not valid" is still matter of dispute between historians of Roman jurisprudence, but for now is of little importance for our concerns.[19] The equality of the parties involved was presupposed and was at least partially responsible for the inability to reach an agreement. Precisely because the parties were equal, neither had an upper hand in deciding what is right and what is wrong.

Jean Bodin tackled the question of equality in compromise in connection with the issue of sovereignty in his famous *Les six livres de la république* published in 1576. In Book 1, chapter 7, when discussing the proper distinctions between subject, citizen, protégé, and sovereign, he emphasizes that a sovereign prince, even if he puts himself under the protection (or arbitration) of another through an alliance, does not lose thereby his sovereignty.

It would seem that if he recognizes a greater than himself, he is no longer sovereign. Nevertheless I hold that he does remain a sovereign and in no sense becomes a subject. The point is settled by a passage in the civil law which is unique. There are various readings of it, but I follow the original of the Pandects at Florence where it is said that in treaties of alliance between sovereign princes, those who put themselves under the protection of one greater than themselves do not become his subjects.[20]

Using the examples of the Swiss confederates, the alliance made by the Romans with other cities of Italy, and especially the leagues of cities in Ancient Greece, he insists that despite the inequality of size and power, the voluntary submission to the arbitration of an alliance for deciding controversies does not affect the equality of the parties as far as sovereignty is concerned.

Icy on peut dire, que toute la Grece n'estoit qu'une Republique, veu la puissance des estats Amphictyoniques: et neantmoins c'estoyent toutes Republiques separees, ne tenans rien les unes des autres, ni des estats Amphictyoniques, sinon qu'ils eussent compromis, comme les Princes ont accoustumé de compromettre, et choisir pour arbitres leurs alliez: ce que n'avoyent pas faict les Lacedemoniens, ni les Phocenses: aussi les

---

[17] George Long (1875), "Recepta," in *A Dictionary of Greek and Roman Antiquities*, ed. William Smith (London: John Murray); emphasis added. See also Derek Roebuck and Bruno de Loynes de Fumichon (2004), *Arbitration, the Roman Way* (Oxford: HOLO Books).

[18] Stein, "Review of *Ricerche*," 247.

[19] See, e.g., different arguments presented in ibid., 248.

[20] Jean Bodin (1955), *Six Books of the Commonwealth*, abridged and translated by M.J. Tooley (Oxford: Basil Blackwell), 24.

Phocenses pour faire entendre aux Amphictyones, qu'ils n'avoyent point de puissance sur eux, ils arracherent, et casserent l'arrest des Amphictyones, affiché aux colonnes du temple de Delphes.[21] (Emphasis added)

It is worth noticing that the first English translation, from 1606, by Richard Knolles, uses "promise" instead of "compromise, which is revealing for the way in which in British promise and compromise were already used interchangeably."[22]

Here might one say, That all Greece was but one Commonweale, considering the power of Amphyctioniques: and yet neverthelesse there were almost as divers Commonweales, as cities, holding nothing one of them of another, neither of the states of the Amphictioniques; but that they had *to promise* one to another, as princes haue accustomed *to promise* among themselues, and *to chuse their allies for their arbitrators*: which neither the Lacedomianians, nor the Phocenses had done, neither could against their wils be of right thereunto enforced. Yea the Phocenses to giue the Amphictioniques to vnerstand that they had no power ouer them, pluckt downe and tore in peeces the decrees of the Amphictioniques, fastened vnto the pillers of the temple of Delphos.[23]

The assumption of equality in compromise is also indicated explicitly in the first French dictionaries: to compromise signified "*s'égaler a quelqu'un*," made oneself equal to somebody else. Richelet (1680) and Furetiere (1690) insist that one cannot compromise with an inferior: a lord should not compromise with a bourgeois; a master should not compromise with his servants, and so on. By definition, then, the practice of compromise rested on three main assumptions: (1) the *recognized* authority of the arbitrator to *equally represent* the interests of both parties; (2) the willingness to *accept the risks* involved in a third party's judgment; and (3) the basic *equality of the parties* involved in the dispute.

The same meaning of settling differences through an accepted arbitration, this time translated into Greek, is found in two Byzantine documents from the sixth century AD.[24] As soon as the empire started to disintegrate, *compromissum* became an even more valuable practice for it implied a willing acceptance of authority at a time when most authorities were in question. By the thirteenth century, in the commercial world of the Mediterranean, for

---

[21] Jean Bodin (1576), *Les six livres de la république*, manuscript published by ARTFL-Frantext, available at http://artflx.uchicago.edu/cgi-bin/philologic/navigate.pl?frantexto509.63, accessed January 6, 2010.

[22] This offers a perfect example on how carefully these texts must be considered. Tooley, for example, uses in his versions "[Aristotle] compromised with the view of various people" (3), and "this would seem to compromise the sovereign power of the prince" (83), yet the word does not appear in either the original French or the English translation of 1606. This is but one example among many.

[23] Jean Bodin (1962) [1606], *The Six Bookes of a Commonweale – Writen by I. Bodin, a famous Lawyer, and a man of great Experience in matters of State. Out of the French and Latine Copies, done into English by Richard Knollers*, London (Cambridge: Harvard University Press), 79.

[24] H. Haarurer (1978), *S.M.E. Van Lith Corpus Papyrorum Raineri, Band VI, III* (Vienna: Verlag Bruder Hollinek).

example, compromise came to be the paralegal practice *par excellence*, because it avoided both judicial fees and court delays.[25] One can already identify its political potential for times so devoid of centralized political authority as the medieval. The revival of jurisprudence in the High Middle Ages restored at least partially this authority, eradicating (as the compilers and glossators of the *Corpus Juris Civilis* from the school of Pavia seem to indicate) the difference between *compromissarius* as *arbiter* and *judex*.[26] And yet the *compromissarius* still enjoyed a greater degree of freedom in arbitration than a regular judge, and therefore more authority in the eyes of the parties involved in the compromise.[27]

3.2. COMPROMISSUM AS ELECTIO

Parties to disputes resolved by a *compromissarius* were not necessarily physical persons. Sometimes they were juridical persons, that is, corporations. According to Roman and canon law, a corporation (or *universitas*) could act legally as a private person, defending both the rights of its individual members and the *universitas* as a whole. As a matter of fact, the acknowledged ability to appoint a representative – be this *syndicus*, *actor*, *procurator*, or *compromissore* – represented for a *universitas* the formal recognition of its legal person.[28] The use of compromise in connection with corporations as legal parties tied compromise ever more closely to politics and offered a second meaning for *compromissum*, that of *electio*. It also reveals something we tend to forget – namely the fact that any election is, directly or indirectly, a means to resolve a dispute. We have elections because we need arbitrators whenever we fail to reach a reasonable conclusion.

This second meaning of compromise, rather forgotten today, was however widely in use during the Middle Ages. It is often missed or downplayed how important and widespread elections were in this period.[29] All church offices

---

[25] John H. Pryor (1981), *Business Contracts of Medieval Provence*, 127.

[26] Paul Vinogradoff (1968) [1929], *Roman Law in Medieval Europe*, with a new foreword by Peter Stein (Cambridge: Speculum Historiale), 58–59.

[27] For Cicero's argument that the difference between an 'arbiter' and a 'judge' are a mere legal quibble, "an idle subtlety of the jurists," see William A. Hunter (1880), *A Systematic and Historical Exposition of Roman Law in the Order of a Code: Embodying the Institutes of Gaius and the Institutes of Iustinian*, trans. by J. Ashton Cross (London: William Maxwell & Son), 795–796. See also Pryor, *Business Contracts*, 286–287.

[28] For an excellent discussion on the legal and practical differences between these types of representatives, see Gaines Post (1964), *Studies in Medieval Legal Thought: Public Law and the State, 1100–1322* (Princeton: Princeton University Press).

[29] The following paragraphs are based mainly on Josep M. Colomer and Iain McLean (1998), "Electing Popes: Approval Balloting and Qualified Majority Rule," *Journal of Interdisciplinary History* 29, no. 1: 1–2; Alexander Murray, "Review of (1992) *Wahlen und Wahlen in Mittelalter* by Reinhard Schneider and Harald Zimmermann [Sigmaringen: Thorbecke]," *English Historical Review* 107, no. 425: 956–958.

from the papacy down were elective, as were early monarchies, and even later on the communes. For example, in late thirteenth-century Bologna, as many as eighteen hundred positions were filled through elections. However, the widespread of elections during Middle Ages is not to be misinterpreted as a modern democratic trend. In fact, 'election' at that time could be more appropriately described as 'selection'; elections fulfilled a radically different function than today.

We moderns tend to see elections as the democratic method *par excellence*. Our perspective, therefore, puts the accent on finding 'the people's choice,' that is, their 'will.' Once this is identified and quantified as the 'sum of individuals' wills,' the qualifications of the chosen individual are at best of secondary importance. One must realize that in medieval times, the conception of elections was completely different. The *method* of election was of secondary importance – by vote, appointment, recommendation, vocal support, or compromise. What really counted was not the *beginning* of the process, that is, the method, but its *final result*, which had to correspond ideally with the requirements of the office – that is, with the 'principle' directory of the office, with its *telos*. The emphasis was not on *the will* of the electors, not even on the elected, but on *the rationality of the position* to be filled. It was, one may say, a teleological, 'top-down' perspective on the electoral process. Thus, Jean Nicot's *Trésor de la langue française* (1606) offers as definition of 'election' the choice of the best solution (*soluta optio eligendi*).

"*L'élection, dit-on*" – writes also Chapelain in 1623 – "*est appelée bonne lorsqu'elle est proportionnée au dessein que l'on a, et mauvais au contraire; comme qui pour faire un palais choisirait un lieu propre, des matières convenables et des outils pour les disposer a cet effet, celui-là serait dit bien choisir pour ce qu'il aurait égard à la fin de son bâtiment, a quoi toutes ces choses se rapportent et sont nécessaires.*"[30]

(Election, it is said, is good when it is in accordance with the design one has, and bad if not; as of somebody who, wanting to build a palace, chose the proper site, the convenient materials and the tools appropriate for this purpose, one would say he chose well for he kept in mind the aim of his construction, to which all these things answer and are necessary.)

It goes therefore without saying that inside the Catholic Church, starting with the pope, elections were meant to discover God's will, since he was the *telos* of the Church. As such, the election was supposedly guided by unanimous choice – "the only rule that could assure the participants that their decision was right. Hence the maxim '*vox populi, vox Dei*.'"[31]

---

[30] Jean Chapelain (1623), *Preface de l'Adon du Marin*. Of course, the subject matter in this case is theater, not politics, yet I found the formulation helpful in offering great insight in the mentality of the epoch.

[31] Colomer and McLean, "Electing Popes," 3. The council of Antioch forbade the practice of bishops choosing their successors in 341.

To anyone who thinks religiously a proper *electio* can only be made by God. Human election then consists in finding out, with prayer, how God has made it. In the Middle Ages this was the main reason for the rule that elections be unanimous: *in scissura mentium Deus non est*, as Gregory the Great put it.[32]

Not surprising, unanimity was often hard to reach, and as a result the process frequently produced conflicts and schisms. The present Catholic Church recognizes 159 popes from AD 32 to 1122, but different factions recognized at least thirty-one 'anti-popes' during those times. "From the mid-ninth to the mid-tenth century, from a total number of twenty-six popes, twelve were removed from office, five sent into exile, and five killed."[33] Things started to change in 1075, when Pope Gregory VII's *Dictatus Papae* asserted the primacy of the pope over political powers. No longer under imperial control, papal primacy required legislative innovation. Four enlarged canon laws were approved, and after 1311 no new canon law codes were adopted until 1918.

In 1215, the Fourth Lateran Council instituted three ways to achieve unanimous agreement in the event of dissension among electorate: 'acclamation,' 'scrutiny,' and '*compromissum*.' The method was in use even earlier, but the Council formalized it as one of the official methods of elections. Elections "by acclamation" were quite rare, although closest to the idea of 'quasi-inspiration.' Scrutiny or 'suitability' (*idoneitas*) was meant to discover, through a general vote, the best candidate for the job. "Compromissum signified the delegation of final choice to a small commission whenever long sessions and repeated failures showed unanimous agreement to be unlikely."[34] However, it is important to emphasize that such 'delegation of final choice' did not equal a delegation of authority. As it will become evident soon, while the decision was 'delegated,' authority kept flowing 'top-down.'

Worried that *scrutinium* presupposed a fixed number of electors and was easily liable to fraud, the English jurist Laurence of Sarmacote, writing four years before the 1258 Oxford parliament, considered it a procedure 'full of dangers.'[35] As far as he was concerned, he preferred '*compromissum*.'[36]

Matters could be argued to a finish. The wide medieval use of compromissum is one of the surprises in store ... most of all in relation with parish clergy.... [T]he methods of their elections after 1200 show how small was the role of 'collators,' bishops included, and how large that of elections, especially by compromissum. One or more *compromissores* would be chosen for each recognized interest: by the *populus* or *universitas parrochianorum*, rich and poor, women as well as men; others by local powers, say a

---

[32] Murray, *Wahlen und Wahlen*, 956.
[33] Colomer and McLean, "Electing Popes," 5.
[34] Ibid., 6.
[35] It might be interesting to note here that *The Oxford English Dictionary*, while mentioning "elections by compromise," provides as the earliest reference a quote from 1726.
[36] Mentioned in Murray, *Wahlen und Wahlen*, 957.

monastery and/or a secular magnate.... Only when such local compromise – in our sense – failed, would choice pass up the hierarchy.[37]

"For each recognized interest": the specification is important for showing that the emphasis was not on the wills of individuals but the common interest of each group, *universitas parrochianorum*. The dispute between the masters and chancellor of the University of Paris between 1210 and 1213 exemplifies how this 'new' *compromissum* could be essential for the legal recognition of a *universitas*.

The dispute started when the chancellor tried to prevent the masters from electing a procurator *ad litem,* supposedly because the university did not have yet a seal and therefore might have not have been considered an 'authentic person.' However, Pope Innnocent III granted the university permission to appoint one "*ad agendum et respondendum*." After prolonged wrangling between Paris and the papal chancery, the matter was finally resolved in France through a *compromissum*. Each party delegated three arbitrators *ad compromissum* (plus the procurator, giving the University a numerical advantage) and the terms of agreement were ratified by the bishop of Paris and then the judge delegate. Only then, through compromise, did the University of Paris became a *universitas,* a legal person properly speaking.[38] German princes also borrowed the procedure for electing the "King of Romans," and though the number of electors varied largely, it was this procedure of *compromissum* that gave birth to the Electoral College by the thirteenth century. If the Catholic Church borrowed heavily from secular Roman law, legal influence in the reverse direction was strong during the High Middle Ages, when secular political formulas and principles were informed by the Church's expertise.

Compromissum proved the most successful of the three methods imposed by the Fourth Lateran Council. Between 1218 and 1316, for example, in the election of the bishops of Scotland, election 'by inspiration' (*per viam Spiritus Sancti*) was for obvious reasons used only twice.[39] The numbers of elections by *scrutinium*, that is, by the majority of votes, surpassed that of elections by inspiration by only a small number. The numbers might stagger a modern, considering that it seems the most democratic method of election, but not if one takes into consideration the medieval rationale behind election. For *scrutinium*, three trustworthy members were selected as 'examiners' or *scrutatores* to take the secret vote of each member of the chapter. The numbers were then compared and the majority of the votes designated the elected. There was, however, a 'glitch' in this method – the majority was not simply numerical. Canon law stated that it should be the '*major et sanior pars*.' The provision '*et sanior*' was open to interpretation and, as a result, whenever '*pars major*'

[37] Ibid., 957.
[38] Post, *Studies in Medieval Legal Thought,* 5–7.
[39] This paragraph is informed by J. Dowden (1909), "The Appointment of Bishops in Scotland during the Medieval Period," *Scottish Historical Review* 7, no. 25: 1–20.

did not coincide with '*pars sanior*' the elections could be contested. Not surprisingly, during the period examined by Dowden, election by *compromissum* remained the method of choice. To prevent a stalemate, there were clear
provisions that the number of *compromissarii* (or *compromissores*) should be
odd, as made clear in *Regiam Majestatem* by Sir John Skene, the most influential medieval treatise in Scottish legal thought: "*Debet autem compromitti
in numerum imparem, quo numero Deus gaudet, scilicet in unum, aut in tres,
et sic de similibus.*"[40]

In the case of *compromissum*, as in secular *arbitratio*, *compromissum* as
electio was to be used only whenever people could not agree – yet here the disagreement was not between two parties, but between multiple factions. Once
again, as in the case of arbitration, it depended heavily on the pre-existing
authority of the *compromissores*.[41] They possessed the wisdom required for
"arguing the matters to a finish," that is, until a unanimous decision was
met. People from each faction ought to have agreed beforehand which was
the most trustworthy to represent the group. A man was not trustworthy
because he had been designated *compromissarius*; rather, he was designated
one of the *compromissores* because he was already trustworthy.[42] This is
manifest in two provisions: first, the *compromissarius* ought to be elected
by unanimous vote; second, if the community did not find somebody trusted
enough to secure unanimity among its own ranks, they could select one from
outside.[43]

In both cases of *compromissum* there was no question of individuals being
represented by the *compromissores*. In *arbitratio*, as we have seen, they represented unbiased justice or, at best, the interests of both parties. In *electio*, they
represented groups, *universitates*, or the interests of these *universitates*. These
specifications are important because they help understand how the negative
connotations of the concept could arise. If by the end of the sixteenth century
the French were already overtly *méfiants* of compromise, one can safely assume
that one or more of the prerequisites for a successful compromise (i.e., the
acknowledged authority of the arbitrator, willingness to accept the risks of an
arbitration, and equality of the parties involved) could no longer be met under
normal circumstances.

---

[40] Quoted in ibid., 15. See also Peter Stein (1969), "The Source of the Romano-Canonical Part of
Regiam Maiestatem," *Scottish Historical Review* 48, no. 146: 107–123.

[41] *The Oxford English Dictionary* notes, using a text from the eighteenth century, that as a method
of election, compromise "in beneficiary matters … signifies an act, whereby those who have
the right of election, *transfer it* to one or more persons, to elect a person *capable of the office*,"
1727–1751, CHAMBERS *Cycl. Compromise*, quoted in *The Oxford English Dictionary*, 1933
ed. (Oxford: Clarendon Press), 746; emphasis added.

[42] The distinction between representation and authority is largely discussed in Hanna Fenichel
Pitkin (1967), *The Concept of Representation* (Los Angeles: University of California Press),
38–59.

[43] For more details, see Dowden, "The Appointment of Bishops."

3.3. THE FRENCH *MÉFIANCE* ABOUT COMPROMISE

The classic meaning of compromise passed into Middle French as '*compromis*' around the fourteenth century. The first mention of '*compromis*' I was able to track down dates from 1402 and was used by Christine de Pizan (ca. 1364–ca. 1431) in a political context: "*Et dessus vous en sont en compromis/Les parties d'un debat playdoye*"[44] ("And above you there are in compromise/The self-pleading parties of a debate"). In this poem, 'the first professional woman writer,' as she is often acknowledged, has the king of France serve as the impartial arbiter of the forces that rule the entire universe, Nobility, Chivalry, Wealth, and Wisdom, debating in the heavens about the qualities of the ideal prince. There are no surprises here. The emphasis is on the wisdom of the arbitrator – *la sagesse* is, and will continue to be for a long time, the central theoretical requirement of any political life. For Christine de Pizan, as for all authors of that period, politics is inseparable from wisdom, that is, philosophy. In another poem, *L'Avision Christine*, she makes the connection between philosophy and politics even clearer, as she addresses Dame Philosophy: "*Tu es politique, car tu aprens a bien vivre*"[45] ("You are political, because you teach how to live well"). The ideal prince can serve as a trustful *compromissarius* between Nobility, Chivalry, Wealth, and Wisdom because he shares all these qualities, but first and foremost because he is wise. Wisdom, not nobility, chivalry, or wealth (which rather are consequences of wisdom), ensured the authority of the arbitrator.

The sense of compromise as arbitration persisted through most of the sixteenth century. Even in 1606, Nicot (*Tresor de la langue française*) offers as definition for *compromis* the classical sense of agreement upon an arbiter (*accorder de quelque arbitre*). Yet as early as 1566 Louis de Masures (1523?–1574) expressed concern about compromising one's faith (*la foy compromise*) in his *David fugitif*. We have already seen that in 1576 Jean Bodin deemed compromise an acceptable yet less than ideal method for solving disputes between equal sovereigns. Around 1585 Guy Coquille, a constitutionalist, also mentions compromise as a less than ideal solution. He argues that kings were established as a last resort by the people in order to avoid the confusion resulting from everyone's participation in deliberation and the decision-making process.

Des le commencement le peuple a établi les Rois comme par voie de compromis, pour éviter la confusion qui seroit, si en chacune affaire d'importance il fallout rechercher l'avis de tous pour délibérer et conclure.... Nos prédécesseurs François a ce premier établissement n'ont pas transféré aux Rois indistinctement et incommutablement tout pouvoir: dont nous appercevons aujourd'hui quelque ombre demeurée de reste, qui est

---

[44] Christine de Pizan (2000), *Le livre du chemin de lonc estude*, ed. Andrea Tarnowski (Librairie Generale Française, Le Livre de Poche Lettres gothiques), quoted in "The Project for American and French Research on the Treasury of the French Language (ARTFL)," available at http://humanities.uchicago.edu/orgs/ARTFL/.

[45] Christine de Pizan (1994), *The Book of the Body Politik*, ed. and trans. Kate Langdon Forhan (Cambridge: Cambridge University Press), xxiv.

de l'assemblée des Etats: avec lesquels de tout temps les Rois avoient accoutumé de délibérer és affaires, étans de l'essence de la Couronne.[46]

(Since the beginning, the people had established the kings by way of compromise, to avoid the confusion that would have resulted if in each important affair one should have looked for the opinion of all to deliberate and conclude.... Our French predecessors at this first establishment did not transfer all power to the kings without distinction and unchangeably: of which [power] we observe today some remaining shadow, which is the assembly of Estates; with whom from all times the kings were accustomed to deliberate matters of state, [this] being of the essence of the Crown.)

The passage is revealing not only for its reference to compromise as a last resort method, but also for the underlying assumptions that will become important later: if not for the confusion resulting from huge numbers, direct participation in public debates and decision-making processes was presumably 'natural.' If this transfer of power was only comparable to a compromise ("by way of") yet not a full-fledged compromise, it is precisely because the transfer was never fully complete – yet another distinction that will become relevant later on.

Without a doubt, the domain in which the French were the most suspicious about compromise was the personal. Under no circumstances should a man compromise (submit to the arbitration of another) his conscience, honor, reputation, and the like. As both Montaigne and Charron make clear, and their works were among the most influential in the seventeenth century,[47] even defending oneself from false accusations could so debase a man as to accept the very possibility of judgment by others and thereby allow the possibility of letting others decide over your most valuable possession – yourself. "I ordinarily assist the unfair presumptions against me that fortune sows about by a way I have always had of avoiding justifying, excusing, and interpreting myself, thinking that *it is compromising my conscience* to plead for it."[48] For both authors the model to be followed remained Socrates who, falsely accused, refused to properly 'defend' himself before the crowd.

Aux faulses accusations et mauvais soupçons qui courent et se font hors justice, il se trouve double finesse. L'une, qui est aux interessez, accusez et soupçonnez, c'est de se justifier et excuser trop facilement, soigneusement, et quasi ambitieusement.... C'est trahir son innocence, mettre sa conscience et son droict en compromis et en arbitrage, que de plaider ainsi: ... Socrates en justice mesme ne le voulust faire ny par soy ny par autruy, refusant d'employer le beau plaider du grand Lysias, et ayma mieux mourir.[49]

---

[46] Guy Coquille (1611), *Questions and reponses sur le coutume de France* (Paris), 125, col. 1. The book was published after his death and was written some time between 1585 and 1595.

[47] Charron's *La sagesse* was reissued dozens of times between 1601 and 1672.

[48] *The Complete Works of Montaigne: Essays, Travel Journal, Letters*, (1958) trans. Donald M. Frame (Stanford, Calif.: Stanford University Press). "*J'aide ordinairement aux présomptions injurieuses que la fortune sème contre moi, par une façon que j'ai des toujours, de fuir a me justifier, excuser et interpréter, estimant que c'est mettre ma conscience en compromise, de plaider pour elle*," *Essais de Michel de Montaigne* (1957), vol. 3 (Paris: Imprimerie Nationale), 395.

[49] Pierre Charron (1601), *De la sagesse; Trois livres* (Bordeaux) 26.

(Faced with false accusations and evil suspicions that spread and are made outside justice, one finds two subtleties. One, which belongs to the interested ones, accused and suspected, is to justify and excuse themselves too easy, with too much care, and almost with ambition.... It is to betray one's innocence, putting one's conscience and right to compromise and arbitration, if one pleads like this: ... Even in justice, Socrates did not want to do it by himself or by somebody else, refusing to use the beautiful pleading of the great Lysias and preferred rather to die.)

It is true that during the entire span of the seventeenth century, every now and then as if by accident one encounters 'compromise' used in its classical sense. One still recalls compromise as one of the three methods of election inside the Church, "*l'inspiration, le scrutin & le compromis*"[50] ("inspiration, scrutiny and compromise"): "*son election se fit par voye de compromis, au mois de Septembre de l'an 1416*"[51] ("his election occurred by compromise, on the month of September of the year 1416"). Also, in books of jurisprudence dealing with Roman law, *compromis* appears with the judicial Latin sense intact.[52] But even here, the method of compromise came with a strong caveat. Thus, in *La jurisprudence de Digest conférée avec les ordonnances royaux, les coutumes de France, et les décisions des cours souveraines* ... (1677) one finds the following warning: "*Le Préteur veut qu'on s'en tienne au jugement de l'arbitre, soit qu'il soit juste ou injuste, parceque celuy qui a compromisé doit s'imputer à soy-meme d'avoir choisi pour compositeur de ses differens, celuy, ou qui n'en étoit pas capable, ou qui étoit capable de faire une injustice.*"[53] ("The Praetor wants the judgment of the arbiter respected, *regardless if it is just or unjust*, for he who compromised ought to blame himself for choosing as composer of his differences one who is not capable, or is capable of committing an injustice.") In speaking of foreign countries, say Italy, one uses 'compromise' as contract of marriage – a sense still in use in contemporary Italian (*compromesso* = engagement). In *La Guerre d'Aenée en Italie appropriée à l'histoire du temps* ..., published in Paris in 1650, Barciet writes of "*compromis, ou bien contrat de mariage*" ("compromise or contract of marriage"). Yet by and large the French attitude toward compromise remained suspicious, to say the least, for the entire century.

Examples of the French distaste for compromise during the seventeenth century are far more numerous; a few will suffice to demonstrate the point. For all practical purposes the sense of compromise as rational arbitration disappears, being replaced by the negative connotations. In 1619, in *L'Astree*, Honore d'Urfe (1567–1625) talks about the lovers' risks of being compromised: "*Considerez, Alcidon, quelle resolution a esté la mienne, de mettre mon honneur et vostre*

---

[50] Louis Moreri (1683), *Le grand dictionnaire historique, ou Le mélange curieux de l'histoire sacrée et profane*, 3rd ed., vol. 2, part 1 (Lyon), 377.

[51] François Pommeraye (1667), *Histoire des archevesques de Rouen* ... (Rouen), 553.

[52] Claude de Ferrière (1677), *La jurisprudence du Digeste conférée avec les ordonnances royaux, les coutumes de France, et les décisions des cours souveraine*, vol. 1 (Paris: J. Cochart).

[53] Ibid., 184; emphasis added.

vie en un si grand hazard; car vous permettre de me venir trouver en ce lieu, et à ces heures, n'est-ce pas mettre et l'un et l'autre en compromis?[54] ("Think about it, Alcidon, what resolution I made, placing my honor and your life in such serious hazard; for allowing you to come and find me in this place, at this time, is that not to put both of us in compromise?") In 1623, François Garasse (1584–1631) described a France devastated after the civil wars: "*ses villes saccagées, ses eglises ruinées, ses rivieres empourprées du sang de ses enfans, ses provinces desolées, ses princes divisés, son estat en compromis et ses armes escartelées*"[55] ("its cities pillaged, its churches ruined, its rivers purpled with the blood of its children, its princes divided, its estate compromised and its armies disbanded"). He also comments on those who "*abusent des termes, et mettent la providence divine en compromis*" ("abuse terms and put the divine providence in compromise"), warns against the danger of putting the Holy Spirit in compromise with human beings and entering in defiance of its fidelity (*mettre le Sainct Esprit en compromis avec les hommes, et entrer en deffiance de sa fidelité*), and asks his readers:

Faut-il que nous soyons si mal-heureux, et si mal fondez en nostre religion, que le desespoir d'un homme enragé, puisse esbransler nos esprits et mettre en compromis la stabilité de nostre creance? Si nous estions si foibles, le diable auroit un beau jeu, et un grand ascendant par dessus nous.[56]

(Should we be so miserable and so ill-founded in our religion that the despair of one enraged man can shake our spirits and put to compromise the stability of our credence? If we were so weak, the devil would have a nice game and a great ascendancy over us.)

In 1627 André Mareschal talks about "*mettre son honneur en compromis*"[57] ("putting one's honor to compromise"), and the abbey Michel de Pure in 1656 warned against the dangers of exposing '*les soins, les peines, les chagrins*' ('the worries, the pains, and the sorrows') of love: "*c'est faire injure à son rang, à sa grandeur et à sa fortune, que de les exposer, et de les compromettre à qui que ce soit au monde*"[58] ("it is injuring one's rank, one's grandeur and one's fortune, by exposing and compromising them to whomever in this world"). In 1637 Corneille is concerned "*qu'on put a jamais me reprocher d'avoir compromis ma reputation*"[59] ("that one can ever reproach me of having compromised my reputation"). For Moliere too, in 1663, a brave man is one who "knows that

---

54 Honoré d'Urfé (1966) [1619], *L'Astree*, vol. 3 (Geneve: Slatkine), 112.
55 François Garasse (1623), *La doctrine cvrievse des beavx esprits de ce temps, ov, Pretendvs tels* (Paris: S. Chappelet), 17.
56 Ibid., 345, 538, 653.
57 André Mareschal (1634) [1627], *La chrysolite* (Paris: A. de Sommaville), 127.
58 Michel de Pure (1938) [1656], *La prétieuse*, ed. Émile Magne (Paris: Librarie E. Droz), 68.
59 Pierre Corneille (1961), *Theatre choisi de Corneille* (Paris: Editions Garnier Freres), "Avertissment," in *Le Cid*, 8. Interestingly, Racine, Corneille's junior contestor who replaced heroic tragedy with tragedy 'gallante,' never used the word "compromise" in his oeuvre.

generous hearts do not put people in compromise for them"[60] ("*il sait que les coeurs généreux ne mettent point les gens en compromis pour eux*"). Examples could be endless.

Obviously, compromise in a political context meant no more and no less than endangering the entire community, that is, *universitas*, that one stood for. For example, in a *discours* presented by an "old French cavalier to the Monseigneur Duc de L'Orleans, unique brother of the King," Louis XIII is bluntly accused of putting the entire nation of France to compromise in a futile war while *also* endangering his conscience: "*Apres la Paix d'Italie le Roy n'avoit-il pas assez de Gloire d'avoir mis ses subiets rebelles à la raison, restably la Religion Catholique dans toutes le villes de son Royaume, maintenu son allié le Duc de Mantoüe contre le forces de l'Empereur, d'Espagne & de Savoye? Pourquoy le fallot-il engager au peril de sa conscience en une guerre etrangere, & mettre la France en compromise ...?*"[61] ("After the Peace of Italy, the King did not have enough Glory for restoring his rebel subjects to reason, reestablishing the Catholic religion in all the cities of his Kingdom, supporting his ally the Duc de Mantoue against the forces of the Emperor of Spain and Savoy? Why should he have engaged, *endangering his conscience, in a foreign war, & putting France in compromise?*"). 'Compromising' meant doubting, something that even the critics of Marie de Medici, the mother of Louis XIII – probably the most unpopular figure of the time after Richelieu – could not dare but suggest by denying. In the spirit of the epoch, her faults could not have been their faults. Her faults belong to her advisers:

Ayant eu l'honneur d'etre sa mere, elle y est bien obligée devant Dieu & les homes, nous ne mettons point en compromise qu'elle n'est s'acquitte de ce devoir: mais concedons qu'elle ait qu'elle est cy-devant donné des témoignages de son affection vers le Roy & l'Etat, les mechans qui l'enuironnent l'empechent par leurs mauvais conseils....[62]

(Having the honor of being his mother, she is strongly obliged by God & men, we are not putting it to compromise that she is not fulfilling this duty: but even if we concede that she forthright gave proofs of her affection toward the King & The State, the villains who encircle her prevent her by bad counseling....)

Since compromise involved by necessity the equality of the parties, for a sovereign to compromise with his subjects was always a risky enterprise. "*Une sage Prince ne doit jamais mettre son autorité en compromis, ny s'exposer au hazard de n'etre pas obey*"[63] ("A wise Prince should never put his authority in compromise, nor expose himself to the risk of not being obeyed"). Even

[60] Molière (1873) [1663], "Le dépit amoureux: Comédie réprésentée sur le théâtre du Palais Royal," in *Oeuvres completes*, ed. E. Despois (Paris: Hachette), 512.
[61] Mathieu de Morgues (1644), *Recueil de diverses pièces pour servir à l'histoire de France sous le règne de Louis XIII, roy de France et de Navarre ...*, vol. 2 (Anvers), 93.
[62] Ibid., 64.
[63] Jean de Silhon (1662), *Le ministre d'Estat, troisième partie: De la certitude des connaissances humaines...* (Amsterdam: A. Michiels), 184–185.

Richelieu, in his *Testament Politique*, indulges himself in reminding the king, although in a circumlocutory manner, that by being too weak a compromising sovereign endangers not only his own conscience, but by the same token his honest followers as well:

Celle qui vous a fait endurer aussi long-tems que le Bien de L'Etat & votre Conscience l'ont pû permettre, la Malice & la legereté, qui ont porté plusieurs fois le Duc du Lorraine à s'aremer contre vous, est une Vertu qui se trouvera dans l'Histoire avoir peut fort d'Exemples.... Beaucoup estimoient avec raison qu'il ne pouvoit revenir, sans mettre en Compromis la seureté de vos plus fidéles Serviteurs; & et cependant ils étoient seuls à vous solliciter de le retirer du peril où il s'étoit mis.[64]

(That which has made you endure for such a long time the terms that the Good of the State & your Conscience could allow, the Malice & the easiness, that have pushed several times the Duke of Lorraine to arm against you, is a Virtue of which there are not many Examples in the History's books.... Many had estimated with good reason that he could not return, without putting to Compromise the security of your most trustful Servants; and yet they were the only ones to ask you to pull him out from the danger in which he had placed himself.)

Despite his fame, Cardinal Richelieu was eager to warn the king that it is better to lose his own life and even harm the interests of the State than to lose his honor or reputation, because by compromising his honor he will compromise in the long run the State as well. The connection between compromise, representation, and self-representation here is obvious. As John Morley does a couple of centuries later, Richelieu goes after the moderates and compromise-prone Politiques, worried about the excess of compromise. A king ought to keep his word and be extremely severe with the representatives (ambassadors and other negotiators) allowed to speak *in his name*, for the representatives can compromise the sovereign. By compromising one's reputation one may compromise the reputation of the State as well:

Je sçais bien que beaucoup des Politiques enseignent le contraire; mais ... je soûtiens que puis que la Perte de l'Honneur est plus que celle de perdre la Vie, un Grand Prince doit plûtot hazarder sa Personne, & même l'Intérêt de son Etat, que de manquer à sa parole, qu'il ne peut violer sans perdre sa Réputation, & par conséquent la plus grande Force des Souveraines. L'Importance de ce Lieu me fait remarquer, qu'il est tout-à-fait nécessaire d'être Exact aux Choix des Ambassadeurs, & d'autres Négociateurs; & et qu'on ne sçauroit être trop Sévère à punir ceux qui outrepassent leur Pouvoir; puis que par telles Fautes, ils mettent en Compromis la Réputation des Princes, & les bien des Etats tout ensèmble.[65]

(I know very well that many Politiques teach the opposite; but ... I maintain that since the Loss of Honor is more than losing Life, a Great Prince should better endanger his Person, & even the Interest of the State, than to break his word, which he cannot violate

[64] Armand Jean du Plessis Richelieu (1688), *Testament politique d'Armand du Plessis, Cardinal duc de Richelieu* ... (Amsterdam: H. Desbordes), vol. 1, pp. 41–42.

[65] Ibid., vol. 2, p. 45.

without losing his Reputation, & by consequence the greatest Force of Sovereigns. The Importance of this point makes me observe that it is absolutely necessary to be precise in the Choice of Ambassadors, & other Negotiators; & that one cannot be too Severe in punishing those who overstep their Power; for by such Faults, they put to Compromise the Reputation of Princes, & the good of States altogether.)

Not surprisingly, the French dictionaries of the seventeenth century are fully aware of these negative connotations. Pierre Richelet (1680) in his *Dictionnaire de la langue françoise ancienne et moderne* mentions the new sense, "*mettre en compromis son credit, son honneur, & ce qu'on a de cher & de considerable*" ("compromising one's credit, honor, & what one holds dearest & most considerable"), while warning that "*il ne faut pas qu'un honnête home se compromette avec des coquins*" ("an honest man should not compromise himself with rascals"). Antoine Furetiere, in his *Dictionnaire universelle* from 1690, is even more explicit about the reason why "*on dit aussi qu'il ne faut pas mettre son honneur au compromis, c'est a dire au hasard*" ("it is also said that one should not place one's honor in compromise, meaning at hazard"): "*On ne doit point mettre en compromis avec les inferieures, pour dire avoir des paroles ou des querelles avec eux*" ("One should not put oneself in compromise with those who are inferior, that is to say have words or quarrels with them"). "*Compromettre signifie aussi s'égaler a quelqu'un, contester avec quelque personne indigne*" ("*Compromettre* also signifies to make yourself the equal, to contest with an unworthy person"). The first edition of *Dictionaire de l'Academie Française* (1697) mentions as well, "On dit figur. *Mettre quelqu'un en compromis, pour dire, Le compromettre. Et l'on dit aussi fig. dans le meme sens, Mettre la dignité, l'authorité de quelqu'un en compromis*" ("It is said figuratively. *Putting someone in compromise, for saying, compromising him.* It is also said figuratively, with the same meaning, *Putting the dignity, the authority of someone in compromise*").

This usage remained predominant in the eighteenth century, and successive editions of the *Dictionaire de l'Academie Française* as well as Jean-Francois Feraud's *Dictionaire critique de la langue française* (1787–1788) make extensive references at such negative connotations. In their writings, Abbé Prévost, Diderot, Montesquieu, Voltaire, and Rousseau, to mention just a few of the most famous, are also repeatedly worried about: "*être obligée de compromettre ma famille*" ("being forced to compromise my family"), "*nous avoir compromis tous deux sans aucune utilité*"[66] ("being both compromised without any utility") (Prevost); "*compromettre l'honneur, l'état, la fortune, la liberté, le repos*" ("compromising honor, the state, fortune, liberty, tranquility"), "*d'être traversé, mal entendu, calomnié, compromis, déchiré*"[67] ("being crossed,

---

[66] Abbé Prévost (1751), *Lettres angloises, ou Histoire de Miss Clarisse Harlove. T. 1* (Amsterdam), 194, 444.
[67] Denis Diderot (1956) [1754], "*De l'interpretation de la nature*," in *Oeuvres Philosophiques*, ed. P. Verniere (Paris: Garnier), 233.

misunderstood, defamed, compromised, torn apart") (Diderot); *"comprom-ettre l'académie"*[68] (compromising the academy) (Montesquieu); *mettant ainsi ses droits en compromis par de vains discours mal reçus"* ("placing his rights in compromise by vain discourses ill received"), *"mettre l'ancienne religion en compromise"* ("putting the ancient religion in compromise"), *"compromettre son autorité"*[69] ("compromising his authority") (Voltaire); *"toutes les fois que l'autorité souveraine voudra s'interposer dans les conflits de l'honneur et de la religion, elle sera compromise des deux côtés"* ("every time that the sovereign authority would want to interpose between conflicts of honor and religion it will be compromised from both sides"), *"on a compromis l'autorité royale"* ("the royal authority was compromised"), *"peur de la compromettre"* ("fear of compromising"), *"craignant de se compromettre"*[70] ("afraid of being compromised") (Rousseau). In *Julie ou La Nouvelle Heloise*, for example, Rousseau uses the term a dozen of times with negative connotations, but never, not even once, does "compromise" appear with a positive meaning or even the neutral sense of "bargain."[71] At best, compromise remains dangerous because it ties the hands of the promissory. Since every author uses 'compromise' consistently in the same context, this can hardly be a coincidence. The fact is even more surprising considering that some of these authors, Montaigne and Voltaire, for example, were passionate Anglophiles fully aware of the British usage of compromise. So what was the difference?

3.4. THE VIRTUES OF BRITISH COMPROMISE

The fact that during the second part of the fifteenth century and the first of the sixteenth the first known mentions of compromise in English follow the classical meaning of arbitration by a third party is not unusual. John Lydgate

---

[68] *Correspondance de Montesquieu* (1914) [1755], ed. F. Gebelin and A. Morize (Paris: Champion), 190.

[69] Voltaire (1756), *Collection complette des œuvres de M. de Voltaire* (Geneve: Cramer), 354, 222.

[70] Jean-Jacques Rousseau (1948) [1758], in *Lettre à Mr. d'Alembert sur les spectacles*, ed. M. Fuchs (Lille: Giard; Geneve: Droz), 92, 97; Jean-Jacques Rousseau (1925) [1761], *La nouvelle Héloïse*, ed. D. Mornet (Paris: Hachette), 131, 208. See also Jean-Jacques Rousseau (1964) [1764], "*Lettres écrites de la montagne*," in *Oeuvres completes*, T.3. (Paris: Gallimard).

[71] Jean-Jacques Rousseau (1761), *La nouvelle Héloïse*: "*peur de la compromettre*"; "*votre hon-neur n'est point intéressé*"; "*que vous compromettez le mien*"; "*et n'ai pu trop m'humilier devant ce qu'elle aime, ne pouvant, sans la compromettre, m'adresser à sa personne*"; "*Je sais qu'il est des amitiés circonspectes qui, craignant de se compromettre, refusent des con-seils dans les occasions difficiles*"; "*Les spectateurs eux-mêmes sont devenus si délicats, qu'ils craindraient de se compromettre à la comédie comme en visite*"; "*Celui qui, pour son intérêt particulier, pourrait compromettre un ami mériterait-il d'en avoir?*"; "*qu'il ne compromet personne*"; "*l'honneur compromis d'un père*"; "*c'est toujours vous compromettre que de vous nommer*"; "*J'espère que tu comptes assez sur ton amie pour croire que ce sera sans te compromettre.*"

(1370?–1451?), for example, wrote about a father so afraid "that peace and mercy do not compromise in him as judge":

> Thy fader is so ferful wel thou wost
> That pees and mercy dat not compromyt
> In hym as juge and eke the hooly goost
> In whome al grace godenes & trouthe is knyt
> Dame trouthe & ryght for juge wyl not admyt
> For wel they wote that he is mercyes frend
> Wherfor thy self of this must make an end.[72]

The most recently updated Middle English Dictionary presents four forms of the word: *compromis* (n.); *compromisen* (v.); *compromission* (n.); and *compromitten* (v.). All of them have the sense of 'mutual agreement,' 'promise,' or 'arbitration' – but again no negative connotation is ever mentioned. ('Being compromised' meant in effect 'being in agreement.')

A few examples will demonstrate the point:[73]

(ca. 1450): "Þei consented all and mad compromisse on-to his persone þat, whom he wold name, þei schul consent on-to him."[74]

(ca. 1460): "Both parties consentid that þe compromisse i-maade togedur..bytwene þem..be i-cancellid."[75]

(ca. 1464): "Horbury sais that ye and the minister stand in comprimise to abide the award of Sir John Malivera."[76]

(?1435): "For the pesyng off the seyde querelles..as yt ys conteyned more pleynly in a compromesse made thervpon."[77]

(1440): "Þe whiche matier and all oþer, as wele spirituell as temporell, bytwix þoe partyes..were putte in compromyse."[78]

(1447): "The which maters..hath honged and yet hongeth yn compremys be fore the lordis."[79]

---

[72] John Lydgate (1480), *Explicit liber primus de curia sapiencie* (Westminister: Printed by William Caxton).

[73] The following examples are from the online Middle English Dictionary, available at http://quod. lib.umich.edu/cgi/m/mec/med-idx?size=First+100&type=orths&q1=comprom*&rgxp=constra ined – accessed on 11.12.09.

[74] (c1450) Capgr.St.Aug. (Add 36704): *John Capgrave's Lives of St. Augustine and St. Gilbert of Sempringham ...*, ed. J. J. Munro, Early English Text Society 140 (1910; reprint 1987).

[75] c1460 Oseney Reg.: *The English Register of Oseney Abbey*, by Oxford, ed. A. Clark, Early English Text Society 133, 144 (1907, 1913; reprinted as one vol. 1971).

[76] c1613(v.d.) [1839]: *Plumpton Let.: Plumpton Correspondence*, ed. T. Stapleton (London: Printed for the Camden Society), 4.

[77] 1435? *Lond. Chron. Jul.* (Jul B.2) [1905]: *Chronicles of London*, ed. C.L. Kingsford (Oxford: Clarendon Press), 1–97, line 26. *Memorials of the Reign of King Henry VI: Official Correspondence of Thomas Bekynton ... from a MS.... at Lambeth, with an Appendix of Illustrative Documents* (1872), ed. G. Williams (London), vol. 1, RS 56.1.

[78] Ibid.

[79] *Letters and Papers of John Shillingford ...* (1871), ed. S. A. Moore (London: Printed for the Camden Society, n.s. 2).

The same usage of compromise as arbitration is found repeatedly in the writings of Richard Arnold (d. 1521?): "...on that other party bienther of hem for the pesing off the sayd quarelle & debatis takyn and chosyn in maner and fourme as it is conteyned more playnly in a comprimise made thervpo~ of the whiche the tendere sweth in this fourme"[80] (1503);

> In wines of whiche thyng to this present compromise my sayd lorde of glouceter hath sub stribid his name wyth his owne hand Hunfroy glouceter And in semblable forme my lorde of winchester in a nother compromise substribid w^t his hand vndir the worde of presthode to stond at the aduyse ordinaunce and arbitrement of ye parsons aboue sayd. (1521)

Thus far, there is nothing surprising – both Frenchmen and Englishmen stick with the classical usage of compromise. What is surprising is that by the second half of the sixteenth century and thenceforward all through the seventeenth, at a time when the French are increasingly using compromise with a negative label, no such trend is detectable across the Channel. In 1561, John Jewel makes reference to compromise as "agreement between parties" *and* as a Church method for solving disputes outside the formal legal system: "In déede by way of compromisse, and agréement of the parties, maters were sometimes brought to be hearde, and ended by the Bishoppe of Rome, as also by other Bishoppes: but not by any ordinarie processe, or course of Lawe."[81] A few years later one finds again compromise as a method of election inside the Church.

> The order of choosing their bishops in the primitiue Church by the Clergie and people was neuer so much respected but that they might many waies forsake and loose their right; as *by petition*, when they had none of their owne; *by compromise*, when they could not agree; *by deuolution*, when they neglected their time aboue six moneths, or transgressed the Lawes or Canons either in the fourme of their election, or in the person elected.[82]

---

[80] Richard Arnold (1503), *In this booke is conteyned the names of ye baylifs custos mairs and sherefs of the cite of londo[n] from the tyme of king richard the furst ...* (British Library).

[81] John Jewel (1565), *A replie vnto M. Hardinges ansvveare by perusinge whereof the discrete, and diligent reader may easily see, the weake, and vnstable groundes of the Romaine religion, whiche of late hath beene accompted Catholique. By Iohn Iewel Bishoppe of Sarisburie.* Copy from Henry E. Huntington Library and Art Gallery.

[82] Thomas Bilson (1593), *The perpetual gouernement of Christes Church Wherein are handled; the fatherly superioritie which God first established in the patriarkes for the guiding of his Church, and atfter continued in the tribe of Leui and the prophetes; and lastlie confirmed in the New Testament to the Apostles and their successours: as also the points in question at this day; touching the Iewish Synedrion: the true kingdome of Christ: the Apostles commission: the laie presbyterie: the distinction of bishops from presbyters, and their succcssion from the Apostles times and hands: the calling and moderating of prouinciall synodes by primates and metropolitanes: the alloting of dioeceses, and the popular electing of such as must feed and watch the flocke: and diuers other points concerning the pastorall regiment of the house of God; by Tho. Bilson Warden of Winchester Colledge. Perused and allowed publike authoritie....* Emphasis added.

Yet perhaps most revealing is the fact that by the sixteenth century the authority of the *compromissores* in England was already 'provided' through and by the agreement of the parties and *did not* predate the actual compromise, as *Thesaurus linguae Romanae & Britannicae* from 1578 seems to indicate: "Compromissum, compromissi. *The authoritie graunted the arbiter by consent of the parties: compremisse.* (*See also* Compromitto, compromittis, compromísi, pen. prod. co~promissum, compromíttere. *To put in compremisse, or to the arbirrement of any indifferent iudge.*)"[83]

The author who may offer the best insight into the usage of compromise during the sixteenth century is probably John Heywood (1497?–1580?). Largely ignored or dismissed as a minor Tudor writer until the last decade, Heywood's work enjoys today a much-deserved rehabilitation. A poet, musician, and dramatist, part of Thomas More's circle, he was also a devoted Catholic who nevertheless managed to survive the political and religious turmoil of his day through court patronage despite the radical changes on the English throne.[84] His plays, interludes, and poems are today reread not just from a literary perspective but also from a political one – which is the one of interest here.

What had been interpreted in the past as rather frivolous, apolitical, or downright confusing has recently been reconsidered as reflecting rather accurately the desperate attempts of Heywood's age to make sense of the seemingly endless confrontations between Catholics, Protestants, and Anglicans, landlords and tenants, supporters of the Parliament and supporters of the King, and other warring factions.[85] His writings "are structured, generally, as unresolved (and even unresolvable) debates" – ones in which each side appears to make equally weighty arguments and a clear-cut solution is impossible to reach. "Good and bad arguments are so evenly distributed among the debaters

---

[83] Thomas Cooper (1578), *Thesaurus linguae Romanae & Britannicae tam accurate congestus, vt nihil penè in eo desyderari possit, quod vel Latinè complectatur amplissimus Stephani Thesaurus, vel Anglicè, toties aucta Eliotae Bibliotheca: opera & industria Thomae Cooperi Magdalenensis.... Accessit dictionarium historicum et poëticum propria vocabula virorum, mulierum, sectarum, populorum, vrbium, montium, & caeterorum locorum complectens, & in his iucundissimas & omnium cognitione dignissimas historias.* Copy from Henry E. Huntington Library and Art Gallery.

[84] For details, see *The Plays of John Heywood* (1991), ed. Richard Axton and Peter Happe (Cambridge: D. S. Brewer), 1–10; and A.W. Reed (1926), *Early Tudor Drama: Medwall, the Rastells, Heywood, and the More Circle* (London: Methuen), 29–71.

[85] See, e.g., Robert Bolwell (1921), *The Life and Works of John Heywood* (New York: Columbia University Press); Robert Carl Johnson (1970), *John Heywood* (New York: Twayne); Ian Maxwell (1946), *French Farce and John Heywood* (Melbourne: Melbourne University Press); Lois Potter (1975), "The Plays and the Playwrights," in *The Revels History of Drama in English*, ed. Clifford Leech and T.W. Craik, 8 vols. (London: Methuen), 83, vol. 2, pp. 167–172; F.P. Wilson (1968), *The English Drama, 1485–1585* (Oxford: Oxford University Press), 27–32. For an updated list of references on Heywood, see James Holstun (2004), "The Spider, the Fly, and the Commonwealth: Merrie John Heywood and Agrarian Class Struggle," *English Literary History* 71, no. 1: 53.

that the plays raise the question whether anyone can, or should, judge in favor of one character."[86]

From this perspective, *The Spider and the Flie: A Parable of the Spider and the Flie* (1556) is particularly relevant. The fable is also open to multiple interpretations in terms of the true intent of the allegory and of the historical characters described under the disguise of spiders, flies, ants, butterflies, and so on.[87] Except for the maid who appears at the very end to restore 'the ancient order' – thanks to the author himself she is easily identifiable as the Catholic Queen Mary – a consensus seems impossible. Some scholars even argued that, because the poem (456 pages quarto with preface and conclusion encompassing 98 chapters) was composed over a period of more than twenty years, there was enough time for Heywood to change his mind about the allegory and characters several times. An exasperated William Harrison wrote in *The Description of England*: "One also hath made a book of the spider and the fly, wherein he dealeth so profoundly, and beyond all measure of skill, that neither he himself that made it, neither anyone that readeth it, can reach unto the meaning thereof."[88] Despite the multitude of possible interpretations about who represents whom, most authors agree that the flies stand for commoners or yeomen, the spiders for the ruling English class.[89]

For what is of interest to us, this alone should suffice. The action is rather simple. Buz, "the fly of flies," is one day caught in a window claimed by "Spider." He defends the rights of all flies to these holes by making appeal to customary law that he has learned by buzzing around "Westminster Hall," while the Spider claims the right to all holes in lattices and, by consequence, the right to slay all intruders in accordance with other customary laws. It goes without saying that while the debate proceeds, each side brings forward the system of justice he finds more advantageous – for Spider the matter ought to be decided by a judge, for Buz by a jury in Westminster Halls. Each proposal is refuted by the other party: Spider argues against juries, because "Thou wouldst bring forth a thousand flies for thee,/Where no one spider for me may make show," while Buz complains that if the trial takes place in the spider's web, he will be "Plaintiff, pleader, juror, Judge, and jailor."

[86] Candance Lines (2000), "'To take on them judgmente': Absolutism and Debate in John Heywood's plays," *Studies in Psychology* 97, no. 4: 401.

[87] Most of the following quotations are from John Heywood (1966) [1908], *The Spider and the Flie: Together with an attributed interlude entitled Gentleness and Nobility*, ed. John S. Farmer (New York: Barnes and Noble). However, the quotations that include 'compromise' are taken from the original manuscript, in order to preserve the original 'flavor' and to make sure that no nuance has been lost.

[88] Georges Edelen, ed. (1968), *The Description of England by William Harrison*, Folger Documents of Tudor and Stuart Civilization (Ithaca, N.Y.: Cornell University Press), 338. Cited in Judith Rice Henderson (1999), "John Heywood's The Spider and the Flie: Educating Queen and Country," *Studies in Philology* 96, no. 3: 241.

[89] For different possible interpretations of the characters, see Holstun, "The Spider, the Fly, and the Commonwealth."

Trying to avoid the pitfalls of the formalized judiciary system, they agree on the second best measure – a compromise. This decision comes at little surprise once one remembers that one of the main roles of classical compromise was precisely to avoid the courts of law.

> The beste waie in my minde when all waise are caste,
> Is that one (quoth the flie) that I touched twyse.
> To haue bene our triall, in all cases paste.
> Whiche was: to put the whole in comprimise.
> Flie: this laste one case: to be tride in that wyse.
> I graunte thee. I thanke you (quoth the fly) praiyng,
> That we maie name our daisemen in this daiyng.

Spider calls in Antony Ant as his '*compromissore*,' while Buz calls Bartilmew Butterfly. However, despite prolonged attempts, several witnesses, and debates, a compromise cannot be reached and the dispute ends in a stalemate. War erupts. Five thousand flies and five hundred spiders die as a result. Ant, held prisoner by the flies, is initially threatened with hanging but finally is sent to appease the spiders. He partially succeeds, in that the spiders agree to let the flies use half of the holes; but, as the flies are about to find out, the so-called half represents in effect only one-sixth of the entire surface. Despite the obvious inequity of the deal, the flies are forced to comply. Spider claims his right to slay Buz, the fly commander, who is still his captive. But before the actual execution takes place, the Maid of the House arrives, frees Buz, destroys most of the webs and, deaf to the Spider's pleas, crushes him.

The allegory is revealing not just because it mentions 'compromise' more than any other text from the sixteenth century, but also presents several 'anomalies' when compared with the classical compromise. Such anomalies signal that a change was under way – at least in sixteenth century England. To begin with, it is the first depiction of compromise as a method to solve disputes at a national level, for the 'spiders' (Lords) and the flies (Commoners) covered the entire political spectrum of sixteenth century England. The Spider *argues* with Buz, instead of simply disposing of him. Clearly, spiders belong to the powerful elite. They fortify a castle and are addressed by flies as "sir," "masters," or "lords," while in return they address flies as "good fellow" or "good men," using the pronouns "thou," "thy," and "thee." And yet, Spider defends his "lordship" to a commoner at length, which indicates at least a certain degree of equality before law – as one remembers, the first prerequisite for a successful compromise. The only possible explanation is that as corporate bodies, both spiders and flies are equal – as any corporate bodies in a *compromissum* as *electio*. There is, however, a twist. The dispute did not start between corporate bodies, that is, between the communities of spiders and flies. It started off as a private dispute between two (representative, to be sure) individuals. Only *after* the two agree to compromise does the conflict involve the corporate bodies of spiders and flies. Furthermore, the two *compromissores* are of unequal authority, yet Ant attempts to convince Butterfly to the contrary:

> Before we futher wade, master butterfly –
> No master sir: I am but a yeoman (quoth he).
> That's no matter (said th'ant) as the case doth lie;
> But, gentleman or yeoman, whatever ye be,
> Since we two come hither these two to agree,
> Let us be agreed on the next and best way
> To bring them agreed, in matter here to say.

The drive to equality (and its dangers) is even more evident when compromise fails. War erupts at least in part because of a radical "coking fly" that in the third round of debates confronts another warmonger, "the quarrelling spider," and asks for a "turning of the tables":

> When Adam dolve and Eve span,
> Who was, in those golden days, a gentleman?
> If yeomen flies were put in authority,
> We should rule as well as spiders gentlemen.

From a classical perspective this compromise was bound to fail because not only did it not entail an odd number of *compromissores*, but also because each *compromissarius* is a blood relative of his party (Ant is a cousin of Spider, Butterfly is an uncle of Buz). Despite the fact that both understand the formal requirement of impartiality ("We both must banish all partiality ... [b]y affinity or consanguinity"), in truth, "the ant's drift was the butterfly to drive/ from affectionate standing on the fly's side,/indifferently to stand, while himself contrive/to be partial with the spider." To complicate matters even further, the authority of each *compromissarius* to represent the other side impartially is not acknowledged by either Spider or Buz – and for good reasons: Spider's *compromissarius*, Ant, is nothing but a "cunning clerk" (a lawyer, according to some interpretations), suspected by Spider himself of being "opened to bribery" ("But promise formerly,/Of known reward at end, to flee the ill/Of suspect bribery"), while the less witty Butterfly obeys his nephew's instructions and is fully committed to protecting his relative's rights.

Luckily, this time peace and justice are restored by the last-minute intervention of The Maid. But how would individuals manage to solve their disputes if no higher authority is acknowledged? In the end, the parable manages to convey a powerful message to its contemporaries: absent a successful compromise, the only alternative left is open violence and civil war. Obviously, Heywood was not the only Englishman to praise compromise as the ultimate alternative to open violence.

Shakespeare uses the word mainly as agreement or truce, even in its reflexive form[90] ("When Laban and himselfe were compremyz'd That all the eanelings

---

[90] This is an important observation since in present-day English the passive or the reflexive form normally indicates blame or criticism.

which were streakt and pied Should fall as Iacob hier" – *Merchant of Venice*, 1, iii).[91] He was neither the first nor the last to use compromise in this sense. John Bridges (d. 1618), Raphael Holingshed (d. 1580?), Dudley Fenner (1558?– 1587), Arthur Hall (1539?–1605), Vincent Alsop (1629 or 1630–1703), or Daniel Williams (1643?–1716) are just a few authors of hundreds of examples of 'compromise' used in a positive light. During the sixteenth and seventeenth centuries, all English writers use compromise in the sense of 'arbitration,' 'making a deal,' 'contract,' 'covenant,' 'mutual obligation,' 'association,' 'bargain,' or 'election,' meant primarily to avoid open violence. Nobody appeared worried about the possibility of compromising himself, his honor, or his virtue.

Even Christ appears willing to 'compromise' various 'interests.' For example, in 1676, one could read such expressions as "All these things does the Lord Christ alone compromise, adjust all these Accounts, and reconcile these Intrests."[92] After the Fall, men are at variance with God and only a compromise or a covenant can save the people from God's wrath. "Let us compromise all Difference between us and God." "One of the Parties at variance is in the earth, the other in Heaven." But thanks to the sacrifice of Christ, "Heaven and Earth are at an accord, and the great quarrel between us and God is compromised and taken up.... The Grounds and Foundation of this peace: And that is by the blood of the everlasting covenant, which is the only propitiatory Sacrifice which could appease God, and give his Justice full satisfaction and recompence for our Offence."[93]

That at that time compromise was assimilated to a covenant and/or alliance is obvious also in the description of Abraham's people's tribulations for green pastures. Whenever they pitched their tents near a city, they obtained the right to graze their animals "through Purchase, Covenant and Compromise." "They either made some Purchase, or some Confederacy, or Compromise, with the Princes or people there, to preserve an inviolable peace amongst them." Furthermore, compromise did not operate only between men or between men and Heaven, but in Heaven as well. Only through "a certain compromise betwixt the Father and the Son, our Blessed Lord and Saviour exercised all his Offices of King, Priest and Prophet, and was so obeyed and believed in (according to the measure of revelation) before he was incarnate."[94]

Not surprisingly then, compromise appears not just "fair," but also "desirable," a "blessing" or even a "virtue," as efficacy and operative power.[95] Robert

---

[91] For Shakespeare's usage of 'compromise,' see also *The Merry Wives of Windsor*, I, I; *John*, V, I; *Richard II*, II, I.

[92] Vincent Alsop (1676), *Anti-sozzo, sive, Sherlocismus enervatus in vindication of some great truths opposed, and opposition to some great errors maintained by Mr. William Sherlock* (London: Printed for Nathanael Ponder).

[93] Thomas Manton (1693), *A fourth volume containing one hundred and fifty sermons on several texts of Scripture in two parts ...*, (J. D. and are to be sold by J. Robinson), 147, 690.

[94] Thomas Tanner (1683), *Primordia, or, The rise and growth of the first church of God described by Tho. Tanner ...* (Ric. Chiswell) 150, 154, 174.

[95] For "fair compromise," see Nathaniel Bacon (1689), *An historical and political discourse of the laws & government of England from the first times to the end of the reign of Queen*

Brady (1627?–1700) in *A Continuation of the Complete History of England Containing the Lives and Reigns of Edward I, II & III and Richard the Second* uses the term "compromise" four times, always in a commendatory context: "by virtue of this Compromise, he should have and enjoy"; "made by virtue of the Compromise unto him; ... by virtue of the Compromise made by both." He who compromises is a "peace-maker": "A peace-maker hee was to compromise, and to end vnchristian controuersies."[96] The examples could be endlessly continued. Compromise was also assimilated with a mutual contract, as in L'Estrange's history of the reign of King Charles: "Our King having advice of this misemployment of his Ships repugnant to their prime *destination by compromise and mutual contract*, sent an expostulatory message to his Brother, demanding the cause of this violation of his Royal parole."[97]

The Parliament accepted compromise as a formalized procedure (*Modi of Parliament*) whenever "the Estates could not agree (or the greater part of the Knights, Proctors, Citizens, &c.) There, by consent of the whole Parliament, *the Matter might be compromised* to 25 chosen out of all Degrees, and to fewer, till at length it might come to 3 who might determine the Case, except that being written it were corrected by Assent of Parliament and not otherwise."[98] It was in effect the classical method of solving disputes through compromise (notice how the diminishing number of *compromissores* is always odd). However, not everyone agreed that all differences could be compromised. After the Glorious Revolution, which posed so many constitutional problems and (as will be shown later) was solved through several compromises, a brave "person of honour" wrote a tract against what was perhaps the most persuasive theory of justification at that time, namely that a king *de facto* was also a king *de jure*. As long as he provided protection for his subjects, it was God's will that he would be the king. Yet not everyone was ready to accept that might makes right.

But when it was observ'd, that neither our Law-Books, nor Bibles, by all the artful application of ill-affected Lawyers, and Priests, could be perswaded to spread a sheltring Umbrage over that shameful Paradox of theirs, which the denial of King WILLIAM's Right forc'd them to devise, some more refin'd Philosophers, with a particular Court-like Address, thought to save its Credit. The Throne (say they) being fill'd, [no matter

---

Elizabeth: with a vindication of the ancient way of parliaments in England: collected from some manuscript notes of John Selden, Esq, by Nathaniel Bacon ..., Esquire; for "desired compromise," see Sir Richard Baker (1643), *A'chronicle of the Kings of England, from the time of the Romans goverment unto the raigne of our soveraigne lord, King Charles.*

[96] John Bowle (1615), *A sermon preached at Flitton in the countie of Bedford at the funerall of the Right Honourable Henrie Earle of Kent, the sixteenth of March 1614. By I.B. D.D.* (London: Printed by William Stansby for Richard Woodroffe).

[97] Hamon L'Estrange (1655), *The reign of King Charles an history faithfully and impartially delivered and disposed into annals* (London: Printed by E.C. for Edward Dod), 57; emphasis added.

[98] John Sadler (1682), *Rights of the kingdom, or, Customs of our ancestors touching the duty, power, election, or succession of our Kings and Parliaments* (London: Printed for J. Kidgell), 316; emphasis added.

how] we are protected by it, and the benefit of Protection requires the reciprocal duty of Obedience. By this one Argument, they would have us believe, *that all Differences may be compromiz'd, their Consciences sav'd, and the Government in no danger.*[99]

One has to keep in mind, however, that the British praise of compromise did not exclude awareness of the negative connotations of the term. In translations from French or Italian into English, one finds the 'continental' sense of compromise intact. A translation from French in 1615, for example, mentions that "it was not thought conuenient, that the Patriarch should with his person put the reputation of the Holie See to compromise,"[100] while a 1626 translation from Traiano Boccalini (1556–1613) also mentions compromise in a clearly negative context:[101]

But much more was his Maiestie astonished, when he vnderstood, that men now a dayes were growne to such a height of folly, that they vsed to call that thing a Play or Game, whereat they dealt so cruelly in good earnest. And further that they esteemed it a delight, sport, and pastime *to put in suspence and to doubtfull compromise that money,* which was gotten with so much toyle and cares, and serued so necessary for such great vses, that without it, this present world would take *Aristotle* to bee an ignorant foole, and *Alexander* the Great a base *Plebeian.*[102]

Yet such awareness is not reflected in the English dictionaries of the time. It is a striking difference one finds in what compromise signifies in the first French and English dictionaries. The French dictionaries of 1680 and 1690, for example, after enumerating the classical senses of the word, add: "*On dit aussi qu'il ne faut pas mettre son honneur au compromis, c'est a dire au hasard*" (Antoine Furetiere, Dictionnaire universelle – "It is also said that one should not put one's honor to compromise, meaning to hazard").[103] However, their

---

[99] [Person of Honour] (1697), *A free discourse wherein the doctrines which make for tyranny are display'd the title of our rightful and lawful King William vindicated, and the unreasonableness and mischievous tendency of the odious distinction of a king de facto, and de jure, discover'd / by a Person of Honour* (London: Printed for John Lawrence ... and Richard Baldwin), 64; emphasis added.

[100] Pierre d'Avity, sieur de Montmartin (1615), *The estates, empires, & principallities of the world Represented by ye description of countries, maners of inhabitants, riches of prouinces, forces, gouernment, religion; and the princes that haue gouerned in euery estate. With the begin[n]ing of all militarie and religious orders. Translated out of French by Edw. Grimstone, sargeant at armes* (London: Printed by Adam Islip for Mathewe Lownes and Iohn Bill).

[101] Such translations aside, *The Oxford English Dictionary* mentions as the first negative usages of compromise in 1696, Phillips s.v.: "*It behov'd him not to Compromise his Honour and his Reputation.*"

[102] *The new-found politicke Disclosing the secret natures and dispositions as well of priuate persons as of statesmen and courtiers ... And now translated into English for the benefit of this kingdome* (1626) (London: Printed [at Eliot's Court Press] for Francis Williams, neere the Royall Exchange); emphasis added.

[103] See also Pierre Richelet (1680), *Dictionnaire de la langue francoise ancienne et moderne*: "*Mettre en compromis son credit, son honneur, & ce qu'on a de cher & de considerable*" ("Putting in compromise one's credit, honor & what one has more dear & of consideration").

English counterparts – Phillips Edward (1658), Thomas Blount (1670) – make no reference to this sense.

Indeed, to find the continental usage in English dictionaries, one must wait until the eighteenth century, when the sixth edition of *The New World of Words; or, Universal English Dictionary* (1706) mentions that, in a figurative sense, compromise may signify "to put to hazard of being censured, *as It behaved not to compromise his Honour and Reputation*" (emphasis added). That this usage was not common in English is shown by the fact that ten years later (1719), the second edition of *Glossographia Anglicana Nova* makes no reference to this figurative sense ("Compromise – in Law, is a Promise of two or more Parties at Difference, to refer the Deciding their Controversies to the Arbitrement of one or more Arbitrators"). *The Imperial Lexicon of the English Language* (1850) also mentions "to put to hazard" as a possible meaning. Yet in 1877, *A Dictionary of the English Language* (Samuel Johnson) has once more no reference to this negative connotation.

The Revised and Enlarged Edition of *The Century Dictionary and Cyclopedia* (1911, first edition 1889) offers a possible explanation. According to it, "to expose to risk or hazard, or to serious consequences, as of suspicion of scandal" represents "a recent meaning for which *compromit* was formerly used." Yet, interestingly, my research on the documents of sixteenth and seventeenth century has not so far revealed 'compromit' as being used with this sense either, but rather with the most specific sense mentioned in the Imperial Lexicon: "To pledge or engage, by some act or declaration, which may not be a direct promise, but which renders necessary some further act. Hence, to put to hazard by some previous act or measure, which cannot be recalled." The sense here is still predominantly judicial – with little or no connection to "compromising your honor or your conscience."[104]

Such a discrepancy begs for an explanation, one that takes into consideration both the individual and the political level, handling not only the understanding of political representation but the representation of the self as well. Why were the French so worried about compromising themselves while their English counterparts embraced compromise as a virtue? To solve this puzzle one has to return to the individual. After all, it is the individual who fears (or not) to compromise himself, his honor, his reputation, or even the State. How did a pre-modern individual perceive her- or himself? How did she or he identify as an "I" and how did this self-identification affect the ways in which she or he grappled with the issue of being represented? The next chapter will address precisely these questions.

---

[104] On this issue see also *The Oxford English Dictionary*.

4

The Dialectic of the Individual

The wise is wise for self and is the first to drink from his wells. Start therefore the meditation with yourself! But this is not enough. It ought as well to end up with you.... You are for yourself the first and the last one.

Pope Urban II

The previous chapter traced the genealogy of compromise from its origins in Roman law as a private verbal contract meant to solve a particular dispute by accepting the arbitration of a third party. It also revealed the political potential of compromise stemming from not only the complete authority of the arbitrator, which was unconstrained in his decisions by any laws, but also the double meaning of compromise during the Middle Ages, *arbitratio* and *electio*. This double meaning serves to remind us of the oft-forgotten assumption that we share about elections as, after all, a method of arbitrating disagreements.

The chapter also identified the approximate period during the second half of the sixteenth century when the usage of compromise diverged on either side of the English Channel and ended with the question: Why were the French afraid to compromise while the English were so willing to? To properly address this puzzle one must first examine how the individual understood her- or himself *before* this crucial moment. Obviously, something changed in the self-perception of the individual across the Channel during that period of time. Yet, before even tackling the 'why' of this change, one has to clarify *what* exactly changed. How was the individual conceived of before this split? Since compromise, as I have tried to show, is a concept at the crossroads between representation and self-representation, the latter becomes crucial for understanding the former.

That the self-definition of the individual in relation to the community is neither modern nor straightforward can be asserted by any reader of Sophocles's *Antigone* or Plato's *Apology of Socrates*. And yet the opinion previously generally agreed upon was that the question of 'individuality' is essentially a modern

one. Earlier scholars, such as Jacob Burckhardt and Otto von Gierke, claimed
that during the Middle Ages man was known solely in terms of collectives (race
or nationality, corporation, family, the people, and the like) and that the 'true'
personality remained 'the group' until the Italian Renaissance. This perspective
decisively influenced the work of historians and sociologists of the twentieth
century looking for clues indicating the emergence of an autonomous individual. However, contemporary scholars beg to differ.[1]

To their merit, a few American historians pioneered this unorthodox
approach. Back in the 1920s (although with little impact at that time), Charles
Homer Haskins was the first to speak of the "Renaissance of the Twelfth
Century," and in an essay published in 1972 Colin Morris considered the
period 1050–1200 a time of "rediscovery of the individual."[2] Their works were
reevaluated at the end of the twentieth century and the beginning of the twenty-
first in light of an impressive body of evidence in their support. The transition
to greater individual self-awareness was explained in terms of Neoplatonism,
Aristotelian naturalism, Ockham's nominalism, Christianity, and the like. Yet
probably the most important change in the interpretation of the period was the
acceptance of the idea that individuals and groups are not opposed but rather
constitutive of each other.[3]

Ce n'est pas seulement dans un sens anthropologique trivial d'interdépendance entre
individu et société, mais aussi dans celui d'une légitimation religieuse, morale et poli-
tique du groupe ou du 'corps' par ses membres, du tout par les parties et vice versa, que
la sociologie historique peut relever le caractère essentiel de l'individu – et ce, même au
Moyen Âge.[4]

(Historical sociology is able to reveal the essential character of the individual, even during the Middle Ages, not only in a trivially anthropological sense of interdependence
between individual and society, but also in the sense of a religious, moral, and political
legitimization of the group, or 'body,' by its members, of the whole by its parts and vice
versa.)

Or, as Antony Black put it, "it would make little sense to talk of the individual
having claims *against* the community; the latter upheld his claims."[5] Therefore,

---

[1] Jacob Burkhardt (1966), *Civilisation de la Renaissance en Italie*, French trans. (Paris: Livre de
  Poche), 157; Otto von Gierke (1868), *Das deutsche Genossenschaftsrecht*, vol. 1: *Rechtsgeschichte*
  der deutschen Genossenschaft, Weidmannsche Buchhandlung (Berlin: Weidmann) quoted in
  Anthony Black (1991), "The Individual and Society," in *The Cambridge History of Medieval*
  Political Thought, c. 350–c. 1450, ed. J.H. Burns (Cambridge: Cambridge University Press).
[2] Charles H. Haskins (1927), *The Renaissance of the Twelfth Century* (New York: Barnes and
  Noble, reprint 1964); Colin Morris (1972), *The Discovery of the Individual*, quoted in (2005)
  L'Individu au Moyen Age: Individuation et individualization avant la modernite, ed. Brigitte
  Miriam Bedos-Rezak and Dominique Iogna-Prat (Paris: Edition Flammarion), 11.
[3] Peter von Moos (2005), "L'Individu ou les limites de l'institution ecclésiale," in Bedos-Rezak and
  Iogna-Prat, *L'Individu au Moyen Age*, 271.
[4] Ibid., 271; my translation.
[5] Anthony Black (1991), "The Individual and Society," 591.

before deciding where exactly to place the 'emergence of the individual' one should first understand better what kind of individual we are talking about. If we are talking about the modern man as "an 'atom' situated in a society where each member is a universe unto himself, protecting and pursuing his own interests, self-determined, a rational calculator of his own best interests," then the medieval individual was definitely more sophisticated than many of us would care today to admit.[6] He was apprehended and apprehended himself both as a unique and independent individual and as a member of one or several corporate bodies. However, most scholars are still working with the dialectic of the individual against the collective with little or no attention to another, more significant dialectic situated *inside* the individual between *forum internum* and *forum externum*. Yet without understanding the interplay between the two fora, one cannot understand why the first references to the negative connotations of compromise are related with a simplified version of *forum internum*, that is, with one's conscience, one's virtue, or one's honor.

The first part of this chapter analyzes the ambivalence planted at the heart of Christianity toward uniqueness and sameness as revealed by the Christian understanding of all the words that we associate today with individuality. The ways in which this ambivalence was formalized in the two fora, *internum* and *externum*, around the twelfth century, is analyzed in the second part. The third part shows how the dialectic between the two fora was reflected in the tension between the two requirements of the Church: the salvation of individual souls and the maintenance of the mystical body of Christ. The same interplay between the individual and the collective was present not only inside of the Church but also in the worldly *res publica*, as shown in the fourth part analyzing the medieval dialectic between *lex publica* and *lex privata*. The chapter concludes with a review of the classical concept of representation, understood as descendent, especially when the representation of people was involved. I will show that the individual could have been represented, and therefore could compromise, only in his *forum externum*. *Forum internum* remained out of bounds, with consequences for the general attitude toward political compromise.

4.1. THE AMBIVALENT CHRISTIAN

While it is easy to dismiss the Christian frame of mind as a vestige of an antiquated Weltanschauung, that would be a mistake if we really want to understand the way people thought during those times. The Western view of the individual owed a great deal to Christianity.[7] In medieval Europe, Christian imagery provided the all-bounding horizon of intellectual and moral life. All

---

[6] Janet Coleman (1996), preface to *The Individual in Political Theory and Practice*, ed. Janet Coleman (Oxford: Clarendon Press), xii.

[7] C. Morris (1972), *The Discovery of the Individual, 1050–1200* (Society for Promotion of Christian Knowledge, Toronto: Toronto University Press), 10.

of the words that we typically associate with the modern concept of the individual, despite their Roman origins, were indelibly marked by their Christian use and the challenging dogma of the Trinity was crucial in shaping the understanding of the relationship between uniqueness and similarity, autonomy and conformity. One cannot accept the counterintuitive idea of one God in three persons, each person in turn the 'whole' God, without consequences for the ways in which one understands oneself. One cannot daily use words meant to describe individuality, as we understand it today, but which at the same time point toward sameness and community, without being influenced by them. A few examples will demonstrate the point.[8]

Identitas, chiefly understood today as a 'permanence of the self' and therefore a marker of individuation, was for centuries employed by Christians to indicate the features shared by the three persons of the Trinity, in opposition to *alteritas, singularitas*, and *diversitas*. As such, it was already a designation of both singularity and plurality. One has an *identity* precisely because one was *identical* with somebody or something else. God the Father has an identity distinct from both the Son and the Holy Spirit *because* all three are identical in essence.

If society was perceived as a play of characters, the *persona* was a mask, but one that reveals more than conceals the true essence. Christ is *persona Paterni* – the image, the face, of the Father. By *re-presenting* the Father, the Son shared also in his *essence*. Once again, the incomprehensible Trinity forces people to conceive of different personas sharing the same substance. From here to the human persona, so identified because it shared with all of mankind the same rational nature, was but a small step. Boethius (ca. 480–524): "What one says to properly pertain to the person is the indivisible substance of the rational nature" (*"personae proprie dicitur naturae rationalis individua substantia"*). One was a person precisely because one shared with everybody else the same substance or essence.[9] The Church was a *persona* because it was a *universitas*. With Innocent IV (d. 1254), who proscribed collective excommunications, the group is 'a representative person' precisely because it enjoyed its own rationality beyond the rationality of the individuals composing it. The distinction became not only conceptual, but also ontological.[10]

Subiectus (subject) is, even more evidently, another ambivalent term. Today, little attention is paid to the genealogy of 'subjectivity' from '*subiectio*' (that which is placed underneath). In Medieval Latin, *subiectus* designated that which was subjected, obeisant, but also the support, in which sense it was assimilated

[8] The following paragraphs are informed principally by Dominique Iogna-Prat (2005), introduction générale to Bedos-Rezak and Iogna-Prat, *L'Individu au Moyen Age*, esp. 25–29.
[9] Although extremely important from the perspective of theology and philosophy, if one considers Heidegger's distinction between the Greek *ousia* 'Being' and *sub-stantia* 'being/standing under,' the distinction between substance and essence is less important for us here, as it probably was for the lay Christian during the Middle Ages.
[10] Anthony Black (1991), "The Individual and Society," 599.

with the substance (sub-stantia), to be differentiated from its 'accidents.' The great sacramental debates of the twelfth and thirteenth centuries surrounding the proper signification of the Eucharist would witness an appeal to the opposition between *subiectivum* and *obiectivum* in order to explain the interior transformation of bread and wine without a mutation in their substances.

Last but not least, by "individual" (*individuus, -a, -um*) Latin designated the quality of being indivisible. The atom was *individuum*, that is, nondivisible. The Trinity, of course, was one and indivisible, despite its three persons, as well as the Church, despite its obvious plurality. In fact, scholastic Latin saw the creation of the noun *individuatio* (that which makes a being a singular existence) and the verb *individuare/individuari*, plus a proliferation of qualifications thereof, such as *individium signatum* and *individuam demonstrandum*.[11] And yet, interestingly enough, the medieval Latin did not use 'individual' for persons, but rather *persona singulus, civis, fidelis*, and so on. I suspect that the reason is to be found precisely in the forgotten dialectic of the individual.

This interplay between uniqueness and sameness was manifest at various levels and came under different forms. Around the twelfth century one observes the emergence and consolidation of family names, heraldic signs, signatures, seals, portraits, and iconography. They were all conceived as methods to identify the individual and yet, *at the same time*, not as an isolated individual, but as a member of a certain group (*universitas*). Such 'markers of individualization' ('*marqeurs de l'individuation*'), as Bedos-Rezak termed them, "have no *raison d'être* but in reference to a group."[12] The surname, for example, emerges by the eleventh century, replacing the practice of a single given name. It indicated either genealogy (*nomen paternum*), place of birth, or occupation – all meant to *identify* but also to *situate* the individual inside a larger community ("the son of...," "the tallest one," "the butcher," or the like). The same applies to armors and heraldic signs. One may claim that such signs were meant to distinguish the individual on the battlefield. Yet they were less a way of identification and more a way of *situation*. The warrior is both a particular individual and a part of the knighthood as a whole, with a given rank inside it. The seal too was more "a measure of the social status than of the individual character."[13] Further examples are far too numerous to be mentioned here.[14]

The surest way then to affirm one's individuality was, paradoxically from a modern point of view, through conformity. In the medieval texts *imitation* was meant to reveal *individuality*. One is tempted today to rate those writers more highly who parted radically with classical Latin style, despite their differences (Fredegaire, ca. 660; Saint Bernard, 1090–1153; the Franciscan

[11] For a more detailed discussion of these terms, see Iogna-Prat's introduction to *L'Individu au Moyen Age*, esp. 25–29.
[12] Ibid., 25.
[13] Bedos-Rezak and Iogna-Prat, *L'Individu au Moyen Age*, 54.
[14] For detailed discussions on all these subjects, see the contributions of Brigitte Miriam Bedos-Rezak, Claude Jeay, Joseph Morsel, and Benoît Grévin in ibid.

Salimbene, 1221–1288 or 1289), because of their display of what we today call 'originality.' Yet the writers perceived by *their* contemporaries as being the most 'original,' such as Mussato (1261–1329), Dante (1265–1321), and Pogge (1380–1459), were praised and flattered themselves for best imitating the style of the classics.[15] One was closer to one's 'true self' so long as one followed the precepts laid down by classical authorities. Not surprising, many of the revolutionary ideas of the sixteenth and seventeenth centuries were presented as *renovatio*, a returning to uncompromised origins. Innovation in these matters was not only unnecessary but also dangerous.

Considering this Christian ambivalence it is easy to see how, from a classical perspective, the individual was subject to an inherent yet fruitful tension between uniqueness and sameness, between the individual in his singularity and the individual as member of some community – in other words, between his *forum internum* and his *forum externum*.

4.2. ONE INDIVIDUAL, TWO FORA

The formalization of the distinction between *forum internum* and *forum externum* can be traced at least back to the conciliar literature, apparently dating from sometime after 1140 but probably even older. The revival of Roman law and the distinction between public and private law (*lex publica* and *lex privata*) made the distinction almost 'natural.'[16] It referred to "the two broad arenas in which the Church's canon law was operative: the external forum of ecclesiastical courts and the internal forum of conscience and of penance."[17] Although the wording sometimes differs, the sense remains the same. For most of the Middle Ages, instead of *forum internum* one finds, for example, *forum conscientiae* or *forum poenitentiale*, while for the *forum externum* one also finds the usage *forum judiciale*. Thomas Aquinas, for example, in *Scriptum Super Sententiis*, uses *forum conscientiae* interchangeably with *forum poenitentiale*, while for the *forum externum* he prefers *forum judiciale*, yet the idea is unchanged: while *forum externum* is formalized, with specific procedures, regulated by trained professionals, *forum internum* is rather informal and less concerned with procedures:

Ad secundum dicendum quod sacerdotus parochiales habent quidem juridictionem in subditos suos quantum ad forum conscientiae, sed non quantum ad forum judiciale;

---

[15] Benoît Grévin, "L'écriture du latin médiéval (XIIe–XIVe siècle). Les paradoxes d'une 'individualisation' stylistique," in ibid., 102–103.

[16] Vittor Ivo Comparato (2006), "A Case of Modern Individualism: Politics and the Uneasiness of Intellectuals in the Baroque Age," in Coleman, *The Individual in Political Theory and Practice*, 149.

[17] Joseph Goering (2008), "The Internal Forum and the Literature of Penance and Confession," in *The History of Medieval Canon Law in the Classical Period, 1140–1234: From Gratian to the Decretals of Pope Gregory IX*, ed. Wilfried Hartmann and Kenneth Pennington (Washington, D.C.: Catholic University of America Press), 379–380.

quia non possum coram eis conveniri in causis contentiosis. Ed ideo excommunicare non possunt, sed absolvere possunt in foro poenitentiale. Et quamvis forum poeniten-tiale sit dignius, tamen in foro judicale major solemnitas requitur; quia in quo operter quod non solum Deo, set etam homini satisfat. (4.18.2.2.1 ad 2)[18]

While the external forum is mandatory (you are compelled to appear before an ecclesiastical court if called) the internal is entirely voluntary: nobody can force anybody else to confess and repent, although at least theoretically the Fourth Lateran Council made at least one annual confession mandatory for both men and women. There is a vast body of canonical literature meant to educate confessors on how to deal with penitents, but also to teach penitents how to prepare for repentance. Yet these details are of little importance for us. "When every allowance has been made for the humdrum character of ever-repeated, every day experiences, the great fact remains that the *forum internum* is and remains a tribunal of love, and not a tribunal of law."[19] In the internal forum, unlike the external one, the individual "is simultaneously plain-tiff and defendant."[20] In the *forum internum* one is one's own master and one's conscience is the only judge.

It would be a mistake, however, to focus solely on the growing acceptance of an autonomous *forum internum* without taking into account the other face of the coin, that is, one's *forum externum*. As I will try to show, such distinctions are better understood not as oppositions but rather as mutually constitutive poles in a sometimes more delicate, sometimes more roughly displayed dialec-tic. Note that I use the metaphor of the two fora in a looser sense than did the canonists of the twelfth century, just as most of their contemporaries probably did: by *forum internum* I understand the forum in which the individual is char-acterized by authenticity and autonomy (in the etymological sense of giving one's own laws, *auto-nomos*), while by the *forum externum* that in which the uniqueness of the individual was ensured by his membership in some *univer-sitas* – not just the Church, but also the village, the city, the province, even the *populus*, as Baldus would have it.[21]

From a Christian perspective this ambivalence was not as hard to handle as it might seem. As Kantorowicz observes, interpreting Dante, "[b]oth Adam and Christ were man in a peculiarly double fashion,"[22] both unique and identical with the whole of mankind. Not surprisingly, "theology emphasized both the community of divine love and the individual's personal relation with Christ."[23] True, the Church was a mystical community that comprised all the believers,

---

[18] Quoted in ibid., 380.
[19] Werner Stark (1965), "The Routinization of Charisma: A Consideration of Catholicism," *Sociological Analysis* 26, no. 4: 208.
[20] Goering, "The Internal Forum," 380.
[21] See the examples offered in Ernst Hartwig Kantorowicz (1997), *The King's Two Bodies* (Princeton: Princeton University Press), 209–210.
[22] Ibid., 482.
[23] Black, "The Individual and Society," 592.

past, present, and future (as Augustine wrote in his *City of God*), but this body ensured the distinctiveness and uniqueness of each of its members precisely because of their quality as 'members.' The hierarchy, visible *and* invisible, between Christians was not an impediment; quite the contrary. Because each member, regardless of his or her position in the hierarchy, fulfilled a unique function, envy was, theoretically speaking, precluded: a pinky, say, cannot replace an eye, but neither the eye can replace a pinky.

[In the City of God] there will be no envy of the lower for the higher, as there is no envy of angel for archangel – for this is one of the great blessedness of this blessed City. The less rewarded will be linked in perfect peace with the more highly favored, but lower could not more long for higher than a finger, in the ordered integration of a body, could want to be an eye. The less endowed will have the high endowment of longing for nothing loftier than their lower gifts.[24]

One was at once created in God's image (therefore identical with any other human being) as the primary cause, and by one's biological parents as a secondary cause. One was at once a morally independent individual *and* a member of the Church. And yet it would be a mistake to simplify this dialectic of the individual by attributing uniqueness solely to the *forum internum* and sameness exclusively to the *forum externum*. For the medieval man the interplay between uniqueness and sameness was present in both fora. The uniqueness of each individual was secured in the *forum internum* by the fact that one was a morally independent individual, accountable only to God and in the *forum externum* by performing a unique function inside the *universitas*. At the same time, the sameness among individuals was preserved in the *forum internum* by the fact everyone was created in God's image, and in the *forum externum* by everybody's membership in the same *universitas*.

Since man was man on account of being God's creation and sharing in God's image and his rationality, the closer he got to the 'proper' representation, the more he shared in the divine essence and the truer to his real nature he was. True independence and authenticity in the private sphere required conformity in the public. "Individuals only entered the picture as occupants of certain 'offices' performing appropriate 'duties (*officia*)': bishops, kings, laborers. Once again, the individual as such did not confront society."[25] If the accusation of heresy remained the most serious one during the entire Middle Ages, this was precisely because it threatened at the same 'the soul' of the individual *and* 'the soul' of the community by calling into question this entire dialectic. Orthodoxy, that is, conformity, remained for a long time the surest path to individuality – and despite appearances, in many cases it still is. One was an 'I' because one was a 'member' and one could be a 'member' only to the extent to

24 Augustine (1958), *City of God*, introduction by Etienne Gilson (New York: Image Books) XXII.30, 541.
25 Black, "The Individual and Society," 593.

which one was an 'I.' If one focuses solely on one or the other pole one risks missing half of the story.

In search of the 'discovery of the individual,' many scholars of the medieval period focused on the monastic and mystical literature in order to emphasize the importance of the *homo interior*, that is, the inner man. Ineke Van't Spijker, for example, focuses almost exclusively on the mystical search for and/or creation of the inner chamber of the mind (or heart). Spijker rightly observes that "in the monastic developments of the early Middle Ages this tradition of the desert [i.e., of the Desert Fathers] was not forgotten," and "the distinction between outer and inner life did not disappear, but seemed to be of little relevance compared with the significance of the ritual, which encompassed both without distinguishing between them" until in the West Benedictine monasticism brought it once again to the forefront.[26] "The mind and its devout activities become a place of concentration and a refuge from the world."[27]

However, since she analyzes her texts with contemporary assumptions, the distinction between the *forum internum* and *externum* is presented in terms of a dichotomy, regardless of the context. Yes, the medieval man in general and in particular the monk in search of mystical revelation were much aware of the distinction between the two and the hypocrisy and deception implied in the distinction between the inner and the outer, in taking care of only the exterior while neglecting the inner self, "content with the mere clothes of this profession."[28] But this is not to say that the two fora are inherently opposed. As the following quotation demonstrates, ideally this 'dichotomy between inner and outer' should be resolved dialectically. By performing certain acts in the 'outer,' one may influence the 'inner' and vice-versa. What appears striking, "the close connection between the outer and the inner man," suddenly makes perfect sense.[29]

The most interesting point in *De Institutione* is Hugh's [of Saint Victor; twelfth century] reason for paying so much attention to outward behavior: in this instruction to young people, modeling the outer man is seen as the starting point for changing the corresponding inner attitudes. Just as uncontrolled behaviour (listening, for instance) betrays a chaotic interior, controlling this behaviour will contribute to reforming the inner chaos into a state of order and harmony. There is thus a strong emphasis on the interconnection between outer and inner, an interconnection which not only works at the level of the novice trying to form his life, but which, as we shall see, runs through the whole world, where outer, visible things, point to the world of the invisible.[30]

Furthermore, once one takes into consideration the interplay between sameness and uniqueness at work in *both* fora and removes the contemporary

---

[26] Ineke Van't Spijker (2004), *Fictions of the Inner Life: Religious Literature and Formation of the Self in the Eleventh and Twelfth Centuries* (Turnhout, Belgium: Brepols Publishers), 19.

[27] Ibid., 45

[28] Peter Damian, *Epistola* 153, quoted in Van't Spijker, *Fictions of the Inner Life*, 45.

[29] Van't Spijker, *Fictions of the Inner Life*, 63.

[30] Ibid., 69.

glasses, what startles Spijker, namely that "realizing one's inner man, in a context where the goal is the restoration of a universally valid Image, does not imply a striving for a distinct individuality," becomes rather logical: "[T]he universality of the goal and the community of fellow monks or hermits prevents the homo interior from becoming a lonely individual, as would be the case in some forms of Protestantism, according to Weber."[31]

We must thus recover this dialectic of the individual, so 'normal' then and yet so strange today. Since the fear to compromise appeared in obvious connection with the fear of compromising one's uniqueness, it is crucial to understand how the dialectic of uniqueness and sameness between and inside the two fora played out in the religious and the political spheres.

4.3. TWO FORA, ONE CHURCH

If this ambivalence about individuality was so deeply embedded in the heart of Christianity, it should come at little surprise if, at the same time that the Church reinforced its institutional hierarchy starting in the twelfth century, it also strengthened some of its most 'individualistic' principles. At least for a while the two tendencies went hand in hand. The Fourth Lateran Council (the same one that introduced *compromissum* as a method of election inside the church) also banned public confession and collective excommunications. In his *forum internum* the individual was not only free but also personally responsible. "Twelfth-century theological and philosophical texts had already emphasized a kind of *ethical personalism* by focusing on the sphere of private, individual intention behind acts." Not surprising, this Council is seen by many historians, including Janet Coleman, as one of the turning points in the path toward modern individualism.

> Out of this concern for private intention arose the expanded practice of private confession as stipulated in the decrees of the Fourth Lateran Council of 1215.... With the elevation of marriage to a Church sacrament during the twelfth century, the marriage contract was seen as a typical expression of two consenting individuals, male and female, to a binding relationship which could only be cemented at the age of reason, the age of consent.[32]

Even today, the *Corpus Iuris Canonici* ends with the canon "*salus animarum in Ecclesia suprema semper lex esse debet*" ("the salvation of souls ought to be always the supreme law in the Church"). At first sight, this appears to be in direct (and intentional) opposition to the fundamental principle of Roman law: "*salus publica suprema lex esto*." For the medieval Church, however, there was no contradiction between the two – ideally, that is. One should keep in mind

---

[31] Ibid., 12.
[32] Janet Coleman (1996), "The Individual and the Medieval State," in *The Individual in Political Theory and Practice*, 16.

that at the level of the Church, there was an ambivalence manifested between the requirements for the salvation of individual souls and the maintenance of the mystical body of Christ. Both requirements ought to be met for the Church to fulfill its mission. Theoretically at least, the Church was accountable for preserving the balance between the two. This was not an easy task.

Practically, because of the inherent corruption of this world, the two requirements clashed often, sometimes even radically, and so the history of the Church was marked by hard-fought battles for one or the other. As Peter von Moos points out, the tension between the two visions, present from the very beginning, exploded during the thirteenth century "when the papal demands for full power were at their height and the ideas of Joachim de Flore (1135–1202) on the coming of a Church of Holy Spirit became widespread and mixed with the Franciscan appeal to a return to a primitive church."[33]

The balance (if ever there were one) was upset, and in the arguments brought forward by each camp can be seen the precursors of the centripetal and centrifugal individualisms of the future. I call 'centripetal individualism' the one that focuses on the *forum internum*, 'centrifugal individualism' the one that focuses on the *forum externum*.[34] Those who favored the *forum internum*, like the canonist Nicolas de Tudeschis, archbishop of Palermo (or *Panormitanus*), favored also the rule *fides in uno solo* (the faith of one) and the personalized communication of each believer with the Holy Spirit. In terms of the relationship between *forum internum* and *forum externum* he does not hesitate to assert: "Against the law of the conscience one has not to obey any superior, not even the pope." If the laws are two (*duae sunt leges*), then the private law (the law of the conscience) is more powerful than the public (*private est potentior publicae*).[35] Even Pope Urban II (1088–1099) in a text attributed by Gratian (ca. 1140) seems to favor private over public law:

There are two laws, one public, the other private. The public law contains all that the Saint Fathers have written or confirmed, of which the right canon was established to fight against the transgressions. The private law is that which, by the inspiration of the Holy Spirit, is inscribed in the heart.... If someone ... touched by the blow of the Holy Spirit wants to save his soul in a convent, because he is guided by the private law, there is no reason why he should be prevented by the public law. For the private law has more dignity than the public one.... Who could resist the Holy Spirit with dignity?[36]

Yet the author who can safely be considered the forerunner of centripetal individualists of the sixteenth and seventeenth century, emphasizing the

---

[33] Moos, "L'Individu ou les limites de l'institution ecclésiale," 274.

[34] See Alin Fumurescu (2011), "Lost in Translation: Centripetal Individualism and the Classical Concept of Descending Representation," *European Journal of Political Theory* 10, no. 2.

[35] Panormitanus, *Commentaria in V Decretalium libros*, in c. 6 X, I 31, and in c. 44 V, 39, n. 3, Venetiis, 1617, quoted in ibid., 283.

[36] Gratien, *Decretum*, II causa XIX, qu2, 2, ed. Friedbeerg I. Lepzig, quoted in ibid., 278; my translation.

necessity to refocus on the *forum internum*, remains Bernard de Clairvaux. In the twelfth century, in his *De consideratione* he warns his former friend and pupil, now Pope Eugene III, that being the head of the Church, responsible for the salvation of so many souls, should not mean neglecting his own – quite the contrary:

> About the fruits of consideration, one should meditate four things, one after the other: yourself, what is below you, around you, and above you. Your attention ought to be directed firstly on yourself and not to be distracted someplace else.... What good is it then to win over the entire world if you ruin yourself, who are unique?... When you will know all the mysteries, the width of earth, the height of heavens, and the depth of seas, would you ignore yourself you would resemble a man who built with no foundation, preparing not the edifice, but ruin. Everything that you've built outside yourself will be but a handful of dust in the wind. The wise is wise for self and is the first to drink from his wells. Start therefore the meditation with yourself! But this is not enough. It ought as well to end up with you.... You are for yourself the first and the last one.[37]

It goes almost without saying that the success of such self-centered visions of the individual could not remain without a counterreaction, lest the Church be resigned by the fourteenth century to fragmentation into as many private devotees as were believers having a one-on-one relationship with God. The vision of the organic body of the Church would have been irremediably shattered. In 1331, Pope John XXII openly attacked the scholastic trend elevating the personal experience of the divinity at the expense of the communitarian side of the Church. If all that counts is the beatitude of the individual soul immediately after death, what good is the Final Judgment? If one got one's reward (or punishment) so soon, what is left to Christ to judge the second time? According to the second Avignon Pope, true beatitude in the presence of God is not possible until the whole body of the Church is reunited, that is, only after the coming of the Kingdom of God on earth. This was not a singular interpretation, but one very much in line with the Fathers of the Church. Augustine also claims that heaven "will be the fulfillment of the Sabbath ... that ultimate Sabbath that has no evening ... but only in the Lord's day – that eighth and eternal day." "Then only shall we be filled with Him and when He will be all in all."[38]

For John XXII, there were also some more mundane implications: the Pope remained the undisputed earthly vicar of Christ until the coming of the Kingdom of God. Until then he was to enjoy *plenitudo potestatis*. Balancing on the other side, his successor, Pope Benedict XII (Jacques Fournier) turned this interpretation almost entirely upside-down, focusing once again on the *forum internum* of the believer. After that, the entire history of the Church, culminating in but not ending with the Reformation, can be seen as an attempt to deal

---

[37] Bernard of Clairvaux (1963), "*De consideratione* II, 3, 6," in *Sancti Bernardi opera*, vol. 3, ed. J. Lecclerq and H. Rochais (Rome: Cisterciennes Editions), 414–415, quoted in Moos, "L'Individu ou les limites de l'institution ecclésiale," 272.

[38] Augustine, *City of God*, 543–544.

with this dialectic of an individual caught between his *forum internum* and his *forum externum* – and with its excesses.

And yet, the Church was not the only *universitas* having troubles finding the proper balance in this unstable dialectic.

4.4. ONE *RES PUBLICA*, TWO FORA

Historians of the Middle Ages have long argued how to properly interpret the distinction between *lex publica* and *lex privata*. Since, for example, corporations were accepted as legal persons, were their rights private or public? What about the 'highest corporation of all,' namely the state (*Imperium, Regnum, Res publica*, or *Civitas*)? While some have argued that there was no proper distinction between public and private law with both merged in the office of the king, others claim only that the two were so interwoven that drawing a line of demarcation is extremely challenging. Some have argued that the success of corporatism prevented the emergence of the state, while others have begged to differ. In his seminal book *Studies in Medieval Legal Thought*, Gaines Post observed, not without humor, after reviewing most of these debates: "The public law, of course, should have as its province what is public as opposed to the private; but sometimes it is as difficult to distinguish between public and private as it is to separate clearly the realms of body and soul."[39] The same can be said for the distinction between *forum internum* and *forum externum*. But, once again, this difficulty should not lead to the conclusion that such distinctions are useless. They obviously were not for the medieval man, who used them on a regular basis, and they should not be for us.

By the twelfth and thirteenth centuries, both France and England were considered not only *res publicae* or *civitates* but also, and probably foremost, *universitates*, in the same way as the Church. Although essential for the development of political thought, the conflict between Church and secular powers is of less importance to our discussion, as are the distinctions between kingdoms and the empire. What is revealing is that the same conceptual apparatus informed both the Church and the kingdom (or the empire) and that Roman legal terminology was used to describe relationships inside all of them; the imagery was the same. As Jean Charlier de Gerson concluded in his *On Ecclesiastical Power* presented to the Council of Constance in 1417, the pope was the equivalent of the king, the cardinals of the nobles, "and every level of the church was represented in the general council, which, embracing pope and cardinals along with the rest, corresponded to the entire body politic."[40] If in

---

[39] Gaines Post (1964), *Studies in Medieval Legal Thought: Public Law and the State, 1100–1322* (Princeton: Princeton University Press), 7.

[40] J.H.M. Salmon (2007) "France," in *European Political Thought: 1450–1700*, ed. Howell A. Lloyd, Glenn Burgess, and Simon Hodson (New Haven and London: Yale University Press), 461.

the case of the Church, *lex publica* dealt with "the state of the Church" (*"status Ecclesiae"*), in the case of the kingdom it dealt with "the state of the realm" (*"status regni"*).

However, as in the case of the Pope – and indeed any bishop – the borders between private and public were blurred in the case of the king. For commoners, this proved both an advantage and a disadvantage. Popes and bishops were first and foremost persons, so they had to care for their *fora interna*. As we have seen in the case of the recommendation of Clairvaux to Eugene III, even the Pope should first consider his *forum internum*, and only afterward the *forum externum*. Yet Pope Innocent II said that a bishop cannot "resign his office to save his own soul if he is needed to help others to salvation."[41] In a similar way, the king (or the emperor) was both part of the kingdom and its head. The office that he filled in his *forum externum* came with certain limitations. He could not donate the keys of the kingdom or empire "because he would be the murderer of his office."[42]

But the emperor cannot divest himself or sell the property [of the empire], because he does not possess it in his own right but by right of the *lex regia*, and because it is not transferred to him and therefore cannot be alienated by him. Indeed, the emperor is the main *procurator* of the empire: he is not, however, the empire's absolute owner, but rather an officer.[43]

He was both a private man *and* a public person. The *fiscus* (treasury), for example, was both public, because it belonged to public authority, and yet "also a private right of the emperor as a private person."[44] Under normal circumstances, the *fiscus* was regulated by *lex publica,* while private property (dominium) was regulated by *lex privata.* The king had no rights over the property of his subjects. But if *status regni* or *utilitas publica* was at stake in such extraordinary circumstances as wars, the king had the right to demand extraordinary taxes or to seize property for the defense of the whole community under *lex publica.* As Baldus de Ubaldis (the disciple of Bartolus de Sassoferrato, with whom he shared fame and influence among the Commentators) asserted in the fourteenth century, it is possible for the emperor to impose a tax for the defense of a province, providing that it touches all equally, in proportion to their wealth.[45]

"Note that all fiscal rights belong to the prince and that he can concede them to anyone. But the rights of individuals do not belong to the prince, nor do they come into his possession ... unless the prince by his absolute power

41 Post, *Studies in Medieval Legal Thought*, 13.
42 Baldus, X. 2. 19.0, n. 7 (fol. 248r), quoted in Joseph Canning (1987), *The Political Thought of Baldus de Ubaldis* (Cambridge: Cambridge University Press), 87.
43 Baldus, *Cons.*, 3.277, fol. 84v, ed. Brescia, 1491, quoted in Canning, *The Political Thought of Baldus de Ubaldis*, 86–87.
44 Post, *Studies in Medieval Legal Thought*, 14.
45 Ibid., 15. See also Salmon, "France," 461.

and for a reasonable cause should make other special provision [D.31.I.78, 3; D.40.II.3]."[46]

Yet the fact that in such cases the boundaries between public and private disappeared was not only a disadvantage for commoners, for it was a two-way street. It also meant that the Roman canonical principle of *private* law, "*quod omnia tangit debet ab omnibus approbari*" ("what touches all must be approved by all") became a principle of *public* law, *lex publica*. Obviously, 'all' in the case of a *universitas*, such as the Church and the kingdom, was not the same as the 'all' in *lex privata*, namely, a collection of individuals. The people were *persona universalis*. As Baldus put it: "It is ... a corporate person which is understood as one person, but consists of many bodies, like the people, as in [D.46.I.22]; and this person similarly is regarded as corresponding to one man and is considered to be an individual body ... [D.4.2.9, 1] is relevant to this."[47]

Baldus, following Aristotle, "maintains that natural man by virtue of his membership of the political *populus* is imbued with political characteristics which he could lack when considered as an isolated individual."[48] He is also explicit in emphasizing that the people cannot and should not be understood as a mere collection of individuals: "Therefore separate individuals do not make up the people, and thus properly speaking the people is not men, but a collection of men into a body which is mystical and taken as abstract, and the significance of which has been discovered by the intellect."[49] In other words, in his *forum externum*, the individual was 'political' by virtue of membership. "If he is considered in congregation, then natural man would be made political."[50] As many other commentators, Baldus follows Thomas Aquinas here, who also asserted that man is what he is in virtue of his membership in the state, though this civic virtue is rather passive; there is no connection with the idea of political participation. One is political by simply being a part of the 'state' and fulfilling one's duties in the *forum externum*. And yet this 'passivity' in the fulfillment of one's office helps also in the *forum internum*. "Since every man is part of the state, it is impossible for any man to be good unless he is well proportioned to the good of the whole; and the whole can only be constituted out of parts that are proportioned to it" ("*Cum igitur quilibet homo sit pars civitatis, impossibile est quod aliquis homo sit bonus nisi set bene proportionatus bono communi; nec totum potest bene consistere nisi ex partibus sibi proportionatis*").[51]

If the individual, regardless of his status, had little or no political weight, the story was completely different when it came to the people as a *universitas* (*universitas, idest populus*). Throughout the Middle Ages most thinkers would

---

[46] Quoted in Canning, *The Political Thought of Baldus de Ubaldis*, 81.

[47] Baldus, C.6.26.2 (fol65r), quoted in ibid., 189.

[48] Canning, *The Political Thought of Baldus de Ubaldis*, 161.

[49] Baldus, C.7.53.5 (fol. 236r), quoted in ibid., 187.

[50] Baldus, C.7.53.5 (fol. 263r), quoted in ibid., 159.

[51] Thomas Aquinas, *Summae Theologiae*, 12/11ae.92.1 ad 3, quoted in Black, "The Individual and Society," 600.

have agreed "that the people were prior to the state in the sense that they had created it by setting up the king over themselves and instituting the laws which regulated the life of the state and limited the discretion of the ruler."[52] And, since the authority of the whole is always higher than even the authority of the head, in the sixteenth century Etienne Pasquier could safely conclude: "When I say the authority of the pope is below that of councils, I follow the greatest theologian we ever had, Master Jean Gerson."[53] The same applied to kings and emperors. "Relatively speaking," wrote Baldus in the fourteenth century, "the emperor is said to be like a father and just as his subjects are bound to obey him well, he is also bound to rule them well." If the emperor failed to provide for the common good and became a tyrant, the people had a right to resist. Theories of resistance of the late sixteenth century have surprisingly earlier precedents. "It is to be noted therefore that the original intention in creating the empire was the public good and advantage rather than private, say that of the emperor Charles. If therefore the emperor were to turn his anger on the [Italian] republics, to shake off his yoke of such servitude would not be contrary to natural reason."[54]

The big question to be solved then, both theoretically and practically, was of *who* can act "in the name" of the people, if "*quod omnia tangit debet ab omnibus approbari.*" There was no easy answer. Precisely because the people constituted a *conceptual* whole, "the significance of which has been discovered by the intellect," no answer was beyond disputation: kings, General Estates, *parlements*, or superior magistrates, all could claim to represent 'the people' – and at one time or another they all did. The solution found by thirteenth century legists came once again from Roman law via Church precedents.

Long before Henri III summoned delegates with full powers to Parliament in 1268, the precedent for his writ was created in Roman-canonical court and ambassadorial procedure. Since the Church is a *universitas* and a *universitas* as any corporation is a legal person, then that person can be represented by agents (*procuratores* or syndics) who were given full powers (*plena potestas*). "*Plena potestas* meant simply that the proctor 'fully represented his principal so that the latter's right was brought into issue.'"[55] If a corporation granted to its representative (proctor) *plena potestas* he could act as defendant or plaintiff, but also as *compromissarius*. The consent to act "was given in the terms of the mandate before the negotiation started" because, as we have seen, the representative (*compromissarius*) was deemed already trustworthy, enjoying the necessary authority.[56] It is time therefore to consider the relationship of the

---

[52] William Farr Church (1941), *Constitutional Thought in Sixteenth Century France: A Study in the Evolution of Ideas* (Cambridge and London: Oxford University Press), 86.

[53] Quoted in Salmon, "France," 461.

[54] Baldus, Cons. 3.283, fol 88r, ed. Brescia, 1491 (= Cons., I, 333, ed. Venice, 1575), quoted in Canning, *The Political Thought of Baldus de Ubaldis*, 91.

[55] Post, *Studies in Medieval Legal Thought*, 93.

[56] Ibid., 107.

individual caught in this dialectic between his *forum internum* and his *forum externum* and the concept of representation. After all, "concepts are never held or used in isolation, but in constellations which make up entire schemes or belief systems."[57] And since compromise involves both representation and self-representation, this connection is worth considering.

4.5. INDIVIDUALS AND REPRESENTATION

Representation, as a word, comes also from Latin (as in the case of 'compromise,' the Greeks had no word for 'representation'), and its original meaning "had nothing to do with agency or government or any of the institutions of Roman life."[58] As with the word 'compromise,' representation "is extended in the literature of Christianity to a kind of mystical embodiment ... but its real expansion begins in the thirteenth and fourteenth centuries, when the Pope and the cardinals are often said *to represent the persons of Christ and the Apostles. The connotation is still neither of delegation nor of agency.*"[59] Once again, the Fourth Lateran Council proved a milestone. Pope Innocent III was the first pope to summon proctors to represent chapters and convents in the General Council.[60] By the sixteenth century the idea of representation came to signify representation of persons as well; yet, apart from England, the classical top-down understanding of representation remained for a while unchallenged. The idea of representing 'inferiors' had yet to be discovered. One could represent only something of superior or equal status, never an inferior. If *fideles nuntii* or *procuratores* were sent as ambassadors to popes and monarchs as representatives, they were obviously representatives of a superior. If they were sent as representatives of corporations, these corporations were also of a superior status than their procurators. The representative always had a lower status than the represented, as with any re-presentation of the original.

In sixteenth- and seventeenth-century France, for example, one finds hundreds of mentions of representation: representations of God, of dreams, of incredible beauty, of heroic characters, of nature, of the loved ones, or of indescribable pains. The list of examples is practically inexhaustible. Marc Vitruve Pollion talks in 1547 about *"representer l'Harmonie celeste"*[61] ("representing the heavenly Harmony"); Joachim du Bellay in 1552 about *"representer en ses vers tous les accidens divers de l'humaine tragedie"* (representing in his

---

[57] James Farr (1989), "Understanding Conceptual Change Politically," in *Political Innovation and Conceptual Change*, ed. Terrence Ball, James Farr, and Russel L. Hanson (Cambridge: Cambridge University Press), 33.

[58] Hannah Fenichel Pitkin (1967), *The Concept of Representation* (Los Angeles: University of California Press), 241.

[59] Ibid., 241; emphasis added.

[60] Post, *Studies in Medieval Legal Thought*, 89.

[61] Marc Vitruve Pollion [1547], *Architecture ou art de bien bastir, autheur Romain antique; mis de Latin en Francois par Jan Martin ...* (Paris), 74.

verses all the divers accidents of the human tragedy) or *"ung coeur vicieux"* (a vicious heart);[62] the same year, Pierre de Ronsard asks *"Morfée, s'il te plaist de me representer Cette nuit ma Cassandre"*[63] (Morphee, if you like to represent me this night mine Cassandre); in 1566 Louis des Masures claims *"ces personnages donc, pour les cognoistre mieux, ay-je voulu ici* representer *aux yeux des benins spectateurs"*[64] ("these characters then, for knowing them better, I wanted to represent here to the eyes of kind spectators"); in 1607 Honoré d'Urfé wrote that *"L'estonnement de Bellinde ne se peut* representer"[65] ("the astonishment of Bellinde cannot be represented"); and so forth. In the compass of a single work from 1610 Pierre de Deimier uses the term 'representation' eighteen times, and yet the idea of representing individuals of an inferior condition is never mentioned anywhere.[66] As Nicot, *Thrésor de la langue française*, mentions in 1606, there is only one conceivable way one could represent 'lay individuals' – as a community (*Representer la communauté des citoyens, Personam ciuitatis gerere*). The king or his magistrates did represent the people, or another specific community. As I will show in the following chapters, the story was quite different across the English Channel.

Despite an excellent analysis of the concept of representation *starting* with Hobbes, Pitkin for example fails to consider the possibility that the English evolution of the concept remained for at least a couple of centuries peculiar to England (and later to its American colonies). A possible explanation for this oversight might be found in Pitkin's interpretation of the uncomfortably large gap between the French and the English understandings of representation between the thirteenth and the sixteenth centuries.

Not until the sixteenth century do we find an example of "represent" meaning "to take or fill the place of another (person), substitute for"; and not until 1595 is there an example of representing as "acting for someone as his authorized agent or deputy." Did the development in the meaning of "represent" that took place in Latin in the thirteenth and early fourteenth century, and that was at least under way in French in the thirteenth century, really not take place in English until the sixteenth century?[67]

Although Pitkin suggests a more mundane answer to this question (English was less used in legal, juristic, and political works than Latin and French until the sixteenth century), she also entertains the possibility that the French acquired an earlier understanding of representation as 'representation of

---

[62] Joachim Du Bellay (1552), *Oeuvre de l'invention de l'autheur*, ed. D. Aris and F. Joubokovsky (Paris: Bordas), 42, 101.

[63] Pierre de Ronsard (1993) [1552], *Les amours*, ed. Henri Weber and Catherine Weber (Paris: Classiques Garnier), 144.

[64] Louis Des Masures (1907) [1566], *Epistres au seigneur Lebrun*, ed. Ch. Comte Cornely et Cie (Paris: Cornely & Cie), 8.

[65] Honoré d'Urfé (1607), *L'Astrée, Tome I* (Paris), 396.

[66] Pierre de Deimier (1610), *L'Académie de l'art poétique* (Paris: J. de Bordeaux).

[67] Pitkin, *The Concept of Representation*, 243.

another person,' and in doing so were the first to open new political, more modern venues for the concept. The diagnosis might be correct if amended. As Pitkin's own examples confirm, whenever 'representation' is used in early French as 'representation of a person,' it is either "for the way in which a magistrate or attorney stands and acts *for the community*," or for a single person with *a higher status*: "a bailiff can be spoken as representing the person of his lord."[68]

As a matter of fact, the 1690 French dictionary makes this interpretation explicit:

Représenter – tenir la place de quelqu'un, avoir en main son autorité. Le pope représente Dieu sur la terre. Les Ambassadeurs représente le Prince. Le Magistrates représente le Roy. On dit aussi dans la cérémonie du Sacre, un tel Seigneur représentais le Duc de Normandie, le Comte de Champagne. On dit aussi dans les successions qu'un petit-fils représente son père décédé pour venire partager avec ses oncles a la succession d'un ayeul.

("Representing – keeping somebody else's place, having his authority in your hands. The Pope represents God on earth. The Ambassadors represent the Prince. The Magistrates represent the King. It is also said in the ceremony of the Sacre that a certain Lord represented the Duke of Normandy, the Comte de Champagne. It is also said during the successions, that a grandson represents his dead father when he comes to divide with his uncles in the succession of an elder.")

In 1694, the first *Dictionaire de l'Academie Française* offers a similar definition:

On dit, que Les Ambassadeurs representent les Souverains qui les envoyent, pour dire, que Par leur caractere, ils sont revestus en quelque façon de la dignité & des prerogatives de ceux de la part desquels ils sont envoyez. Ce qui rendoit cette assemblée encore plus illustre, c'estoit le grand nombre des Ambassadeurs qui representoient les plus grands Rois de la Chrestienté. les Ambassadeurs ont caractere pour representer leur maistre. On dit aussi, qu'Un Viceroy, qu'un Gouverneur de Province represente le Roy, le Prince dont il a pouvoir. Etc.

(It is also said that the Ambassadors represent the Sovereigns who send them, for saying that according to their character, they assume in certain ways the dignity & the prerogatives of those in whose name they are sent. What made that assembly even more illustrious was the great number of Ambassadors who represented the grandest Kings of Christianity. The Ambassadors have the character to represent their master. It is also said that a Viceroy, a Governor of a Province represents the King, the Prince from whom he has power.)

From this perspective, there is no change in the meaning of representation between the thirteenth century and the end of the seventeenth. As with compromise, representation remains top-down: The person to be represented is of a higher status or has greater authority than the 'representative,' never the

---

[68] Ibid., 242–243; emphasis added.

other way around. Among other things, this has important consequences for accountability in representation, for according to the classical understanding representatives (be they elected through compromise or otherwise, designated, or simply acknowledged as such) were accountable *not* to individuals but to the higher authority they were elected or designated to represent: God, the king, the princes, a certain community, or even the *populus*. Representation was not a matter of will, but one of reason. Even if an emperor enjoyed authority in his *forum externum*, there was still a compelling authority in his *forum internum* by the simple fact that he was human, and therefore a creature of both God and nature.

> By positive law the emperor is obliged by the dictates of reason, because he is a rational animal, and therefore the emperor is a rational animal, and therefore the emperor is not freed from reason. For no authority, whether of the emperor or the senate can make the emperor other than a rational and mortal animal, or free him from the law of nature or from the dictates of right reason or the eternal law [D.7.5.2].[69]

If representatives failed in their mission of representation, it was through failing to properly represent this higher principle or authority, *not* individuals, and could be removed by the *universitas* even if they were kings or popes.[70] And yet, as shown before, the individuals who chose, designated, or accepted the representatives did not grant (or create) any authority in the process. Their authority was not delegated bottom-up but top-down. In the same way as the individual was created by God as primary cause and born to his parents as secondary cause, the king or the emperor received his authority from God and yet was 'elected' by the consent of the people. Yet even the people as *universitas* were not *auto-nomos*. They were not above law. According to the medieval interpretation, no corporation could emerge as such without the tacit or express consent of a superior authority.[71] In terms of the potential abuse of power, nobody, not even the people, as source of authority, was above suspicion. "Tyranny whether by the monarch or by the people was universally condemned as infringing *utiltas publica*."[72] For Baldus, for example, "the constitutive element was not the ruler's command or the people's consent alone, but that will exercised in accordance with moral, religious and rational criteria. Thus Baldus considers that the *ius naturale, ius gentium* and *ius divinum* are so

---

[69] Baldus, C.3.34.2 (fol. 190v), quoted in Canning, *The Political Thought of Baldus de Ubaldis*, 77.
[70] Eric Voegelin (1952), *The New Science of Politics* (Chicago: University of Chicago Press), talks about the "transcendental" type of sense of representation, the sense in which a society is or can be "the representative of something beyond itself, of a transcendent reality," "a transcendent truth" (54, 75). Yet, as will become clear later, there are differences between Vogelin's transcendental representation and the interpretation that I propose. In his account, "a society must articulate itself by producing a representative that will act for it" (41).
[71] See, e.g., Post, *Studies in Medieval Legal Thought*, 29.
[72] Black, "The Individual and Society," 463.

axiomatic that there can be no debate about whether the princes can infringe them – if he does do so, his law is not valid."[73]

The consequences of this understanding of authority and representation will become obvious in time. For one thing, the entire "mandate–independence controversy," as presented by Pitkin, or "agent" versus "representative" in Voegelin's account – a controversy that has fascinated the Anglo-American world almost from the beginning – raises little concern in continental Europe. It makes little or no sense to ask whether a representative should follow to the letter the indications and the wishes of his 'constituency,' or whether he is allowed the independence of thought and decision making that Burke (or Hegel, for that matter) requires. Being a representative of a higher principle, the person does not fall under either of the two terms of these equations, mandate versus independence. The mandate to represent comes from the people, yet the representative is 'dependent' on the principle he is mandated to represent since his authority comes from it. Once again, representation has to be informed by reason, not by will(s).

Second, as principles, ideologies, interests, and the like demanding 'representation' multiplied in the modern world, the political scene in continental Europe became ever more fragmented. Since it was not individuals but their 'interests' or 'ideologies' that were to be represented, the emphasis was never on representing individuals, let alone individuals' wills. Unfortunately, this crucial distinction has been overlooked by most scholars.[74] A possible explanation might lie in the confusion between what Hwa-Yong Lee, following Walter Ullmann, labeled as the 'ascending' and 'descending' conceptions of representation during the Middle Ages. "The former sees that power in society ... was ascribed to the community or the people," while "in contrast, the descending conception of government and law supposes that governmental authority and law-creating power were given by one supreme agent."[75]

The confusion here is between 'people' understood as a whole or *universitas*, and 'people' understood as a collection of individuals. In the first

---

[73] Canning, *The Political Thought of Baldus de Ubaldis*, 76.

[74] As a matter of fact, the only examples I am aware of are Lucien Jaume (1986), *Hobbes et l'etat représentatif moderne* (Paris: Presses Universitaires de France), esp. 201–211; Quentin Skinner (2005), "Hobbes on Representation," *European Journal of Philosophy* 13, no. 2: 155–184; Quentin Skinner (2007), "Hobbes on Persons, Authors and Representatives," in *The Cambridge Companion to Hobbes' Leviathan*, ed. Patricia Springborg (Cambridge: Cambridge University Press); Quentin Skinner (2009), "A Genealogy of the Modern State," *Proceedings of the British Academy* 162: 325–370. Quentin Skinner too makes a distinction between representing the people as whole and representing people as a collection of individuals, in place during the seventeenth century. He also stresses that the representation of 'the people' as a conceptual whole was of French inspiration. In an exchange with Prof. Skinner, we agree that there are many similarities between our interpretations, but also some important differences in emphasis. See further.

[75] Hwa-Yong Lee (2008), *Political Representation in the Later Middle Ages: Marsilius in Context* (New York: Peter Lang), 34.

interpretation, representing a community relies on the *descending* rather than *ascending* understanding of representation – the whole being *always* apprehended as being above the individual. "The whole body was prior to and greater than the king, greater though he might be than any individual member of the realm."[76] Only in the second case, in which the people are conceived of as a collection of autonomous and equal individuals, can one properly speak of a reverse with long-lasting consequences in the direction of representation.

This confusion was facilitated by the medieval dialectic of the individual. In terms of representation of the individuals, apparently there was no clear-cut demarcation line – sometimes individuals (emperors, kings, and popes, but also bishops and lower magistrates) appear to be personally represented, at other times it seems that such persons were represented only in virtue of the communities they represented in turn. If, say, a king could represent his people, then he could also send out an ambassador (or even a *compromissarium*) to represent him. As in the case of the distinction between *lex publica* and *lex privata*, scholars have argued about *who* exactly was represented. Yet once one considers the dialectic between *forum externum* and *forum internum* the problem fades away.

For medieval man, regardless of his status, *forum internum* could never be represented. As nobody could represent one's 'inner self,' regardless of how one defined it, no representation could involve both fora, that is, the whole individual. The *forum internum* is the forum of conscience, and therefore is dominated by reason. Nobody could represent either your conscience or your personal relationship with God. Thus, nobody could have compromised it either. On the other hand, *forum externum* is the forum of the acting individual, the forum informed by the moving will, which drives individuals to fulfill the requirements of their 'offices.' Only in this capacity could the individual have been represented and/or compromised. The king, for example, was represented by his officers and represented the people by virtue of his office. The magistrate represented the king also in virtue of his office, that is, in his *forum externum*. And when it came to representing corporations, the individual was represented by virtue of his membership to a certain *universitas*. Obviously, the dialectic between the two fora was reflected in the medieval dialectic between reason and will: reason is moved by the will, yet this will, in turn, has to be informed by reason.

---

[76] Howell A. Lloyd (1983), *The State, France and the Sixteenth Century* (London: George Allen & Unwin), 153. One can see why until now it has been generally assumed that the ascending theory of representation spread much sooner all over Europe. The ambiguity of the term "people" was as present during the sixteenth and seventeenth centuries as it is today. Not only could it signify a multitude as well as a whole but also it could have been used to designate either a conceptualized community (*populus*) or the lowest, uneducated, and undisciplined part of society (*plebs*). See Hubert Carrier (2004), *Le labyrinthe de l'état: Essai sur le débat politique en France au temps de la Fronde (1648–1653)* (Paris: Honore Champion Editeur), 121–122.

Ratio habet vim movendi a voluntate ... Sed voluntas de his quae imperantur, ad hoc quod legis rationem habeat, oportet quo sit aliqua ratione regulata. Et hoc modo intelligentur quod voluntas principis habet vigorem legis; alioquin voluntas principis magis esset iniquitas quam lex.[77]

Reason has its power of moving from the will ... but in order that the will has the reason of law in those things that it commands, it is necessary that it be informed by some reason. And in this way the will of the prince can be said to have the force of law; otherwise the will of the prince would be a sin rather than a law.

As the ideas of individuality, community/conformity, and representation were so tightly wrapped together in the medieval and early modern psyche, it is now time to inquire into the relationship between individualism and absolutism in the particular context of sixteenth and seventeenth century France. The aim is to discover how French absolutism could have had an effect in forging private individuals so afraid of compromising themselves in the public sphere.

I advance as working hypothesis the possibility that the crises of authority of the time served as a catalyst, upsetting the balance between the two fora. Two different attempts to solve these tensions developed on the two sides of the Channel: a French one emphasizing the *forum internum* ('centripetal individualism'), and a British one focusing more on the *forum externum* ('centrifugal individualism').

By impacting the self-representation of the individual, they affected by the same token the understanding of what political representation is or ought to be and the attitude toward compromise.

---

[77] Thomas Aquinas, *Summa Theologiae* 1.2 q.90.i, quoted in K. Pennington (1991), "Law, Legislative Authority and Theories of Government, 1150–1300," in Burns, *Cambridge History of Medieval Political Thought*, 430.

5

Compromise and Centripetal Individualism

[Y]ou are running out, you are scattering yourself; concentrate yourself, resist yourself; you are being betrayed, dispersed, and stolen away from yourself.

Montaigne

As shown in the previous chapter, earlier conceptions of modern scholars about the medieval individual proved one-sided. Far from turning passively like a wheel in a huge mechanism, he was apprehended and apprehended himself both as a member of a *universitas and* as a distinct and unique individual. The medieval man managed, most of the time that is, to strike a balance between his *forum internum* and his *forum externum* – a balance that was reflected in the workings of the entire society. Not surprisingly then, his attitude toward compromise was neutral. Both as *arbitratio* and as *electio* compromise remained a useful tool to solve a particular problem, and nothing more. It did not involve the entire 'I' of the individual but only his *forum externum*. If *forum internum* could not be represented, neither could it be compromised. And yet, as we have seen, from the end of the sixteenth century through the seventeenth, one witnesses a remarkable cross-Channel split in the usage of compromise: while the French became increasingly worried about compromise, the British embraced it as a virtue. Obviously then, during that period something happened to affect the dialectic between the two fora differently in the two countries. I claim that in France the explanation is at least in part to be found in the exacerbation of the difference between the *forum internum* and *forum externum*. The increased pressure for conformity applied by absolutism on the *forum externum* had as a counterreaction a withdrawal of the individual into his *forum internum* which came to be understood – mistakenly, from a medieval perspective – as the sole repository and last bastion of uniqueness and authenticity, hence the fear of compromising one's inner self. *Forum externum* became more of a costume that would not affect the 'true self.'

There is a large body of literature dealing with what historians have called 'the crisis of the sixteenth century' and 'the crisis of the seventeenth century,' respectively. If these crises marked the beginning of what we label today as early modernity it is primarily because underneath the medieval camouflage the elements that define modern states had started to emerge: by the end of the sixteenth century, 'reason of state' became a widely accepted justification, state regulatory powers increased, legislative sovereignty was tentatively asserted. "The state ideology made it possible for rulers to justify actions in 1700 that would have been considered tyrannical and immoral in 1500."[1] In her seminal book *Philosophy and the State in France*, Nannerl Keohane uncovers something close to a paradox: French absolutism bred a peculiar form of individualism that manifested disregard for civic involvement. "Even at the height of participatory humanism a few men of letters (including Rabelais) and a few jurists (including La Boétie) expressed contempt for politics and advocated some version of a life devoted to pleasant learning and good company."[2] Yet the same individualism managed somehow to provide a fertile ground for a theory of effective participation that exploded during the French Revolution. "[T]he French political culture in the age of Henry IV, Louis XIII, and Louis XIV is a phenomenon that needs explaining, not one that was somehow fore-ordained before Enlightenment and the Revolution drew men into action."[3] By the eighteenth century the passive member of the ancient corporations moved without hesitation into politics and was not content with an illusory delegation of authority through representation, unlike his British counterpart. Not only was he suspicious of compromise, he also refused the idea of being represented. How was this possible?

I suspect that the explanation runs deeper than the generally accepted alliance of the nascent modern individual with the nascent modern state against old forms of corporatism such as parishes, guilds, and the like.[4] Frenchmen of all ways of life refused to be compromised and to be represented qua individuals, because in both cases they felt their uniqueness, that is, their *fora interna*, would be endangered. On the one hand, the newly discovered state managed to surpass in importance the ancient *corps* and communities, yet remained an entity transcending individuals.[5] "No 'mere conglomeration of individuals,' far

[1] Daniel Engster (2001), *Divine Sovereignty: The Origins of Modern State Power* (DeKalb: Northern Illinois University Press), 4.

[2] Nannerl Keohane (1980), *Philosophy and the State in France: The Renaissance to the Enlightenment* (Princeton: Princeton University Press), 87.

[3] Ibid., 121.

[4] See, e.g., Walter Ullmann (1966), *The Individual and Society in the Middle Ages* (Baltimore, Md.: Johns Hopkins University Press). See also most of the authors in Janet Coleman, ed. (1996), *The Individual in Political Theory and Practice* (Oxford: Clarendon Press), or in Brigitte Miriam Bedos-Razak and Dominique Iogna-Prat (2005), *L'Individu au Moyen Age* (Aubier: Editions Flammarion).

[5] See Howell A. Lloyd (1983), *The State, France and the Sixteenth Century* (London: George Allen & Unwin), 20–23.

more than the sum of its parts, the state was reality in its most developed form, the supreme 'unity of universal and particular.'"[6] On the other hand, as we have seen, the interplay between *forum internum* and *forum externum* was not by any means new. Yet the series of crises – religious, intellectual, social and political – that dominated the period served as a catalyst that helped restate by simplifying the dialectic between the two to the point of perceiving them as opposites.

Absent this dialectic one cannot understand why people from different intellectual, religious, and social venues took their desire for intellectual liberty and their disdain for the 'common people' so seriously, while at the same time stressing the importance of direct participation in politics and trying at any opportunity to apply this participation to an extreme. One cannot understand the paradoxes that will later mark the French Revolution if one fails to take into consideration the almost obsessive focus on the *forum internum* and the authenticity of the self coupled with a drive toward conformity and unity in the *forum externum* that was already in place more than a century before. Furthermore, one cannot understand why political representation as representation of individual wills – an understanding that we take for granted today – was not at all appealing to early modern Frenchmen. Simply put, Frenchmen refused to choose between "a polity composed of individuals loosely bound together by subordination to the same rules and recognition of one another's liberties, and a community of persons united by shared love of their fellowship."[7] They wanted a polity in which uniqueness and the private sphere are protected and yet citizens are still bound together by more than mere self-interest. They wanted, so to speak, to have their cake and eat it too. As Bossuet had put it, two apparently contradictory truths ought not to be reconciled. Suffice it to hold strongly "the two ends of the chain, even though one cannot always see the middle through which the chain continues."[8]

If "at the beginning of the [sixteenth] century England and France alike may be said to have but just reconstituted central government after long anarchy" and yet "the lines on which political thought proceeded in the two countries rapidly diverged," it is difficult to determine to what extent these differences in understanding were the cause or the result of structural changes.[9] It is more than the need of monarchs and elites for new ideological justifications of the legitimacy of their power.[10] If changes in the social, economic, and political fabric influenced the individual dialectic between *forum internum* and *forum externum*, it is

---

[6] Ibid., 22.

[7] Ibid., 462.

[8] Jacques-Bénigne Bossuet (1966), *Traité du libre arbiter*, ch. 4, quoted in Jacques Truchet (1966), *Politique de Bossuet* (Paris: Armand Colin), 12: "*les deux bouts de la chaîne, quoiqu'on ne voie pas toujours le milieu par où l'enchaînement se continue.*"

[9] J.W. Allen (1957), *A History of Political Thought in the Sixteenth Century* (London: Methuen & Co), xv.

[10] See, e.g., Engster, *Divine Sovereignty*, 5.

obvious that a different understanding of the individual and his relationship with the state influenced the lineaments of the entire society as well.

Parallel with the rapid changes in the social structure, there occurred a definite development of political concepts which corresponded roughly to the evolution within society. Yet this alteration of accepted constitutional doctrine was not caused exclusively by factual considerations; intellectual currents, philosophical as well as legal, exercised marked influence upon theories of state.[11]

Historians have offered several explanations for these differences, ranging from structural explanations focusing on class relations to political economy. However, since this research centers on the different usages of compromise, I will discuss such aspects only to the extent that they relate to different apprehensions of the individual and issues of political representation. Thus, the historical aspects will serve more as an illuminating background than as straightforward causes. There are suggestive correlations, but as many scholars agree it is difficult if not altogether impossible to reduce intellectual changes to environmental causes (or vice versa).[12]

Old hierarchies and forms of authority were increasingly challenged by new ones, which, in turn, lacking the force of tradition, were forced to mimic old forms and arguments. Considering this crisis of authority, one of the main questions of the time became: *Who shall be judge?* Who could serve as the impartial arbitrator, endowed with the reason required for justice and the will to implement it? In other words, who shall be the *compromissarius*?

At least partially in response to the social, economic, and political turmoil, the development of absolutism, which is not to be mistaken for totalitarianism, appeared a suitable solution. The centralization of power promised stability in an otherwise insecure world. One witnesses therefore the emergence of the first professional armies, needed to conduct foreign policies efficiently (mainly through wars) and to compete economically with the surrounding powers. New methods of taxation were devised in response to the financial crisis that plagued monarchies during this period. And yet, despite the similarities between France and England at the beginning of the sixteenth century, by the end of the century it was clear that the two countries had taken different evolutionary paths. The success of the English Revolution during the seventeenth century and the defeat of the Fronde in France only confirmed the existence of divergent responses to otherwise rather similar challenges.

---

[11] William Farr Church (1941), *Constitutional Thought in Sixteenth Century France: A Study in the Evolution of Ideas* (Cambridge: Harvard University Press), 4.

[12] See, e.g., Allen, *A History of Political Thought*, xvii: "Explanation of the genesis of this thought, begotten by desire on circumstance, is strictly impossible; we can do little than note suggestive correlations." See also Lloyd, *The State, France and the Sixteenth Century*, xviii: "Such an answer would seem to imply that between environmental and intellectual developments there is a straightforward correlation, such that changes in the conditions in which men live simply induce corresponding degrees of change in their ideas."

However, to only stress the changes of the sixteenth and seventeenth centuries and disregard the undeniable continuities with the medieval world would be a mistake as well. As Lloyd put it, "continuity is not less important than change – above all continuity of consciousness."[13] The more that change challenged the stability of the medieval order, the more people tried to find stability in ancient models. As Salmon argues, "constant reiteration of the principle of renewal was a way of protesting against the processes of change.... *Renovatio* concealed *innovatio*."[14] There was an enduring belief that underlying all these twists of fortune, all these events in flux, there still was an order discernible by the keen observer.

Bernard du Haillan, historiographer of France under the last Valois king and the first Bourbon, maintained that "although persons change, the world nevertheless does not change at all."[15] Chaos was just an appearance. Properly grasped, these *accidens* should prove *phenomena* revealing an organized whole. It is therefore no coincidence that during the sixteenth century historical studies developed in France with an intensity never before witnessed. People "surveyed the past and contemporary events (as 'exemplarists'), their institutions (as philologists and jurists), and their society (as political philosophers)" yet "for the exponents of all three models, philosophical considerations were of first importance. It was by reference to universal ethical principles that they vindicated their study of history."[16]

Translated in the plan of self-awareness, this complex interaction between continuity and change was manifested in what Lloyd calls the "two paramount traits": this consciousness was both "markedly metaphysical in its orientation" and "profoundly impressed by a sense of the mutability and instability of human affairs."

[T]he influences that informed the metaphysical sphere ought always to be exemplified, as far as was humanly possible, in the institutions that controlled men's lives, in the leadership and authority to which men were required to defer, and even in the groups to which men belonged. The metaphysical was thus intimately linked with the ethical; and the state – a term that itself implies stability – emerged as a response to ethical exigencies at a time when the contemporary sense of insecurity had grown acute.[17]

We ought therefore to pursue our investigation of continuity and change on two distinct yet related levels: that of the individual, with the interplay between *forum internum* and *forum externum*, and that of the newly emergent state. After all, the intimate connection between self-representation and political representation should not be overlooked. If the Frenchman was *méfiant* toward

---

[13] Lloyd, *The State, France and the Sixteenth Century*, xviii.
[14] J.H.M. Salmon (1975), *Society in Crisis; France in the Sixteenth Century* (New York: St. Martin's Press), 14.
[15] Quoted in Lloyd, *The State, France and the Sixteenth Century*, 8.
[16] Ibid., 5.
[17] Ibid., xix.

compromise, French society as a whole was *méfiante* as well. Compromise could have become, as it did in England, a political practice not just widely accepted but embraced as the only alternative to violence, yet it never did. The reason, I suspect, is in the French refusal to understand political relationships in terms of individual contracts – for contracts and compromises presuppose an equality of wills, disregarding the obvious inequality of wisdom.

The way in which individuals reacted to this developing absolutism, that is, the increased pressure for conformity in the *forum externum*, is analyzed in the first part, where a wealth of examples demonstrates how the gap between the two fora was widened as the result of a simplified dialectic: since *forum externum* came to be apprehended as mostly informed by conformity, its counterpart, *forum internum*, came in turn to be assimilated with the true self, the last bastion of authenticity, hence the need to protect it at all costs. The increased awareness of the distinction between the two fora of the individual, together with the reduction of their dialectic to a simple opposition, is evident in the writings of the most famous thinkers of the time, despite their otherwise totally different perspectives, from Montaigne and Charron to Pascal and Corneille. Furthermore, it is not an accident if precisely during that period the casuistry of 'mental reservation' enjoyed an almost disturbing popularity. It is this almost obsessive focus on the *forum internum*, I shall argue, that helps explain not only the French *méfiance* toward compromise, but also the otherwise paradoxical insistence on participatory politics, as soon as conjecture appeared to allow it.

The second part of this chapter will consider the emergence of absolutist theory in France as evinced in the works of Seysell, Pasquier, l'Hospital, and Bodin. In the same way in which the medieval dialectic of the individual was changed yet not destroyed, their works were far from marking a radical departure from medieval theories, relying on a similar framework, not only in terms of descending representation, but also as far as the relationship between reason and will was concerned. A will uninformed by reason, especially in the case of the absolute sovereign, remained unacceptable. As a matter of fact, as we shall see, both sovereignty and state were concepts worked out by reinforcing some medieval ideas at the expense of others. Among other consequences of this simplified dialectic, such a perspective resulted in an increased awareness of the distinction between the equality of wills inherent in any compromise, and the obvious inequality of reasons that made compromise a dangerous political practice. From this perspective, Bodin, for example, proves an early precursor of Guizot's criticism of representation understood as a 'mechanical counting of wills.'

The third part will consider the rivalry between two competing conceptual wholes – namely, the people and the state – from both theoretical and practical perspectives in order to explain why in France 'the people' as *universitas* lost the battle for sovereignty with the newly emergent state instead of being assimilated with it. I argue that, despite a practical reinforcement of the importance of smaller *universitates* (communes, fraternities, local parishes, and the like) starting in the second half of the sixteenth century, 'the people' as an all-encompassing concept had simply too many competing claimants – parlements, estates, and magistrates. All pretended to be the best equipped to speak in the people's name, for better understanding its 'true' interests. Thus, since the very concept of sovereignty presupposed a unity not only of will but also of reason, there was no clear-cut solution for deciding who is right and who is wrong. From this perspective, the embodiment of sovereignty in the king and the development of the absolutist state followed the path of least resistance. Obviously, it was much easier for a king than for an entire people to claim "*l'État c'est moi*"!

The last part deals precisely with these conjectures when Frenchmen, regardless of their religion or their social status, thought they had the opportunity for hands-on politics. What is revealing is that the roots of the excesses of the French Revolution and of the unwillingness of the French revolutionaries to compromise were obvious more than a century before, during the Fronde(s). If Rousseau's peculiar version of the social contract, his dispraise of both political representation and compromise, and his distinction between the General Will and the will of all took such a hold on the French revolutionary spirit, the reason, I shall claim, is to be found in this exaggerated gap between *forum internum* and *forum externum*.

5.1. THE EMERGENCE OF CENTRIPETAL INDIVIDUALISM

As Vittor Ivo Comparato points out, the revival of the classical distinction between private and public entailed by this individualism represented not just a mere *renovatio*, "but something more intimate and self-reflective regarding the moral value of the decision whether or not to accept any degree of integration between the personal and public spheres."[18]

Despite differences in emphasis, historians generally agree that during this period the French manifested a peculiar disregard for civic or political involvement, at least when compared with their British counterparts. If one does not take into consideration the dialectic between *forum internum* and *forum externum*, one cannot understand why people from different intellectual, religious, and social venues took, as Comparatto put it, "their desire for intellectual autonomy, their scorn for all compromise, their disdain for the 'common people' and for common sense to extremes," while at the same time continually stressing the importance of direct participation in politics – and tried to apply this principle 'to an extreme' whenever they got the chance. One cannot understand the paradoxes that later marked the French Revolution if one fails to take into consideration the almost obsessive focus on the *forum*

[18] Vittor Ivo Comparato (1996), "A Case of Modern Individualism: Politics and the Uneasiness of Intellectuals in the Baroque Age," in Coleman, *The Individual*, 149.

internum and the authenticity of the self that was already in place more than a century before coupled with a drive toward conformity and unity in the *forum externum*. Thankfully, the widespread French stubbornness against the idea of compromising may help in illuminating the overlooked side of the same story.

The wars of religion had as an unintended consequence an enlargement of the gap between the two fora. In the political sphere, the zealots, as Charon points out, managed to give Christianity a bad name. "*Quelles exécrables méchancetés n'a produit le zele de religion?... Cette guerre intestine ... est un venin qui consomme toute l'humanité.*"[19] ("What atrocious meanness was not produced by the zeal of religion?... This intestinal war ... is a poison for all of humanity.") The Huguenot François de la Noue is even harsher.

Si on demande qui a produite telle génération (d'incroyants et de libertins), on ne répondra pas mal que ce sont nos guerres pour la religion qui nous a fait oublier la religion. Et ne faut point que ni les uns ni les autres dissent: c'est le parti contraire qui engendre les athéists, car toutes parts y se rencontrent.[20]

(If one asks what has produced such a generation (of unbelievers and libertines), one will not answer wrong that it is our wars for religion that made us forget religion. And it is useless for the one [party] or the other to say: it is the opposite party that engenders the atheists, for all parties are involved.)

But this was only half of the story. These wars of religion paradoxically also had the effect of turning men and women alike toward *forum internum* through private prayer and meditation. "Individual piety developed and grew stronger, among clergy and laity alike, as increasing emphasis was laid on *examen de conscience*, confession and the prayerful study of certain devotional works."[21] Thus, for a variety of reasons that cannot be exhausted here, by 1600 the new individualism, suspicious about public involvement, was already well under way and manifested itself under a variety of forms. Scorning the irrationality of the zealots in the public sphere while stressing the authenticity of individual piety were two sides of the same coin, in the same way in which the scorn for the multitude was doubled by praise of the conceptualized 'people.'

From different perspectives, to be sure, authors such as Seysell, Bodin, Montaigne, Charron, and Pascal agreed that the individual fully manifested himself only in the confines of the private sphere. Only here, in what Montaigne called "the back room of the mind," was he able to preserve space for his freedom of conscience. "The wise man should withdraw his soul within, out of the crowd, and keep it in freedom and power to judge things freely."[22] Here, there

---

[19] Quoted in John Cruickshank (1996), "A Note on Lay Piety in the Early Seventeenth Century," in *Ethics and Politics in Seventeenth-Century France*, ed. Keith Cameron and Elizabeth Woodrough (Exeter: University of Exeter Press), 31.

[20] Quoted in ibid., 31.

[21] Ibid., 33.

[22] Montaigne, I, 23 (146), in *Les essais* (2009), édition complete, adaptation en français moderne par André Lanly (Paris: Gallimard), translated in Keohane, *Philosophy and the State in France*, 110.

was no other authority than his conscience (and, eventually, God). "My reason is not trained to bend and bow," he said.[23] Here, in the back room of his mind, he was what he really was. Here, his true self could be explored and, most important, could be *protected*. The centrifugal temptations of public sphere ought therefore to be resisted for the sake of the self.

C'était un commandement paradoxe que nous faisait anciennement ce Dieu à Delphes: Regardez dans vous, reconaissez-vous, tenez-vous à vous, votre esprit et votre volonté qui se consommé ailleurs, ramenez-la en soi; vous vous écoulez, vous vous répandez; appilez-vous, soutebez-vous; on vous trahit, on vous dissipe, on vous dérobe à vous.[24]

(It was a paradoxical command that was given us of old by that god of Delphi: Look into yourself, know yourself, keep to yourself; bring back your mind and your will, which are spending themselves elsewhere, into themselves; you are running out, you are scattering yourself; concentrate yourself, resist yourself; *you are being betrayed, dispersed, and stolen away from yourself.*)[25]

Pascal launches a strikingly similar warning when he develops the theme of *divertissement* – the distraction that switches the focus from the true self to the imaginary, narrow one: "We are not content with the life we have within us, in our own being; we wish to live an imaginary life in the minds of others, and we force ourselves to appear other than we are.... We work incessantly to embellish and maintain our imaginary being, and neglect the true one."[26]

As Comparato points out, "the need to distinguish spiritual from temporal jurisdiction led to the establishment of a clear-cut boundary between individual conscience and that which is subject to the law."[27] When it came to an individual's true self, no 'arbitration' or judgment by somebody else could be a more appropriate judge, for only conscience can read even the most secret intentions of the heart. "So wonderful is the power of conscience [that] it makes us betray, accuse, and fight against ourselves, and for want of other witnesses, to give evidence against ourselves," says Montaigne.[28] (*"Tant est extraordinaire la force de la conscience [qu']elle nous force à nous trahir, à nous accuser et à nous combattre nous-mêmes, et, à défaut de témoin étranger, elle nous produit nous-mêmes [comme temoins] contre nous."*) And since conscience was the best judge of the self, it goes without saying that it should not be disgraced through any kind of compromise.

[23] Montaigne, III, 8 (714), quoted in Keohane, *Philosophy and the State*, 110.
[24] Montaigne, III, 9 (332), in *Essais de Michel de Montaigne* (1998), présentation, établissement du texte, apparat critique, et notes par André Tournon (Imprimerie Nationale Éditions). See also Montaigne, III, 9 (1211), in *Les Essais*.
[25] Montaigne, III, 9. See also I, 3, and III, 12. Translated in Keohane, *Philosophy and the State*, 100; emphasis added.
[26] Blaise Pascal (1995), *Pensées*, ed. Léon Brunschvig (New York), 147.
[27] Comparato, "A Case of Modern Individualism," 104.
[28] Montaigne, "On Conscience," in *Les essais*, 452.

Confession was the best way to preserve the integrity of one's *forum internum* and therefore of one's true self. In *Les éloges et les vies des reynes, des princesses et des dames illustres en piété, en courage et en doctrine* ... (1647), Hilarion de Coste urges his readers: "*Confesse, ie te prie, confesse-toy hardiment; car le delay de la Confession met en Compromis ton salut, en danger la vie de ton ame, & en confusion tout ce qui est de toy*"[29] ("Confess, I pray you, confess yourself without mercy; for the delay of Confession puts in Compromise your salvation, in danger the life of your soul, & in total confusion all that is of yourself"). By now, *forum internum* had come to be totally assimilated with the true self. The dialectic between the two was lost. *Forum externum* remained rather a costume having nothing to do with the authentic self. If one compromises one's *forum internum,* one compromises one's salvation. Unlike the *forum externum,* by definition, nobody (in this world, that is) can arbitrate over one's *forum internum.* Being willing to compromise meant being willing to accept not only the pre-existing authority of the *compromissores,* but also the lack of distinctiveness – if I am your equal, I am no different from you. (Remember the caveat from *La jurisprudence du Digeste:* you have to respect the decision of the *compromissarius,* regardless if it was just or not. The fault of choosing the wrong arbiter is entirely yours.)

Since the distinction between the two fora had become so dramatic, the question of 'trustworthiness' returns over and over again, in different settings. I believe it is not mere coincidence if the casuistry of 'the mental reservation' enjoyed such popularity in France precisely between the second half of the sixteenth century all the way toward the end of the seventeenth century, differentiating yet once again France from England across religious lines.[30] Spelled out for the first time in 1515, by Sylvester, in his *Summa summarum,* it grew increasingly in popularity in the next fifty years, reaching the pick of its popularity in the decades surrounding 1600. In sum, the doctrine asserted that if one is speaking the truth in one's mind, by mentally adding a few words to the spoken ones in dire situations, one is not committing the sin of lying. Being true to oneself in one's *forum internum* was all that mattered. Thus, a Catholic priest could deny being a priest in front of his persecutors as long as he adds in his mind "of Apollo." Yet despite being commonly associated with the Jesuits, the casuistry of 'mental reservation' and 'equivocation' was cutting in effect across the Catholic–Protestant divide in continental Europe. The British case was different.[31]

[29] Hillarion de Coste (1647), *Les éloges et les vies des reynes, des princesses et des dames illustres en piété, en courage et en doctrine...,* 611.

[30] I am indebted to my colleague at Tulane University, Gary Remer, who pointed out this connection.

[31] For an in-depth discussion, see Albert R. Jonsen and Stephen Tolumin (1988), *The Abuse of Casuistry – A History of Moral Reasoning* (Berkeley: University of California Press). For the peculiar case of English casuists, see esp. ch. 8. For a different insight, see Johann P. Sommerville (1988), "The 'New Art of Lying': Equivocation, Mental Reservation, and Casuistry," in

Obviously, such a doctrine was able to undermine even (com-) promises and oaths. In Sylvester's casuistry, if a man is waylaid by thieves and compelled to promise to pay some money in the future, he is not obliged to do so as long as he had mentally added some clause. Thus, internal actions become 'truer' than the external ones, for revealing the 'true self.' For Hobbes, as we will see, this is precisely what one cannot do. According to him, promises and/or contracts are to be kept even if, threatened by thieves, one does it out of fear, for (a) contracts imply a transfer of rights, and the transfer of a right is a declaration of will, and (b) without (com-) promises and contracts there can be no society.

From here probably stems the obsession of the seventeenth century with discussions of hypocrisy – after all, one has to be sure that the other party does not simply fake virtue – and also the differences between France and England: while in England such discussions remained confined to hypocrisy in its religious dimension, in France there was an increased worry about hypocrisy in all the domains of public life.[32] In the *forum externum*, claimed Charron, the natural hypocrisy of men makes them "more scrupulous about external actions, which are on display, yet ... less important" (*"l'on est plus scrupuleux aux actions externs, qui sont en montre, mais ... peu importants"*). On the contrary, internal actions, which are "secret and of no display, yet truly required and necessary ... are much more difficult. On them depends the reformation of the soul, the moderation of passions, the regulating of life; while from the acquisition of the external ones one ends up neglecting the internal" (*"secretes et de nulle montre, mais bien requises et necessaires ... sont fort difficiles. D'icelles dépend la reformation de l'ame, la moderation des passions, le reglement de la vie: voir par acquit de ces externs l'on vient à une nonchalance des internes"*).[33]

Not surprisingly then, the first reaction of most French intellectuals was to refuse to compromise themselves in the public sphere. The model of excellence was Socrates, and not only for Montaigne or Charon. In a letter to Méré, La Rochefoucauld wrote:

La véritable vertu se confie en elle-même, elle se montre sans artifice et d'un air simple et naturelle, comme celle de Socrate. Mais le faux honnêtes gens, aussi bien que les faut dévots, ne cherchent que l'apparence, et je crois que, dans la morale, Sénèque était un hypocrite et que Epicure était un saint.[34]

Conscience and Casuistry in Early Modern Europe, ed. Edmund Leites (Cambridge: Cambridge University Press), 159–184.

32 Jacques Bos (2002), "The Hidden Self of the Hypocrite," in *On the Edge of Truth and Honesty: Principles and Strategies of Fraud and Deceit in the Early Modern Period*, ed. Toon Van Houdt, Jan L. DeJong, Zoran Kwak, Marijke Spies, and Marc Van Vaeck (Leiden and Boston: Brill), 65–84. See also G. Goedecke (1968), *L'hypocrisie, le vice du siecle: eine Darstellung des Problems der Heuchelei in der französischen dramatischen Literatur des 17. Jahrhunderts* (Berlin).

33 Pierre Charron (1986) [1604], *De la sagesse*, text revu par Barbara de Negroni (Fayard), Livre Premier, 53, 342.

34 Quoted in William D. Howarth (1996), "'Alternative' Ethical Systems in France during the *Grand Siècle*," in *Ethics and Politics in Seventeenth-Century France*, ed. Keith Cameron and Elizabeth Woodrough (Exeter: University of Exeter Press), 26.

(True virtue is confined to itself; it shows without artifice and with a simple appearance, as that of Socrates. But false honest people, as well as false devouts, look only to the appearance, and I think that, from a moral point of view, Seneca was a hypocrite and Epicurus was a saint.)

"The Epicurean exhortation to abstain from participation in public life could be spontaneously accepted by the individual when he had rationally understood the deep meaning of politics and discovered that it is not the summit of human activity, but the occasion of a supreme alienation of the individual from himself."[35] As many historians have observed, in seventeenth-century France, civil and political spheres became estranged from one another.[36] And yet this judgment applies almost exclusively to just one side of the individual, his *forum internum*. As I will show shortly, the case of the *forum externum* was entirely different. Unless one takes into consideration the distinction between the two fora, the French insistence, from Montaigne to Pascal, on *both* individualism and absolutism might appear quite schizoid.

To compromise your conscience, to leave it to the arbitrage of others was unacceptable for (1) the public sphere had no business interfering with the private one, (2) the competency and trustworthiness of the outsiders was dubious to say the least, and therefore (3) no authority from outside was ever conceivable when it came to one's *forum internum*. Under these circumstances, none of the three preconditions for the acceptance of compromise – the authority of the *compromissores*, the willingness to risk the judgment, and the equality of the parties involved – was met. But if conscience (and therefore individuality) could be protected from the outside world by simply refusing its judgment in the private sphere, what happened with the individual when such a strategy was no longer possible, for he could not (and should not) remain forever confined in it? The solution was to devise different strategies for different forums. Far from being schizoid, such an attitude was in effect quite logical.

The inner world is free and regulated by reason. By contrast, the external world is dominated by the conventions which allow political communities to survive and to last: religion, customs, and law. But the cultivated man is capable of creating a world of authenticity within himself, where the values of freedom, truth, and friendship are held in high esteem.[37]

If, as we have seen, customary laws were no longer viewed as embodying the wisdom of the people, it does not follow that they ought not to be followed in the *forum externum*. Quite the opposite: precisely because times were so turbulent, everyone was expected to obey the laws, no questions asked, dutifully performing his assigned function in the *universitas* that was the state. Centripetal individualism required conformity in the *forum externum*. Authentic thinking was to be disconnected from external actions.

---

[35] Comparato, "A Case of Modern Individualism," 166.
[36] See, e.g., Keohane's discussion of this phenomenon in *Philosophy and the State*, 121–123.
[37] Comparato, "A Case of Modern Individualism," 161.

[L]e sage doit, au dedans, *retirer son âme de la foule et la maintenir dans la liberté et le pouvoir de juger librement des choses, mais que,* au dehors, *il doit suivre entièrement les façons [de faire] et les usages reçus.* La société public n'a que faire de nos pensées, *mais le reste, c'est-à-dire nos actions, notre travail, nos situations sociales, et notre vie propre, il faut prêter et livrer cela à son service et aux opinions communes, à l'exemple de ce bon et grand Socrate qui refusa de sauver sa vie en désobéissant à l'autorité des lois et même de lois très injustes et très iniques.*[38]

([T]he wise man should withdraw his soul *within*, out of the crowd, and keep it in freedom and power to judge think freely; but as *for externals*, he should wholly follow the accepted fashions and forms. *Society in general can do without our thoughts*; but the rest – that is, our actions, our work, our fortunes and our very life – we must lend and abandon to its service and to the common opinion, just as the great and good Socrates refused to save his life by disobedience to the magistrate, even to a very unjust and very iniquitous magistrate.)

As Bodin pointed out, as soon as the individual "goes forth out of his own house where he commands, to negotiate and traffic with other heads of families about that which concerns them all in general," he becomes a *"companion, equally and fellow-like with others."*[39] Once he enters the sphere of *la chose publique*, he loses his individuality, becoming a *member* of a pre-existing community, defined mainly by his role in this larger structure – the corporate body. In such a community the member enjoyed *equality* – the precondition of compromise – but endangered his *individuality*. The only thing that ensured his distinctiveness in this commonly defined public realm was his honor, that is, his reputation among his peers. To clarify this point, Arendt's description of life in the ancient polis offers a nice parallel and deserves a lengthy quotation:

[The] modern equality, based on the conformism inherent in society … is in every respect different from equality in antiquity, and notably in the Greek city-states. To belong to the few "equals" (*homoioi*) meant to be permitted to live among peers; but the public realm itself, the *polis*, was permeated by a fiercely agonal spirit, where everybody had constantly to distinguish himself from all others, to show through unique deeds or achievements that he was the best of all (*aien aristeuein*). The public realm, in other words, was reserved for individuality; it was the only place where men could show who they really and inexchangeably were.[40]

The same applies in the case of early modern French society. As Keohane observes, by the seventeenth century, the ethic of *la gloire,* the ethic of Corneille, Balzac, and Descartes, provided a different strategy, "an alternative to the retiring and skeptical sage who was the *libertine's* ideal."[41] In the public sphere,

[38] Montaigne, I, 23 (146), in *Les essais*, translated in Keohane, *Philosophy and the State*, 110; emphasis added.
[39] Jean Bodin (1577) *Les six livres de la republique*, I.6, 46–47, quoted and translated in Keohane, *Philosophy and the State in France*, 69; emphasis added.
[40] Hannah Arendt (1998), *The Human Condition*, 2nd ed. (Chicago and London: Chicago University Press), 41.
[41] Keohane, *Philosophy and the State*, 186.

honor, glory and reputation became the equivalent of conscience in the private realm, and therefore *defining* attributes of individuality to be protected "*à tout prix*." To compromise (or even to be suspected of willingness to compromise) one's honor or one's reputation was to abandon one's individuality in the public sphere, to make oneself one among many, part of the unruly multitude.

> The sage rises above the mass of ordinary people and protects himself from the two opposing stumbling-blocks on which the mad and the common herd founder: that is, stubborn obstinacy, shameful reversals, repentances, and changes, and stays free with a liberty of spirit which the wise man never allows to be taken from him.[42]

The many ideological forms this way of thinking embraced are proofs of its resilience and versatility. "Individualism dominated French ethics and psychology from the end of the sixteenth century well into the seventeenth, and proved for a time an admirably efficient ideology for the subjects of an absolutist state."[43] Faced with absolutist dogma and corporatist thinking, the French 'obsession' with the preservation of the distinctiveness and thus the 'authenticity' of the individual can be traced down in otherwise sharply opposed ethical ideals: not only of the aristocratic hero praised by Corneille, or the *libertines* of whom Montaigne and Charron are the most prominent figures, but also the Jansenists *solitaires*, of whom Pascal was perhaps the perfect embodiment. As Keohane keenly observes, "there were similarities within these teachings that make it unwise to treat them as wholly distinct."[44] They all shared a common language – the language of 'virtues' (although not necessarily 'civic virtue') as opposed to the language of 'rights.'

The almost pathological fear of individuals to 'compromise themselves' created a paradoxical attitude toward politics. On the one hand, they claimed in a classical vein that each man should participate in the protection of the common good according to his station in life ("in his degree and according to his quality"),[45] yet on the other hand they warned against the dangers of taking this involvement at a personal level. In other words, they cautioned against the dangers of mistaking the *forum externum* with the *forum internum*. They were no idealists. On the contrary, most of them were skeptics aware of the fact that politics required a different kind of morality and a different kind of virtue "assigned to the affairs of the world" ("*a virtue affectée aux affaires du monde*"), a "virtue with many bends, angles, and elbows, so as to join and adapt itself to human weakness" ("*une vertu avec beaucoup de plis, d'encoignures et*

---

[42] Pierre Charron (1824): "*Par lesquelles le sage excelle par dessus le commun, se garde des deux escueils contraires, ausquels tombent les fols et populaires; scavoir testues opiniatrez, honteuses desdites, repentirs et changements, et se maintient libre, liberte d'esprit que jamais le sage ne laissera ravir,*" quoted and translated in Comparato, "A Case of Modern Individualism," 164.

[43] Keohane, *Philosophy and the State*, 83.

[44] Ibid., 186–187.

[45] Ibid., 80, quoting Bodin. I was unable to track down the exact expression in his *Six Books*, Book I.

de coudes pour s'appliquer et s'ajuster a la faiblesse humaine").[46] One still has
two personae, but the one in the *forum externum* is no longer revealing for the
'true self.' It becomes a mask that does not reveal, as the skin, but conceals, as
a costume.

[One has to know] how to distinguish and separate ourselves from our public charges.
Each one of us plays two roles and has two personae, the one alien and in appearance
only, the other our own and essential to us. It is important to know the difference
between the skin and the costume. The skilful man will perform his office well but never
forget to judge clearly the folly, the vice, the knavishness he finds there. He will exercise
his charge because this is the practice in his country; it is useful to the public and can be
also to himself; this is the way the world runs, and he should do nothing to damage it.
One must make use and avail oneself of the world as one finds it, but nevertheless consider it as a thing alien to oneself, know how to enjoy oneself apart from it, commune
confidently with one's own good, and at the worst, walk by oneself.

*[Il faut] bien sçavoir distinguer, et separer nous mesmes d'avec nos charges publiques;
un chacun de nous joüe deux roolles et deux personages, l'un estranger et apparent,
l'autre proper et essential. Il faut discerner la peau de la chemise: l'habile home fera
bien sa charge, et ne laissera pas de bien juger la sotisse, le vice, la fourbe, qui y est. Il
l'exercera, car elle est en usage en son pays, elle est utile au public, et peut ester à soy, le
monde vit ainsi, il ne faut rien gaster. Il se faut server et se prevaloir du monde tel qu'on
le trouve; Cependant le considerer comme chose estrangere de soy; sçavoir bien de soy
joüyr à part, et se communiquer a un sien bien confident, au pis aller à soy mesme.*[47]

The *"raison d'état,"* which advocated a sharp distinction between private
and public morality, could trump any other moral consideration and therefore
was dangerous for the individual. There is no reason to envy the sovereign,
argued Charron (himself a supporter of the absolute sovereignty via Bodin):
he is forced to actually sacrifice his *forum internum* in order to comply with
the requirements of the *forum externum*. "If grandeur and sovereignty are so
desired by everyone it is because all the good that is there appears on the *outside*, and all its evil is *inside*" (*"La grandeur et souveraineté est tant desirée
de tous, c'est pource que tout le bien qui y est paroit dehors, et tout son mal
est au dedans"*). The advantages are just appearances. "The name and title of
sovereign, the display and its *outside* are beautiful, pleasant and ambitious,
but the task and its *inside* are tough, difficult and quite thorny.... It is a public
and honorable servitude, a noble misery, a rich captivity" (*"Le nom et titre de
souverain, la montre et le dehors est beau, plaisant, et ambitieux, mais la charge
et le dedans est dur, difficile et bien épineux.... C'est une publique et honorable
servitude, une noble misère, une riche captivité"*).[48] From this perspective, the
high office of the king implied the most important self-sacrifice, namely the sacrifice of the *forum internum* on the altar of the *forum externum*. Unlike others,

---

[46] Montaigne, III, 9 (1199), in *Les essais.*
[47] Charron, *De la sagesse*, Livre Second, 2, 415. English trans. in Keohane, *Philosophy and the
State*, 136–137.
[48] Ibid., Livre Premier, 69, 322–323.

the king ought, so to speak, to renounce his own duality. Speaking about this sacrifice, Le Moyne emphasizes that "all his glory is *to abandon himself*, and to sign all of his interests over to the public."[49] The cardinal Le Bret is even more straightforward: "The main responsibility of the prince is to rid himself of his own interests ... *to take himself away from himself* in order to give himself entirely to the public."[50]

It is worth reminding oneself that surprisingly (or not, depending on how one chooses to consider his statement), Richelieu, a forerunner of *Realpolitik*, tried in his *Testament politique* to present the king with a more convenient interpretation: the Prince ought not to sacrifice his reputation and honor, because these attributes are essential parts of his sovereignty. By compromising one's honor, one compromises in the long run the state as well. Thus, for Richelieu, safeguarding the *forum internum* of the king meant safeguarding the 'true,' not the conjectural, *raison d'état*. Thus, "one cannot be too Severe in punishing those [representatives of the king] that overstep their Power; because by this kind of Fault, they put in Compromise the Reputation of Princes, & the good of the States altogether" (*"qu'on ne sçauroit être trop Sévére à punir ceux qui outrepassent leur Pouvoir; puis que par telles Fautes, il mettent en Compromis la Réputation des Princes, & le bien des Etats tout ensemble"*).[51]

Thanks to this French centripetal individualism and the endurance of a descending understanding of representation, the king's sacrifice of the *forum internum* never amounted (as it did in England) to embracing the idea of the king's two bodies. As tempting as it might be to equate the two, the dialectic between the two fora is not to be confounded with that of the king's two bodies. If the first was accepted all over continental Europe, writes Kantorowicz, "it was nevertheless in England alone that there had been developed a consistent political, or legal, theory of the 'King's Two Bodies,' just as the correlative notion of 'the corporation sole' was a purely English device."[52] Once one takes into consideration the split of this dialectic between centripetal and centrifugal (and peculiarly British) individualisms around the beginning of the seventeenth century, one can also understand why solely in Britain did the idea of the king's two bodies take such hold on the national psyche and why "the legal fiction of the King's Two Bodies was a distinctive feature of English political thought."[53] As we will see in the next chapter, only here, thanks mainly yet not only to a

---

[49] Pierre Le Moyne (1665), *De l'art de reigner* (Paris: Cramoisy), iv, quoted in Ellen M. McClure (2006), *Sunspots and the King Sun: Sovereignty and Mediation in Seventeenth-Century France* (Urbana and Chicago: University of Illinois Press), 59; emphasis added.

[50] Cardin Le Bret (1689), "*De la souveraineté du roy*," in *Les Oeuvres de Messire C. Le Bret* (Paris: Charles Osmont), 1, quoted in McClure, *Sunspots and the King Sun*, 45; emphasis added.

[51] Armand Jean du Plessis Richelieu (1688), *Testament politique d'Armand du Plessis, Cardinal duc de Richelieu...*, Partie 2 (Amsterdam: H. Desbordes), 45.

[52] Ernst Hartwig Kantorowicz (1997) [1957], *The King's Two Bodies* (Princeton: Princeton University Press), 446.

[53] Ibid., 42.

powerful national Parliament, the classical understanding of representation as 'descending' was replaced by the modern ascending one, as representation of individual wills.[54] Absolutist as he was, the King of France was also a "victim," for having to sacrifice his *forum internum*, "to take himself away from himself," as Cardinal Le Bret has put it. Not only did he not enjoy "two bodies," but he had "no soul."

Under such circumstances, the French individual *qua* individual had no choice but either to distance himself from politics altogether or to accept the position of a representative of the king by occupying a public office, for "such a professional bureaucracy did not represent the community governed but, rather, was an extension of the king or regional prince and his procedures"; or do both at the same time – as did Montaigne.[55] While filling several important administrative positions, Montaigne was also carefully pointing out that to accept a public office was to run almost unacceptable risks, "because in every government there are necessary offices which are not only abject but also vicious" ("*dans tout gouvernement il y a des functions nécessaires qui sont non seulement viles, mais encore entachées de vices*"). However, since such offices are necessary for the smooth running of the government, he sarcastically conceded to "let this part be played by the more vigorous and less fearful citizens who sacrifice their honor and their conscience ... for their country's good" – who are, in other words, willing to compromise themselves ("*il faut laisser jouer ces rôles par les citoyens plus vigoureux et moins craintifs*").[56]

Paradoxically at first sight, it was precisely the corporatist perspective inherited from medieval times coupled with the monarchocentric and hierarchical vision of the public sphere that allowed the survival (or rather the safe hibernation) of the individual in the absolutist seventeenth century. As Comparato put it bluntly, "Absolutism becomes something more than a background issue: it is the very condition for private freedom."[57] When, by the eighteenth century the idea of individuals having a saying in the political process finally gained momentum in France too (more than a century after England), this suddenly politically awake individual took it "*à la lettre*" and would not be satisfied with a more or less fictional delegation of authority through representation. He demanded a more direct involvement – but at the same time remained cautious against "wills without reason." Even the fact that *Declaration of the Rights of Men and Citizens* (1791, 1793) distinguishes between man as man and man

---

54 Ibid., 447: "It seems, however, that the notion's of the 'King's Two Bodies' cannot be severed from the very early development and the lasting momentum of Parliament I English constitutional thought and practice. Parliament was, by representation, the living 'body politic' of the realm."

55 Janette Coleman (1996), *The Individual and the Medieval State*, 6. See also Walter Ullmann (1966), *The Individual and Society in the Middle Ages*, 91–95.

56 Montaigne, III, 1 (956), in *Les essais*.

57 Comparato, "A Case of Modern Individualism," 163.

as citizen, that is, in his public capacity (a distinction that will fascinate Marx, for example), points toward the fact that the distinction between the two fora, although probably unconscious by then, was more resilient that we would care to admit. Without this seventeenth century 'hibernation,' the peculiar French stubbornness with regard to direct democracy can hardly be explained, but neither can the suspicion against the 'tyranny of majority.' And yet signs of this dual attitude were present well before.

5.2. *PLUS ÇA CHANGE, PLUS C'EST LA MÊME CHOSE –* SOVEREIGNTY: BETWEEN WILL AND REASON

Few historians would dispute that starting with the sixteenth century the French manifested an individualism centered on the authenticity of the self in secular, religious, and philosophical settings, or that this individualism was somehow connected with the rise of absolutism and the nascent modern state.[58] However, the explanations for this connection differ. I argue that the history of compromise and the dialectic between the *forum internum* and *forum externum*, between reason and will, and between private and public helps us better understand this peculiarity. The insistence on a will informed by reason made compromise a dubious practice and especially so at a political level. One can easily claim an equality of wills, but less so in the case of access to reason. The absolutist state appeared to offer a solution, yet neither absolutism nor the idea of an abstract entity named 'the state' emerged *ab nihilo* during the sixteenth century. They were both developments of ideas widely spread and accepted during medieval times.

If one looks for the author who captures best the amalgam of continuity and change that characterize this century, Claude de Seysell will probably be the first to qualify. Allen argues that there is no better way to understand the development of political thought in France in the sixteenth century than by reading Seysell's *Le Grant Monarchie de France* since "much of the controversy that followed can be read as a commentary on or an expansion, on one side or another, of the views of Seysell." Church too claims that "students of French political thought in the sixteenth century are fortunate in having their point of departure well defined" in the work of this one man.[59] In a sense, his work bridges the medieval theory of kingship with the yet-to-emerge absolutist theory.

There is no need to fully analyze Seysell's constitutional thought; there are several excellent such analyses already.[60] What we are interested in are the

---

[58] See, e.g., Keohane, *Philosophy and the State*; Lloyd, *The State, France and the Sixteenth Century*; or Comparato, "A Case of Modern Individualism."

[59] Allen, *A History of Political Thought*, 275; Church, *Constitutional Thought*, 22.

[60] Just a few examples: Allen, *A History of Political Thought*, 275–279; Church, *Constitutional Thought*, 22–42; Keohane, *Philosophy and the State*, 32–49.

three aspects of his theory directly related with the history of compromise: the source of political authority/legitimacy, the directionality of representation, and the understanding of 'the people.' With his training as a legal scholar and as a practitioner of politics in his capacity as ambassador and negotiator in several European countries, Seysell was more interested in the legal and practical aspects of government than in philosophical argumentation, which makes his assumptions somewhat less clear and open to interpretation. *"Telles choses,"* he wrote, *"se connaissent mieux par la pratique que par la théorique"*[61] ("Such things are known better by practice than by theory").

Although Allen, for example, claims that "his *grant monarchie* rests not on divine right in any sense or degree, but on custom and expediency," I suspect that Seysell's position is a bit more complex.[62] Following in the footsteps of the Gallican tradition he finds the ultimate source of political authority of kings in God's authorization. *"Le Prince et monarque ... est esleu et députe par la diuine prouidence à cette dignité si grand et si honorable principalment pour maintenir et faire justice, qui est le vray office des princes"*[63] ("The Prince and monarch ... is elected and deputed by the divine providence to this dignity so grand and so honorable mostly to maintain and do justice, which is the true office of princes"). The emphasis here is on the office of the crown, less so the person of the monarch. While opening the door for a more forceful assertion of the divine right of kings, he is still working inside the medieval frame of thought. If Allen claims that his monarchy does not rest on divine authority it is because Seysell makes clear repeatedly that men choose rationally between monarchy, aristocracy, and democracy (popular government).[64] And yet, as we have seen in the previous chapter, the simple fact that the political regime is men's choice does not exclude a divine authorization. Quite the contrary: men's choice serves as a vehicle for God's choice. The directionality of representation (and therefore of authority) remains a top-down one. In the same vein, the three bridles of the monarch, that is, religion, justice (*iustice*), and *la police*, are all but restatements of old and widely accepted understandings of the just monarchy.

As shown before, precisely because kings are granted their authority by a superior power (God through the consent of the whole people, as Seysell also implies), they are bound to obey both God's commandments and the requirements of more abstract justice. If they overstep the bounds of religious commandments and of justice (as they are often tempted to do), they are subject to remonstration by clerics or any religious man (*"il est loisible à vn chascun*

[61] Claude de Seysell (1510), *La monarchie de France et deux autres fragments politiques*, texts établis et présentés par Jacques Poujol (Paris: Librarire D' Argences, 1961), vol. 2, pp. 17, 155.
[62] Allen, *A History of Political Thought*, 275.
[63] Claude de Seysell [1519] (1558), *La grande monarchie de France*, 33a–33b, quoted in Church, *Constitutional Thought in Sixteenth Century France*, 24. See also Seysell, *La monarchie de France*, vol. 2, pp. 15, 150.
[64] See, e.g., the beginning of the *Prohème*, or the beginning of the first chapter of *La monarchie*.

prelate ou à autre home religieux")[65] in the first instance, and by the *Parlements* in the second. The order of the bridles is not merely Seysell's lip service to the powers that be, as many scholars seem to assume. If Justice *"fait les princes régner et dominer, et sans laquelle les royaumes sont appelés larcins"* ("makes princes rule and master, and without which kingdoms are called thieveries") and if it is *"le premier et le plus digne trésor de ce royaume"* ("the first and the most dignified treasure of this kingdom") it is still *"après la religion dont j'ai parlé ci-dessus"* ("after the religion of which I've spoken above").[66] If one gives up the modern lenses, Seysell's theory cannot but rest on certain metaphysical foundations.

The third bridle, *la police*, is both the most complex and the most vaguely defined, and for good reason. This ambiguity is deliberate, not necessarily because Seysell wanted to avoid the anger of a king contested openly in his *absolue* power, as some have suggested,[67] nor because he wanted to imply that the monarch's power was *absolue* "only to a certain sphere of action appropriate for the king."[68] *La police* included not only the long-time established organized structure of the state, but also the estates – the Nobility, the *Peuple Menu*, and the *Peuple Gras* – and the laws established initially by the kings themselves that through usage and custom had become the very essence of the monarchy (i.e., the constitution of the state). Theoretically and legally speaking, monarchs were not bounded to observe any of the customary laws. Practically, though, they did, because they realized (or were reminded to do so) that "this moderation and bridling of the absolute power of kings is to their own great honor and profit."[69] Once again, this understanding, which might sound strange to modern ears, made perfect sense inside the Christian Weltanschauung.

[T]out ainsi que la puissance de Dieu n'est point jugée moindre pour autant qu'il ne peut pécher ni mal faire; ainsi en est autant plus parfaite. Et sont les rois beaucoup plus à louer et priser de ce qu'ils veulent en si grande autorité et puissance être sujets a leurs propres lois et vivre selon icelles, que s'ils pouvaient à leur volonté user de puissance absolue.[70]

([J]ust as the power of God is not thought to be the less because he cannot sin or do evil, but is thereby more perfect. And in the same way, kings are to be praised and prized much more when they choose in their great authority and power to be subject to their own laws and live according to them, though they could at will make use of their absolute power.)[71]

---

[65] Seysell, *La grande monarchie de France*, 10b, quoted in Church, *Constitutional Thought*, 24. See also Seysell, *La monarchie de France*, vol. 1, pp. 9, 116.
[66] Ibid., vol. 2, pp. 15, 149.
[67] See Allen, *A History of Political Thought*, 278.
[68] Keohane, *Philosophy and the State*, 37.
[69] Quoted in ibid., 38.
[70] Seysell, *La monarchie de France*, I, 12, 120.
[71] Trans. in Keohane, *Philosophy and the State*, 38.

The single will of the monarch was the main *practical* reason why Seysell preferred monarchy to other forms of government, popular or aristocratic. From a more theoretical perspective he would have probably preferred aristocracy, as long as it was not understood as the rule of a hereditary group, but "a government of notable and eminent persons based upon some system of selection."[72] *"[Aristocracy] semble être plus raisonnable et plus louable, pour autant qu'il est plus perdurable, mieux fondé et plus tolérable, étant les personnages choisis & élus par l'assemblée du peuple ou de partie d'icelui & sujets à correction & mutation"*[73] ("[Aristocracy] seems to be more reasonable and more praiseworthy, as long as it is more enduring, better founded and more tolerable, being the persons selected & elected by the assembly of people or by parts of it & subjects to correction & replacement"). Yet as a practical man he was also convinced that all political bodies, *les corps mystiques*, will decay like any natural body once plagued by multiple judgments and repugnant and discordant wills (*"plusieurs entendements et volontés discordantes et répugnantes"*).[74] A compromise in the classical sense between "multiple judgments and repugnant and discordant wills" is, obviously, impossible.

Keohane notices that "the notion that it is a grave disadvantage for government to be subject to the partial wills of those who are governed are, that such subjection is not a source of liberty but of chaos and destruction, distinguishes French theory from the beginning of the sixteenth century and sets it apart from Anglo-Saxon modes of thought."[75] Since factions won't be willing to compromise, the result will be the destruction of the political body. "All authority flows from the king, all institutions are organized around the throne. The patterns of activity in the *corp mystique* do not flow upwards, the only connections are from the top downward, in a pyramidal fashion."[76] The observation is correct if we keep in mind that the French theory was not an outlier. Quite the contrary, Seysell does nothing but follow medieval tradition: if a political society is to be apprehended as a mystical body, the king was "the fountain and the source from which emanate and flow all the streams of good policies," while the kingdom *"la Chose publique divises et départis entre tous les Etats proportionnellement, selon leur condition et un chacun d'iceux garde en sa prééminence et qualité, s'en ensuit une harmonie et consonance qui est cause de la conservation et augmentation d'icelle Monarchie"*[77] ("the Public thing [*res publica*, state], divided and partitioned among the all Estates proportionally, according to their condition and each of them preserving its preeminence and equality, it causes a harmony and consonance which is the

---

[72] See Allen, *A History of Political Thought*, 276.

[73] Seysell, *La monarchie de France*, vol. 1, pp. 1, 103. Although the last part is not included in the original manuscript from 1510, it is present in the editions of 1519, 1541, and 1557.

[74] Ibid., vol. 1, pp. 3, 108.

[75] Keohane, *Philosophy and the State*, 34.

[76] Ibid., 41.

[77] Seysell, "Prohème d'Appien," in *La monarchie de France*, 84.

cause of the conservation and augmentation of such Monarchy"). Ideally, there should be no tension between reason and will. As God's reason coincides with his will, so too the ideal monarch will blend reason and will. However, in this world, such an ideal situation was far from frequently met. As in the case of any mortal individual, there will always be at least a partial difference between his *forum internum* and his *forum externum*, between reason and will.

Since the will of the sovereign, which ought to be one, should not be disordered and rushed ("*volonté désordonée ni soudaine*"), but informed by reason, princes are in obvious need of guidance, as even Moses did, by God's command. "*Car il n'est possible qu'un seul homme, ni encores un petit nombre de gens, quelque accomplis qu'ils soient, puissent entendre et manier tout les affaires d'une si grand monarchie*"[78] ("For it is not possible that one single man, not even a small number of men, no matter how accomplished they might be, could understand and manage the affairs of such a grand monarchy"). Once again, the exemplary model is Jesus Christ, "*à l'exemple duquel l'on doit faire toutes choses que l'on peut*"[79] ("of whose example one should follow in all things that one can"). Christ had his own "*Grand Conseil of LXXII*," a second, secret *Conseil* of 12 apostles, and a third one, composed of "*saint Pierre, saint Jean et saint Jacques, auxquelles il communiquait les choses les plus intrinsèques et les plus hautes mystères – comme celui de sa Transfiguration*"[80] ("to whom he communicated the things the most intrinsic and the highest mysteries – as that of his Transfiguration"). Kings should do the same, relying on the advice of the wisest servants of the kingdom.

For Seysell, as for any medieval man, the source of authority (reason) is not to be mistakenly confounded with its vehicle (will). As we have seen, according to the medieval understanding, reason, which ought to inform *forum internum*, ought to inform will, and there is no way that kings, aristocracy, or even the entire people can always ensure the proper balance between the two without error. Corruption can be postponed but not avoided altogether, and the best way to do so is to not mistake one for the other. If the sovereign will should be one, the access to the proper reason necessary to inform that will can be ensured through several vehicles: counselors, prelates, estates or parlements. Since in this world there is simply no clear-cut recipe for grasping always and without failure reason and/or truth, one should focus more on the aim and less on the method. All one can hope is that by refining the instrument or the vehicle of the decision-making process (decision which, as Aristotle has it, combines reason and will) one will delay the inevitable corruption. From this perspective at least, our medieval predecessors proved more skeptical than we. As one was aware of one's imperfection ("*connaissant mon imperfection, ensemble celle de plusieurs autres*," "knowing my imperfection, altogether with those of many

---

[78] Ibid., vol. 2, pp. 4, 134.
[79] Ibid., vol. 2, pp. 4, 134.
[80] Ibid., vol. 2, pp. 4, 135.

others") one was aware as well of the imperfection of any political body.[81] There were no grand illusions, neither about the individual nor about political institutions. An imperfect world cannot have a perfect solution.

In the later part of the sixteenth century, political, social, and religious turmoil increased dramatically with two major consequences: on the one hand, the instability of the world created a renewed quest for order and stability; on the other hand, the same instability required an increase in adaptability – customary laws were no longer able to keep pace with the transformations taking place at all levels. As a result, the study of history increased even further, with the hope of finding some pattern of order underlying all these changes. Customary laws were no longer perceived as embodiments of some universal reason, but just for a particular time and place. Authors such as Chancellor L'Hospital and Etienne Pasquier were among the first to insist that such laws ought to be followed not necessarily because they were intrinsically just, but because they were just for the French people at that specific time. "*Il ne faut considerer seulement si la loy est juste en soy,*" stated L'Hospital before the Estates General in 1561, "*mais si elle est convenable au temps et aux homes pour lesquelz elle est faicte*"[82] ("One should not consider only if the law is just in itself, but if it is propitious for the time and the men for whom it was made"). Pasquier also claimed that "Whatever the diversity of the law, it is necessary to live according to those of one's own country, and to consider that since they are established, we ought to judge them to be good."[83] "Such a sentiment," observes Keohane, "was characteristic of French social theorists, from Montaigne to Montesquieu."[84] But since these customary laws ought to be interpreted and eventually adapted to a changing context, such interpretation needs the advice of parlements, counselors, prelates, and jurists. Pasquier observed, as did Seyssel before him, that it is a "truly great thing, and worthy of the majesty of the prince, that our kings, to whom God has given full and absolute power, have by ancient institutions *willed to submit their wills* to the civility of the law."[85] Once again, the *will* of the king is just so long as it is informed by *reason* and wills to will what is good. The problem was that there were too many competing claims to the 'right' interpretation and, as we have seen, the claims to reason cannot compromise as easily as the claims to equal wills.

Being the first to attempt to fully conceptualize state sovereignty in his *Six livres de la république*, Jean Bodin refined even further the interplay between reason and will. For him, statutes and customary laws have no authority unless

---

[81] Ibid., vol. 2, pp. 14, 148.

[82] Chancellor L'Hospital (1561), "*Harangue à l'assemblée des états-généraux, à Saint-Germain-en-Laye,* Aug. 26, 1561," in *Oeuvres,* vol. 1, 450–451, quoted in Church, *Constitutional Thought,* 206.

[83] Etienne Pasquier, "Letter to Eschacier," xix, 7, 554, quoted in Keohane, *Philosophy and the State,* 45.

[84] Keohane, *Philosophy and the State,* 45.

[85] Etienne Pasquier, II, 4, p. 8, quoted in ibid., 46; emphasis added.

the sovereign confers it. If law can break custom, custom cannot derogate from the law, and "thus the force of both statutes and customary laws derives from the authorization of the prince."[86] If Bodin is so emphatic that sovereignty cannot be divided, it is because will cannot be divided. In many respects, however, Bodin is no innovator – he just pushes to extremes assumptions otherwise largely embraced by his predecessors. He agrees that a *res publica* can be founded by force or by consent, yet it is quite clear that sovereignty comes, as in the old medieval tradition, from God and is handed by the people to the acknowledged sovereign as a "true gift, being at once unconditional and irrevocable."[87] Bodin carefully distinguishes between reason and will. If the sovereign's edicts and ordinances conclude with the formula 'for such is our good pleasure,' it is because "the laws of a sovereign prince, *even when founded on truth and right reason*, proceed simply from his own free will."[88] And yet, once again, such emphasis on the sovereign's sheer will should not be misinterpreted.

It is far otherwise with divine and natural laws. All the princes of the earth are subject to them, and cannot contravene them without treason and rebellion against God.... The absolute power of princes and sovereign lords does not extend to the laws of God and of nature. He who best understood the meaning of absolute power, and made kings and emperors submit to his will, defined his sovereignty as a power to override positive law; he did not claim power to set aside divine and natural law.[89]

The role of reason in informing will is undeniable. If Bodin favors monarchy instead of democracy or aristocracy it is not mainly because the single monarch becomes symbolically identical with the unified legislative will, as many scholars have suggested. He makes clear that since sovereignty can be held by one person, by several, or by many, the unity of the will was not his main concern. What (only apparently paradoxically) worried him was the lack of unity of the reason that informed that will or, more specifically, a will uninformed by the right reason. The problem with a popular government, Bodin claims, is that it asserts an equality of reason where, in effect, there is just an equality of wills. And absent such equality, no compromise is possible. Such equality of reason

is contrary to the laws of nature, for by nature some are wiser and more inventive than others, some formed to govern and others to obey, some wise and discreet, others foolish and obstinate.... As to natural liberty, which is so much cried up in the popular state, if such a condition were realized anywhere, it would preclude the existence of any magistrates, laws, or form of state, since it presupposes inequalities. As for the common good, it is quite clear that there is no form of commonwealth where it is less regarded than in a popular state.... *In popular assemblies votes are counted, not weighed*, and the number of fools, sinners, and dolts is a thousand times that of honest men.[90]

[86] Jean Bodin (1955), *Six Books of the Commonwealth*, abridged and trans. by M.J. Tooley (Oxford: Basil Blackwell), I.10, 44.
[87] Ibid., I.8, 27.
[88] Ibid., I.8, 29; emphasis added.
[89] Ibid.
[90] Ibid., VI.4, 192–193; emphasis added.

In the same vein, aristocracy might appear both theoretically and practically the more desirable political regime, since it is between democracy and monarchy, and yet "the golden mean that everyone is looking for *is not secured by a numerical calculation*, but in the sphere of morals means the rule of reason, as all the philosophers agree."[91] True, it would seem that in effect both democracy and monarchy are some form of aristocracy, since in a popular government, more often than not, a handful of people end up imposing their agenda, while in a monarchy most decisions are in the hands of a senate or some sort of privy council. But, argues Bodin, such interpretation implies a huge confusion between reason and will. Reason might come from a handful of people, yet the sovereign will is *not* in their hands. If the monarch, as Seysell for example argued as well, needs the council of the wisest men of the kingdom, one should not mistake 'counsel' with 'command.' "It is better to take opinion of many than one in all matters of counsel, for it is said that many understand better than one. But for taking a decision and issuing an order, one is always better than many."[92]

Since the distinction between will and reason is so central to his argument, it is probably no accident that, after explaining how sovereigns are bound by the laws of God and nature, Bodin goes to some length to distinguish between covenants and laws, for "many have been led astray by confusing the laws of the prince with covenants entered by him." A sovereign may "set aside the laws which he has promised and sworn to observe if they no longer satisfy the requirements of justice," because such promises are unilateral and justice comes first. They are not compromises, not contracts that oblige because they set equality between the parties involved. They do not *create* justice but *discover* it. Things are different in the case of covenants or compromises, which involve reciprocity.

> A law and a covenant must therefore not to be confused. A law proceeds from him who has sovereign power, and by it he binds the subject to obedience, but cannot bind himself. A covenant is a mutual undertaking between a prince and his subjects, *equally* binding on both parties, and neither can contravene it to the prejudice of the other, without his consent. *The prince has no greater privilege than the subject* in this matter.[93]

The specification helps us to begin understanding the French *méfiance* about compromise, at least at a political level. If compromise is a contract that ought to be respected, it is because it establishes a voluntary equality of wills. In compromises, both parties enter as equal wills, regardless of the differences in terms of power or reason. The justness of the compromise was created by this very acknowledgement of equality. If, as we have seen, according to Bodin, compromises between princes, despite their differences in power, will not affect the

---

[91] Ibid., VI.4, 194; emphasis added.
[92] Ibid., VI.4, 198. For a similar observation, see Keohane, *Philosophy and the State*, 74–75.
[93] Jean Bodin (1955), *Six Books of the Commonwealth*, I.8, 30; emphasis added.

sovereignty of the weakest party, it is because sovereign wills were accepted as equal. But in a compromise between a prince and his subjects, the sovereign's will has to voluntarily lower itself to the level of his subjects' wills – a decision that obviously must be undertaken with extreme caution.

With Bodin absolutist thought received the theoretical support that it needed to flourish throughout the seventeenth century. The absolute monarch appeared the best suited to literally embody the paradoxical relationship between the *forum internum* and the *forum externum* of the mystical body which was the state. While constitutive of each other and thus interdependent, the two fora had also to be kept not too far removed from one another lest they become estranged, yet not too close lest they become impossible to distinguish. "Absolutism required on the one hand an intense *personalization* of kingly power, an incarnation of pure authority in a single human individual to be adored and obeyed, and on the other hand *abstraction* from any human qualities in the intangible symbol of the state, pure authority and public purpose organized without human frailty."[94] If this conceptualization of the relationship between reason and will at a political level proceeded rather easily in the case of the absolute monarch, it proved more difficult and ended less successfully for another mystical body in need of theoretical clarification during the late sixteenth century, namely 'the people.'

5.3. STATE VERSUS PEOPLE

Apparently, it should have been easy and somehow natural to assimilate the state with 'the people,' since both concepts refer to some abstract or mystical entity representing more than a mere collection of individuals. In effect, it was this similarity that made them competing concepts and the emergence of the abstract concept of sovereignty, different from authority and/or power, tipped the balance decisively in favor of the state. Here, the single monarch had the upper hand when compared with several competing claims about the people.

During the sixteenth century, the French had for a long time been accustomed to the ubiquitous *universitates*, and even the radical and structural changes wrought in their substance were not able to challenge their form. If the cohesion and the unity of different *universitates* suffered in practice, they were still accepted in theory. The 'metaphor of orders' was "a description not of society as it actually was, but of an ethical system by which it was ideally informed."[95]

This was a century of intensified population-pressure upon material resources, of price-inflation, of modified property-relations – a century, too, when customary laws were being consolidated and local institutions assimilated more rigorously to systems

---

[94] Keohane, *Philosophy and the State*, 17.
[95] Lloyd, *The State, France and the Sixteenth Century*, 23.

of authority directed from above. Upon a society that was apparently disintegrating from within, governmental authority was being brought to bear more immediately and more onerously than ever before. And yet amid conditions of change later-medieval and sixteenth-century Frenchmen maintained in their conduct of social and political affairs a powerful sense of continuity.[96]

As a matter of fact, as a result of these changes, some of these corporations not merely survived but even acquired an increased role. At parish level, for example, the *communauté d'habitants*, composed of the heads of the major households, had long been responsible for managing collective affairs, common pastures, and access to common lands. But as the royal taxes came to be regularly imposed and the seigneurial *tailles* were abolished, the role of these *communautés* in negotiating these taxes, maintaining collective rights, and ensuring each household the access to the common land necessary for bare survival increased – at least for a while. The Counter-Reformation also ended up stressing the role of the parish in maintaining the symbolic unity of the congregation. The French parish priest not only kept the registers for both secular and ecclesiastical authorities, but also was expected to reinforce attendance at mass on Sundays and to maintain the Catholic faith untainted by possible heresies.

In the same way that on a theoretical level the existing turmoil created a renewed quest for an underlying order and the restoration of a golden-age political body, on a more practical level the sixteenth-century crisis pushed men in need of psychological or economical protection to seek the comfort of *universitates*, large and small. The poor formed fraternal communities (*frérage, frérèche, affrèrement*) wherever they had the opportunity, pooling property and land, which gave them access to more resources and lessened the burden of taxation. Professional soldiers became true 'brothers in arms,' creating *compagnies d'ordonnance*. The religious wars forced men to take sides and join religious confraternities, both Catholic and Protestant, that were explicitly designated in terms of kinship and did not overlap with the parishes. They had their own collective rituals, offices, statutes, and assets. And even if the relationships between feudal lords and their followers changed in nature to patronage-clientage, they preserved the terminology and forms of kinship.[97]

That Seysell viewed both the French people and the French state as composites of various *corps mystiques* organized in a pyramidal fashion is not surprising. What is somehow dazzling is that even Bodin or Richelieu, the two main promoters of the idea of state sovereignty, kept using the same metaphor

---

[96] Ibid., 34–35.
[97] For a wealth of details about this development, see Lloyd, *The State, France and the Sixteenth Century*, especially ch. 2, "Men in Groups." See also Salmon, *Society in Crisis*, esp. part I; and Michael S. Kimmel (1988), *Absolutism and Its Discontents: State and Society in Seventeenth-Century France and England* (Oxford: Transaction Books), esp. the beginning of ch. 2.

of an order of orders. For Bodin, the state was a federation of federations: "[A] group of families bound together by mutual trust forms a corporate association or community, and a group of corporate associations and communities bound together by sovereign power forms a commonwealth."[98] Not mere interest or even formal justice bound these *universitates*, guilds included, but love – a love that can be developed only through practice.

> Justice is never pitiful. Involving as it does strict exaction of rights, it often makes enemies of friends. But mutual affection leads men to make concessions, and this secures that natural justice shall prevail. The sole end of all laws divine and human is to foster love among men, and between men and God, and this is best secured by intercourse and daily association.[99]

For Richelieu too, men could not be apprehended but as parts of smaller corporations that in turn functioned as parts of the whole state. "The people exist to perform their functions as farmers, soldiers, merchants, so that governing them requires treating them as working parts of the whole state."[100] So if the people as *universitas* played such an important role, why did it lose the conceptual battle for sovereignty with the state?

The advantage of the state was that it was a concept much more abstract than 'the people,' despite the fact that in the beginning it expressed the same tendency in the political sphere. Thus, according to Mousnier, in the last two centuries of the *ancien régime* France was "essentially a society of *corps* and communities"; and from the social groups constituting the society emerges a public corporation or collectivity, willing and acting on behalf of society and in its name. This public corporation, this moral and judicial person, is the State, an organization that realizes the unity of a plurality of individuals.[101]

If the state of the fourteenth, fifteenth, and even the first half of the sixteenth centuries could be approximated with 'the people,' by the end of the century this was no longer the case. "[F]rom the seventeenth century onwards the state as *persona moralis* was endowed with attributes that distinguish it increasingly, and categorically, from the *corpus mysticum republicae* of organological tradition."[102] Richelieu's state was not the same as Bodin's state. It was far more removed from the individuals than any *universitas* could have ever been. It did not just encompass individuals, it transcended them. It was no longer centered on virtue and bounded by love, but by cold-calculated interest.

This new understanding of the state as an abstract instead of organic entity and the emergence of the concept of sovereignty overlapped with the move

---

[98] Bodin, *Six Books of the Commonwealth*, VI.4, 97.

[99] Ibid., VI.4, 98–99.

[100] Keohane, *Philosophy and the State*, 179.

[101] R. Mousnier (1974), *Les institutions de la France sous l'ancien régime (1598–1789)*, vol. 1: Société et l'état (Paris), 496, 498, quoted in Lloyd, *The State, France and the Sixteenth Century*, 22.

[102] Lloyd, *The State, France and the Sixteenth Century*, 22.

of other concepts, such as 'reason of state' and 'interests' "from the periphery to the heart of the ethical discourse" of the seventeenth century.[103] As Albert Hirschman argues in *The Passions and the Interests*, interest occupied a no-man's-land between reason and the passions. Since the passions are nothing else but will uninformed by reason, and since sovereignty presupposes the opposite, that is, a will informed by reason, there is no surprise that both interests and 'reason of state' came to be associated with the concept that better addressed both requirements, that is, the modern state.

The concept of 'the people' had problems becoming the site of sovereignty because its strengths constituted also its weaknesses. Taking advantage of the feeble royal authority in place beginning with 1559, absolutist theories were challenged by the old constitutionalist theories claiming that the people were prior to the king. For a while, both arguments enjoyed a relatively equal popularity. And yet, confronted with the more abstract sovereignty, the concept of the people proved unable to compete with the king. "France in the mid-sixteenth century did not lack a theory of its constitution to oppose that of royal absolutism: the mischief was that it had too many such theories." I believe that Allen is right claiming that, when confronted with similar issues a century later, England was dealt an easier hand than France. "In England the issues were relatively simple. There, opposition to the claims of the King focused naturally in Parliament. There was no such single focus in France."[104]

During the late sixteenth and seventeenth century in France there were simply too many institutions advancing competing claims to represent both the will *and* the reason of 'the people.' In other words, the concept of the people had two major problems in fulfilling the main requirements of sovereignty – to keep will and reason distinct and yet not too far removed from one another. First, since in France nobody really challenged the institution of monarchy, not even at the height of rebellion, the will of the people had to connect somehow to the will of the monarch, for according to the requirement of sovereignty, the will ought to be singular. Second, in terms of reason, who was to be considered 'the people'? Differently stated, who had better access to reason, that is, to the natural and divine laws that ought to inform human laws? This was more than a philosophical problem. "Because of their intimate association with political concepts, these higher principles were not simply remote ideals serving as aims and ends but were directly fused into every important political problem."[105] As L'Allouette wrote in 1597, "all these [human] Laws, if they are to be valued and received as good and just, had to have their movement and origin in reason and righteousness, much higher than human fantasy, passing through the circles of divine right and justice, which makes them valid and legitimate" (*"toutes lesquelles Lois pour les faire valoir et receuoir pour bonnes et iustes,*

103 Keohane, *Philosophy and the State*, 152.
104 Allen, *A History of Political Thought*, 287.
105 Church, *Constitutional Thought*, 79.

il faut qu'elles ayent leur mouuement et origine de la raison et droiture, de plus haut qu'en la fantasie humaine, passant par les circles de droiture et iustice Diuine, qui les rendent valuables et legitimes").[106]

The first, almost 'natural' contenders for the sovereignty of the people were the parlements – mainly lawyers assembled to decide if new laws corresponded to reason. From a modern perspective they were totally unrepresentative bodies, being neither elected nor composed from people from all the estates. But if even the king accepted that it was their role to assert if his edicts were in accordance with customary laws, it was because nobody thought they ought to represent numerical people, or some people's will. They had to represent reason. Unless formally accepted and registered by the parlements, royal edicts had no judicial power. In 1560, Etienne Pasquier claimed that the Parlement of Paris and not the Estates represented the ancient assemblies of the Champs de Mai.[107] The quandary the parlements presented was simply that there were too many, each sovereign in a certain district. Therefore, the problem was not their weakness but their strength. If an edict were to become law applicable to all France, it had to be accepted and registered by all parlements, and refusal to register royal edicts was as a matter of fact quite frequent. The famous Edict of Nantes, for example, took ten years to be registered by all the parlements of France. Under these circumstances, any compromise in the modern sense was almost impossible. Allen captures well this paradox hidden in the heart of the French parlements and deserves a rather lengthy quotation:

The claim of the Parlement to veto royal edicts tended, it must be observed, not only to place sovereignty actually in their hands, but to divide France permanently. It tended to make the Parlement of Rouen sovereign in Normandy, that of Rennes in Britanny, that of Bourdeaux in Guienne, that of Toulouse in Languedoc, that of Aix in Provence, that of Grenoble in Dauphiné and that of Dijon in Burgundy! It was partly, at least, for this reason that the claim never received any great amount of support. But there were other reasons. The noblesse were at once jealous and contemptuous of the claims of gens de robe; while the Huguenots were hostile to bodies that were one and all Catholic. Not only so, but the Parlements themselves were all more or less dominated by the ideal of a national government. Their claims were in conflict with their ideal. They were in conflict also with the claims made on behalf of States-General.[108]

On the other hand, the Estates General were revived after 1560 and there was a strong tendency common to Catholics, Huguenots, and *politiques* to support them as the true 'representative' of the people, since they mirrored better than the parliaments the organic vision of the people as a hierarchical yet symphonic combination of different *universitates*. In a sense, they were much

---

[106] François de L'Alouette (1597), *Des affaires d'état: Des finances, du prince, de la noblesse* (Metz) 10, quoted in Church, *Constitutional Thought*, 79.

[107] Etienne Pasquier (1560), *Recherches de la France*, I, quoted in Allen, *A History of Political Thought*, 288.

[108] Allen, *A History of Political Thought*, 289.

more representative of the people, indeed to such an extent that sometimes they were literally identified with it, as for example Guy Coquille did: "Since the beginning, *the people had established the Kings as by way of compromise*, for avoiding the confusion that would have resulted if in each important affair one should have looked for the opinion of all to deliberate and conclude."[109] According to this constitutionalist, the transfer of power between the people and the king was never complete but it was done, *faute de mieux*, for practical reasons and the Estates remained 'the shadow' of the people. As Coquille wrote, in effect it is the people who make the laws (*"mais en effet, c'est le peuple qui fait la loi"*).[110] Furthermore, if disputes arise between two pretenders to the crown, it is the people, that is, the Estates, that serve as arbiter. *"En certains autres cas les Etats sont appelez non pas comme simple Conseillers, mais comme ayans plein et entier pouvoir; comme si la Couronne etoit en débat antre deux prétendans ... auquel cas se faut representer le même temps qui etoit quand les François établirent sur eux un Roy"*[111] ("In specific cases the Estates are called not as simple Consulters, but as having full and entire power; as if the Crown would be in debate between two pretenders ... in which case one has to represent [remember] the same time that was when the François established over them a King").

In 1577 the Estates of Bois sent emissaries to Henry of Navarre declaring that religious unity, that is, Catholicism, was a fundamental and inviolable law not only because it was customary, but also because it was instituted by *king and people* in the Estates General. Such laws, they claimed, "cannot be made but in the general assembly of the entire kingdom ... with the common accord and consent of all the people from the three estates, and of those that can attend and have a voice in such assemblies; and since then, in the same way [such laws] cannot be changed or in any way modified" (*"elles ne peuuent ester faictes qu'en generale assemblee de tout le gens de trois estats, et de ceux qui peuuent assiter et auoir voix aux dites diettes, aussi depuis ne peuunet ester changees n'y en façon quelconque alterees"*).[112] In 1588, even the king, Henri III, acknowledged in his opening speech of the session of the Estates that a fundamental law ought to be passed by the joint decision of the monarch and of the estates. "I am of opinion that for making it more stable, that we make it one of the fundamental laws of the Kingdom, and that on the next day of Tuesday, in the same place and in the selfsame notable assembly of all of my Estates, we swear it all, so nobody can never pretend not to know it" (*"ie suis d'advis pour le render plus stable, que nous en facions une des lox fondamentales*

---

[109] Guy Coquille (1611), *Questions et reponses sur le coutume de France*, 125, col. I; emphasis added. The book was published after his death, and was written sometime between 1585 and 1595.

[110] In ibid., 125.

[111] Histoire de Nivernois, 445, quoted in Church, *Constitutional Thought*, 280.

[112] *Instruction des gens des troys estats ... à ... leurs deputez vers le roy de Nauarre* (Blois, 1577), quoted in Church, *Constitutional Thought*, 89.

du Royaume, et qu'à ce prochain iour de Mardy, en ce mesme lieu et en ceste mesme et notable assemblée de tous mes Estats, nous la iurions tous, a ce que jamais nul n'en pretendent cause d'ignorance").[113]

In a period that served as the cradle of absolutist theory, it is surprising to observe how many authors agreed with Guy Coquille: the transfer of sovereignty from 'the people' to the king was nothing else but a compromise, a second-best solution to a direct democracy in which everyone had a voice. Furthermore, the very existence of the parlements was a proof of another compromise: since the Estates were assembled but intermittently, the Parlement was the representative of the Estates, which in turn were the representative of the people. "Because it was impossible to gather whenever necessary a body composed of so many scattered here and there … this authority truly supreme was reserved for a final remedy … – the Parlement, which may be called an epitome of the Estates of France" (*"[P]arce qu'il estoit impossible d'assembler à toutes occurrences vn corp composé de tant de members espars ça et là … ceste authorité vrayement supreme a esté reseruee pour un dernier remede … – ce Parlement, qu'on peut appeler vn abregé des Estats de France"*).[114] As Church observes, the idea that the Parlement "was the permanent representative of the Estates General, or of the three social classes at large, was not confined to a few theorists but appeared in the pronouncements of the two institutions themselves."[115] For example, in 1593, the Parlement declared itself to be an "epitome of the Three Estates, image and miniature of all the Orders of the Kingdom" (*"abrégé des Trois Etats, image et raccourci de tous les Ordres de Royaume"*).[116]

Historians have wondered why, if the Estates General were more or less successful for over half a century, they did not end up becoming as central to French politics as their counterpart across the Channel. Most of the explanations amount to the argument that their increased influence was 'too little, too late.' Some point fingers at the lack of tradition, the extreme regionalization of France compared with England, the unwillingness of the delegates to travel so far and at great expense to participate in such assemblies, or to the conflicts between Catholics and Protestants inside the Estates at the apex of their political influence.[117] All of these explanations are correct, and yet a larger one may encompass all of them: if both the estates and the parlements of France failed in their attempt to embody the sovereignty of the people, it was because they were simply unable to compromise – within and among themselves. The reason why they were unable to do that should be clear by now; the three core requirements of a classic compromise could not be met: (1) political relationships

---

[113] *Sommaire de toutes les harangues, edits et ordonnaces … en ses estats tenus à Bloys* (1588), 808, quoted in Church, *Constitutional Thought*, 90.

[114] Simon Marion, *Plaidoyez*, 268–269, quoted in Church, *Constitutional Thought*, 137.

[115] Church, *Constitutional Thought*, 138.

[116] Maugis, quoted in ibid., 138.

[117] See, e.g., the excellent study of P.S. Lewis (1962), "The Failure of the French Medieval Estates," *Past and Present*, 23: 3–24.

were not perceived in terms of contracts; (2) the parties involved – kings, parlements, and estates – were by definition not equal; (3) if the problem of will
would have been somehow manageable, there was no consensus about who
ought to represent reason once and forever.

Absolutism became, logically, the easiest solution. It followed the path of
least resistance. The king proved much more able to juggle the two requirements of sovereignty – a unified will informed by a metaphysical reason.

5.4. CENTRIPETAL INDIVIDUALISM AND HANDS-ON POLITICS

As we have seen, the idea of representation being necessarily top-down was
never challenged during this time, not even by the strongest supporters of the
sovereignty of the people. During the sixteenth and seventeenth centuries the
idea that the parlements or the Estates could possibly represent individuals
never occurred. Nobody wanted that – certainly not the nobility, nor either the
peuple gras or the *peuple menu*. As per the classical understanding, representing inferiors would have been demeaning, and being represented as individuals
would have been impossible in the *forum internum*. While Frenchmen trusted
the conceptualized communities in the *forum externum*, they were also highly
suspicious of the claims to political authority of other individuals as well as
other representative bodies. Simply put, they rejected the idea of somebody else
speaking 'on their behalf.'

In practice, this distrust often manifested itself in sporadic conflicts between
aristocrats and the central government or in local rebellions of the economically disadvantaged, some of them quite large, both in numbers involved and
violence wrought. As a matter of fact, the end of the sixteenth century and a
good part of the seventeenth were marked by various popular or aristocratic
upheavals. However, the orthodox interpretation, as we have seen, is that from
a political perspective all these open conflicts, including the Fronde, amounted
to little if anything. "[W]hat was lacking among all these groups, and also
among the officials and commercial bourgeoisie was an ethic of positive commitment to the activities of the polity.... In its place was the radically individualistic ethic of the 'dissociated man.'"[118]

I argue that this is an overstatement that overlooks historical realities simply
because they do not fit in the picture of an individual removed from the political life. This 'radically individualistic ethic' did not automatically translate into
a refusal of politics or of 'positive commitment,' but rather in a refusal to commit to a political life via intermediaries, that is, via fictional representatives. In
the same way that the Church has one body and one personality not because
it comprises anonymous body parts but rather specific and distinct members,

[118] Keohane, *Philosophy and the State*, 122. For the "dissociated man," see Anna Maria Battista,
Sul rapporto tra societa e stato nello Francia dell' assolutisma, quoted in Keohane, *Philosophy
and the State*.

the body politic ought to be comprised of distinguishable (and distinguished?) individuals. The revolts at the end of sixteenth century and those of the Fronde during the seventeenth prove that the French were quite committed to acquiring a voice in government and to contesting the status quo, so long as the two classical requirements were met. First, the individual ought to act in his capacity as member of some community and for the interests of that community. Second, the will of such an individual and of the community as a whole ought to be informed by the 'proper' reason. It goes without saying that these were not easy requirements, certainly not ones to be met without contest. If the main cause for the failure of the Fronde is generally considered to be the multiplicity of irreconcilable and partial interests, and if most historians claimed that the *frondeurs* lacked all political coherence as far as their political ideals were concerned, the explanation had to be sought in an inability to agree on the proper representation of the people. From this perspective, what at first sight appears as paradoxical, namely praising *the* people while despising *people*, begins to make sense.

The closer one gets to the conceptualized people, the more one starts worrying about the actions of the faceless multitude, that is, the irrational "beast with a thousand heads." Hubert Carrier is right when he observes that despite the apparent differences among most of the ideas of the *frondeurs*, there is an underlying commonality that ensures at least some degree of coherence. Regardless of the fact that the parties – Court, Princes, Parlements or even *le peuple menu* – could not agree on whom and how ought to represent 'the people,' there was at least a point of consensus: the sum of individual wills do not make the people *a* people. Even the partisans of the most radical participatory versions of politics were careful to avoid confusion between the will of the people and the arithmetical counting of wills.

For example, as I will discuss in more detail in Chapter 7, the basis of the theory of Huguenot resistance with its decentralized, federal plan of government "was a system of checks and balances between the various aspects of government, and an elective method and system of recall which *made chosen leaders at every level, and regardless of their rank, subject to the sovereign community*." [119] What is even more impressive is that on the first anniversary of the St. Bartholomew's Day massacre the deputies of the southern protestant churches meeting at Montauban decided to put this theory into practice. They divided the province of Languedoc into two districts with Montauban and Nimes as their respective capitals and started to sketch a system of councils at different levels, to be elected by popular vote regardless of the social rank, which in turn would name delegates to a general assembly. The details were worked out in a second meeting, held at Milau on December 16, 1573, getting the entire project even closer to the propositions made in *Reveille Matin*. As a matter of fact, according to the author of the second part of *Reveille Matin*,

---

[119] Salmon, *Society in Crisis*, 189; emphasis added.

the original proposals "were taken from town to town and discussed before the early meetings."

A quote from J.H.M. Solomon offers a detailed picture of the radical democratic intentions of the participants.

This programme had outlawed pluralism and venality of office, and declared that all officials should be elected for annual terms *on the basis of merit* and without regards to hereditary claims. In each town and region popular assemblies were to choose a civil government of an elder (*maieur*) and a council of twenty-four, who would send electors to a central assembly. These electors were in turn to appoint a supreme *maieur*, 'whether from the nobility or the people,' an executive council of twenty-four, and another council of seventy-five, who, in conjunction with the *maieur* and the twenty-four, would form a council of one hundred to act as an interim legislature and a court of last appeal. No member of the hundred might assume military command without resigning from the council.... At any level an ordinary citizen had the right to accuse an official of corruption, and the accusation must be heard. Should the official prove innocent, the accuser himself was liable to punishment.[120]

There were two more Protestant constituent assemblies, the last one in 1575, and both reaffirmed the same constitution. The fact that this constitution did not survive for long should not diminish the importance of its radical democratic assumptions. In effect, all the popular uprisings from the end of the sixteenth century through to the end of the seventeenth were for all practical purposes all but failures. However, what is of interest to us is that they all reveal a surprising array of direct democratic features, regardless of the social status or religious allegiance of their leaders, and hard to explain from the orthodox perspective. The examples are too numerous to be exhausted here, but a few cases will demonstrate this point. The Razats of Provence revolted in 1578 against the abuses of soldiers of every political persuasion and included peasants of both faiths. In 1579 they massacred a force of 600 noblemen, sacked and burned several chateaux and subjected the region to their own taxation system. Other peasant revolts, most notably that of the Croquants, followed in the 1590s with similar results. Undoubtedly, the weakness of the crown and the growing hostility both between and within the social orders were responsible for many of these revolts. But their radical democratic features are hard to ignore.

The Parisian Sixteen, for example, were Catholic revolutionaries who took their name from the committees of public security established in each of the sixteen *quartiers* of Paris after the murder of Henri de Guise. They did not include nobility of the sword and were more than willing to challenge the existing social order, arguing in favor of *le peuple menu* against *le peuple gras*, as revealed in *The Dialogue between the Courtier and the Labourer*.[121] Probably

---

[120] Ibid., 191–192.
[121] For more details on this various movements, see ibid. The following paragraphs are partially informed by this extraordinary book.

written sometime later (1593?) by Cromé, the satire proposed to abolish hereditary ranks and establish an elite of virtuous Catholic zealots. Popular assemblies were commonplace during these times of insurrection. The provincial councils created by the League all over France "represented a new concept of participatory government created by the revolutionary situation."[122]

During the Fronde the same dualism in praising the conceptualized people while mocking people as a mere crowd manifested in the pamphlets of the time.

Ce que les pamphlets frondeurs rédigés entre 1648 and 1653 nous révèlent avant tout, c'est cette ambivalence du peuple, un peuple qui, lorsqu'il est conceptualisé, est perçu comme une communauté primordiale; alors que, lorsque les libellistes décrivent le peuple vivant et s'agitant sous leurs yeux, cet aspect disparaît, laissant la place à un peuple assimilé à un multitude bestiale.[123]

(What the Frondist pamphlets composed between 1648 and 1653 reveal above all is this ambivalence of the people, a people that, when it is conceptualized, is perceived as a primordial community; yet when the pamphleteers describe the people that live and bustle under their eyes, this aspect disappears, leaving in place a people assimilated to a bestial multitude.)

Once again, the distinction is made in terms of a differentiated access to reason and wisdom (*sagesse*). The multitude is not to be trusted, for it lacks the ability to know what it wants and why. Therefore, *this* people is not reliable and is easy to manipulate.

Enfin, vous revenez, et le peuple s'en plaint.
Mais sait-il ce qu'il veut? Mais sait-il ce qu'il craint?
Il croit aisément tout ce que l'on lui persuade.
C'est sans raison qu'il aime, et sans raison qu'il hait.[124]

(Finally, you returned, and the people is complaining.
But does it know what it wants? But does it know what it fears?
It easily believes everything one persuades it
It is without reason that it loves, and without reason that it hates.)

"*La voix du peuple,*" one also reads in *Le Remède aux malheurs de L'État*, "*n'est la voix de Dieu qu'à condition d'entendre par peuple 'les gens de bien, savants et expérimentés' et non 'la populace et la lie des hommes'*"[125] ("The voice of the people is the voice of God only if one understands by it 'good men, savants, and the experimented,' not 'the populace and the dregs of humanity'").

---

[122] Ibid., 252.

[123] Bernard Biancotto, quoted in Hubert Carrier (2004), *Le labyrinthe de l'état: Essai sur le débat politique en France au temps de la Fronde (1648–1653)* (Paris: Honore Champion Editeur), 121–122.

[124] *Réflexions politiques et morales publiées par Scarron* (1652), quoted in Carrier, *Le labyrinthe de l'état*, 152.

[125] Quoted in Carrier, *Le labyrinthe de l'état*, 203.

So deeply rooted was the mistrust in individuals that during the Fronde the general aversion for all republican regimes ("the popular governments") was manifested even among its supporters. For almost everybody, a popular republic was a synonym for chaos, as demonstrated by the tracts of the time.[126] The unwise and unruly multitude could even *compromise* its leaders.

Thus, in *Les Sentiments du vrai citoyen sur la paix* (1649), Bertaut, a moderate Frondist, warns his readers against "*cette dangereuse liberté qui se rencontre parmi le peuple, non seulement de mal interpréter les actions et la conduite des chefs, mais encore de les exposer et les mettre en compromise quand bon leur semble*"[127] ("this dangerous liberty that is found among the people, not only to misinterpret the actions and behavior of the leaders, but also to expose and *put them in compromise* whenever they feel like it"). Rebellion was an act of resistance by individuals and as such ought to be condemned. Insurrection, on the other hand, was legitimate because it was done by the whole people raised against tyranny. "*Autre chose est quand tout le peuple, par un mouvement et par un intérêt commun, se soulève contre l'oppression; car alors ce n'est plus une rébellion et une désobéissance*"[128] ("It is a different thing when an entire people, in one movement and in one common interest, raise against the oppression; for then it is no longer rebellion and disobedience").

Nonetheless, in the rare instances when people took power in their own hands during the Fronde and established a democratic government, as when in Bordeaux in 1653 they took the expression *Vox populi, vox Dei* quite literally and established an "authentic dictatorship of the proletariat" *avant la lettre*, as Carrier put it. If the King had forbidden the Parlement of Bordeaux in 1649 and 1650, he by this very act provided legitimacy for the popular assemblies that administered the city – but as assemblies, not as a collection of individuals.

Sa Majesté ayant retiré de ce Parlement l'autorité qu'il lui avait communiqué n'a pas entendu que la société des homes retournât dans son premier chaos et dans l'horreur de ces brutales et inciviles façons des premier homes; mais, nous ayant défendu de lui obéir, il a laissé son peuple dans le droit naturel de se rendre justice, dans sa franchise et dans ses privilèges.[129]

(By taking away the authority of this Parliament, His Majesty did not mean the society of men to return to its original chaos and to the horrors of those brutal and uncivilized manners of the first men; but being prevented from obeying him, he left to his people the natural right of rendering themselves justice, in its exemption and its privileges.)

Not surprising, such radicalism ended in Bordeaux as elsewhere in a blood bath, as would the French Revolution a century later. What is surprising is

---

[126] See ibid., 93–133.
[127] Quoted in ibid., 132.
[128] Text from 1652, quoted in ibid., 215.
[129] *Apologie pour Ormée*, in the Municipal Library of Bordeaux, H 2856, 35, quoted in Carrier, *Le labyrinthe de l'état*, 148.

that its contemporaries did not fault their excesses, but their lack thereof. In other words, at fault was the penchant toward compromise. "*En matière de soulèvement, on n'est coupable que d'avoir eu trop de moderation,*" concludes Montandré in *Le Point de Ovale*[130] ("In matters of uprising we are guilty only of having too much moderation"). He was not the only one to think this way. Marigny too wrote in 1653, when the end of the Fronde was in sight, that "moderation leads only to sure and unavoidable peril" ("*la modération ne conduit qu'à des précipices assurés et inévitables*").[131]

Across the Channel, the English begged to differ – with much more efficient and less bloody results.

---

[130] Quoted in Carrier, *Le labyrinthe de l'état*, 136.
[131] Ibid., 136.

6

Compromise and Centrifugal Individualism

> I am here in a country [England] which hardly resembles the rest of Europe.
>
> Montesquieu

> I have always been astonished that a fact, which distinguished England from all modern nations and which can alone explain the peculiarities of its laws, its spirit, and its history, has not attracted still more than it has done the attention of philosophers and statesmen, and that habit has finally made it as it were invisible to the English themselves.
>
> Alexis de Tocqueville

In early 1519, a group of King Henri VIII's young companions, who had been on embassy to France and spent the previous Christmas at the court of Francis I, returned to England. According to the chronicler Edward Hall they arrived home: "all French in eating, drinking, and apparel, yea, and in French vices and brags so that nothing by them was praised, but if it were after the French turn." The young men's newly acquired Francophilia and Hall's rather sour reaction typify the range of English responses to France in the sixteenth century and in the five centuries since.[1]

As Richardson showed in his survey of the most recent research on sixteenth century Franco–English relationships, the middle of the sixteenth century witnessed a radical change. "From being openly hostile they became more ambivalent in the true meaning of the word."[2] The competition was not just political and military but also cultural and, as a result, the intellectual exchanges between the two countries increased accordingly. "Under the Tudors a pattern of reciprocal contact and comparison between the two nations was

---

[1] Glenn John Richardson (2008), "England and France in the Sixteenth Century," *History Compass* 6, no. 2: 510.

[2] Ibid., 510.

established, or rather re-established, after the Hundred Years War."[3] This trend increased during the seventeenth century. James I, for instance, was extremely concerned with his continental (and especially his French) reputation. He intervened in continental scholarly disputes, both theological and political, and in more worldly affairs, acting for example as *compromissarius* in a dispute about the theological doctrine of justification between the French Protestants Du Moulin and Tilenus.[4] Other examples include Hobbes and Locke, who spent several years in France and were deeply influenced by the French culture. And yet, if by the second half of the sixteenth century Michel de Montaigne and Louis de Masures were already worried about the possibility of compromising one's conscience or one's faith, no such worries were to be found across the English Channel, which suggests that this increased commerce did not manage to overcome deeper differences. Sure, many Puritans, Anabaptists, and so forth were concerned about the dangers of worldly burdens that might corrupt the soul, yet the question remains: Why was the fear of a corrupted soul never backed up by a fear of compromising oneself, one's virtue, reputation, and the like, as in the French case? There might be here more than meets the eye.

It is the aim of this chapter to provide further evidence for the distinct English development, despite the indisputable intellectual exchanges of the time. This is not an easy task. As Gerhard Dilcher points out, "the most difficult investigation ... would have to include social reality and consciousness, self-interpretation, and interrogation into a universal value structure."[5] It would be an impossible and rather useless effort to enter into all the intricacies of British history in the sixteenth and seventeenth centuries; the literature on this period is more than impressive and increases by the year.[6] And yet, this seeming disadvantage may become an advantage when looking for answers to specific questions. Since one tries to solve only one particular puzzle, this abundance of historical material and analysis can provide a wealth of evidence for or against a given hypothesis – in this case, that English compromise, while retaining some of its original sense, acquired a new one, thanks to particular developments in the understanding of representation.

[3] Ibid., 521.

[4] J.P. Somersville (1991), "James I and the Divine Rights of Kings" in *The Mental World of the Jacobean Court*, ed. Linda Levy Peck (Cambridge: Cambridge University Press), 59–60.

[5] Gerhard Dilcher (2006), "The City Community," in *The Individual in Political Theory and Practice*, ed. Janet Coleman (Oxford: Clarendon Press), 282.

[6] A few examples should suffice: Robert Zaller (2007), *The Discourse of Legitimacy in Early Modern England* (Stanford, Calif.: Stanford University Press); David Armitage, ed. (2006), *British Political Thought in History, Literature and Theory, 1500–1800* (Cambridge: Cambridge University Press); Victor Stater (2002), *The Political History of Tudor and Stuart England: A Sourcebook* (London and New York: Routledge); J.G.A. Pocock, ed. (1993), *The Varieties of British Political Thought, 1500–1800* (New York: Cambridge University Press); J.H. Hexter, ed. (1992), *Parliament and Liberty from the Reign of Elizabeth to the English Civil War* (Stanford, Calif.: Stanford University Press).

All one needs do is check the preconditions of compromise as they have been identified in the previous chapters: (1) the *acknowledged* authority of the arbitrator to *equally represent* the interests of both parties, (2) the willingness to *accept the risks* involved in a third party's judgment, and (3) the basic *equality of the parties* involved in the dispute. To this list of requirements one may add a fourth – the impossibility of solving the dispute through other means and the looming alternative of open violence. Such preconditions could have been met if, for a variety of political, social, and religious reasons, England developed quite earlier a peculiar form of individualism and a different understanding of representation than in continental Europe. I suspect that the distinction between the two fora, *internum* and *externum*, collapsed here sometime around the second half of the sixteenth century, and individuals started to apprehend themselves and be apprehended primarily in terms of individual wills. In close connection with this development, representation came to be understood as an ascending representation of individuals. If so, then all the preconditions for the wholehearted embrace of compromise could have been met. Therefore, this chapter will investigate these assumptions.

The first part of the chapter examines the English peculiarity when compared with continental Europe, a distinction of which both Englishmen and foreigners appeared to be fully aware even before the end of the sixteenth century. Part two further considers how this individualism created a peculiar form of commonwealth – no longer understood in an organic way, but as a voluntary assembly of free and equal individuals. Part three analyzes the collapse of the two fora, *internum* and *externum*, and the consequent emergence of a centrifugal individualism that apprehended itself mostly in terms of public office, while part four retraces the connection between this centrifugal individualism and contractarianism. It shows not only the unprecedented explosion of contractualist language but also of contractarian practices – from secular and theological covenants to oaths of allegiances – and how such contracts and covenants were often assimilated with compromises. Here, an analysis of the Hobbesian distinction between the two fora in favor of *forum externum* (or *foro externo* as he had it), in both *De cive* and the *Leviathan*, will serve as example.

For the first time, the political body, that is, the commonweal, was understood as the result of a voluntary contract – a compromise based upon equality of wills. This is the time when one witnesses the emergence of an ascending understanding of representation as representation of individual wills. The embodiment of this ascending representation was, undoubtedly, the Parliament. Its characteristics contrasted with those of the French Estates, and the apprehensions and self-apprehensions of the MPs as representatives of each and every single Englishman are analyzed in part five. The chapter ends with a survey of the ways in which compromise became a central political practice as the seventeenth century progressed, focusing more specifically on the overlooked reasons for which many scholars came to consider the Great Revolution as a Great Compromise.

One more specification should be mentioned here. It should be clear by now that I uses the terms 'English' and 'British' indiscriminately. Such practice may appear careless or outdatedly Anglo-centric, since most historians agree today that in dealing with Britain of the sixteenth to eighteenth centuries one must remember that one is dealing in effect with three kingdoms – England, Ireland, and Scotland – and the 'history of Britain' does not always reflect the complexities and particularities of the 'multiple-kingdoms' approach. The 'English bias' has been made evident especially through recent works of the Center for the History of British Political Thought. Yet the same scholars agree that "there is no point in trying to force a Three-Kingdoms approach where one does not make sense."[7] This is one such case.

6.1. "AND THE BRITISH BEING UTTERLY DIVIDED FROM THE WHOLE WORLD"

In sixteenth and seventeenth century England, political and religious turmoil made it increasingly difficult for people to convene on an undisputable source of authority and legitimacy. Most historians agree that "early modern England was a society in transition, and its modes of discourse were in flux, not to say in turmoil" – something that we have already seen reflected in Heywood's allegory of the spider and the fly.[8] Different factions wrestled with the many problems of the Reformation and 'post-Reformation' period: The increasing competition for authority and legitimacy between Parliament and Crown, the disruptive forces of confessional differences manifest in theories of resistance, millenarianism, civil war radicalism, and so on. The establishment of the Anglican Church and the existence of the dissenters further complicated the British picture. Not surprisingly then, "public discourse in the second half of the sixteenth century was carried on through an extraordinary confusion of tongues."[9] As David Hume also noticed as early as the eighteenth century, around 1600 the appearance of consensus during the reign of Elizabeth began to display incoherence.[10] People found it increasingly difficult to agree upon a common set of principles – indeed, the only thing they *could* agree upon is that there was no such common ground. As for the ever-present threat of violence, suffice it to remember that "the era between the onset of the English reformation and the outbreak of the English

---

[7] Tim Harris (2006), "In Search of a British History of Political Thought," in Armitage, *British Political Thought*, 90. For a more detailed discussion on this subject, see, in the same volume, the articles by J.G.A. Pocock, Gordon Schochet and Lois G. Schworer, John Morrill, and Colin Kidd.

[8] Zaller, *The Discourse of Legitimacy*, 3.

[9] Donald R. Kelley (1993), "Elizabethan Political Thought," in Pocock, *The Varieties of British Political Thought*, 47.

[10] David Hume (1983) [1778], *The History of England*, vol. 5, p. 18 et passim; mentioned also in Pocock, *The Varieties of British Political Thought*, 6.

civil war" has been characterized "as the period that generated England's bloodiest domestic conflict, its last royal execution, and its lone experiment in republican government."[11]

It is important to note that the peculiar British usage of compromise coincides with the replacement of Latin with English in the liturgy of the English Church. While the decision was reversed by Queen Mary and reinstated by Queen Elizabeth, between 1550 and 1650, when English finally came to replace French in the proceedings of the common law, there was an increased awareness about the need to transform English from a second-hand language into "the king's English," as Shakespeare phrased it in his *Merry Wives of Windsor* where Sir Hugh Evans gladly offers, in Act I, Scene I, "to make atonements and compremises" in order to redress Falstaff's "disparagements." There was a feeling, expressed by several authors, that English should become a language worth of the emerging empire. In 1599, for example, Samuel Daniel wrote the poem *Musophilus* in which he manifested a rather unusual optimism concerning the fate of his language. "And who in time," asks Daniel,

> knows whither we may vent
> The treasure of our tongue, to what strange shores
> This gain of our best glory shall be sent,
> T' enrich unknowing nations with our stores?
> What worlds in the yet unformed Occident
> May come refined with the accents that are ours?[12]

An increased feeling of distinctiveness at the level of self-perception doubled this emphasis on the preeminence of English. The most common observations about a distinct English development were then as now made with reference to the Parliament and to the peculiar common law in opposition to the Roman and canon law that dominated continental Europe. Sir John Fortescue (ca. 1395–ca. 1477) took his time to explain in great detail to the young Prince the reasons why the *Laws of England* are far superior to the civil laws popular on continental Europe. "[T]hey are necessarily replete with prudence and wisdom, since they are promulgated by the prudence not of one counselor nor of a hundred only, but of more than three hundred chosen men."[13] In the same vein, Sir Thomas Smith argued that in *De republica anglorum* he had "set forth almost the whole of its form, especially those points in which [this commonwealth] differs from the others."

[11] Zaller, *The Discourse of Legitimacy*, 1, following Lawrence Stone (1986), *The Causes of the English Revolution, 1529–1642*, 2nd ed. (London: Routledge).

[12] Samuel Daniel (1965) [1930], *Poems and a Defence of Ryme*, ed. Arthur Colby Sprague (Chicago: University of Chicago Press), 96, quoted in Richard Helgerson (1988), "Language Lessons: Linguistic Colonialism, Linguistic Postcolonialism, and the Early Modern Nation," *Yale Journal of Criticism* 11, no. 1: 289–299.

[13] Sir John Fortescue (1997), *On the Laws and Governance of England*, ed. Shelley Lockwood (Cambridge: Cambridge University Press), 27.

But it differs in almost all.... I have furnished fruitful argument for those who would debate ... whether what is held here and in those regions which are administered in accordance with the Roman Law. For all things, almost, are different.[14]

Sir Edward Coke, the most prominent constitutionalist of the seventeenth century, used (as did many of his contemporaries) the quote from Virgil's first *Eclogue* extremely popular among Englishmen, *toto divises orbe Britannos*, in close connection with the uniqueness of British common law. If Roman law imposed itself all over continental Europe regardless of differences and particularities, England's common laws were 'tuned' to respond specifically to the needs of the Englishmen.

Here our common lawes are aptly and properly called the lawes of England because they are appropriated to this Kingdome of England as most apt and fit for the government thereof, and have no dependancy upon any forreigne law whatsoever, no not upon the civill or cannon law other then in cafes allowed by the laws of England, as partly hath been touched before: and therefore the Poet spake truly hereof, *Et penitus toto divises orbe Brittannos* (*and the British being utterly divided from the whole world*): so as the law of England is *proprium quarto modo* (*property in the fourth degree*) to the Kingdome of England; therefore forrein precedents are not to be objected against us, because we are not subject to forrein lawes.[15]

Most contemporary scholars tend to agree. Indeed, all across Europe, whenever local, customary law was not able to solve a judicial problem, "the *ius commune* of Roman and canon law applied. [But only] in England local law developed into common law."[16] "On the whole ... Roman law failed to take root in England."[17] "Common law triumphed over canon and papal law" and helped increase the role of the Parliament.[18] The connections between common law and the originality of English political thought and practice have been emphasized from a variety of perspectives.[19]

Because of the peculiar success of customary law in England, scholars are still arguing if this particularity is to be interpreted as a preservation of the medieval features or, on the contrary, as an early social contract between equals, opposed to the feudal contracts between unequals.[20] One observation

---

[14] Sir Thomas Smith (1906), *De republica anglorum: A Discourse on the Commonwealth of England*, ed. L. Aston (Cambridge: Cambridge University Press), 142, quoted in Zaller, *The Discourse of Legitimacy*, 224.

[15] Sir Edward Coke (2003) [1606], "Statute of Merton," in *Selected Writings of Sir Edward Coke*, vol. 2, ed. Steve Sheppard (Indianapolis, Ind.: Liberty Fund), 98.

[16] Dilcher, "The City Community," 282, footnote.

[17] Kelley, "Elizabethan Political Thought," 64.

[18] John Guy (1993), "The Henrician Age," in Pocock, *The Varieties of British Political Thought*, 22.

[19] See, e.g., Clive Holmes (1992), "Parliament, Liberty, Taxation, and Property," or Charles M. Gray, "Parliament, Liberty, and the Law," in Hexter, *Parliament and Liberty*.

[20] See P. Anderson (1974), *Passages from Antiquity to Feudalism* (London), 150–151, 194–195; J.C. Holt (1992), *Magna Carta*, 2nd ed. (Cambridge: Cambridge University Press); Janet Coleman, "The Individual and the Medieval State," in Coleman, *The Individual*, 9–11.

is generally accepted: while on the continent, and particularly in France, the increasing power of the King came to be assimilated with the more abstract "state," thus checking the resistance of feudal lords, in England the same lords managed to be assimilated *with* the king and thus *with* the state, checking the king's powers and increasing commoners' rights but, by the same token, maintaining them outside the formalized political sphere.[21]

As DeLolme astutely observed in the eighteenth century in his *Constitution of England*, the differences between England and France can be traced back to feudal times. In France, the liberty enjoyed by the barons prevented their alliance with the people, which cleared the road for absolute monarchy, while in England, paradoxically, "the Lord, the Vassal, the inferior Vassal, all united" in Parliament in order to check the royal power. The "people," by the same token, "instructed by the examples of their Leaders, ... insisted that for the future, every individual should be intitled [*sic*] to the protection of the law; and thus those rights to which the Lords had strengthened themselves, in order to oppose the tyranny of the Crown, become a bulwark which was, in time, to restrain their own."[22] Despite the rather rosy and 'whiggish' picture that he promotes, DeLolme's insight is worth noticing for its help in understanding the peculiar long-run development of England. "The Representative of the Nation, and of the whole Nation, were now admitted into the Parliament."[23] "[B]oth crown and Parliament expanded in scope and [assumed] authority in the century after the Reformation, and that what happened in 1640 was a migration of legitimacy from the former to the latter, a revolution *within* the state."[24]

As will become increasingly evident, this development forged a different kind of individualism than the French version. Unlike in France, in England the state was not assimilated with some transcending entity, but with the product of (although not by any means exclusively) individual wills. "The entire span of English history between 1529 and 1689 constituted a single revolutionary arc, on one side of which was polity still communitarian in its outlook, and on the other one deeply infused with the principle of personal interest."[25] Zaller is not the only one to observe the peculiar English penchant toward a more practical form of individualism. This is something on which the supporters of the contextual approach and the 'revisionist' school can agree – both the royalists and their parliamentarian opponents were strong defenders of private property and of the liberties of free-born Englishmen,

---

[21] Howell A. Lloyd (1983), *The State, France, and the Sixteenth Century* (London: George Allen & Unwin).

[22] Jean Louis DeLolme (2007) [1774], *The Constitution of England; or, An Account of the English Government*, edited and with an introduction by David Lieberman (Indianapolis, Ind.: Liberty Fund), 32.

[23] Ibid., 38.

[24] Zaller, *The Discourse of Legitimacy*, 5.

[25] Ibid., 2.

"though by those terms they did not necessarily mean the same things as their opponents."[26]

Following in the footsteps of Sir F. Pollock and F.W. Maitland, Alan Macfarlane, for example, observes "that England as a whole was different from the rest of Europe" and at least in what concerns 'individualism' it "stood alone."[27] He expresses strong doubts that English feudalism even then "fit into the Continental, particularly French, model."[28] To back up this claim, he provides evidence from a variety of perspectives – from the peculiarity of English witchcraft within Europe, to the singularly English unconcern about incest, to the keeping of diaries and the nature of peasant society.

[I]t is no longer possible to 'explain' the origins of English individualism in terms of either Protestantism, population change, the development of a market economy at the end of the middle ages, or other factors.... Individualism, however defined, predates sixteenth century changes and can be said to shape them all. The explanation must lie elsewhere, but will remain obscure until we trace the origins even further than has been attempted in this work.[29]

In the light of previous chapters and the pages to follow his argument is of particular importance for understanding the different usages of compromise across the English Channel. Macfarlane argues that for the British, unlike their continental counterparts, notably the French, "society [was] constituted of *autonomous, equal, units, namely separate individuals, and that such individuals are more important, ultimately, than any larger constituent group.*"[30] To check the accuracy of the description of England as "a society in which almost every aspect of the culture was diametrically opposed to that of the surrounding nations," he offers "notable accounts or statements, first by foreigners who wrote about England, and secondly by Englishmen who were comparing their own society with those around them."[31] Samples of travelers' diaries, from Frederick, Duke of Wirtemberg (1592), and Paul Hentzner from Germany, to an Italian physician, Cardano (1552), or Emmanuel van Metereren from the Low Countries, among many others, are offered in this context.[32] For the English perspective, one finds John Alymer (1559), Sir Thomas Smith (1565), or Sir John Davis

---

[26] Glenn Burgess (2007), "England and Scotland," in *European Political Thought, 1450–1700: Religion, Law, and Philosophy*, ed. Howell A. Lloyd, Glenn Burgess, and Simon Hodson (New Haven and London), 333.

[27] Alan Macfarlane (1979), *The Origins of Individualism: The Family, Property, and Social Transition* (New York: Cambridge University Press), 5; F. Pollack and F.W. Maitland (1968), *History of English Law before the Time of Edward I*, 2nd ed. (Cambridge: Cambridge University Press).

[28] Macfarlane, *The Origins of Individualism*, 206.

[29] Ibid., 197.

[30] Ibid., 5; emphasis added.

[31] Ibid., 165.

[32] Ibid., 170–175, quoting from W.B. Rye, *England as Seen by Foreigners in the Reign of Elizabeth and James the First* (1865).

(1612).[33] In the end, Macfarlane makes an interesting observation that merits a somehow lengthy quotation:

> Those accepting the conventional wisdom are forced to argue that almost all those who wrote about England up to the nineteenth century, both those who lived there and those who visited the country, were deluded. They are forced to take the view that those who studied their own past and their own present were under a massive misapprehension.... Yet it is surely more reasonable to assume that when they argued that England was somehow different ... they knew, in general, what they were doing.[34]

6.2. THE COMMON WEAL OF INDIVIDUALS

Not surprisingly, this peculiar form of individualism created a peculiar form of commonwealth as well – a voluntary one based upon the supposed equality of the parties. The requirement of equality for the parties involved in compromise is probably the crucial one. As we have seen in the previous chapter, the major worry of the French about compromise was tied with the fear of having to compromise with inferiors and/or to subject oneself to the arbitration of unworthy *compromissores*. There is only one conceivable situation when *everybody* is willing to compromise wholeheartedly – once everybody agrees *in principle* that on some abstract legal level (not economic, nor social, to be sure), all individuals are of equal worth. Only then will one not run the risk of 'compromising' with someone unworthy.

The well-known case of the Magna Carta (1215) is particularly revealing. No other English legal document has enjoyed such long life, and none has pretended (and to a large extent succeeded) in *stating* customary law while also becoming *part* of it. As J.C. Holt put it, "Magna Carta has been preserved not as a museum piece, but as part of the common law of England, to be defended, maintained or repealed as the functions of the law required."[35] It is not the aim of these pages to analyze the ways in which this document has been used in turn by antiquarians, radicals, or by the supporters of natural rights theories to promote the development of Parliament, and within it of the House of Commons. As mentioned in the beginning of this chapter the dispute between different schools of historical interpretation is of little interest for our concerns. What is important, however, is the famous chapter 29 (Cap. 39 in the 1215 version), stating that no free man is to be imprisoned, dispossessed, outlawed, exiled, or damaged without lawful judgment of his peers or by the law of the land. The statement was devised mainly in the interest of the aristocracy and the "free men" as a class formed but a small proportion of the population of thirteenth-century England. Yet the opportunity was not wasted. In the earlier statutes of

---

[33] Ibid., 176–183.
[34] Ibid., 203.
[35] Holt, *Magna Carta*, 2.

Edward III of 1331 and 1352, the words 'no free man' became simply 'no man,' but in 1354 in the statute that refers for the first time to 'due process of law,' 'no free man' became 'no man of whatever estate or condition he may be.'[36]

Compared with the rest of Europe, this was a huge leap forward in individual equality and it remained an important reference and source of precedents all the way through the seventeenth century, despite all the vicissitudes of royal opposition or the increasing appeal to concepts such as natural law and natural rights that had less need for precedent. Already by the sixteenth century these men, equal before the law 'whatever their estates or conditions,' formed a particular form of *res publica* – a commonwealth. The word can be misleading as seeming to emphasize the 'community,' the unity of the political body, at the expense of individuals – and some people found the translation worrisome precisely for this reason. In 1513, in *The Boke named the Governour*, Sir Thomas Elyot opposed the translation of *res publica* as 'commonwealth' because it implied "that everything should be to all men in common, without discrepance of any estate or condition.... [A]ll men must be of one degree and one sort" (he preferred the expression 'public weal').[37]

Sir Elyot must have worried too much, for most people understood exactly what the 'commyn wele' was, namely a collection of individuals of different conditions who nevertheless were "quietly & peasybly passing theyr lyfe, ychone [= each one] loving other as partys of one body, every parte dowing hys duty & office reqyryd therto," as Thomas Starkey put it in 1532.[38] Yet if these loving 'fingers,' 'feet,' 'ears,' and so forth formed a body, as they were taken to do in sixteenth-century France as well, it was certainly a very strange one. Instead of growing together – as according to the organic theory presumably their French counterparts did – these body parts walked for a while the Earth equal and free until suddenly they decided, nose, ears, heart, and stomach alike, to come together *and covenant* to form a body. At least this is the image that Sir Thomas Smith appears to be conceiving. For him a commonwealth is "a society or common doing of a multitude of free men collected together and united by common accord and covenauntes among themselves, for the conservation of themselves aswell [*sic*] in peace as in warre."[39]

Such a vision of free, deliberative individuals forming a commonwealth has little to do with medieval *universitates* – the corporate bodies, guilds, estates, and so on – as described for example by Bodin.[40] As a matter of fact one can

[36] Ibid., 10.

[37] Sir Thomas Elyot (1962), *The Book Named the Governor*, ed. S.E. Lemberg (London), 1–2, quoted in Burgess, "England and Scotland," 336.

[38] Thomas Starkey (1989), *A Dialogue between Pole and Lupset*, ed. T.F. Mayer (London), 37, quoted in Lloyd, Burgess, and Hodson, *European Political Thought*, 336.

[39] Smith, *De republica anglorum*, 20, quoted in Zaller, *The Discourse of Legitimacy*, 225.

[40] See, e.g., Ellen Meiskins Wood and Neal Wood (1997), *A Trumpet of Sedition: Political Theory and the Rise of Capitalism, 1509–1688* (New York: New York University Press), 48–50.

safely argue that one faces a proto-social contract between individuals enjoying juridical equality. But if men are created equally free, this does not automatically exclude inequality. In Smith's account, for example, this original equality in freedom does not preclude the ulterior political divisions of the commonwealth between 'gentlemen' (king, nobles, knights, squires), 'citizens' (elected town burgesses, backbenchers in Parliament), 'yeomen' (the forty-shillings freeholders, not "medd[ling] in publike matters and judgments but when they are called, and gladde when they are delivered thereof") and 'laborers.' This last yet most numerous category in England, "the fourth sort of men which doe not rule," comprised "day labourers, poore husbandmen, yea merchants or retailers which have no free lande, copyholders, and all artificers." But even men in this category filled some positions, as churchwardens, constables (an office "that toucheth more the common wealth"), or members of juries (hence Spider's reluctance in Heywood's fable to undergo trial by jury).

To his merit, Smith does not see these categories as immutable – quite the contrary.

For the nature of man is never to stand still in one maner of estate, but to grow from the lesse to the more, and decay from the more againe to the lesse, till it come to the fatall end and destruction, with many turnes and turmoyles of sicknesse and recovering, seldome standing in a perfect health, neither of a mans bodie it selfe, nor of the politique bodie which is compact of the same.[41]

Working hard, a yeoman could place his child one step higher on the social ladder, translating wealth into a new social position. Later, Tocqueville will make a similar observation, pointing toward English early social fluidity as an explanation for its peculiar development.

England was the only country in which the system of caste had not been changed but effectively destroyed. The nobles and the middle classes in England followed together the same courses of business, entered the same professions, and what is much more significant, inter-married.[42]

Tocqueville's observation about the high degree of social mobility that makes any talk about distinctive social groups rather difficult is confirmed by much more recent studies. At one end of the spectrum, the Crown was eager to knight rich merchant creditors. At the other, the identity of yeomen and freeholders became more and more imprecise, with an impact on the number of electors in county constituencies. "There are signs that service on a grand jury was sufficient to bring recognition of social arrival even to quite poor men in the counties; in the towns, membership of the corporation, or sometimes of the aldermanic bench (especially in smaller communities), brought the label 'Mr.'"[43]

41 Smith, *De republica anglorum*, 12–13.
42 Alexis de Tocqueville (1956), *L'Ancien régime*, trans. M. W. Patterson (Oxford: Oxford University Press), 89.
43 Derek Hirst (1975), *The Representative of the People? Voters and Voting under the Early Stuarts* (Cambridge: Cambridge University Press), 5.

Such mobility could not but reinforce the individualistic and egalitarian self-perception of the Englishmen. Thus, starting at least with the sixteenth century, the English commonwealth differs dramatically – not just in practical terms, but also in self-apprehensive ones – from the French political 'body.' If there is an organic vision it is not based on 'natural growth,' but on the body parts' wills. The result is a strange and unusual body, to say the least. Of course, the 'strangeness' of this assumption is not evident to the people involved, although the English peculiarity is obvious for both Englishmen and outside observers. Not surprisingly, languages are still mixed, authors often disagree or contradict themselves, and the distinction between the 'whole realm' or the 'people' and the consensual association of free and equal individuals is not always easy to discern. In 1587, for example, the puritan John Field could affirm that "it is the multitude and people that bring the discipline to pass which we desire."[44] What is evident, though, is that the central precondition for a successful compromise – the equality of the parties – was met on a scale unprecedented in continental Europe. As Overton put in a speech to Parliament, "by natural birth all men are equal, and alike born to like property and freedom."[45]

6.3. COLLAPSING THE TWO FORA

The question to be tackled now is: How did this peculiar individualism manifest itself from a political perspective? A few years ago, Conal Condren proposed a radically new reappraisal of moral and political theory in early modern England. He claims that the relationships between private and public then are at odds with the concepts that we take for granted now. One cannot talk, argues Condren, about the emergence of some sort of a Habermasian public sphere during that time since language was fluid and there was no clear-cut distinction between one sphere and the other.[46] On the contrary, each borrowed heavily the terminology of the other. There is much to support this thesis. For example, James I, in a speech to parliament in 1604, argued for the union with Scotland using well-known domestic imagery:

What God hath conjoined the joined then, let no men separate. I am the husband, and all the whole isle is my lawful wife; I am the head and it is my body; I am the shepherd and it is my flock: I hope therefore no man will be so unreasonable as to think that I, that am a Christian king under the Gospel, should be a polygamist and husband to two wives; that I, being the head, should have a divided and monstrous body; or that being

---

[44] Quoted in ibid., 13.

[45] Richard Overton, *An Appeal from the Commons to the Free People*, quoted in A.S.P. Woodhouse, ed. (1951), *Puritanism and Liberty* (Chicago: University of Chicago Press), 323.

[46] Conal Condren (2006), *Argument and Authority in Early Modern England: The Presupposition of Oaths and Offices* (Cambridge: Cambridge University Press); Conal Condren (2009), "Public, Private, and the Idea of 'Public Sphere' in Early-Modern England," *Intellectual History Review* 19, no. 1: 15–28.

the shepherd to so fair a flock (whose fold hath no wall to hedge it but the four seas) should have my flock parted in two.[47]

On the other hand, the domestic, private sphere was often described with the help of public, political metaphors. "The general vocabulary through which the familial or the domestic was conventionally described made its *personae* accountable therefore, in the same terms of moral disapprobation as mayors, priests and princes: husbands might be tyrants, wives and children rebels."[48] If the private was not trustworthy it was mainly because of its secrecy. It suggested the illicit and conspiratorial or "could designate a worthless residue, life at the bottom of the bottle," as John Hitchock for example put it, in *A Sanctuary for Honest Men* (1617).[49] If hypocrisy, as we have seen in Chapter 4, for medieval man meant taking care only of the exterior while neglecting the inner self, "content with the mere clothes of this profession," now the exterior becomes revealing while the interior remains suspicious.[50] Condren concludes that for early modern Englishmen "moral autonomy was neither sought nor celebrated." What mattered, what helps explaining institutional change and state formation in early modern England, was the concept of political or public office, for "no man," as Edmund de Bohun put it in 1684, "is without office, not aspect of life without rule."[51]

And yet, despite an impressive analysis and a wealth of examples gathered from political, literary, and theological sources, Condren fails to grasp what would constitute the most logical explanation: if the distinction between the private and the public started to evanesce in favor of the latter, it was because of the collapse of the *forum internum* into the *forum externum*. All the examples that he offers – and there are several hundreds – start to make sense once one considers this dialectic. *Forum internum* started to lose the 'competition' with *forum externum*. Englishmen started to define themselves exclusively in terms of wills and office. Only with this centrifugal individualism can one understand why "what was private could be no more than the absence of a right in a given situation" and why "the only liberty was liberty of office."[52] Only if the *forum internum* came to be assimilated with *forum externum* can Condren's observations begin to make sense:

We might now need to postulate some inner self as a moving *explanans* for the diversity of social identity, but there is little to suggest people in the early modern world actually

47 Quoted in J.D. Tanner (1930), *Constitutional Documents of the Reign of James I, A.D. 1602–1625, with an Historical Comment* (Cambridge: Cambridge University Press), 26–27.

48 Condren, "Public, Private,'" 26.

49 Condren, *Argument and Authority*, 72, quoting John Hitchock, *A Sanctuary for Honest Men: or an Abstract of Human Wisdom* (1617).

50 Peter Damian, Epistola 153, quoted in Ineke Van't Spijker (2004), *Fictions of the Inner Life: Religious Literature and Formation of the Self in the Eleventh and Twelfth Centuries* (Turnhout: Brepols), 45.

51 Edmund de Bohun, *The Justice of the Peace, His Calling: A Moral Essay* (1684), quoted in Condren, *Argument and Authority*, 54.

52 Condren, *Argument and Authority*, 73.

did so. Rather, what was taken to be a moral person was the constitution of offices. This may seem to us now suggestive of a moral schizophrenia, but to think of it in such terms is itself a case of *petito principii*: it presupposes the very unity we now routinely expect.... Moreover, from what I have outlined of the way in which people wrote of the soul, they left little or no space for selves, or individuals to provide sites for this unity, or to occupy zones of moral autonomy.[53]

The king's case is probably one of the most revealing for this displacement of emphasis from *forum internum* to *forum externum*. In the previous chapter we saw how, even in the case of French centripetal individualism, the king's position remains a particular one. If he ought not to be envied it is because, unlike anyone else, he must sacrifice his *forum internum* for the sake of the *forum externum* and of the public good. In the context of this peculiar British centrifugal movement, the case of the king of England is even more radical. Here, the king's *forum externum* became truly external: It became corporeal. Kantorowicz's observation that the metaphor of the king's two bodies remains a peculiar British one is to be apprehended in this context. "[T]he English judges in the sixteenth century tried to conjoin again what they had separated and declared that the body politic [of the king] was incorporated with the body natural, and vice versa."[54] "At any rate, the theory of 'the King's Two Bodies,' in all its complexity and sometimes scurrilous consistency, was practically absent from the Continent.... Nowhere did the concept of the 'King's Two Bodies' pervade and dominate the juristic thinking so generally and so enduringly as in England, where, not to mention other aspects, that notion had also its important heuristic function in the period of transition from mediaeval to modern political thought."[55] Although Kantarowicz argues that "any effort to 'explain' a historical phenomenon ... remains a hopeless task," he is also eager to point out that the explanation is to be found in a distinct understanding of political representation:

It seems, however, that the notion of the King's Two Bodies cannot be severed from the very early development and the lasting momentum of Parliament in English constitutional thought and practice. Parliament was, by representation, the living 'political body' of the realm. This is to say, the English Parliament was never a *persona ficta* or a *persona repraesentata*, but always a very real *corpus repraesentans*.[56]

I will try to demonstrate in the following pages that Kantorowicz's insight proves correct. Unfortunately, Condren's analysis totally ignores any possible dialectic of the individual and, by focusing on the collapse of the private with the public almost exclusively from the perspective of office holding, he is forced to claim the absence of "zones of moral autonomy." And yet, such a claim has

---

[53] Ibid., 80–81.
[54] Ernst Hartwig Kantorowicz (1957), *The King's Two Bodies: A Study in Mediaeval Political Theology* (Princeton: Princeton University Press), 441.
[55] Ibid., 447.
[56] Ibid.

difficulties explaining a phenomenon that has heavily marked the development of early modern England – the practices of oath-taking, vows, and covenant theology translated in the secular sphere in the language of contractarianism. For Condren, who dedicates almost a third of his book to this topic, this is another proof of the importance of the ethics of the office. And yet to claim, as he does, that no autonomy was involved in such practices is a little bit far-fetched. I argue that far from disappearing because of the collapsing of the two fora, the sphere of moral autonomy that before belonged to the *forum internum* and was informed by reason moved into the *forum externum* and came to be informed predominantly by the will. Taking an oath, argued Selden in 1686, is like taking a bitter pill. It is an act of will and one should not even try to "chew" it. "Now Oaths are so frequent, they should be taken like Pills, swallowed whole; if you chew them you will find them bitter; if you think what you swear, 't'will hardly go down."[57]

On this point, recourse to Hobbes proves quite illuminating. As mentioned in the Introduction, Hobbes was credited by Carl Schmitt and other scholars as well for introducing the distinction between *forum internum* and *forum externum*.[58] When discussing – both in *De cive* (ch. 3) and in the *Leviathan* (ch. 15) "the other laws of nature," he concludes that "a law of nature gives rise to an obligation in *the internal Court* [*in Foro interno*] or in conscience always and everywhere; but in *the external court* [*in foro externo*] it gives rise to obligation only when it can be kept with safety."[59] At first sight, one may think that Hobbes is still working inside the classical dialectic of the two fora. Furthermore, one may even have the impression that, as Montaigne or Charron before him, he is just simplifying the two, presenting *forum internum* as the only forum of authenticity. However, this is to badly misinterpret his intentions. A closer look reveals that far from concentrating his energies on *forum internum*, Hobbes does everything in his power to persuade the reader that, at the end of the day, *forum externum* is everything that matters.

To begin with, in preserving the laws (of nature) the fulfillment of the law may consist in what may appear as its violation – stealing from thieves, for example. But what is more important is that in any conceivable (by Hobbes) situation, *forum internum* would carry no weight when confronted with the requirements of *forum externum*. In the state of nature, it is simply irrational to act according with the dictates of reason, that is, of the *forum internum*: "If

---

[57] Selden, *Table Talk* (1686), para. 94, quoted in Condren, *Argument and Authority*, 233.

[58] Carl Schmitt (1996), *The Leviathan in the State Theory of Thomas Hobbes: Meaning and Failure of a Political Symbol*, foreword and introduction by George Schwab, trans. George Schwab and Erna Hilfstein (Westport, Conn.: Greenwood Press), esp. ch. 5. For a recent emphasis of Hobbes's 'inovation,' see David Ragazzoni (2011), "Identity vs. Representation: What Makes 'the People'? Rethinking Democratic Citizenship through (and Beyond) Carl Schmitt and Hans Kelsen," *Perspectives on Federalism* 3, no. 2.

[59] Thomas Hobbes (1998), *On the Citizen*, ed. and trans. Richard Tuck and Michael Silverthorne (Cambridge: Cambridge University Press), 54.

a few men, more modest than everybody else, practiced the fairness and consideration which reason dictates, and the rest did not do so, they would certainly not be acting rationally," for they would destroy themselves, thus destroying the law of self-preservation.[60] The same argument will be repeated almost ad verbatim in the *Leviathan*.

But the argument won't stop here. In both *De cive* and the *Leviathan*, Hobbes makes clear that if "reason teaches that peace is good," men can never be sure neither about the means, nor about what is actually good. For what man calls 'good' and 'evil' will be subject to disagreements. Thus, the only solution out of this conundrum is – as I will explain in more detail in Chapter 8 – the willing acceptance of a contract that will create not only 'the people' as a whole, but also (and foremost) the authority of an arbitrator. Hobbes's insistence upon 'will' instead of 'reason' is, as we have seen, no accident. Will is the manifestation of *forum externum* and entering a contract is an act of will. Thus, respecting a promise or a contract, even when entered when 'forced' by fear, becomes for Hobbes a necessity.

As was shown in the previous chapter, in early modernity European casuistry embraced the doctrine of mental reservation. Since by that time *forum externum* was apprehended as merely a costume, what mattered was to remain truthful in one's inner self, that is, in one's *forum internum*. The outspoken words carried no weight insofar as they were 'adjusted' by some inner complements. Thus, if a person is robbed on a highway by a band of robbers who make him agree that he will pay a further amount of money if released, he is not bound by his verbalized promise as long as the promise is doubled by a mental reservation. Using exactly the same example, Hobbes is adamant both in *De cive* and in the *Leviathan* that fear or coercion cannot make a promise or a contract invalid. On the contrary, "we are obligated by agreements motivated by fear."[61] One can easily understand now why the British casuists were so horrified by their counterparts. Once one accepts the doctrine of mental reservation, all oaths, contracts, and compromises stand on very shaky foundations and therefore cannot be trusted. Hence, no civil society and no government are possible.

Once the sovereign is created, to will is to act according to the law. 'Conscience' is "a willingness to act in conformity with the judgment of one's sovereign."[62] Put differently, in the state of nature, *forum internum* ought to be ignored, for the sake of self-preservation. Under civil laws, it has to become one with *forum externum*, in accordance with the will of the sovereign. Hence, far from being the 'inventor' of the two fora, as other scholars have it, Hobbes was about to deliver the final modern blow to this delicate dialectic. If, for

---

[60] Ibid., 53.
[61] Ibid., 39. See also *Leviathan*, Book I, 14:27.
[62] David Runciman (2008), *Political Hypocrisy: The Mask of Power, from Hobbes to Orwell and Beyond* (Princeton: Princeton University Press), 32.

the French, *forum externum* became just a costume, while *forum internum* was the sole repository of the true self, for Hobbes the costume is to be taken seriously, for, after everything is said and done, the costume *is* the man.[63] After him, Locke will make a brief reference to *forum internum* in part I of *An Essay Concerning Human Understanding*, chapter 3, only to dismiss the existence of any innate principles. Faced with centrifugal individualism *forum internum* had thrown the towel, will took preeminence over reason, and compromise came to be assimilated with a contract, both of them of a new sort, and both in theory as well as in practice.

6.4. CENTRIFUGAL INDIVIDUALISM, COMPROMISE, AND CONTRACTUALISM

By the beginning of the seventeenth century, in England the language of contractualism was in full flower. As Victoria Kahn observes, "Parliamentary debates, sermons, and theological tracts show an explosion of the language of contracts in these years." She even goes as far as to assert that "[i]n this light, the juridical murder of the king in 1649 appears less as an anomaly than as the logical conclusion of the new discourse of contract and, in particular, of the king's perceived breach of contract in taking up arms against his subjects in 1642. By 1652 Robert Filmer would claim disapprovingly that 'original power by nature in the people ... is the only theme now in fashion.'"[64] Despite being incomplete and rather one-sided, Kahn's description captures well the extent to which the language of contracts dominated British political life. On 1688, the Convention accepted the Parliament's resolution after James II's fall, using an unequivocal contractarian vocabulary. "King James the Second, having endeavored to subvert the Constitution of the Kingdom, by breaking the original Contract between King and People, and by the Advice of Jesuits and other wicked Persons, having violated the fundamental Laws, and having withdrawn Himself out of this Kingdom, has abdicated the Government; and that the Throne is thereby vacant."[65] However, one should notice that the right to "rebellion" was formulated not, as Locke would have had it, under the principles of the social contract, but under the ones of the old-fashioned govermental one, between a people and its rulers. The importance of this distinction will become obvious in the following chapters.

By that time, however, the British contractarian vocabulary had a well-established tradition. In 1627, in the parliamentary debate about the Five

---

[63] I am fully aware that this interpretation of Hobbes is likely to stir some scholarly debates. Yet I side with David Runciman's reading of the Hobbesian handling of the two fora. See further.

[64] Victoria Kahn (2004), *Wayward Contracts: The Crisis of Political Obligation, 1640–1674* (Princeton: Princeton University Press), 3.

[65] *Journal of the House of Lords* (1688–1689), 110, quoted in Martyn P. Thompson (1987), *Ideas of Contract in English Political Thought in the Age of John Locke* (New York and London: Garland Publishing), 12.

Knights Case, the liberty of the subjects, and the habeas corpus, Sir Robert Phillips (or Phelips) stated as a generally accepted fact the reality of the contract between the king and his (voluntary) subjects: "It is well known, the people of this state are under no other subjection, than what they did voluntarily consent unto, by the original contract between king and the people."[66] By the sixteenth century in England the practice of the oath of associations or national covenants was widespread, and it was far from being treated merely as a metaphor or philosophical artifice;[67] it involved actual swearing by actual *individuals*.

Successive Tudor monarchs resort with increasing frequency to nationally subscribed oaths as meaning of testing the religious and political loyalties of their subjects. This process in turn prompted forces opposed to the Tudors' assumption of ecclesiastical supremacy to develop their own counter-oaths. By the end of the sixteenth century, England had turned into a nation in which mass oath taking was an almost customary part of political life and in which even the lowliest members of society were aware of the penalties for swearing falsely.[68]

Thus, religion became intermingled with more secular concerns, not the least of which being the rejection of local allegiances in favor of a national loyalty. "The subscriber was presented as being not only personally involved in the process of religious reformation ... but also as being involved in a secular contract, in which the parliament promised to defend the subjects' rights and liberties in return for their allegiance."[69] By 1602, the conflation of promises (morally binding: "*pacta servanda sunt*") with contracts (legal acts of contracting) became official when common law courts in England started treating broken contracts as breach of promise (Slade's case, extended by *Warbrook v. Griffon* in 1610), promises that before were under the jurisdiction of ecclesiastical courts. "[T]he law was now ready to enforce promises other than those formally recorded," provided there was "some evidence that a contract really existed.... The consideration or inducement must be shown, in return for which the unfulfilled promise was made."[70]

That covenant, contract, and indeed compromise were used interchangeably is proved in a variety of instances. For example, Robert Dudley, Earl of Leicester, a

---

[66] Quoted in Kahn, *Wayward Contracts*, 87.

[67] For what is of interest here, one can at least for now disregard the distinction between 'covenants' and 'contracts.' For two different perspectives on this differentiation, see, e.g., Adela Cortina (2003), *Covenant and Contracts, Politics, Ethics and Religion* (Leuven–Dudley: Peeters), and Kahn, *Wayward Contracts*.

[68] Edward Vallance (2005), *Revolutionary England and the National Covenant: State Oaths, Protestantism and the Political Nation, 1553–1682* (Rochester: Boydell Press), 17. See also Michael Davis (2003), *Actual Social Contract and Political Obligation: A Philosopher's History through Locke*, Studies in the History of Philosophy, vol. 69 (Lewiston: Edwin Mellen Press).

[69] Vallance, *Revolutionary England and the National Covenant*, 5.

[70] Christopher Hill (1983), "Covenant Theology and the Concept of 'A Public Person,'" in *The Collected Essays of Christopher Hill*, vol. 3: *People and Ideas in 17th Century England* (Amherst: University of Massachusetts Press), 301.

fervent partisan of the execution of Queen Mary, is said to have "advised to have her sent into Scotland, and executed on the Borders, yet having compromised his Vote as the major part should determine it, begins to rectifie their method, and puts them upon debate by what Law they should proceed."[71] Clearly, Richard Watson uses compromise in this context as promise, tying compromise even tighter with the will of the majority. As we have seen in Chapter 3, describing a naval incident involving French and British ships, Hamon L'Estrange wrote that the King Charles "having advice of this misemployment of his Ships repugnant to their prime destination *by compromise and mutual contract*, sent an expostulatory message to his Brother, demanding the cause of this violation of his Royal parole, and withall requiring the restitution of his Ships."[72]

Even before incarnation, Christ exercised "all his Offices of King, Priest and Prophet," "by a certain compromise betweext the Father and the Son."[73] Not surprisingly, compromise (or covenant) was seen as essential for maintaining the peace. Thomas Manton (1620–1677) encouraged his readers: "let us compromise all Difference between us and God."[74] Since "one at the Parties in variance is in the earth, the other in Heaven," "the Grounds and the Foundations of this peace ... is by the blood of the overlasting covenant." Christ, therefore, is the Mediator who can "compromise the difference between us and God."[75]

Both secular and religious terms started borrowing from each other's imagery, both emphasizing the role of the individual. Thus, William Perkins, trying to describe why Adam's sins are every man's sins, used the image of a shire represented by an MP: "[A]s in a Parliament whatsoever is done by the burgess of the shire is done by *every person* in the shire."[76] It is speculated that the contractual language of covenant theology was influenced by the growing significance of commercial contracts, as trade developed.[77] One may also argue, following Max Weber, the other way around. Be that as it may, the result is undisputable: the language of contract and promise (compromise) became normal in religious, secular, and political contexts.

The trend continued throughout the seventeenth century with oaths, vows, and covenants. As the tensions between King and Parliament escalated after 1640, so too did the demands for more radical oaths of loyalty (or of association, as they were usually called). Between May 1641 and September 1643 the Long Parliament imposed three main oaths of loyalty: the Protestation, the

---

[71] Richard Watson (1657), *Historicall collections of ecclesiastick affairs in Scotland and politick related to them including the murder of the Cardinal of St. Andrews and the beheading of their Queen Mary in England*, 207.

[72] Hamon L'Estrange (1655), *The reign of King Charles an history faithfully and impartially delivered and disposed into annals*, 57; emphasis added.

[73] Ibid., 174.

[74] Thomas Manton (1693), *A fourth volume containing one hundred and fifty sermons on several texts of Scripture ...*, 147, 690.

[75] Ibid., 690, 961.

[76] Quoted in Kahn, *Wayward Contracts*, 51.

[77] *The Collected Essays of Christopher Hill*, 301.

Vow and Covenant, and the Solemn League and Covenant. There were even proposals for an oath of an extra-parliamentary association, in case the two houses of the parliament decided to soften their position toward the king and his supporters.[78] On June 24, 1643, Charles issued a proclamation condemning the Vow and Covenant (which made no usual claims regarding the defense of the king's person and authority) only to issue three days later his own Sacred Oath or Covenant. Confronted with such a wealth of requests, the Englishmen were forced to seriously consider the implications of actual contracts of allegiances. Some (especially royalists) complained about the imposition of a covenant, arguing that no covenant could be possibly forced, about the age limit being set too low (15 instead of 18, which raised the question of freedom of conscience at such a young age), and so on.[79] The royalist Daniel Featly, for example, argued in 1643 that a forced oath was "a heavy yoke laid upon the Conscience, inconsistent with our Christian Liberty," while Robert Sanderson defined a covenant as a reciprocal contract that had the "voluntary mutuall consent of the Contractors" in making it.[80]

There were many discussions about the proper ways of making such covenants, yet very few disputed their usefulness. For the Pilgrims such contracts were almost a necessity. It is well known, for example, that when the Pilgrims landed in America from the *Mayflower* in November 1620 they resolved: "We do solemnly and mutually, in the presence of God and of one another, covenant and combine ourselves together into a civil body politic." But they were not the only ones. The settlers of Portsmouth did the same thing on January 7, 1638: "We whose names are underwritten do here solemnly in the presence of Jehovah incorporate ourselves into a Bodie Politick, and as He shall help, will submit our persons, lives and estates unto our Lord Jesus Christ." And so did the colonists of Connecticut on January 14 the same year: "We ... doe ... associate and concioyne ourselues to be as one Publike State or Commonwelth and doe, for ourselues and our Successors and such as shall be adionyed tu vs att any time hereafter, enter into Combination and Confederation together," in order to preserve their liberty and the purity of the Gospel of Jesus Christ.[81]

The fact that in the minds of these pilgrims the Body Politic or the Commonwealth was the result of a sum of individual wills is beyond doubt and the references to God are not mere lip service. In Chapter 4 we have seen how the status of the pre-modern man as both a unique person *and* the image of God put in motion a dialectic between uniqueness and conformity, between

---

[78] For more details on this period, see Vallance, *Revolutionary England and the National Covenant*, esp. ch. 2.

[79] Once again, for a wealth of details, see ibid., esp. ch. 3.

[80] Daniel Featley (1661), *The League Illegal* [reprint of letters written in 1643], 2, and Robert Sanderson (1647), *Reasons of the Present Judgment of the University of Oxford*, 2; both are quoted in Vallance, *Revolutionary England and the National Covenant*, 71.

[81] Rhode Island Records, i. 52; Connecticut Records, i. 20–21, quoted in J.W. Gough (1936), *The Social Contract: A Critical Study of Its Development* (Oxford: Clarendon Press), 84. For other examples, see Davis, *Actual Social Contract*.

forum internum and *forum externum*, differently solved on either side of the Channel. For the French, the decision to follow God was but the beginning of a highly personalized journey, one that everyone 'performs' differently. Therefore, while conformity in the *forum externum* – conformity with the requirements of the church or of the powers to be – was assumed as a must resulting from the condition of being a 'member,' freedom, uniqueness, and personal responsibility were undeniable attributes of the *forum internum*, hence the emergence of a centripetal individualism centered on these untransferable attributes. For the English, on the other hand, the confession of faith in Jesus Christ was essentially the only requirement for salvation. Christopher Hill captures well the interplay between the *forum internum* and *forum externum*.

Faith becomes the more important as external material aids to grace (the counters of salvation) lose their usefulness. The relationship between God and man is direct, and emphasis is placed upon promises, mutual covenants between the two parties. That is why the inner state of mind of the Christian was so significant. God is not mocked: in entering into or renewing a covenant it was essential that the intention should be sincere.[82]

Yet the Old Testament covenant between God and 'his people' that served as a model was by now modified in a subtle yet radical way. 'The people' were no longer understood in a corporatist way, but as a collection of individuals. Furthermore, the people could *individually* make a covenant with God, something unthinkable for the classics, for – as I have shown – a contract presupposes the equality of the parties. Even Hobbes stepped back from this idea, arguing that a covenant with God is as impossible as a covenant with a beast, since in the former case one cannot know what God wants (with some exceptions – a lip-service paid to ancient prophets), while in the latter, the beast has no ability to understand the terms of the contract.

Thus, the doctrines of predestination and covenant theology ended up emphasizing precisely what they appear to deny, namely the will of the individual. This "inner of state of mind" was obviously informed by will. "In the logic of covenant theology ... God's gift of grace rectified human incapacity and made a place for will."[83] God accepts the will for the deed. Since no deeds could ever ensure salvation, the willingness to believe became the keystone of faith. "Without a promise there can be no faith," declared Tyndale.[84] (Note how once again contract is assimilated with promise.) *Precisely because* each individual is made after God's image, membership in a church – the true church – was a highly personalized decision. Since one willingly accepted to follow Christ, one must willingly accept the proper ways (i.e., church) to follow him.

Covenant theology thus made room for human agency, even as it seemed to deny it. It authorized scrupulous analysis of the intentions and dispositions of the individual

[82] *The Collected Essays of Christopher Hill*, 302.
[83] Kahn, *Wayward Contracts*, 51.
[84] *The Collected Essays of Christopher Hill*, 302.

believer; it enabled the fallen sinner through the divine gift of a contract; it made the activity of interpreting Scripture an obligation of faith; and it licensed the metaphorical or equitable interpretation of the law.[85]

If, as we have seen, for Montaigne conscience was rightfully entitled to be the harshest judge and guardian of one's true self because of its central position, for his contemporary, William Perkins (*Discourse of Conscience*, 1596), conscience was not only self-accusatory but self-wounding as well. It was, in Kahn's words, "the lawyer of the prosecution": it "stirre[s] up sundrie passions and motions in the heart," especially shame, "sadness and sorrow," "feare" (the attribute of a guilty conscience), "desperation," and "perturbation."[86] Only through grace can the accusing conscience become an excusing conscience, offering joy and serenity. Thanks to this divine grace, *forum internum* could remain at peace while the focus switched to *forum externum*. "The transition was from the ineluctable inheritance of sin, to a definable contractual relationship.... The element of choice, of freedom of will, is restored."[87] Centrifugal individualism was born.

As many scholars have observed, "among English-speaking communities ... on both sides of the Atlantic ... the contract theory of the state seems to have been arrived at much more directly as the result of the development of individualist theory of ecclesiastical organization.... An individualist theory of the state followed naturally from the individualism of their ecclesiastical theory."[88] For the Independents and other separatist Churches it was clear that "when a church was to be gathered, such as desired to be members *made a confession of their faith in the presence of each other and signed a covenant*, obliging themselves to walk together in the order of the gospel, according to certain rules and agreements therein contents."[89] Men voluntarily associated with others to form congregations, in the same way that they contracted to enter into a political society of their choice.[90]

Without entering into all the complexities of the British denominational landscape of the seventeenth century, it would be, however, an exaggeration from a contractualist perspective to put emphasis solely on the churches excluded from the national church.[91] Despite their doctrinal differences, most churchmen from a variety of denominational backgrounds supported the idea of a

---

[85] Kahn, *Wayward Contracts*, 55.

[86] William Perkins (1966), *A Discourse of Conscience*, in *William Perkins*, ed. Thomas F. Merrill (Nieuwkoop, the Netherlands), 39, quoted in Kahn, *Wayward Contracts*, 66.

[87] Ibid., 303.

[88] Gough, *The Social Contract*, 82–83.

[89] D. Neal, *History of the Puritans* (1822), vol. I, p. 103, quoted in Gough, *The Social Contract*, 82; emphasis added.

[90] See also *The Collected Essays of Christopher Hill*, vol. 3, ch. 14.

[91] For the difficulties raised by the very term "puritans," for example, and their role in the Parliament, see Conrad Russell (1979), *Parliaments and English Politics, 1621–1629* (Oxford: Clarendon Press), 26–32.

national covenant. And even though some of them protested about the *form* taken, for example, by the Solemn League and Covenant, they did not dispute the *idea* behind it. Even if the passing of the Covenant troubled 'Independents and Brownists,' there was no explicit repudiation of it, as even the heresiographers conceded. As a matter of fact, these dissenters claimed in fact to follow the true intentions of the Covenant.[92]

The idea of an actual national covenant was taken seriously and politically by both Diggers – of whom the most famous is probably Gerrard Winstanley – and by the Levellers. Winstanley interpreted the Solemn League and Covenant and a social contract that obliged both parties, the people as well as Parliament, because of its reciprocal nature. In *The True Levellers Standard* (1649) he complained that the Parliament had "made the people take a Covenant and Oaths to endeavour a Reformation, and to bring in liberty, every man in his place; and yet while a man is in pursuing of that Covenant, he is imprisoned and oppressed." The Parliament, he argued, should agree to the True Levellers' demands precisely because of their "Covenants and Promises."[93] The reinterpretation of the Solemn League and Covenant by Independent and Leveller writers culminated with the Levellers' proposal, "Agreements of the People." "Just as baptism is the symbol of entry into church covenant, of access to the means of grace, so acceptance in the Agreement of the People was the means by which men (or some men) would have contracted into the refounded English state if the Leveller program had been accepted."[94] This was supposed to be a written constitution to be signed by every single Englishman, not by the Parliament, because "[n]o act parliament is or can be unalterable, and so cannot be sufficient security ... from what another parliament may determine" and because "parliaments are to receive the extent of their power, and trust[,] from those that betrust them."[95] Although the initiative was never realized it was quite seriously debated, and it is indicative not only of the English tendency to take such contracts as seriously and formally as possible, but also of the extent to and seriousness with which they considered the possibility that *every man*, regardless of his status, should be entitled to have an equal voice in elections.

There are many other examples, but in all of them two aspects of this mélange of religion and secularism of the time are constant.[96] First, that this understanding of contract as actual contract helped the transition from understanding the people as a whole to a discrete collection of (politically)

92 For more details on this matter, see Vallance, *Revolutionary England and the National Covenant*, esp. chs. 6 and 8.

93 *The Works of Gerrard Winstanley* (1941), ed. G.H. Sabine (New York), 255–257.

94 *The Collected Essays of Christopher Hill*, vol. 3, p. 301.

95 Don M. Wolfe (1944), *Leveller Manifestoes of the Puritan Revolution* (New York: Thomas Nelson and Sons), 230, quoted in Davis, *Actual Social Contract*, 136.

96 For more details and further examples, see Vallance, *Revolutionary England and the National Covenant*; Gough, *The Social Contract*; Kahn, *Wayward Contracts*.

equal individuals. "I think," said another Leveller, Thomas Rainsborough, "that the poorest he that is in England hath a life to live as the greatest he; and therefore truly, Sir, I think it's clear that every man that is to live under a government ought first by his own consent to put himself under that government."[97] Second, that because of its religious connotations, the contracts came to presuppose a surrender of rights and liberties. In the same way that by entering the covenant with God man accepted voluntary subjection in order to gain true Christian liberty, so in entering the political (or social) contract, man also came to accept that he must surrender his natural liberty (even if only temporarily) by delegating his rights to his representative(s) in exchange for 'civil or federal' liberty.[98] A passage from John Winthrop is revealing in this case:

This liberty is maintained and exercised in a way of subjection to authority; it is of the same kind of liberty wherewith Christ has made us free. The woman's own choice makes such a man her husband; yet being so chosen, he is her lord, and she is subject to him, yet in a way of liberty, not of bondage.... Such is the liberty of the Church under the authority of Christ.... Even so, brethren, it will be between you and your magistrates.[99]

Yet something was lost in this translation from the religious vocabulary to a more secular and increasingly political one. This covenant – or, as we have seen, compromise – was no longer between God and His people as a whole, but between individuals and God and among individuals in front of God. Furthermore, if allegiance to God came naturally somehow (at least to any man of good faith), and the covenant was only acknowledging the *pre-existing* divine authority, in the case of secular contracts the authority was *created* in the process of contracting. A contract *constituted* relations (social, political, etc.) between the parties – it did not merely *acknowledge* them, as was made clear in the trial of Charles I by John Bradshaw, the judge appointed by Parliament.

There is a contract and bargain made between the King and his people, and your oath is taken: and certainly, Sir, the bond is reciprocal; for as you are the liege lord, so they are liege subjects.... This we know now, the one tie, the one bond, is the bind of protection that is due from the sovereign; the other is the bond of subjection that is due from the subject. Sir, if this bond be once broken, farewell sovereignty![100]

Or, as Buckley put it, the reciprocal promise (com-promise) has to be kept by both parties as in the case of the covenant with God. "The Covenant which

---

[97] *Clark Papers*, i. 263, quoted in Gough, *The Social Contract*, 90.
[98] For a more elaborate discussion on this topic, see Kahn, *Wayward Contracts*, esp. ch. 3.
[99] John Winthrop [1908], *Journal (History of New England), 1639–49*, ed. Homer (New York), ii. 238–9, quoted in Gough, *The Social Contract*, 86.
[100] Quoted in C.V. Wedgewood (1964), *Trial of Charles I* (London), 161.

passeth between God and us is like that which is passeth between a king and his people; the king promiseth to rule and govern in mercy and righteousness, and they again promise to obey in loyalty and faithfulness."[101] Once the metaphor of the contract, as Victoria Kahn put it, broke into the secular world, different strategies for its usage were deployed by politicians, journalists, pamphleteers, and the like. "In the course of these struggles, both sides came to understand contract as a powerful metaphor that could be used to loose as well as to bind, to justify resistance, as well as allegiance."[102] Not surprisingly, as Thompson observes, "Jacobite and Tory appeals to contract in fact turn out to be frequently of a very similar kind to many Whig arguments."

Indeed, in the writings of one of the most colorful characters of the period, Robert Ferguson "the Plotter," we find two very popular pamphlets, both apparently written in good faith, both employing arguments based upon the idea that the English constitution embodied a contract between ruler and ruled, but one was a Whig tract written in defense of William of Orange and the other was a Jacobite tract written in defense of the deposed James II. The arguments were of exactly the same form. But the conclusions drawn were diametrically opposed.[103]

"Practically all the legal arguments for and against the Revolution were at some time or another defended by reference to contract."[104] Historians, theologians, lawyers, and philosophers – almost all made reference to the language of contract. Contract came to be such a prominent term in the political literature of seventeenth century England that even its more vehement critics were forced to mold their arguments in the shape imposed by it. James I, for example (tutored in his youth by the contract theorist George Buchanan), deployed an early (and shrewd) attack, analyzing the very possibility that kingship was created through some sort of contract. Instead of attacking the theory itself, the king went after its consequences: who was to judge a breach in such a contract? In other words, if parties are equal, who shall be the impartial *compromissarius*? Without provisions for a lawful trial, he argued, such contract cannot be brought to bear, unless "*every man* may be both party and judge in his own case, which is absurd."[105] He was among the first forced to react to the popularity of contractualist language. As will be shown in Chapter 8, two other contenders in the intellectual field, patriarchalism and republicanism, could no longer avoid the contractualist challenge. One way or another, they were forced to respond.

[101] P. Buckley, "The Gospel-Covenant: Or the Covenant of Grace Opened" (1646), 435–436, quoted in *The Collected Essays of Christopher Hill*, vol. 3, p. 304.
[102] Kahn, *Wayward Contracts*, 85.
[103] Thompson, *Ideas of Contract*, 15.
[104] Ibid., 33.
[105] Cited in Robert Filmer (1949), *Patriarcha and Other Political Works*, ed. P. Laslett (Oxford: Blackwell), 93; emphasis added.

6.5. PARLIAMENT AND ASCENDING REPRESENTATION

One has now to consider the remaining preconditions of compromise, namely the willingness to accept the risks involved in third-party arbitration and the acknowledged authority of the arbitrators. To do this, one has to turn to what Sir Thomas Smith in *De republica anglorum* defines as being "the most high and absolute power of the realme of Englande"[106] – Parliament, that is, "the ultimate theater of discourse in early modern England."[107] After all, as we have already seen, to accept a *compromissarium* is, simply put, to accept and to trust not just an arbiter but also a 'representative,' especially when more than one *compromissarius* is involved in the arbitration. And what better example of a large-scale representation of the 'entire realm' was there than Parliament? Again, what we have to look for specifically are proofs that during sixteenth and seventeenth century England, both representatives and represented understood representation as representation of individuals from which the authority to represent was derived, not as representation of a collective body or of a higher principle – such as, in France, *Dieu, L'Etat, le peuple, Les Etates, Parlements*, and so forth. If this proves to be the case, then the British politicization of compromise appears as a logical development. If free and equal individuals do not just agree upon one or several representatives, but also concede *faute de mieux* to provide these representatives with their authority, then for the first time the very process of representation becomes a generalized compromise on an unprecedented scale. Furthermore, once the parties provide the authority of the arbiter, this authority becomes undisputable.

One can speculate *ad nauseam* if this peculiar British individualism is responsible for the centrality and endurance of the British Parliament or if the relationship of causality is to be read the other way around. Although fascinating, however, this question remains out of the scope of this inquiry. As far as the history of compromise is concerned it is of little interest if British legal egalitarian individualism has been the cause or the result of the early development of the system of representation. As the usage of compromise began to differ on either side of the English Channel only in the sixteenth century, this is the period from which our investigation ought to begin.

Fortunately, plenty of historical documents dating from that period are extant. The same Thomas Smith who considered the Parliament "the absolute power" of the realm in 1565 has a specification that is nowhere to be found in the French documents of the time regarding political representation: "[E]*verie* Englishman is entended to be there present, either in person or by procuration and attornies ... [a]nd the consent of the Parliament is taken to be *every man's*

---

[106] Smith, *De republica anglorum*, 48.
[107] Zaller, *The Discourse of Legitimacy*, 473.

consent."[108] By that time, this was not necessarily a breakground idea. Citing plenty of historical evidence, Edmund S. Morgan argues that "representation in England began before representative government or the sovereignty of the people were thought of":

> It began in the thirteenth century as a mode of insuring or facilitating, and eventually of obtaining, consent to the king's government. The king summoned representatives from counties and boroughs to come to his Parliament armed with power of attorney to bind their constituents to whatever taxes or laws they agreed to. The power of attorney had to be complete (plena potestas), so that the representative could not plead that he must go back and consult his constituents. His consent, given in Parliament, must be as much theirs *as if they had come in person.*[109]

By the fourteenth century the summoning of commoners to Parliament was regarded as obligatory. Bicameralism developed slowly but surely. The English transfer of power between King and Parliament was a gradual one, marked by a series of ups and downs on each side, depending on the particular conjuncture, yet the direction was unmistakably from King to Parliament. By the fifteenth century, matters had come to such a point that Sir John Fortescue wrote several works on law and government meant to persuade not just the young prince Edward but a larger audience that England, being a *dominium politicum et regale,* was superior to other kingdoms, especially France, which was a mere *dominium regale.* This is not say that the King of England had less power, if unlike the King of France he cannot "by himself or by his ministers, impose tallages, subsidies, or any other burdens whatever on his subjects, nor change their laws, nor make new ones, *without the concession or assent of his whole realm expressed in his parliament*" – quite the contrary.[110] By acting politically, not only does he act with a view to the public good, but he is also compelled to control his own passions and "who can be freer and more powerful than he who is able to vanquish not only others but also himself?" "Hence, Prince, it is evident to you, *from the practical effects*, that your ancestors, who sought to cast aside political government, not only could have obtained, as they wished, a greater power than they had, but would have exposed their own welfare, and the welfare of the realm, to great risk and danger."[111] Suffice it to compare, he argued, the lives of Englishmen and Frenchmen in order to arrive at the same conclusion.

By the sixteenth and early seventeenth centuries, the absolute power of kings came to be challenged, first accidentally, then increasingly programmatically,

---

[108] Quoted in Hannah Fenichel Pitkin (1967), *The Concept of Representation* (Los Angeles: University of California Press), 246.

[109] Edmund S. Morgan (1988), *Inventing the People: The Rise of Popular Sovereignty in England and America* (New York and London: W.W. Norton), 39; emphasis added.

[110] Sir John Fortescue (1997), *On the Laws and Governance of England*, ed. Shelley Lockwood (Cambdridge: Cambridge University Press), 52; emphasis added.

[111] Ibid., 54; emphasis added.

by the authority of the Parliament, and thus of 'the people.' A perfect metaphor is the judo technique of using your adversary's strength to your own advantage. On the one hand, "the Tudors, seeking a counterpoise to the baronage, had done their best to elevate the country gentry and the commercial classes into political importance, and during the sixteenth century these classes had steadily improved their position."[112] On the other hand, by elevating the king to unprecedented heights, Parliament in effect isolated him from the rest of his subjects and above all from Parliament.[113]

The concept of 'the King in Parliament' provided a rather smooth transition. Words are dangerous fictions, as Morgan would have put it. Conceived initially to provide the king's decisions with more authority (and allow King Henry to get a divorce), the idea that only in Parliament would the king have full *potestas* was filled with momentous possibilities, and gradually Parliament squeezed every advantage out of it. For if it was only in Parliament that the king could enjoy his full authority, the logical implication was that, fancy words aside, it was Parliament who represented the ultimate source of authority – and, by consequence, the 'people.' Slowly but surely, *dominium politicum* took over *dominium royale*. The only question remaining in suspense was "what kind of people?" – the people in the organic, French understanding, or people understood as a collection of individuals? Hanging on the answer to this question was the entire concept of political representation.

The transfer of power was doubled by an overlooked transition from 'communities' to 'individuals.' A writ from 1290, from example, specified that the knights summoned at the Court should be empowered "to consent for themselves and for the whole community of the county (*pro se e tota communitate cimitatus illa*)."[114] The distinction between representing 'individuals' and representing 'communities' was not yet seen as being as important and revolutionary as we see it today. But in 1593, Richard Hooker points out concerning consent that "not only [do] they give [it] who personally declare their assent by voice, sign, or act, but also when others do it in their names by right originally at the least derived from them."[115] The transfer of authority from each individual to his representative was by then complete.

The way in which an individual was accepted to represent other individuals "is not altogether clear." "It is possible," speculates Morgan, "that originally a representative could consent only in the name of individuals who specifically empowered him."[116] As an indirect proof he offers the example of the first representative assemblies gathered in England's colony of Maryland in the

---

[112] Tanner, *Constitutional Documents*, 200.
[113] See Morgan, *Inventing the People*, ch. 1.
[114] *Calendar of the Close Rolls Preserved in the Public Record Office ... Edward I* (London, 1900–1908), 135–136 (June 14, 1290), quoted in Morgan, *Inventing the People*, 41.
[115] Richard Hooker (1965), *The Law of Ecclesiastical Polity* (London: Everyman Library), 194.
[116] Morgan, *Inventing the People*, 39.

1630s. In the 1638 assembly "the records show that some free men attended in person while others delegated representation, each of whom was entitled to his own vote and also to all the votes of those who selected him as their representative."[117] Yet by the 1640s the assembly came to be seen as a strictly representative body in which each representative was selected by a majority of votes from his community, and was supposed to represent everyone from that community.

As these elections became increasingly contested – another English peculiarity at that time – so did increased awareness of the fact that an electorate existed and numbers counted. Because of the increasing social mobility unparalleled anywhere else in Europe, the electoral franchise increased as well.[118] "Politicians both locally and in the House of Commons displayed great readiness to allow more and more people in to vote in the towns."[119] Electoral strategies begin to develop. Candidates started to vie for votes, increasing the awareness of individuals' political weight. By the seventeenth century "political consensus and the patronage system broke down, elections and contests ensued, and a surprisingly large social group became involved in legitimate politics."[120] The entire political process became centered on the individual. And from representing individuals to enjoying their authority is but a small step. Richard Tuck rightly emphasizes the peculiar "extent to which individuals were invested with rights that they might surrender them absolutely to the sovereign" – be it the king, Parliament, or both.[121]

Because of the way in which Parliament came to be understood, the balance was tilted in favor of the individual. Statute creations helped erode the borders between public and private interests. Once more the emphasis switched from the private to the public. "It was ... not only possible but essential to represent particular interests in Parliament as public and universal ones."[122]

Since all the acts arose from petitioning the king, all partook of the common front of justice. In this sense the grievance of the whole land *might be construed as that of the single individual multiplied many times over.* Justice was divided among many but indivisible in itself. And since the king was inseparably united with Parliament, the justice done there was the act of the whole land even when it was extended to only a single individual.... The fact that legislation could and did derive from the plaints of the humble no less (if rather less often) than from the interests of the great, from the

---

[117] Ibid., 40.
[118] For a wealth of details on these aspects, see Hirst, *The Representative of the People?*; see also John K. Gruenfelder (1981), *Influence in Early Stuart Elections, 1604–1640* (Columbus: Ohio State University Press).
[119] Hirst, *The Representative of the People?* 7.
[120] Ibid., 4.
[121] Richard Tuck (1980), *Natural Rights Theories: Their Origins and Development* (Cambridge: Cambridge University Press), mentioned also in J.G.A. Pocock (1985) *Virtue, Commerce and History* (Cambridge: Cambridge University Press), 45.
[122] Zaller, *The Discourse of Legitimacy*, 475.

community of the realm as well as from the crown, made it a collectively and uniquely comprehensive expression of the will of all.[123]

During the seventeenth century, the Royalists themselves contributed to the dismissal of the idea of 'the whole people' being represented, "for the people, to speak truly and properly, is a thing or body in continuall [*sic*] alteration and change, it never continues one minute the same, *being composed of a multitude of parts*, whereof divers continually decay and perish, and others renew and succeed their places."[124] 'The people,' most of them argued, was but a fiction, an ever-changing collection of individuals. And if we are to take seriously the idea that individuals delegated whatever powers they possessed to the Parliament, it followed that they could also revoke them. In a speech to the Parliament, Richard Overton makes this exact claim:

While the betrusted are dischargers of their trust it remained in their hands, but no sooner the betrusted betray and forfeit their trust but (as all things else in dissolution) it returneth from whence it came, even to the hands of the trusters. For all just human powers are but betrusted, conferred, and coveyed by joint and common consent; for to every individual in nature is given an individual property by nature, not to be invaded and usurped by any ... for every one as he is himself hath a self property – else he could not be himself – and on this no second may presume without consent.[125]

In 1648, a group of "gentlemen and Freeholders" from a dozen counties, eight cities, and fifty-two boroughs did precisely that. They "addressed their representatives by name, repudiated their actions, and declared that they did 'revoke and resume all that trust, power and authority we formerly delegated and committed to them.'"[126]

That by that time the idea of 'people' was no longer understood as an organic whole but instead as a collection of individuals is proved by a variety of sources. For example, the supporters of religious freedom arguing against the parliamentary regulation of religion made clear that "the people of a nation" are nothing but free individuals. Since a man did not entrust Parliament with the power of regulating religion, Parliament has no right to do so.

The people of a Nation [wrote Walvyn in 1645] in chusing of a Parliament cannot confer more than that power which was justly in themselves; the plain rule being this: That which a man may not voluntarily binde himselfe to doe without sinne: That he cannot entrust or refer unto the ordering of any other.[127]

---

[123] Ibid., 475–476; emphasis added.

[124] Dudley Digges (1643), *A Review of the Observations upon some of his Majesties late Answers and Expresses* (Oxford), 4, quoted in Morgan, *Inventing the People*, 61; emphasis added.

[125] Richard Overton, *An Appeal from the Commons to the Free People*, quoted in Woodhouse, *Puritanism and Liberty*, 323.

[126] *A Remonstrance and Declaration of Several Counties, Cities and Burroughs* (London, 1648), 8, quoted in Morgan, *Inventing the People*, 63.

[127] *A Helpe to the right understanding of a Discourse concerning Independency* (London, 1644/5), 4, quoted in Morgan, *Inventing the People*, 70.

Some, such as Sir Mathew Hale, would still argue in a classical vein that "the community considered as a community is a distinct thing from the particular persons that are integral to that community," but most Englishmen would agree with Richard Cumberlain, who asserted that Hobbes's egoism is not, in effect, opposed to the common good. "The several kinds of public good are no other than (but exactly the same with) the good of the individuals."[128] The public good became the collection of individual goods. The community became the sum of its individuals. As a result, what was before a representation of the entire *populus*, or at least of a significant part of it (baronage, shires, communes, etc.) *as a whole*, had become a representation (virtual, to be sure) of *every* single subject.[129] And from *representing* individuals to *deriving authority* from them is but a short step.[130] By the middle of the seventeenth century it was clear to all parties that the political battles to follow would center on the individual as the provider *par excellence* of political authority. *He* was the one giving away his power, rights, or authority and thus empowering the political leaders, be they kings or members of the Parliament.

In the Succession Act of 1604 (*A most joyful and just recognition of the immediate, lawful, and undoubted Succession, Descent, and Right of the Crown*), the members of the parliament present themselves as the embodiment and representatives of the whole realm and of every "particular member" in it:

Upon the knees of our hearts [we] agnize our most constant faith, obedience, and loyalty to your Majesty and your royal progeny as in this High Court of Parliament, where all the whole body of the realm, and every particular member thereof, either in person or by representation (upon their own free elections), are by laws of this realm deemed to be personally represented.[131]

The humble tone, typical for the time, cannot cover the underlying importance of Parliament as the forum where the "whole body of the realm, and every particular member thereof" was to be considered present by representation. Although not always clear, the transfer from geographical representation ("our country, cities, and boroughs, who hath sent us hither not ignorant or uninstructed of their griefs, of their desires, and hopes") to the individual one ("we, the knights, citizens, and burgesses of the House of Commons

---

[128] Both Hale and Cumberlain are quoted in J.R. Western (1985), *Monarchy and Revolution: The English State in the 1680s* (London: Macmillan), 28.

[129] See, e.g., Eric Voegelin (1952), *The New Science of Politics* (Chicago: University of Chicago Press), 38–39.

[130] Morgan makes a similar observation in *Inventing the People*, 48. And yet by overlooking the essential difference between representing 'the people' and representing 'each and every single individual,' he formulates it differently: "But it was only a short step from representing *the whole people* to deriving authority from *them*." The coupling of 'the whole' with 'them' instead of 'it' is yet another proof of this endurable confusion.

[131] Tanner, *Constitutional Documents*, 11.

assembled in Parliament, and in the name of the whole commons of the realm of England") is rather obvious.[132] The emphasis switched from rationality to the will of the majority. Already by 1566, in his *De republica anglorum*, Sir Thomas Smith reported as a well-established principle not requiring further explanation that in both houses "as the more number doth agree, so it is agreed on, or dashed."[133] Deliberative reason lost preeminence when confronted with the 'arithmetical machine' counting individual wills.[134] "No other kingdom in Europe achieved anything quite like it for another two centuries."[135]

Rousseau's later distinction between the "will of all" and the "general will" represents an excellent exemplification of the difference between 'people' as body and 'people' as a collection of individuals. If the "will of all" is, as Rousseau will claim, a sum of individual wills, the pluses and the minuses will cancel each other out. An insufficiently informed political body, he argued, will break down in "intrigues and partial associations," and deliberation, instead of helping to formulate the general will, will prove self-destructive. To properly understand the British propensity for compromise, it is essential not to disregard such distinctions. Only if British representation came to be understood as representation of equal individuals, providers of authority for their respective arbiters, could compromise have possibly been assumed as the political practice *par excellence*. Only in that case was there nothing to fear in a compromise. The parties involved in an otherwise unsolvable argument were equal, while the authority of the *compromissores* was beyond doubt, since it was created in the very process of compromising.

This was the time when, as Pocock observed, in England the 'vocabulary of virtues' made ever more room for the 'vocabulary of rights,' the language of liberalism. If seventeenth century England was the time "of a heightened awareness of the dialectic between authority and liberty in both the politics and the political thinking of the period," it was precisely because of the newly created distance between the freedom of the individual and the political sphere. By giving away his rights, the individual became the source of king or/and parliament's authority, and yet "sovereignty was extra-civic, and the citizen came to be defined not by his actions and virtues, but by rights to and in things." Under these circumstances, his liberty was essentially a negative one – to be protected as a person and as a proprietor by the sovereign. Having his rights protected, the individual was eager to distance himself from politics. Or virtue, which requires "active self-rule," "cannot be reduced to matter of

---

[132] *Form of Apology and Satisfaction* (20 June 1604), quoted in Tanner, *Constitutional Documents*, 220–221. See also "with these minds, dread Sovereign, your Commons of England, represented in us their knights, citizens, and burgesses," 218.

[133] Smith, *De republica anglorum*, 55.

[134] One may argue that since 'reason' is such an elusive concept, the concept of will is meant to solve otherwise irreconcilable positions. However, a closer look at the concept of will, as I have tried to suggest, proves it at least as hard to define and manage.

[135] Davis, *Actual Social Contract*, 105.

right."[136] Virtue cannot be compromised, for it cannot be arbitrated – by its nature, it "may be developed, but cannot be distributed."[137] As J. Peter Euben remarks: "If politics is a partnership in virtue, how could I designate someone to be virtuous for me?"[138] If in the language of virtue representation "makes no sense," it appears suitable in the language of rights. Unlike virtue, rights can be delegated or trusted to someone else.

6.6. COMPROMISE AS POLITICAL PRACTICE

Words are powerful tools. The ways in which we use them shape our practices and compromise is no exception. The peculiar praise of compromise in England was doubled by the penchant for compromise observed in British politics from the end of the sixteenth century all the way through the seventeenth and beyond. Entering into all of the political intricacies of a period marked by religious and civil wars, the beheading of a king, an interregnum, and like events would be a futile enterprise. There is an impressive literature dealing with this period and scholars still argue about how to interpret the ever-mounting facts. Thankfully, the academic wars between revisionist and anti-revisionist scholars have waned and both camps agree that there is much to learn from the others' findings and interpretations. Hopefully, the following pages will further contribute to this process. If, despite their differences, revisionists and anti-revisionists agree that paradoxically enough this 'revolutionary' period was characterized not only by a surprisingly 'modest' bloodshed compared with the rest of Europe, while the revolutionaries themselves are characterized as 'reluctant revolutionaries,' it might be that the explanation is to be found at least partially in this new discovery of compromise as a generalized political practice.

It is by now generally accepted that Parliament was so successful compared with the French General Estates because it was able to overcome the ideological rifts (political, regional, and religious) that paralyzed its counterpart across the Channel. As, to his merit, DeLolme already emphasized by the eighteenth century, "England was not, like France, an aggregation of different Sovereignties: it formed but one State.... The same laws, the same kind of dependence, the same interests, prevailed through the whole."[139] If the French Estates had to compete not only with the Parlements but also with the regional Estates, the British MPs acquired much earlier the conscience of representing not a specific borough but each Englishman at a national level. "Had it been, like France, divided into several distinct dominions, it would also have had several

---

[136] Pocock, *Virtue, Commerce and History*, esp. the chapter "Virtues, Rights, and Manners."
[137] Pocock, *Virtue, Commerce and History*, 43.
[138] Peter J. Euben (1989), "Corruption" in *Political Innovation and Conceptual Change*, ed. Terrence Ball, James Farr, and Russel L. Hanson (Cambridge: Cambridge University Press), 227.
[139] DeLolme, *The Constitution of England*, 33.

National Assemblies. These Assemblies, being convened at different times and places, for this and other reasons, never could have been acted in concert."[140] "None of the three Elizabethan parliamentary theorists, Sir Thomas Smith, William Lambarde and John Hooker, identified MPs as the representatives of a particular body of electors. As John Hooker said: 'But in the Knights, Citizens and Burgesses: are represented the Commons of the whole Realme, and every of these giveth not consent onely for him self; both for all those also for whom he is sent.'"[141] It is generally believed that Edmund Burke was the first to assert the independence of the representative from his particular constituency and an imperative mandate; however, as Owen Ulph has demonstrated, the idea was present in England as early as the thirteenth century: "[T]here knights have been summoned from each of our counties … in order to deliberate about *the common affairs of our kingdom.*" Again, "we must hold a deliberation … to establish full assurance of peace and tranquility for the honor of God and *the advantage of the whole kingdom,*" and so on.[142]

Furthermore, if the Frenchmen were rather reticent in participating in the assemblies of the Estates (mainly from financial concerns), for their English counterparts to be 'of the parliament' was "a matchless attraction." It meant to be "at the heart of politics, and listen to famous men speaking in the House; to gather news from all quarters of the kingdom and the world. Such a one stood a tip-toe among his neighbours in his return home."[143] The fascination of being at the center of a national representative institution and the influence that came with it did not prevent internal conflicts inside Parliament. But, unlike in France, such conflicts did not coalesce into ideological lines of fracture. As Conrad Russell argued with plenty of examples, "the court-country, or government opposition, split assumed by Parliamentary historians was not only institutionally impossible … – it was also ideologically impossible."[144] Faced with the evidence, even anti-revisionist scholars were forced to accept that although disagreements existed, they did not revolve around matters of principles, but were argued on prosaic, even quotidian matters – war, taxes, ministerial behavior, and the like. If there was an opposition it was one of 'methods,' not of principles, and what method is more suited to solve prosaic disagreements than compromise?[145] Even if one accepts, as does Glenn

---

[140] Ibid., 39.

[141] D.M. Dean and N.L. Jones (1990), introduction to *The Parliaments of Elizabethan England*, ed. D.M. Dean and N.L. Jones (Oxford: Basil Blackwell), 2; see also P.S. Lewis (1962), "The Failure of the French Medieval Estates," *Past and Present Society* 23: 2–24.

[142] Owen Ulph (1951), "The Mandate System and Representation to the Estates General under the Old Regime," *Journal of Modern History* 23, no. 3: 225; emphasis added.

[143] Sir John Neale, *Commons*, 150, quoted in Dean and Jones, *The Parliaments of Elizabethan England*, 6.

[144] Conrad Russell (1979), *Parliaments and English Politics, 1621–1629* (Oxford: Clarendon Press), 9.

[145] Theodore K. Rabb (1981), "The Role of the Commons," *Past and Present Society* 92: 55–78.

Burgess, that there were some principled conflicts, they did not escalate into actual political confrontations. "In the (practical) conflicts between supporters of government policy and opponents of it the issues dividing the two groups were not theoretical. Such theoretical differences as existed were manifest *within* the government (i.e., the Privy Council)."[146] The Commons were forced to compromise among themselves and with the Court and the House of Lords, as the best way to get things done was with the help of a powerful patron, not by going against one. Thus, early Stuart Englishmen, "when they did seek theoretical or ideological justification for their action," sought it in order to solve disputes over particular goals and strategies, rather than theoretical disagreements. "That is to say that conflicts of ideas tended to be over policy rather than over first principles (by which is meant the nature and extent of political obedience)."[147]

The religious differences that proved so toxic for the French Estates of the late 1500s moved the English Parliament instead toward a more secular line of argumentation. "By the 1590s there were signs that irreconcilable theological differences over the purpose and role of government were increasingly making secular considerations the only acceptable way of justifying legislation." This was not mere coincidence or a happy accident. As I have tried to show before, "as the relationship between people and their God became increasingly individualistic, there was less and less need for forcing the community to conform to God's laws." For example, the debates over usury between 1571 and 1640 demonstrate that although biblical arguments and the laws of God were still used, they were mostly used to drape more secular persuasions.[148]

When the Arminian dispute – the first serious ideological and religious fracture – arose in the late 1620s, there were still attempts to find a compromise. Conrad Russell was even more accurate than he believed when he observed: "The one area of common ground through the whole House was the desire for 'accommodation': the Lords, as politicians, wanted to achieve compromise." If they failed it was not "unfortunately," as Russell had it. It was something meant to happen *precisely* because, as he unwittingly observed, "the hardest to bring to a compromise is one about the ultimate source of authority," that is, to find an undisputable *compromissarius*.[149] The British success of the contractarian theory as a method to solve this otherwise insoluble dilemma was nothing else but the solution of the problem of ascending representation, creating through delegation or trust the authority of the arbitrator (or *compromissarius*).

It was a lesson learned the hard way. Because a compromise over the arbitrator proved impossible, in 1629 Parliament was abruptly dismissed for the next

---

[146] Glenn Burgess (1993), *The Politics of the Ancient Constitution: An Introduction to English Political Thought, 1603–1642* (University Park: Pennsylvania State University Press), 112.

[147] Ibid., 169–170.

[148] Dean and Jones, introduction, 12.

[149] Russell, *Parliaments and English Politics*, 371.

eleven years. Yet although in this period many of the leading members of both the House of Lords and the House of Commons died, their ideas did not die with them.[150] Without winning the trust of the electorate in the 1620s, the success of the Long Parliament in raising an army (which the king proved unable to do against the "popish" Irish rebellion) could not have been possible.[151] The penetration of Arminianism to the highest levels of the church – Richard Montagu was made bishop in 1628 and the bishop of London, William Laud, became archbishop of Canterbury in 1633 – prompted a Puritan counterreaction.

It was a paradoxical situation, as John Selden observed in his *Table Talk*. The Puritans, he wrote, "who will allow no free will, but God does all," permitted "the subject his liberty to do or not to do, notwithstanding the king, the God upon earth." On the other hand, "the Arminians, who hold we have free-will, yet say, when we come to the king there must be all obedience, and no liberty must be stood for."[152] This apparently schizophrenic situation makes sense only in light of the dialectic of the two fora. The Arminians were rightfully accused of being "popish," but for the wrong reasons. They did not want to restore the authority of the Pope over the church, but since like the Catholics they allowed freedom in the *forum internum*, they also had to militate for conformity with the powers to be in the *forum externum*. On the other hand, as we have seen, for Calvinists the doctrine of predestination put no emphasis on the *forum internum*. The only 'proof' of salvation was to be discovered in the *forum externum*. As a result, will was not lost by the doctrine of predestination – it was redirected. Therefore, the transformation of centripetal millenarianism into a centrifugal one that so puzzles scholars makes perfect sense in the light of the centrifugal individualism that characterized seventeenth century England.[153]

Although scholars still dispute whether Arminianism was the cause of or just an alibi for the civil war that followed the Long Parliament, it is quite clear that Parliament and king were bound to clash.[154] Even if as late as 1642 "many men yearned for a return to the golden days of Elizabethan compromise and strove to keep peace in their counties," civil war was no longer avoidable.[155] For Englishmen, as shown in the parable of *The Spider and the Flie*, it became clear that the only alternative to compromise remained open violence. The perspective was frightful enough that the Restoration was seen, at least by the Presbyterians, as the compromise needed for the restoration of peace. And even

---

[150] Ibid., 427–428.
[151] Ibid., 432.
[152] John Selden (1892), *Table Talk*, ed. S. Reynold (Oxford), 71, quoted in William M. Lamont (1993), "The Puritan Revolution: A Historiographical Essay," in Pocock, *The Varieties of British Political Thought*, 126–127.
[153] Lamont, "The Puritan Revolution," 120.
[154] For a survey of this scholarly dispute, see ibid., 123–125.
[155] Johann P. Sommerville (1992), "The Liberty of the Subject," in Hexter, *Parliament and Liberty*, 58.

if the Arminians of the Church of England came back with a vengeful agenda, there was nothing it could do to avoid a religious compromise. By 1660 the multiplication of religious sects in England was at an unprecedented level, so in his Declaration of Breda Charles accepted that "no man shall be disquieted or called into question for differences of opinion in matter of religion which do not disturb the peace of the kingdom."[156]

From the Restoration through the Revolution, the rhetoric became increasingly more conservative and politically restrained. "The reason for the shift was that a powerful fear of another civil war operated through the remainder of the century to temper the language of the opposition."[157] Not surprising, by the mid-1680s Lord Halifax could theoretically defend what before had been used as an insult – *The Character of a Trimmer*.[158] In 1682, a Tory supporter, Sir Robert L'Estrange (not to be mistaken with Hammon L'Estrange), probably the most prolific and successful journalist of the late seventeenth century, pointed out to an imaginary character, the Trimmer, that not all agreements (read 'compromises') are necessarily good as long as they solve conflicts. A 'good' agreement should be 'in the right,' not 'in the wrong.' The method cannot trump the principle.

[November 15, 1682]

Trimmer: Is it not a Christian *office* to endeavor a fair understanding betwixt party and party; and to bring differences and disputes into a state of accommodation?

Observator: Yes, it is so; provided you make your business to procure an agreement *in the right, not in the wrong; and in the truth, and reason of the matter*; not in a conspiracy, or faction; for otherwise the more united, the worse...

As mentioned before, the connection between this penchant toward compromise and the ascending understanding of representation as representation of the multitude, not of the whole, is captured by the Observator in another conversation with the Trimmer, dated February 10, 1683:

The people are the nation; and the nation are the people: but do we speak of the multitude, or of the community? If of the community, why do ye not rather call it government? If of the multitude; they have no right of acting, judging, or interposing, otherwise than in obedience and submission to the rules. So that you are telling of people that they may do this or that; is the same thing with telling them, that if they don't like their laws and their governors, they may provide better, and shift for themselves: now here's a sedition, not only licensed, but encouraged: for being couched in this trimming, middling way; it speaks plain English to the rabble.[159]

---

[156] J.G.A. Pocock and Gordon J. Schochet (1993), "Interregnum and Restoration," in Pocock, *The Varieties of British Political Thought*, 173.

[157] Howard Nenner (1993), "The Later Stuart Age," in Pocock, *The Varieties of British Political Thought*, 182.

[158] The *Character of a Trimmer* was written in defense of the species in 1684 and was published in 1688.

[159] Quoted in Steven C.A. Pincus (2006), *England's Glorious Revolution, 1688–1689: A Brief History with Documents* (New York: Palgrave Macmillan), 143.

The fragment captures well the reasons why the classical, descending understanding of representation came to be perceived as outdated and was bound to lose the battle with the modern, ascending one: once the dialectic of the individual between the two fora was lost and man came to be apprehended (and to apprehend himself) as equally unidimensional, the claim that there is a difference between the people as a whole and the people as a collection of individuals, together with the claim that not everyone is equally entitled to speak in the name of the people, lost all traction. It simply did not make any sense.

6.7. THE GLORIOUS COMPROMISE

So powerful was the British penchant for compromise that, as Edmund Burke had it, 1688–1689 was "a revolution not made, but prevented." In his *History of England* written in 1875, the German scholar Leopold von Ranke also concluded that the English intellect was "as far removed from the keen dialectic of the French as from the world-embracing ideology of the Germans; it has a narrow horizon; but it knows how to comprehend and satisfy the requirements of the moment with circumspection and great practical sense."[160] Even today, most scholars would agree that the 1688 'revolution' was in effect "a compromise between Whig and Tory attitudes toward monarchy" and/or a compromise between the claims of the Parliament and the monarchical requests.[161] They are closer to the truth than they ever imagined. It is no accident if almost every stage of the settlement was characterized as a compromise, beginning with William's Declaration of Rights, meant to avoid the alienation of either the Whigs or the Tories.[162] Almost everyone agrees that references to the common law and 'the ancient constitution' proved elastic enough to be used not only by supporters of the parliamentary sovereignty but also by the supporters of the divine rights of kings; not only by the advocates of traditions, but also for the contractarian theorists. "It is, in fact, an irony of seventeenth-century discourse that fundamental law managed to lead an exceedingly protean life all the while that it stood as a monument to immutability."[163] As a result, the

---

[160] Edmund Burke (1837), "Speech on the Army Estimates, 1790," in *The Works of Edmund Burke* (Oxford), I, 454; Leopold von Ranke (1875), *A History of England, Principally in the Seventeenth Century* (Oxford), IV, 500; both quoted in Nenner, "The Later Stuart Age," 183.

[161] Western, *Monarchy and Revolution*; J.R. Jones (1972), *The Revolution of 1688 in England* (London); E.A. Reitan (1970), "From Revenue to Civil List: 1689–1702: The Revolution Settlement and the 'Mixed and Balanced' Constitution," *Historical Journal* 13, no. 4: 571–588; Mark Goldie (1977), "Edmund Bohun and Jus Gentium in Revolution Debate, 1689–1693," *Historical Journal* 20, no. 3: 569–586.

[162] Lois Schwoerer (1981), *The Declaration of Rights, 1689* (Baltimore, Md.: Johns Hopkins University Press); Jonathan Israel, ed. (1991), *The Anglo-Dutch Moment* (Cambridge: Cambridge University Press). For a somewhat different perspective, see Tony Claydon (1996), "William III's Declaration of Reasons and the Glorious Revolution," *Historical Journal* 39, no. 1: 87–108.

[163] Nenner, "The Later Stuart Age," 193.

politics 'of reason' was replaced by the politics 'of experience.' During the confused Convention there were no statements of constitutional principles, but only "housekeeping arrangements."

The new monarchs, therefore, could have been understood to be king and queen by right of election, conquest, a tortuous rendering of heredity, an all-embracing and undefined notion of providence – or by some combination of the above. It was an impressive variety of options made possible by unprecedented circumstances, a need for ambiguity, and, more important, by a rule of succession which for all that had happened was still uncertain.[164]

Since the legitimacy of any political power had died for the royalists in 1649, for the republicans in 1653, and for Jacobites in 1689, there was one only possible way out – creating the political authority through an individual delegation of rights, that is, through a compromise at a national level. Revisionist scholars have tried to demonstrate that in effect it was not the contractarian vocabulary that is relevant for the disputes of the time but rather the much more popular theories of conquest and 'abdication' as James's rational and voluntary choice. And yet, although both alternatives were very widely circulated during this period, more recent studies demonstrate beyond doubt that in effect even such alternative theories were framed in such a way as to imply at a certain point some sort of consent of the parties, and therefore a contractarian perspective.[165] At that time, the insistence on the king's abdication or desertion of the throne did not necessarily imply a voluntary, one-sided gesture on the part of the deserter. Adopted from the Latin *'abdicare filium'* a father could 'abdicate,' that is, forsake his son. The son was, in effect 'abdicated,' not the other way around. He was not the actor but the 'acted upon.' Sir Thomas Elyot wrote: "And sometimes the father to restreigne the prompte disposicion that he seeth in his children to vicious qualities, doeth abdicate nowe and tahne one, that is to saie, putteth them out of his familie." In 1689, John Calvin also wrote that "he who divorces his wife, abdicates his son-in-law."[166] Clearly then, abdication was a two-way road: one could abdicate or one could have been abdicated. "It takes no contortion of thought to realize that the committee meant to say that James broke a Lockean type of original contract when they listed the reasons why 'abdicated' was a necessary element of their resolution."[167]

As the records of the period reveal, the question "what the original contract is and whether there be any of such or not" was generally answered in positive. "Atkyns pointed out that even James I had believed there was a 'paction between prince and the people.' Levinz thought that 'you may call it an original contract, though you know not when it began, because there are

---

[164] Ibid., 200.
[165] For a review of the literature on these debates, see Thomas P. Slaughter (1981), "'Abdicate' and 'Contract' in the Glorious Revolution," *Historical Journal* 24, no. 23: 323–337.
[166] Both quoted in ibid., 327.
[167] Ibid., 332.

oaths on both sides, king and people, one to govern, the other to obey.' Nelville said that even a government founded by conquest 'in a little time becomes an original contract.'"[168] The fact that there was no perceived contradiction between conquest and contract is demonstrated, as will be shown in Chapter 8, by the writings of Gilbert Burnet as well. The examples could be endlessly extended. As far as the hereditary right of monarchy being endangered by a contractarian theory, there were no worries. The Jacobite Bishop Turner held "that the hereditary succession to the crown was a law which formed part of the 'original contract' and could be altered only by a new law. The line of succession had, it is true, been broken seven times since the conquest, but more recently the oath of allegiance had been modified by statute so that it extended not merely to the existing ruler but to his heirs and successors." Treby, despite being a Whig lawyer, was in agreement: "That this kingdom is hereditary, we are not to prove by precedent.... The laws made are certainly part of the original contract; and by the laws made, which establish the oath of allegiance and supremacy, we are tied upon to keep in the hereditary line."[169]

During the Convention the greatest effort was dedicated to binding William and Mary and their successors by some sort of contractual relationship. One of the very few acts passed by the Convention was to make sure that the coronation oath took the form of a binding contract. "Legitimacy, as a result, was turned from a concept of government based in traditional right and hereditary monarchy, to government that was anchored instead in its acceptance by the subject in return for protection."[170] It goes without saying that not everyone was pleased with the results. As previously mentioned, "a person of honour" wrote in 1697 that William's coronation was the result of the Calvinists who thought that everything that happens, even the most vicious sins, are part of God's plans and therefore excusable.

But the Defenders of the De facto Notion applied to King WILLIAM, are not afraid to make God the Author of Usurpation. They Blasphemously affirm, That Allegiance is due, not to legal Right only, but to the Authority of God who sets up Kings, without any regard to legal Right, or humane Laws.... Umbrage over that shameful Paradox of theirs, which the denial of King WILLIAM's Right forc'd them to devise, some more refin'd Phoilosophers, with a particular Court-like Address, thought to save its Credit. The Throne (say they) being fill'd, [no matter how] we are protected by it, and the benefit of Protection requires the reciprocal duty of Obedience. By this one Argument, they would have us believe, *that all Differences may be compromiz'd, their Consciences sav'd, and the Government in no danger.*[171]

---

[168] Quoted in Western, *Monarchy and Revolution*, 310.

[169] Quoted in ibid., 313.

[170] Nenner, "The Later Stuart Age," 206.

[171] Person of Honour (1697), *A free discourse wherein the doctrines which make for tyranny are display'd the title of our rightful and lawful King William vindicated, and the unreasonableness and mischievous tendency of the odious distinction of a king de facto, and de jure ...*, 62, 64; emphasis added.

It was, however, too late. The contract understood as compromise required no divine blessing. Neither compromise nor contract can any longer be considered in terms of 'right' or 'wrong.' The only remaining question therefore was how many rights this newly discovered one-dimensional individual would give away. For some, as Richard Overton or John Crook – as did just a few decades later John Locke – maintained that this "giving away" of one's liberty has more than one limit. "Free man can give away their freedom no further then as it conduceth to justice universal and particular."[172] For others, like Hobbes, this granting was total except for the right to self-preservation. Yet regardless of the answer almost everybody agreed that 'the people' was nothing but a collection of individuals each endowed with his own will. The whole became the sum of its parts. This self-confidence of the individual in his political power and his basic political equality with *all* his fellow countrymen made all the difference.

If the distinction between representing 'the people' and representing 'individuals' is as important as the usage of compromise seems to indicate, one can expect that the most elaborate theories of the time, dealing with the social and/ or governmental contract, should reflect the same difference across the English Channel. The following two chapters will check this hypothesis.

---

[172] Morgan, *Inventing the People*, 71.

7

The Forgotten Road of Representation

Continental Contractarian Theories

> C'est une autorité ... dont le movement est circulaire.... [E]lle vient de Dieu immédiatement sur le Peuple & du Peuple elle monte aux Synodes & aux Evêques, c'est la maniére dont roule l'autorité des Sociétez confédérées.
>
> Pierre Jurieu

In the previous chapters I sought to show the connection between peculiar usages of compromise and different assumptions about individuals and political representation starting from the assumption that, when confronted with the crises of the sixteenth and seventeenth centuries, the dialectic of the individual was differently handled on either side of the Channel. In France, growing absolutism and the imposition of the newly discovered concept of the state as the all-encompassing *universitas* exacerbated the distinction between the two fora, seen now in a rather simplified manner: individuals of different political and intellectuals allegiances came to apprehend the *forum internum* as the sole repository of individual authenticity, while at the same time stressing the importance of conformity in the *forum externum*. The interplay between uniqueness and sameness at work in both fora started to fade away. "For it is sufficient," as Christine de Pizan had put it a couple of centuries before, "to speak of the manner in which everyone ought to do his own part in the order that God has established, that is, nobles do as nobles should, the populace does as it is appropriate for them, and everyone should come together as one body of the same polity, to live justly and in peace as they ought."[1] Far from decreasing in the early modern era, the importance in France of these *universitates* increased for a time. As Tocqueville observed, in pre-Revolutionary France "there was no

---

[1] Christine de Pizan (1994), *The Book of the Body Politic*, trans. Kate Langdon Forhan (Cambridge: Cambridge University Press), 59.

individual who did not belong to a group," one of the "thousand little groups of which French society was composed."[2]

The elevation of the 'conceptual community' of the State went hand in hand with a skeptical attitude toward the competency of the multitude to act as a judge. In theory, as the historian du Hailland affirmed in 1570, "virtue, without which nothing great can be undertaken, engendered France itself" and was embodied in all its institutions.[3] Yet theory and practice were often at odds. The metaphor of 'orders' was "a description not of society as it actually was, but of an ethical system by which it was ideally informed."[4] As we have seen, this coupling of the emphasis on personal virtue with the status of individual qua member of one or several communities led to a rather generalized mistrust of the virtues of *le peuple*, here understood as a crowd, and its judgmental expression, *l'opinion publique*. This is less paradoxical than it seems once one takes into consideration the tension between the conceptualization of the community as a whole and the reality of the unreliable, unstable, and irrational multitude.[5] And if the public sphere was no longer informed by reason, even the representation of *forum externum* became problematic. Hence, the development of a centripetal individualism and the almost unanimous suspicion against compromising and/or getting compromised, that is, of endangering one's uniqueness and one's identity.

On the other hand, in England, a new concept of the individual and a new understanding of his relationship with the political sphere were about to develop. Thanks to a combination of factors difficult to quantify (among which must be noted an increased social mobility and electoral franchise, the heritage of the Magna Carta, and the importance of the national Parliament – unprecedented in Europe at that time), the English movement toward centrifugal individualism enjoyed an early start. As seen in the previous chapter, for the first time one witnesses the collapse of the two fora and a move away from the medieval conceptualization of 'the people,' an organic whole (*universitas*), toward a new understanding as a collection of discrete, free, and (judicially) equal individuals (*societas*). And, as in the case of its French counterpart, the new vision proved resilient enough to be shared by people of different intellectual and political allegiances. Regardless whether they based their political vision on the assent of the people, as did Richard Hooker, or preached the right of individuals to revoke their consent and violently resist the tyranny, as did John Ponnet, or embraced the patriarchal vision of father and children, as did Robert Filmer, the one-dimensional individual occupied a central place

---

[2] Alexis de Tocqueville (1904), *L'Ancien regime* (Oxford), 103, quoted in Howell A. Lloyd (1983), *The State, France, and the Sixteenth Century* (London: George Allen & Unwin), 21.

[3] Du Haillan (1570), *De la fortune et vertu de la France* (Paris), 5, quoted in Lloyd, *The State, France, and the Sixteenth Century*, 45.

[4] Lloyd, *The State, France, and the Sixteenth Century*, 23.

[5] See Hubert Carrier (2004), *Le labyrinth de l'etat: Essai sur le debat polituque en France au temps de la Fronde (1648–1653)* (Paris: Honore Champion), esp. 121–122.

in all these new understandings of politics.[6] Not surprisingly, such (theoretical) equality of individuals coupled with the absence of indisputable judges and arbiters kept compromise as a central and quasi-formalized practice able to create the authority of *compromissarius*, as shown in the writings of John Heywood or Thomas Stapleton. The emphasis on individual wills made almost natural the assimilation of the 'new' compromise with a contract meant to create both a voluntary association and an undeniable political authority through the representations of these individual wills.

To sum up, the split history of compromise was intimately connected with a split understanding of representation and self-representation. In France, even when the king, Parlements, or General Estates came to be apprehended as 'representatives,' the classic directionality of representation remained unchallenged. These representatives were still representatives of something higher – in this case the whole people – since the whole was always higher than any of the parts. It was only in England that individuals qua individuals came to be understood as providers of political authority and legitimacy, thus switching the directionality of representation to a bottom-up, ascending one. As a result, the classical emphasis on the representation of reason gave way to the emphasis on the representation of individual wills.

It is now time to switch once again to the more theoretical aspects, further checking this hypothesis in what represented the most elaborated political theories of the time, namely the contractarian ones. There were many accepted meanings for 'contracts': covenants, promises, compromises, agreements, and so on. "The wide range of synonyms for contract is also evidence of the absence of any single, precise meaning of the word in the political literature of the time."[7] We may therefore expect that, as did the usages of compromise, contract theories too differed sharply across the Channel – if not necessarily in form, then in their basic assumptions. Both Frenchmen and Englishmen started to accept some form of contract as the primary basis for any political authority, yet only the latter came to assimilate this contract with compromise. The only possible explanation is that some fundamental assumptions about such a contract differed in a radical fashion. But before we get into specifics, some general observations are in order.

The body of literature on contract theory is quite impressive in terms of volume, complexity, and the significance of the issues it raises.[8] Furthermore,

---

[6] As I will argue shortly, patriarchalism was in effect a new vision of politics, developed in reaction to the popular contractualist theories, as demonstrated by the study of Gordon J. Schochet (1975), *Patriarchalism in Political Thought* (New York: Basic Books).

[7] Martyn P. Thompson (1987), *Ideas of Contract in English Political Thought in the Age of John Locke* (New York: Garland Publishing), 13.

[8] A few examples should suffice: Otto von Gierke (1958), *Natural Law and Theory of Society, 1500 to 1800*, trans. Ernest Baker (London: Cambridge University Press); J.W. Gough (1936), *The Social Contract: A Critical Study of Its Development*, 2nd ed. (Oxford: Clarendon Press); Harro Höpfl and Martyn P. Thompson (1979), "The History of Contract as a Motif in Political

after a period of relative dismissal, recent years have witnessed a renewed interest in contractualism and several attempts to reinterpret it in order to address both criticisms and new challenges.[9] However, the scope of this book not being an exhaustive survey of the entire contractarian literature, I follow here Pocock's strategy of what he calls a 'tunnel history,' pursuing "a single theme … to the partial exclusion of parallel phenomena."[10] Since I am not trying to solve the debate surrounding the distinctions between 'social' and/ or 'governmental' contracts, 'moral,' 'governmental,' 'legislative,' or 'political' contracts, philosophical versus constitutional contractarianism, and so forth (distinctions which probably would have made little sense for the authors of the time in any case) I prefer using 'contract theories' instead of the much more common yet disputable 'social contract theories.'

Nothing much has changed since Höpfl and Thompson observed that "everyone agrees on the centrality of the contractarian arguments to the political thoughts of the sixteenth, seventeenth, and eighteenth centuries; but, aside from consensus at this trivial level, almost every statement about the history of contract has been met with contradictions."[11] Such disagreements are due not so much to the internal contradictions of these authors' theories – although undisputedly there are plenty of those too – as to differences in scholarly expectations. One usually finds what one is looking for. Pending which contract theory is assumed to be the 'ideal' one, all the others are looked upon from a rather evolutionist perspective, as more or less successful attempts to get closer to the standard. "Many of these differences in judgment may be attributed, at least in part, to disputes about what constitutes the 'proper ingredients,' as it were, of a 'genuine' contract theory."[12] Some scholars chose

---

Thought," *American Historical Review* 84, no. 4; Jean Hampton (1986), *Hobbes and the Social Contract Tradition* (Cambridge: Cambridge University Press); Michael Lessnoff (1986), *Social Contract* (Atlantic Highlands, N.J.: Humanities Press International); Peter J. McCormick (1987), *Social Contract and Political Obligation: A Critique and Reappraisal* (New York: Garland); Martyn P. Thompson (1987), *Ideas of Contract in English Political Thought in the Age of John Locke* (New York and London: Garland Publishing); Ron Repogle (1989), *Recovering the Social Contract* (Totowa, N.J.: Rowman and Littlefield); James Gordly (1997), *The Philosophical Origins of Modern Contract Doctrine* (Oxford: Clarendon Press).

[9] Among recent attempts to 'update' the interpretation of contract theories one should mention Julia Simon (2001), *Beyond Contractual Morality: Ethics, Law, and Literature in Eighteenth-Century France* (Rochester, N.Y.: University of Rochester Press); Michael Davis (2003), *Actual Social Contract and Political Obligation: A Philosopher's History Through Locke* (Lewiston: Eldwin Mellen Press); Adela Cortina (2003), *Covenant and Contract: Politics, Ethics and Religion* (Leuven–Dudley: Peeters); Victoria Kahn (2004), *Wayward Contracts: The Crisis of Political Obligation, 1640–1674* (Princeton: Princeton University Press); Mark E. Button (2008), *Contract, Culture, and Citizenship: Transformative Liberalism from Hobbes to Rawls* (University Park: Pennsylvania State University Press).

[10] J.G.A. Pocock (1981), "The Machiavellian Moment Revisited: A Study in History and Ideology," *Journal of Modern History* 53, no. 1: 53.

[11] Höpfl and Thompson, "The History of Contract," 919.

[12] Ibid., 922.

to emphasize the extent to which rebellion is to be permitted (i.e., how many rights are handed out and under what conditions), while others focused more on the accepted levels of representation (i.e., King versus Parliament or General Estates) or on the extent to which such contracts were understood literally or metaphorically.[13] As far as the scope of this discussion is concerned, such problems, important as they are, are of no concern to us – as they most likely were not for their contemporaries. What I am looking for are the underlying and shared assumptions about individuals' equality and individuals' delegation of rights, regardless of other differences in philosophical assumptions or divergent political allegiances.

In this particular case, a tunnel history implies two restrictions. (1) I will compare and contrast mainly the French and the British contract theories, at the expense of other important authors of the time, such as Grotius, Althusius, Spinoza, and Pufendorf, who will be considered rather briefly. (2) Leaving aside a host of important questions about the different ways contracts were conceived at that time, I will focus almost exclusively on two aspects revealing for the connection between contract theory and a particular understanding (and usage) of compromise: (a) the assumption (or lack thereof) of the equality of all the individuals entering the contract as the precondition of any compromise; (b) the existence (or not) of a moment in which individuals delegate their (political) rights to the hands of a person or a group, thus creating not only an 'artificial' arbitrator, but also, by the same token, the premises of a distinct, 'professional' political sphere. My hope is that despite these restrictions, showing that there were radically different ways of conceiving such contracts is important for more than historical reasons. It also helps in illuminating many contemporary debates surrounding contractarianism as basis for political legitimacy, while revealing overlooked connections with the hotly debated issues of representation and the utility of political compromise.

The reason for the first self-imposed restriction is rather straightforward. An in-depth analysis of the Dutch or German contractarian theories would be rather useless unless backed by a consideration of the socio-political contexts of these countries, followed by a survey of the usage of 'compromise' in everyday language. Such an endeavor goes well beyond the scope of my enterprise and must await a later study. Nonetheless, even a brief survey of such theorists finds a common continental assumption about contracts and representation that transcends the borders of early modern France.

The second restriction is required by the main thrust of the argument pursued: if one can show that the various versions of the French contract lacked at least one criterion required by the 'new' compromise (i.e., the assumption of equality between *individuals* entering the contract *and/or* the moment when these individuals *delegate their rights* to another party, thus creating instead of

---

[13] For a review of this literature until 1979, see Höpfl and Thompson, "The History of Contract."

simply acknowledging the authority of *compromissores*) while in the English versions one can find both, one can safely conclude that the aforementioned equation of contract theory and generalized compromise in England is more than a working hypothesis.

The first part of the chapter considers the first French monarchomachs' theories of the contract (both Huguenots and Catholics), emphasizing the ways in which they have struggled to address new challenges, primarily within a classical framework. What becomes clear quite rapidly in all such theories of resistance is that, in themselves, the differences between the Catholic and the Protestant Weltanschauung are not enough to explain the rapid and radical split in the understanding of compromise and representation. In both cases, the right to rebellion was confined to individuals only insofar as their *forum externum* was concerned, in the same ways in which representation could only involve it. One could never rebel in one's private capacity, but only as member of the threatened *universitas* or as occupant of an office representative of the whole community. The only conceivable situation involving the *forum internum* in which the right of resistance was accepted was if the forum of conscience, that is, the inner autonomy of the individual, was threatened – an idea that, as I shall show later, would horripilate Hobbes. In all cases, however, the contracts that created political leadership remained subject to the recognized authority of reason.

The same distinction between 'contracts of reason' and 'contracts of will' is evinced in other continental contractarian theories surveyed in part two. From Althusius and Grotius to Spinoza and Pufendorf, author after author stresses not only the natural sociality of men but also that the end of any political society is positive liberty; not just the protection of the negative liberty of the individuals entering the contract, but the fulfillment of the requirements of justice. But since access to reason is obviously unequal, they all remain suspicious about the competency of an unwise multitude. Under these circumstances, as shown by Pufendorf for example, compromise was possible only before societies became so large that no wise *compromissarius* could be trusted to arbitrate between conflicting interests.

Finally, the third part of the chapter considers later versions of French contractarianism. By the end of the seventeenth century, persecution forced the Huguenots to turn their attention to contract theories once again. This time they were strongly influenced by British contractarian theory and practice and open supporters of the Parliament against the king. However, despite these influences, the basic assumptions about individuals and representation remained unchanged from the previous century. An analysis of the work of the Goliath of Protestantism, as Pierre Jurieu was called, not only reveals an amazing continuity with his predecessors but also clarifies many aspects otherwise confusing in terms of the directionality of representation, the source of political authority, and the relationship between *forum internum* and *forum externum* by the end of the seventeenth century in France.

7.1. THE FRENCH 'CONTRACTS OF REASON'

To be sure, contract theory was not an invention of the sixteenth century. In one form or another, the idea of some sort of *pactum* between the ruler and the people was quite common during medieval times. Nor were these theories distinctively Protestant, although most scholars agree that by stressing the centrality of the individual, the Reformation is at least in part responsible for the popularity such theories enjoyed starting in the second half of the sixteenth century. Not only did the Catholics of the League use more or less the same theories whenever the tables turned, but most of the arguments of the Huguenots came from constitutionalist (or even ultra-constitutionalist) sources dating sometime before the rise of Protestantism.[14] Not surprisingly then, some scholars find no novelty in the works of the French monarchomachs, arguing that they expose only "quasi-feudal contractualism" and are "medieval rather than Protestant."[15]

Obviously, the underlying assumption in such observations is an evolutionary one: if such theories are not really of scholarly interest it is because they are not 'evolved' or 'modern' enough. As a matter of fact, if there was a *'revolutio'* in their thinking it was one in the original sense of the word – of a returning to the original ways of their ancestors. But perhaps the goal of these theories was a classical yet equally interesting understanding of politics that repudiated the idea of individuals' representation as basis for political legitimacy. Although such approaches ended up engulfed in what we understand today by 'modern representation' as representation of individuals, this does not mean that these alternatives present only an antiquarian interest.

When carefully considered, the resilience of the descending understanding of representation and the preservation of the distinction between the two fora among continental thinkers even *after* they started to grapple with the issues of individual rights and resistance theory is quite impressive. Throughout the Middle Ages most thinkers would have agreed "that the people were prior to the state in the sense that they had created it by setting up the king over themselves and instituting the laws which regulated the life of the state and limited the discretion of the ruler."[16] Yet, as we have seen, 'the people' was conceptualized as a whole rather than a multitude of distinct individuals. And, since the authority of the whole is always higher even than the authority of the head, in the sixteenth century Etienne Pasquier could, as mentioned before, safely conclude: "When I say the authority of the pope is below that of councils, I follow

[14] William Farr Church (1941), *Constitutional Thought in Sixteenth Century France: A Study in the Evolution of Ideas* (Cambridge and London: Oxford University Press), 86.

[15] Lessnoff, *Social Contract*, 32; J.W. Allen (1957), *A History of Political Thought in the Sixteenth Century* (London: Methuen), 303.

[16] Church, *Constitutional Thought*, 86.

the greatest theologian we ever had, Master Jean Gerson."[17] He was not the only one to follow in the footsteps of Gerson. As Salmon points out, Jacques Almain and John Mair, for example, two lecturers in the theology faculty of the University of Paris, made the parallel between the political and the ecclesiastical realm even more evident.

Both Almain and Mair were much more explicit than Gerson ... about the power of the secular community over the ruler. The community retained a constituent power. It could change both the ruler and the form of the constitution for reasonable cause, and with strongest justification when the conduct of the former violated its natural right to self-preservation. These were radical views that were to resurface during the Wars of Religion.[18]

The first monarchomachian theories were written from a constitutionalist perspective meant to emphasize that they were promoting ancient laws and liberties rather than creating radically new interpretations. The leading Calvinist polemicists were not only members of the same personal circle but shared the same legal training and drew upon the same general sources.[19] This is particularly relevant because, as Richard Tuck emphasizes, the legacy of humanist legal theories of the early sixteenth century is evident throughout their works. Although they occasionally considered the 'state of nature,' so central to most contract theories, it remained of little importance to them, since what differentiated men from animals was the rationality that for all practical purposes 'coerced' them to leave this state. It was not *ius naturale* that was of interest, therefore, but *ius gentium* and/or *ius civiles*, "the product of social and civilized man." "Giving the general attitude of humanist lawyers, there was obviously no place in their thinking for natural rights of any kind."[20] François Connan exemplified this approach well in the late 1540s and will therefore be quoted at some length:

The *ius naturale* relates properly to a solitary man, leading his life in the fields with a mate and children. But since he is led by nature itself to the society of other men and association with them, he gradually ventures out, and becomes involved in society first with close relatives, then with friends, with neighbours, and eventually through his commerce with them the whole human race.

Only at this phase do contracts start to play a role, although a secondary one, since they were but among the *results* of society and not its cause. "There

---

[17] Quoted in J.H.M. Salmon (2007), "France," in *European Political Thought: 1450–1700*, ed. Howell A. Lloyd, Glenn Burgess, and Simon Hodson (New Haven and London: Yale University Press), 461.

[18] Salmon, "France," 462.

[19] Ralph E. Giesey and J.H.M. Salmon (1972), editors' introduction to *Francogallia*, by François Hotman, Latin text by Ralph E. Giesey, trans. by J.H.M. Salmon (Cambridge: Cambridge University Press), 4.

[20] Richard Tuck (1979), *Natural Rights Theories: Their Origin and Development* (Cambridge: Cambridge University Press), 37, 40.

was no idea of social contract involved in this, simply because promises took their force from their convenience to social man, just as property did. *Natural man had nothing to contract about: no dominium and no rights to renounce or transfer.*"[21] Here is Connan again:

It was necessary in this process for them to foster justice, to keep contracts (*fidem servare contractum*), to harm no one by word or deed, and to use the same honesty with foreigners and strangers, as they were accustomed to use with their mate and children.... Everyone thus very willingly embraced a *ius* which is called *gentium*; it is distinguished from the *ius naturale* in that the latter relates to man as an animal, prudent and cunning admittedly, but when at home not much different from the beasts. The former relates to man qua man, rational and wise, and fully involved with other men.[22]

As Connan's pupil, François Hotman was also more interested in *ius gentium* than in *ius naturale*. While asserting the preeminence of the people as the ancient source of kings' authority, he never seriously considered its origins and, as a result, did not posit a hypothetical or a historical state of nature. Therefore, many historians of contract and of resistance theory only mention him briefly, if at all. Most of them, such as J.W. Gough, summarize his contributions in a couple of lines. And yet amid the plethora of resistance literature he was quoted extensively and considered a central figure. Whence this discrepancy?

To be sure, Hotman is not someone who easily fits in a box. He occupies a position between medieval and modern times, not fully committed one way or another, yet not lukewarm either. As a matter of fact, this 'uncompromising' yet comprehensive, yin–yang attitude characterizes his entire work. While following the precepts of his humanist education by using historical arguments for the interpretation of laws, he was also suspected (for good reason, one might add) of Bartolist sympathies.[23] "He was both an innovator disguised as a reactionary and a renovator masquerading as a radical."[24]

This is a revealing attitude not only for François Hotman but an entire host of continental thinkers who found themselves at a crossroads, about to adapt old approaches to new challenges. One finds in *Francogallia* a strange mixture of old and new. First, a secular tone is used throughout the book. The arguments made in favor of the Estates General are historical, political, and juridical, with no religious references whatsoever, unlike later works by Beza or Brutus.[25] According to Hotman, the remedies for the afflictions that plagued

---

[21] Ibid., 37; my emphasis.

[22] François Connan (1558), *Commentariorum Iuris Civilis Libri* X (Paris), 19v–20r, quoted and trans. in Tuck, *Natural Rights Theories*, 37.

[23] See Church, *Constitutional Thought*; Tuck, *Natural Rights Theories*. Bartolus (Bartolo) of Sassoferrato (1314–1357) was one of the major commentators of the Justinian Code, who, although acknowledging the sovereign's power to disregard, if needs be, ius gentium, also opposed a justification based solely on free will, without a rational cause (sine aliqua causa).

[24] Giesey and Salmon, introduction to *Francogallia*, 3.

[25] For a similar observation, see Allen, *A History of Political Thought*, 308–309.

France (an obvious allusion to the massacre of St. Bartolomew's Day in 1572) was a return (*renovatio*) to the principles of the original constitution, whose main feature was the rule of the Public Council or Estates General as originated on the *Champ de Mai.*

Although the existence of some sort of governmental contract is implied – since *Francogallia*'s kings were "restrained by defined laws and compacts" (*"sed eos certis legibus et pactionibus obligatos esse"*), of which "the first and foremost ... was that they should preserve the authority of the public council as something holy and inviolate" – in effect this contract was heavily biased *against* the king.[26] With obvious pleasure, Hotman quotes the words used by the general council in appointing the king of Aragon: "we, who are worth as much as you and can do more than you, elect you as king."[27] The implications are clear: if there is a contract of governance, the power remains with the council, not with the king. While the parties are of equal worth, one can *do* more than the other.

In Hotman's account, the three orders presented by Claude de Seyssel in his *The Monarchy of France* are not intended as a description of the ordinary society but as a depiction of a council whose role is not just legislative but executive or governmental as well. The three estates "correspond to the three kinds of government embodied in the council – that is to the regal, the aristocratic and the popular types."[28] The public council had the right to make laws, to decide in matters of war and peace, appoint magistrates, elect and depose kings, and so on, while the kings cannot "depose" the council, simply because it would be absurd to 'depose' the people – the very reason for the existence of kings. In extremis, a people could survive without a king, but a king could not exist without his people.

[J]ust as the pupil is not created for his tutor, nor the ship for the pilot, not the flock for the pastor, nor the army for the commander, but, on the contrary, all these are appointed for the former, so the people are not found and procured for the sake of the king, but rather the king for the people. For there may be a people without a king, who may obey the counsel of the nobility or of themselves (*ut qui optimatum aut suo ipsius consilio paret*), as they do during an interregnum. But the idea of a king without a people is as inconceivable as a pastor without a flock.[29]

Hotman's seeming carelessness in equating 'the people' with 'the public council' or 'the estates' is in fact revealing of a basic assumption shared by many continental thinkers. As we have seen in the case of Guy Coquille as well, the Estates were assumed to *be* the people, instead of merely representing it. "The kings of Francogallia were constituted by the authoritative decision and desire of *the people, that is, of the orders*, or, as we are now accustomed to say,

[26] Hotman, *Francogallia*, 459.
[27] Ibid., 307.
[28] Ibid., 293.
[29] Ibid., 399–401.

of the estates."[30] This was no accident. Once again, the distinction between the conceptualized 'people' and the 'multitude' helps us understand how these thinkers managed to support, with equal strength, a direct political say for the people and a non-egalitarian vision of society. If "it is not lawful for the king to determine anything that affects the condition of the commonwealth as a whole (*ut ne quid quod at statum Republicae in universum pertineat*) without the authority of the public council,"[31] it is "because it is an attribute of liberty that those at whose peril a thing is done should have some say and authority in arranging it, or, as it is customarily and commonly said, what touches all should be approved by all."[32] But what in theory was the whole commonwealth (*Republicae in universum*), in practice should become a selection (yet not an election) of its wisest and more worthy individuals (*optimates*), "lest the council be hindered by the judgment of an inexperienced and vulgar multitude which was incapable of judging anything wisely."[33]

Obviously, to interpret these members of the council (or the Estates) as being 'representatives' of each and every single individual is in fact to misrepresent the people. The conceptualized people cannot be represented but by "*des gens de bien et d'honneur comme representant la personne du peuple, lequel les commet a cela et leur donne cette puissance*" ("men of distinction and honor as if representing the person of the people that commits them to this and give them this power"). Interestingly enough, the wording of this French version from 1574 departs significantly from the Latin text where there is no mention of 'representation' but of 'authorization' – "*optimatum et delectorum auctoritate, quibus eam potestam populus permittit.*"[34] The requirement of excellence is emphasized several times hand in hand with a distrust of the multitude: "A multitude of men ought not be ruled and governed by one of their number, who, peradventure, sees less than others do when taken together, but rather by proven men of excellence, selected with the consent of all, who act by combined advice as if they possessed one mind composed from many."[35]

It goes almost without saying – and the famous Huguenot tract *Le reveille-matin des Francois* spells it out, using *Francogallia* as an authoritative source – that such *optimates* are the supreme magistrates.[36] Yet when the Estates were not in session, the right and duty to bridle the power of kings fell on inferior magistrates. This was the thesis clearly articulated by Hotman's friend, Theodore Beza (Theodore de Bèze). They had been fellow students at

---

[30] Ibid., 231–233.
[31] Ibid., 459.
[32] Ibid., 297.
[33] Ibid., 307.
[34] Ibid., 154. The French version from 1574 is quoted in Allen, *A History of Political Thought*, 311.
[35] Hotman, *Francogallia*, 299.
[36] *Le reveille* is a pseudonymous work, variously attributed to Hotman himself, Theodor Beza, Nicolas Barnaus, or Hugues Doneau.

the University of Orleans who both embraced Calvinism and took refuge in Geneva. The similarities between *Francogallia* and Beza's *Du droit de magistrats* are not mere coincidence. While working on his book Beza was in close contact with Hotman, and it is quite clear that the two read each other's manuscripts before their publication. When the Council of Geneva was pondering the publication of *Right of Magistrates*, Beza said that only two people know the manuscript: his secretary and Hotman.[37] Even the images they are using have a striking resemblance. For Beza too *"les peuples ne sont pas créez pour les magistrats, mais au contraire les magistrats pour le peuples; comme le tuteur est pour le pupille, et non le pupille pour le tuteur, et le berger pour le troupeau et non le troupeau pour le berger"*[38] ("the peoples are not created for the magistrates, but on the contrary the magistrates for the peoples; as the tutor is for the pupil and not the pupil for the tutor, and the shepherd for the flock and not the flock for the shepherd"). As a matter of fact, for both of them the origins of these peoples are of no interest – Beza makes reference to Greeks, as well as to Athenians, Spartans, and so on, with equanimity – only the origins of the magistrates, rulers *y compris*.

One may say that the *Right of Magistrates* ensures the transition between Hotman's *Francogallia* and Brutus's *Vindiciae*. Although in terms of a contractual theory it does not go so far as the *Vindiciae*, Beza's account is much more deeply infused with contractarian references than *Francogallia*.

[J]e di que l'equité mesmes et ce droit de nature duquel depend l'entretenment de toute la societé humaine, ne permet que nous revoquions en doute aucun de ces deux points, assavoir qu'en toutes conventions qui se contractent par le seul consentement des parties, ceux par lequels l'obligation est contractee, la peuvent aussi deffaire quand la raison y est; et par consequent ceux-là ont la puissance de deposer un Roi, qui ont puissance de le creer. Secondement, que s'il y a aucune juste occasion de dissoudre un contract ou convention, et par laquelle une obligation s'annulle d'elle-mesmes, c'est quand les conditions essentielles sont notoirement violees, moiennant lesquelles, et au respect desquelles, proprement l'obligation avoit esté contractee.[39]

(I say that equity itself and the right of nature on which depend the endurance of all human society do not allow us to doubt either of these two points, namely that in all conventions that are contracted by the consent of the parties, those by which the obligation is contracted can also undo it whenever they have reason for it; and by consequence those have the power to depose a King who have the power to create him. Second, if there is any right reason to dissolve a contract or a convention and when the obligation nullifies itself, it is when the essential conditions are obviously violated, in view of which and to respect of which properly speaking the obligation was contracted.)

The two parties of the contract are, of course, the people as a whole and the ruler. And once again, the concept of 'the people' has a particular understanding:

[37] Robert M. Kingdon (1970), introduction to *Du droit de magistrates*, by Theodore de Bèze (Geneva: Librairie Doz), xxvii.

[38] Bèze, *Du droit de magistrates*, 9.

[39] Ibid., 44–45.

what in theory is a whole, in practice becomes the most 'reasonable' part of it. Beza goes further than *Francogallia*, conferring the right to resistance both to the Estates and to the inferior magistrates while *Vindiciae* will focus almost exclusively on these inferior magistrates at the expense of the Estates. The reasons for such a transition are quite obvious: despite their revival by 1550, the idea that the Estates represented the preservers of national sovereignty (with or without the king) never traveled too far among the nobility. Besides, the majority of these Estates being composed of Catholics, the Huguenots had little if anything to gain from such an emphasis.[40]

But while conferring the right of resistance to specific individuals, Beza is also careful not to be interpreted as a supporter of the right of private individuals to rebel. In effect, he specifically rejects any possible associations with the Anabaptists, the Peasants' War, and other popular movements, especially in Germany, precisely on this account. He rages against "the calumnies of those who show no shame in considering us one with these fantasist Anabaptists who abolish the authority of magistrates" ("*les calumnies de ceux qui n'ont point de honte de nous enveloper avec ces fantastiques d'Anabaptistes qui abolissent l'authorité des Magistrats*"). Only the magistrates, superior or inferior, can judge when the contract is broken, precisely because they act for the whole in their public capacity, in their *forum externum*, not as private persons. If Jesus Christ himself, Lord of heaven and earth (*seigneur du ciel et de la terre*), had confirmed that tributes and other taxes are properly due to earthly princes, it is because "he did not come on earth to rule in a human manner, and from this perspective was a private person, making no use of the privileges of the house of David" ("*n'estant venu en terre pour y regner à la facon des homes, ains pour estre en cest esgard personne privee, et non usant des privileges de la maison de David*").[41]

The humanists' legal theories play an important role in this approach, "for if what was important about a right or contract was the action attached to it, then the role of a judge as privileged executor of the law was indeed vital.... A plaintiff had to work through a judge."[42] The same rationale applies to people as well as to the Estates: what in theory is a whole, in practice is the most enlightened part of it, for only this part can properly exercise right judgment about a contract being broken. In other words, such magistrates act as the classical *compromissarius* between the people and the king.

According to Beza there are three categories of subjects: private persons properly speaking ("*personnes du tout privees et sans aucune charge d'Estat*"), inferior officers or magistrates ("*subalternes ou inferieures*"), and superior magistrates, who are ordained to serve as bridles to the sovereign Magistrate, that is, the king ("*encores qu'ils n'aient la puissance souveraine et ordinaire*

---

[40] See Allen, *A History of Political Thought*, 290–291.
[41] Bèze, *Du droit de magistrates*, 60–61.
[42] Tuck, *Natural Rights Theories*, 42.

à manier, toutesfois sont ordonnez pour server comme de bride et de frein au souverain Magistrat").[43] Whenever the tyranny becomes so strong that the Estates are prevented from meeting it is the duty of these magistrates or the sanest part of these Estates (*"la plus saine partie des Estates"*) to ask for the convocation of the assembly, *"sans que les meschans empeschent les bons, les lasches retardant les diligens, ni la plus grande partie retienne la plus saine"*[44] ("without the bad ones preventing the good, the cowards slowing down the diligent, nor the greater part restraining the sanest"). If the majority refuses to follow the voice of reason, the 'sane' minority is entitled to act without waiting for a common assembly. Evidently, there is no question of wills here, for were that so the majority would have the final word. Beza's politics are still 'of reason,' not 'of will.'

That such an understanding of politics was not specifically Huguenot nor necessarily connected to contract theories can be seen in *Le discours de la Servitude Volontaire* of La Böetie (La Boétie), written some decades before but published for the first time in 1576, along with the *Right of Magistrates* and other Huguenot writings, under the title *Mémoires de l'Estat de France sous Charles IX* by Simon Goulart.[45] At first sight these two works could not have been more different, despite the fact that both discussed the subject of tyranny. While Beza was a militant Calvinist careful to prevent any popular revolts, Étienne de la Boétie was (at least formally) a Catholic fascinated with the willingness of millions to follow the orders of one or a few who, in reality, had no power but that handed over by their obedient multitude. *Le discours*, it has been argued with good reason, "was an essay on the natural liberty, equality and fraternity of man."[46] For La Boétie it seems that between a direct democracy and tyranny there are no intermediate regimes. 'Representation' is not a word in his vocabulary, only 'subjection.' A man either has his liberty or does not. There are no gray areas, no intermediaries, no representatives, neither for the individual nor for the people as a whole. The difference between elected leaders and imposed ones is only of nuance:

Les élus du people, le traitent comme un taureau à dompter; les conquérants, comme une proie sur laquelle ils ont tous les droits; les successeurs, comme un troupeau d'esclaves qui leur appartient tout naturellement.[47]

(The elected of the people treat it as a bull to tame; the conquerors, as prey upon which they have all rights; the successors, as a flock of slaves that naturally belongs to them.)

---

[43] Bèze, *Du droit de magistrates*, 15–16.
[44] Ibid., 54–55.
[45] As a matter of fact, in 1574 the *Réveille-matin des François* contained a partial version without the name of the author. The 1576 *Mémoires* mentioned the author and offers the full version but under the title *Contr'Un*. Fearing accusations of Calvinism, Montaigne had to renounce his project to include *De la servitude* in his first edition of his *Essays* (1580).
[46] Allen, *A History of Political Thought*, 314.
[47] Étienne de la Boétie (1976), *Le discours de la servitude volontaire*, texte établi par P. Léonard (Payot: Paris), 188.

Despite its radicalism, or perhaps because of it, this vision embodies the second of the two poles between which the French political thought swung during the sixteenth and seventeenth century, namely absolutism and direct responsibility, respectively. Yet, as we have seen, the two are not as far apart as they might seem. The theoretical focus on the sovereignty of a conceptualized people was counterbalanced in practice by the responsibility for action on the part of rational individuals – the only ones able to properly represent 'the people.' In the case of La Boétie as well, the focus on the individual's liberty and rights does not end up in an atomized society, but on the contrary gives rise to a tight-knit community (as any classical thinker regardless of his particular political preferences would have had it) or possibly even tighter bound together than that, considering the admiration he expresses when mentioning *"la liberté de la république de Platon."*[48] Some paragraphs bear a strange resemblance to Rousseau's *Social Contract* despite a separation of two centuries.

[La nature], premier agent de Dieu, bienfaitrice des homes ... nous a fait, à tous, ce beau présent de la voix et de la parole pour nous aborder et fraterniser ensemble, et par la communication et l'échange de nos pensées nous amener à la communauté d'idées et de volontés; ... elle a cherché, par toutes sortes de moyens à former et resserrer le nœud de notre alliance, le liens de notre société; ... enfin, elle a montré en toutes choses le désir que nous fussions, non seulement unis, mai qu'ensemble nous ne fissions, pour ainsi dire, qu'un seul être.[49]

(Nature, God's first agent, benefactor of men ... gave us all this great gift of voice and speech, for us to approach and fraternize together, and by communication and the exchange of our thoughts to bring us into the community of ideas and wills; ... [nature] had tried by every means to form and tighten the knot of our alliance, the bonds of our society; ... finally, it had shown in all things the desire that we were not only to unite but also that together we form, so to speak, one being.)

It is through speech and the exchange of ideas that the community comes to be 'one being' and the requirement of equality is ensured precisely by the liberty to participate in this process. Does this radicalism of La Boétie translate in a support for the people in a more concrete fashion? Not at all. When it comes to the masses, the friend of Montaigne proves as highly suspicious as his Huguenots counterparts, speaking about *"la partie ignorante et grossière du people"* ("the ignorant and crude part of the people") and using epithets such as *"ces miserables gens"* ("these wretched people").[50] The explanation is to be found in the emphasis that La Boétie places on reason and its close relationship with virtue.

Men are essentially born free and equal because there is in each and every single one *"un germe de raison, qui, réchauffé par les bons conseils et les bons exemples, produit en nous la vertu"* ("a seed of reason, which, warmed by good

48 Ibid., 203.
49 Ibid., 185.
50 Ibid., 202, 212.

advice and good examples, produces in us virtue"). Thus, "if we would live with the rights that we have by nature, following the percepts that it teaches" (*"si nous vivions avec les droit que nous tenons de la nature et d'après les préceptes qu'elle enseigne"*) "we would be naturally submissive to our parents, *subjects to reason, but slaves to no one"* (*"nous serions naturellement soumis à nos parents, sujets de la raison, mais non esclaves de personne"*).[51] If this is obviously not the case, it is because "*le people ignorant et abruti a toujours été de même"* ("the people, ignorant and foolish, has been always the same"): it always falls prey to vices.[52] And thus, "strangled by these vices, the seed of reason and love of freedom is aborted" (*"étouffé par le vices qui trop souvent surviennent, ce même germe avorte"*).[53] Not surprisingly then, "the first reason for voluntary servitude is (bad) habit" (*"la première raison de la servitude volontaire c'est l'habitude"*). Such people can never be citizens, but only subjects. If such bad people get together, as Hobbes would have it, "it is a gang, not a society" (*"entre méchants, lorsqu'ils s'assemblent, c'est un complot et non un société"*). Fearing each other, "they are not friends but accomplices" (*"ils ne sont pas des amis, mais complices"*).[54]

Junius Brutus, the author of *Vindiciae contra tyrannos* (most likely the pseudonym of Philippe Duplessis-Mornay with some editorial assistance from Hubert Languet), shares with La Boétie the assumption that men by nature love liberty and hate servitude, being "born rather to command than obey."[55] However, he differs from La Boétie in accepting that, under certain circumstances, men could have willingly renounced this "privilege of nature" and accepted being governed by others "for some special and great profit that they expected from it."[56] And the only safe way to secure the exchange of liberty for collective security or welfare was through some form of contract, express or tacit, formal or informal.

Apparently, for what we are interested in there is little if any novelty. Once again, the 'people' is understood as a whole, a *universitas*. And once again, "as all the whole people is above the king, and likewise taken in one entire body, are in authority before him, yet being considered one by one, they are all of them under the king."[57] Therefore, Brutus too, as Hotman or Beza, opposes all acts of rebellion initiated by private individuals. Only the entire body of the people can depose a king because it was this body that created him – at least in ancient times. Once again, the assumption of an initial direct democratic election is unmistakable, and is astonishingly similar to Guy Coquille's description

[51] Ibid., 184; emphasis added.
[52] Ibid., 204.
[53] Ibid., 184.
[54] Ibid., 221.
[55] Junius Brutus (1924), *A Defence of Liberty Against Tyrants*, introduction by Harold J. Laski (London: G. Bell and Sons), 139.
[56] Ibid.
[57] Ibid., 127.

of the establishment of Estates "as by mean of a compromise," in order to avoid the impracticability of such an endeavor when considering the numbers:

> But since the kings began to extend their limits, and that it was impossible for the people to assemble together all into one place because of their great numbers, which would have occasioned confusion, the officers of the kingdom were established, who should ordinarily preserve the rights of the people, in such sort notwithstanding, as when extraordinary occasion required, the people might be assembled, or at least such an abridgment as might by the most principal members be a representation of the whole body.[58]

Brutus's usage of history to support his arguments is different from, say, Hotman's and the entire constitutionalist school, signaling a crossroads that deserves special attention. If "we must ... see wherefore first kings were established, and what is principally their duty" it is not because time justifies a custom, but because in a pristine, still uncorrupted situation, one can better grasp its founding principle. "We usually esteem a thing just and good when it attains to the proper end for which it is ordained," he claims, following in the footsteps of Aristotle.[59] Were someone to reply that the 'description' does not fit existing reality, this observation (however correct, implies Brutus) would not affect the validity of the argument. Even though the officers of the kingdom and the people are now in terms of virtue unlike anything that Brutus describes, this does not mean that they have lost their authority, which transcends the king's. A corrupt or wrong attitude is not made rightful by the length of its continuance.

> But peradventure, some one will reply, you speak to us here of peers, of lords and officers of the crown. But I, for my part, see not any, but only some shows and shadows of antiquity as if they were to be represented on a stage. I see not for the present scarce any tract of that ancient liberty, and authority; nay, which is worse, a great part, if not all, of those officers take care of nothing but their particular affairs, and almost, if not altogether, serve as flatterers about those kings who jointly toss the poor people like tennis balls.[60]

The kings and the magistrates become corrupted for using their *forum externum* for private ends, while the people are guilty of forgetting that in their *forum externum* capacity they are to be above and not subject to their representatives. The author of the *Vindiciae* does not duck this charge. He only contests its conclusion.

> What can be answered to this? The business goes thus. The outrageousness of kings, the ignorance of the party, together with the wicked connivance of the great ones of the kingdom, has been for the most part such throughout the world, that the licentious and unbridled power wherewith most kings are transported and which has made them insupportable, has in a manner, by length of continuance, gained right of prescription,

---

[58] Ibid.
[59] Ibid., 139.
[60] Ibid., 118.

and the people, for want of using it, have intacitly quit, if not altogether lost, their just and ancient authority.[61]

At this point of the diatribe, Brutus has an interesting observation – one as modern as possible, considering the free-rider problem in a socialist context: "So that it ordinarily happens that what all men's care ought to attend on, is for the most part neglected by every man; for what is committed to the generality, no man thinks is commended to his custody." Yet this does not bend Brutus. This is a weakness of individuals who have forgotten that *forum externum* ensured membership in the community, not of the principle. Virtue cannot be blamed for its lack. Being aware of men's weaknesses does not equate to denying man's fundamental liberty.

Notwithstanding, no such prescription nor prevarication can justly prejudice the right of the people. It is commonly said that the exchequers do admit no rule of prescription against it, much less against the whole body of the people, whose power transcends the king's, and in whose right the king assumes to himself that privilege.[62]

This is a passage both La Boétie and Beza would have agreed with, although for different reasons. For La Boétie, men would give up their natural liberty only because of vice, deceit, or force – at least until by force or habit they become accustomed to tyranny. Yet from a teleological perspective, even this corruption cannot properly affect the true nature of man. Nature is nature precisely because it cannot be changed. You can corrupt it, you can forget it, you even may make it look like its complete opposite – but you cannot change it. A bonsai oak is still an oak, and a pony still a horse. The body of people is not fully conscious, he argued, if it willingly makes itself a slave to somebody else. Nobody can get rid of himself, as Rousseau would put it later. For Beza, too, a contract by which all men delegate their rights to somebody else without provisions is void by nature, because it is irrational. Unlike modern contracts, for these authors contracts are contracts of 'reason,' not 'will.' Since not everything willed is by necessity rational, it follows that not every contract is valid.

Mais je dirai que, quand memes un Peuple sciemment et de son plein gré a consenti à une chose qui de soi-mesmes est manifestement irreligieuse et contre le droit naturel, une telle obligation ne peut valoir; tant s'en faut qu'on puisse douter si elle est vallable ou non, quand par force ou crainte elle a esté extorquee, ou contractee par surprinse ou fraude manifeste.[63]

(But I would say that even when a People knowingly and of its own will had consented to something which by itself is obviously irreligious and against the natural right, such an obligation has no value; the same applies when one may doubt if it is valid or not, when by force or fear it was extorted, or contracted by surprise or obvious fraud.)

---

[61] Ibid.
[62] Ibid., 119.
[63] Bèze, *Du droit de magistrates*, 45.

As a matter of fact, while most scholars agree that the *Vindiciae* was probably the most influential work of its time, especially in terms of contract theory, they are also eager to point out that this was due not as much to its originality as to its ability to summarize ideas already stated by previous authors.[64] Furthermore, the double contract – one between the people and the king on the one hand and God on the other, the second between the king and his people – was interpreted as a mistranslation for *foedum* and *pactum* (since it does not involve an act of volition but one of acknowledgment), as a typical Calvinistic covenant, rather medieval in its essence, or as downright confusing: after all, are there two contracts or three?[65] Yet it is precisely these 'weaknesses' that might help us better understand what was less an antiquated form of contract theory than an attempt to craft a different understanding of political representation.

The first contract – the one between people and king on the one side and God on the other – is seen as necessary in order to ensure that the parties are bound to a higher principle, namely, the law of God. Only after both people and king acknowledge this higher principle can the proper contract, that between the king and the people, safely take place, because now there is an impartial judge to weigh the validity of the contract. *The problem of finding a proper arbiter – which is the core idea of classical compromise – marks the beginning of modernity.* In ancient times, a man of authority could provide an impartial arbitration in specific cases. It was easy to be found, identified, and acknowledged as such. But, as men multiplied and the very authority of such *compromissores* became questionable, the problem of the arbitrator became an imperious one. The solution, according to the author of the *Vindiciae* is, first and foremost, the law. Because of their objectivity, laws are of a higher authority than even kings, and may serve as impartial and just *compromissores*.

When people began to seek for justice to determine their differences, if they met with any private man that did justly appoint them, they were satisfied with it. Now for so much as such men were rarely and with much difficulty met withal, and for that the judgment of kings received as laws were oftentimes found contrary and difficult, the magistrates and other of great wisdom invented laws, which might speak to all men in one and the same voice.[66]

Kings are nothing else but "guardians and administrators" of the law, "for so much as the laws could not foresee the particularities of actions to resolve exactly, it was permitted the king to supply this defect."[67] Brutus is

---

[64] See, e.g., Laski in his introduction to Brutus, *A Defence of Liberty*; Allen, *A History of Political Thought*; Gough, *The Social Contract*; or Lessnoff, *Social Contract*.
[65] For the critique of the *Vindiciae* along these lines, see esp. Allen, *A History of Political Thought*, and Lessnoff, *Social Contract*. For a more favorable reading, see Gough, *The Social Contract*, or Höpfl and Thompson, "The History of Contract."
[66] Brutus, *A Defence of Liberty*, 144.
[67] Ibid.

adamant that the will of kings is not in itself enough of a justification. Law "is a divine thing coming *from above*" and "the soul of a good king, [that] gives him motion, sense and life. The king is the organ and as it were the body by which the law displays her forces, exercises her function, and expresses her conceptions."[68] Subjecting his will to the rationality of law does not diminish the king's authority – quite the contrary. As for the medieval man, true freedom is the freedom of obeying the higher law, not one's erratic will. Therefore, the king has to acknowledge the law "as his lady and mistress, esteeming nothing can become him worse than that feminine of which Juvenal speaks: *Sic volo, sic jubeo, sic pro ratione voluntas. I will, I command, my will shall serve instead of reason.*"[69]

This way of thinking appears paradoxical, to say the least, for the modern mind. "All these writers insist that though the Prince is an agent and delegate of a sovereign people, he is also an agent and a delegate of God."[70] How so? Yet for a writer such as Brutus, the two sources of authority, God and the people, were complementary and confirmed each other. As God, as the primary cause, creates man while his biological parents act as a secondary cause, God appoints kings while the people establish and reconfirm their authority. 'The people' is, so to speak, the biological parent of the king. Without the latter's confirmation, God's selection could not become manifest. Without the former's appointment, the choice of the people would remain arbitrary. Furthermore, because of this "double-checking," kings themselves are brought to realize that the position they are in is not the result of their own merits. The difference is one of office, that is, of *forum externum.*

We have shewed before that it is God that does appoint kings, who chooses them, who gives the kingdom to them: now we say that the people establish kings, puts the scepter into their hands, and who with their suffrages, approves the election. God would have it done in this manner, to the end that the kings should acknowledge, that after God they hold their power and sovereignty from the people, and that it might the rather induce them, to apply and address the utmost of their care and thoughts for the profit of the people, without being puffed with any vain imagination, that they were formed of any matter more excellent than other men, for which they were raised so high above others.[71]

What appears as downright confusing for modern scholars comes from the different understanding of what 'representation' stands (or should stand) for.[72] As we have seen in the previous chapters, if sometimes nobles represent 'the people' and at other times city magistrates, Parlements, or the Estates do, it is because there is no clear-cut recipe for the representation of the whole: what matters foremost for these writers is who, at any given moment, has a better

[68] Ibid., 145; emphasis added.
[69] Ibid., 144.
[70] Allen, *A History of Political Thought*, 317.
[71] Brutus, *A Defence of Liberty*, 118.
[72] Allen, *A History of Political Thought*, 323.

and unbiased understanding of what the true interests of the people are (or, from a religious perspective, what God's will is). Thus, they insisted that governmental contract were contracts 'of reason' as opposed to 'contracts of will.' The emphasis was on the concept of 'the people,' not on its real-life manifestation. The real-life manifestation of the people, through its kings, Estates, magistrates, nobles, or even through popular assemblies, could still be corrupt, because unreasonable. Reason remains the ultimate arbitrator, the ultimate judge, or if one prefers the ultimate *compromissarius*. Therefore, sometimes the concept of the people is better grasped by a handful of individuals, sometimes by a formal body, elected or not. But at any rate, since representation remains representation of a higher authority, or of a principle, there is no single individual or institution that under all circumstances can claim to be the proper representative of 'the people.' If the monarchomachs were ready to contest (under specific circumstances) the ability of kings to always rightfully represent the people, they were not eager to accept that other, lesser forms of representation – Estates or magistrates – might, on the contrary, be incorruptible.

The Catholics of the League could not but agree, once the Massacre of St. Bartholomew, which had spurred the Huguenots' theories of resistance, met its equivalent in the murder of the two leading members of the house of Guise, Henry, Duke of Guise, and his brother, Cardinal de Guise, on the specific orders of Henry III. The king could no longer be excused as badly advised and misguided. It was the Leaguers' turn to claim that power and sovereignty (*potestas* and *maiestas*) resides with the people; however, because of their mistrust of Gallicanism and the king's attempts to control the French Catholic church, they added a new element in their picture of the governmental contract, the pope. According to most of them, the pope was the real supplier of authority, and able therefore to identify tyrants and demand their repression.

Jean Bouchet, the rector of the Sorbonne and leading member of the League, was no exception. While following the *Vindiciae* in mentioning a contract between God, king, and people, and asserting that kings were constituted by the people, his four books on the *Just Deposition of Henry III from the Kingdom of the French* (*De justa Henricii III abdicatione*), published in 1589, called upon the pope to depose the king, accusing him of all imaginable crimes. As Brutus before him, he did not equate the people with the multitude, that 'beast of many heads,' but with 'men of wisdom and honor,' that is, nobles and senators, the ones who can rightfully decide to constitute or depose kings.[73]

Another tract quite popular at the end of the sixteenth century was *The Just Authority of a Christian Commonwealth against Impious and Heretical Kings* (*Reipublicae Christianae in reges impios et haereticos authoritate*) whose author's identity, Gulielmus Rossaeus, is disputed between Guillaume Rose, Bishop of Senlis, and the English Catholic William Reynolds. Although

---

[73] For more details on Jean Bouchet, see Gough, *The Social Contract*, 57–58, and Salmon, "France," 474–475.

Rossaeus has no explicit contract theory, his argument runs along the same lines. Men were destined by the 'light of nature' to constitute civil societies and therefore no social contract properly speaking was needed. However, political authority was created by the "will and approbation of peoples," from their "free choice and decision." Some societies, such as the Scots, subjected their rulers overmuch to popular whims, while others elevated them too much "and falsely declared that kings can never be punished or deposed by the people." Both extremes are wrong, according to Rossaeus. While the authority of the rulers is not to be contested because of personal injuries, if kings overstep their limits, becoming tyrants or espousing pagan heresy, they can rightfully be deposed.[74]

But these constitutionalist, contractarian, and resistance theories were already too little and too late for the French context of growing absolutism. Yet, as Salmon observes, "these ideas spread rapidly to other parts of Europe, creating the double paradox that something specifically French lost its national context and something essentially religious was adapted to secular institutional ends."[75] It is therefore time to see how these ideas traveled in other parts of continental Europe.

7.2. OTHER CONTINENTAL VERSIONS OF CONTRACT THEORY

The emergence of contract theories by the end of the sixteenth century and their increased popularity during the seventeenth was no mere coincidence. These were, as we have seen, times of religious, economic, and political turmoil all across Europe, and new, more credible formulas were needed to ground authority and legitimacy. It was a two-way street: these new formulas could be used not only to justify the need to obey but also the right to rebel once, under the new definitions, authority and legitimacy became questionable. Not surprisingly, then, Dutch thinkers were among the front-runners of contract theorists. The Netherlands was the place where religious wars had a peculiar political component: at stake was more than just the salvation of souls, but also the creation and the survival of a new republic. The United Provinces had to unify in a coherent and legitimate political body in order to effectively fight the kingdom of Spain and obtain their independence. "Before the Dutch could make common cause against the king of Spain, they had to have a common government; and before a common government, a commonwealth."[76] Johannes Althusius and Hugo Grotius tried to address these challenges.[77]

---

[74] The quotations are from Gough, *The Social Contract*, 58–59, and Salmon, "France," 475–476.

[75] Salmon, "France," 460.

[76] Davis, *Actual Social Contract*, 213.

[77] "Although Althusius was a German, his connections with the Netherlands were so close that he may be described as the foremost political theorist of Dutch Calvinism." Lessnoff, *Social Contract*, 35.

Despite the fact that almost no history of contractualism fails to mention these authors, their specific importance in the genealogy of contract theories is heavily disputed. Althusius, for example, is considered by Höpfl and Thompson as the first author to use contract as the basis of a "self-consciously scholarly political theory" and by Davis as the author of "the first full theory of the civil state as a body entered by individuals upon their own 'agreement.'"[78] At the same time Althusius is counted by Schochet as one of the main exponents of patriarchalism, a follower in the footsteps of Bossuet.[79] Grotius, too, is viewed by Kahn as a major influence on contractarian thinking: "For seventeenth-century readers, the centerpiece of *De jure belli* was Grotius's contractualist account of property, society and government."[80] Yet most scholars considered him rather 'the father of international law' and of natural rights theory than a contractarian theorist in his own right.[81] As we have seen, such disagreements are by no means confined to these two authors and have everything to do with each scholar's vision of the ideal contract theory.

The first element missing from the contractarian picture of Althusius or Grotius is the absence of the atomistic perspective. Both insist upon the innate 'sociability' present in all human beings even before any 'contract' ever took place. Social and political lives are part of man's nature and therefore cannot be avoided.[82] And although Althusius saw all relationships as essentially contractual (*pacta, foedera,* or *conventus*) he was not yet ready to part ways with the organic terminology that suggests that "both society and hierarchy are natural rather than artificial" (if civil society is described as *symbiosis,* citizens are *symbiotes*).[83]

Equality was of no concern to him, since the entire system was based upon a hierarchy of associations, starting from the family all the way up to the state: "the universal and major public association," "people united in one body by the agreement of many symbiotic associations and particular bodies, and brought together under one right."[84] Because the first unit is the family, composed not only of adults, but also of children and the feebleminded, there was no question of equality between individuals and such agreement was necessarily hypothetical.[85] Such a vision of political societies was as far from the

---

[78] See Höpfl and Thompson, "The History of Contract," 935, and Davis, *Actual Social Contract,* 213.

[79] Gordon J. Schochet (1975), *Patriarchalism in Political Thought* (New York: Basic Books), 34–35.

[80] Kahn, *Wayward Contracts,* 36.

[81] See, e.g., Gough, *The Social Contract,* 77, or Charles S. Edward (1981), *Hugo Grotius: The Miracle of Holland: A Study in Political and Legal Thought* (Chicago: Nelson-Hall), 9–10.

[82] For a similar observation, see Schochet, *Patriarchalism,* 34.

[83] Höpfl and Thompson, "The History of Contract," 936.

[84] Johannes Althusius (1964), *The Politics ... An Abridged Translation of the Third Edition of Politica Methodice Digesta,* ed. and trans. Frederick S. Carney (Boston: Beacon Press), 61.

[85] See Davis, *Actual Social Contract,* 216–217.

abstract individualistic perspective as could be.[86] "For all the changes he rang in the concept of covenant, one covenant he did not contemplate – namely a covenant between *individuals* equipped with natural rights."[87] As Althusius stresses repeatedly, the members of all public associations are not individuals but only other associations.[88]

For Althusius, the commonwealth is nothing but a federation of federations. The vision is essentially corporatist, like the medieval one, but the major novelty (as most scholars point out) is that now authority flows upward, from smaller (private or civil) associations to larger ones (public, political).[89] This claim, however, is challenged by those who – rightfully, I claim – interpret Althusius's theory as "a 'contractualized' version of Aristotle, in which the Aristotelian series of human groups is made to depend on successive contracts."[90] In this case, although the state is the completion of smaller associations existing prior in the order of time, it is also "prior in the order of nature to the family and the individual," for "the whole is necessarily prior in nature to the part."[91] Authority, therefore, is still descending, as the classic theory of representation had it. No authority is created through a bottom-up delegation of rights, let alone by individuals.

For Hugo Grotius too, "the desire for society" is "peculiar to men." This desire, which "the Stoics called ... the *domestic instincts*, or *feeling of kindred*" is "a desire for a life spent in common with fellowmen; and not merely spent somehow, but spent in tranquility, and in a manner corresponding to the character of the intellect."[92] The last specification is important, as Grotius goes to explain that this human desire is not to be confounded with an animal impulse. It is not a matter of 'will' or of "seeking own advantage or good" but of conforming to the Natural Law through "a judgment rightly framed; not to be misled by fear or by the temptation of present pleasure, not to be carried away by blind and thoughtless impulse; and that what is plainly repugnant to such judgment, is also contrary to *Jus*, that is, to Natural Human Law."[93]

It is precisely this emphasis on reason and judgment 'rightly framed' that precludes any abstract equality. While "it is conformable to Natural Law to observe compacts" and "Civil Rights were derived from this source, mutual compact," not everybody is equally qualified to exercise this judgment.[94]

---

[86] Höpfl and Thompson, "The History of Contract," 926; Gough, *The Social Contract*, 72–75.

[87] Höpfl and Thompson, "The History of Contract," 936.

[88] Althusius, *The Politics*, 37.

[89] See, e.g., J.W. Gough, Harro Höpfl and Martyn P. Thompson, or Michael Davis.

[90] Lessnoff, *Social Contract*, 38.

[91] Aristotle, *Politics*, I, ii, 12–13.

[92] Grotius (1853), *On the Rights of War and Peace*, abridged and translated by William Whewell (Cambridge: Cambridge University Press), xxiv.

[93] Ibid., xxiv–v.

[94] Ibid., xxvii.

And to this exercise of judgment pertains a reasonable and thoughtful assignment, to each individual and each body of men, of the things which peculiarly belong to them; by which exercise of the judgment in some cases, the wiser man is preferred to the less wise; in others, a poor man to a rich; according as the nature of each act and each thing requires.[95]

Not surprisingly then, "while assuming that all social union is the result of the free combination of individuals who originally lived in isolation, he allows other methods beside contract or consensus by which rights over men can be acquired (e.g. delict, which explains the imposition of servitude by way of punishment), and there can be societies of unequals as well as of equals."[96] As a matter of fact, according to Grotius, the state is a society of *unequal* persons and the mutual obligation between king and the people does not universally hold. The equality of individuals was by no means crucial, as he makes clear from the very beginning of *On the Rights of War and Peace*. "Society is either that of equals, as brothers, friends, allies; or it is unequal, as that of parent and child, master and servant, king and subjects, God and men: and what is just, is different in the two cases. We may call them respectively Equatorial Rights and Rectorial Rights."[97]

Grotius's entire theory is informed by this judicial approach, inspired by the Roman legalistic tradition, which sometimes makes interpretation rather difficult, especially when it comes to relationships between subjects and their government instead of those between sovereigns (as in the international laws). If there is a contract between people and government, either express or tacit, it is "not clear about whether the contracting people is corporate or merely collective," that is, an organic whole or a collection of discrete individuals.[98] Yet when it comes to transfer of rights (for it is more than a mere 'delegation'), the context clearly indicates that 'the people' are understood as a body similar in its wholeness to that of an individual. If "a man may by his own act make himself the slave of any one ... why then may not a people do the same, so as to transfer the whole Right of governing it to one or more persons?"[99] This is not to say that Grotius favors such a complete transfer of right, as Rousseau later will imply, but only that he does not see any juridical impediment to doing so. On this point, Michael Davis makes an important observation:

Grotius does not think it impossible for the people to divide sovereignty with one or a few magistrates nor does he think it impossible for the people to retain the government themselves. What he does think impossible is that the same (corporate) people be at once and for the same matters both sovereign and subject, both ultimate governor (principal or guardian) and one governed by someone else (a mere agent or ward).[100]

---

[95] Ibid., xxv–vi.
[96] Gough, *The Social Contract*, 77.
[97] Grotius, *On the Rights of War and Peace*, 2.
[98] Davis, *Actual Social Contract*, 218.
[99] Grotius, *On the Rights of War and Peace*, 38.
[100] Davis, *Actual Social Contract*, 219

Clearly, for Grotius sovereignty cannot be represented. It is either retained *and* exercised or transferred *and* endured. But if neither Althusius nor Grotius fulfills the two requirements we have been looking for (i.e., equality of individuals and delegation of rights into the hands of one or more representatives), what about Spinoza, arguably the seventeenth century's "most important of the followers of Hobbes" who may even surpass Hobbes in the boldness of his assumptions?[101] It has even been said that Hobbes himself exclaimed that he 'durst not write so boldly' as Spinoza had done in his *Theological-Political Treatise*.[102]

Like Althusius and Grotius, Baruch de Spinoza is a heavily disputed author, now as during his lifetime. For most of his contemporaries he was "a sort of henchmen for the devil," "the supreme philosophical bogeyman of Early Enlightenment Europe."[103] Yet, as in the case of Hobbes, he became an unavoidable philosopher of his century and the following even if only in order to refute his thesis. According to Israel – one of today's most enthusiastic supporters of Spinoza, one might say – he has "fundamentally and decisively shaped a tradition of radical thinking which eventually spanned the whole continent, exerted an immense influence over successive generations, and shook western civilization to its foundations."[104] Today the debate is still continuing. Was he a liberal *avant la lettre*? A radical democrat? A pantheist, deist, or atheist? Fortunately, such questions are once again of no concern to us. We know what we have to look for.

On the question of individuals' equality, Spinoza has a peculiar undertaking. On the one hand, individuals are equal in that each individual, human being or something else, has the same sovereign right to do whatever she or he (or it) can do. On the other hand, this equality does not prevent a natural inequality in terms of access to reason.

And here I do not acknowledge any distinction between men and other individuals of Nature, nor between men endowed with reason and others to whom true reason is unknown, nor between fools, madmen, and the sane. Whatever an individual thing does by the laws of its own nature, it does with sovereign right, inasmuch as it acts as determined by nature, and can do no other.[105]

Like Hobbes, he wanted to break with all philosophers who "conceive of men not as they are, but as they themselves would like them to be." As a

---

[101] Gough, *The Social Contract*, 107; Lessnoff, *Social Contract*, 71.

[102] John Aubrey (1898), *Brief Lives* (Oxford), vol. 1: 357, quoted in Martin van Gelderen, "The Low Countries" in Lloyd, Burgess, and Hodson, *European Political Thought*, 414.

[103] See Brad S. Gregory (1989), introduction to *Tractatus Theologico-Politicus*, by Baruch Spinoza, trans. Samuel Shirley (New York: E.J. Brill), esp. 27–32, 29; Jonathan I. Israel (2001), *Radical Enlightenment: Philosophy and the Making of Modernity 1650–1750* (Oxford University Press), 159.

[104] Israel, *Radical Enlightenment*, 159.

[105] Spinoza, *Tractatus Theologico-Politicus*, 239.

result, they "have never conceived a theory of politics, which could be turned to use."[106] But this was about to change, for Spinoza claimed to have no such illusions. For him, men were essentially subject to passions, not to reason. "In consequence, since all are equally bent on supremacy, they start to quarrel, and do their utmost to enslave one another."[107] Spinoza agrees with Hobbes that "there is no one whose life is free from anxiety in the midst of feuds, hatred, anger and deceit" and "it will become quite clear to us that, in order to achieve a secure and good life, men had necessarily to unite in one body."[108] But, unlike Hobbes (and much closer to the later Rousseau), the individuals transferred their rights not to one person or a body of persons, but to the *entire community*.[109] For what we are interested in, this is a crucial distinction. "They therefore arranged that the unrestricted right naturally possessed by each individual should be put into *common* ownership, and that this right should no longer be determined by the strength and appetite of the individual, but by *the power and will of all together*."[110] Just a couple of pages later, he rephrases and expands upon the idea:

Therefore, without any infringement of natural right, a community can be formed and a contract be always preserved in its entirety in absolute good faith on these terms, that *everyone transfers all the power he possesses to the community, which will therefore alone retain the sovereign natural right over everything*, that is, the supreme rule which everyone will have to obey either of free choice or through fear of the ultimate penalty. *Such a community's right is called a democracy*, which can therefore be defined as a united body of men which *corporately possesses sovereign right* over everything within its power.[111]

The main advantage in a democratic state is that "nobody transfers his natural right to another so completely that thereafter he is not to be consulted."[112] As much as possible, individuals should retain their say in the political process through votes, discussions, debates, and the like. By preserving an equal "voice in affairs," "democracy promised to be the least irrational form of government, opening up for citizens the opportunity to live in accordance with reason, and, in doing so, to become truly free."[113] This is a far cry from the common version of the contract theory, where once individuals delegate their rights the decision-making process becomes the exclusive attribute of their representatives. Furthermore, Spinoza's emphasis on direct democracy is doubled by a deeply communitarian dimension. By acting for the common good, the individual acts

---

[106] Ibid., ch. 1, sec. 1, in A.G. Wernham, ed. (1958), *The Political Works* (Oxford), 261.
[107] Ibid., 277.
[108] Ibid., 239.
[109] The striking parallels between Spinoza's social contract and Rousseau's are worth considering, but beyond the scope of this work.
[110] Spinoza, *Tractatus Theologico-Politicus*, 239; emphasis added.
[111] Ibid., 241; emphasis added.
[112] Ibid., 243.
[113] Gelderen, "The Low Countries," 413.

"therefore for his own good also."[114] Following Quentin Skinner, Israel justly observes the dramatic difference:

Political freedom Spinoza conceives not in the 'negative' sense affirmed by Hobbes, and later adapted in a liberal direction by Locke, but as a tendency or condition of man linked to securing forms of political organization which serve the needs of the community, and the common interest or common good, and are best calculated to preclude corruption and despotism. Consequently, liberty in Spinoza is not negatively defined as an absence of obstacles, or confined to the private sphere, but envisaged, as in Machiavelli and later Rousseau, as a positive good or inalienable potential.[115]

As a matter of fact, Spinoza himself stressed this basic difference between his theory and Hobbes's when bluntly asked about by his friend Jelles, in 1674: "[It] consists in this, that I always preserve the natural right in its entirety, and hold that the sovereign power in a state has a right over a subject only in proportion to the excess of its power over that subject."[116] Apparently this deeply democratic commitment is at odds with Spinoza's similarly deep distrust of the 'multitude,' and the 'masses.'

[T]hose who have experienced the fickleness of the masses are almost reduced to despair; for the masses are governed solely by their emotions, not by reason; they rush wildly into everything, and are readily corrupted either by avarice or by luxurious living.... To guard against all these dangers, to organize a state in such a way as leaves no place for wrongdoing, or better still, to frame such a constitution that every man, whatever be his character, will set public right before private advantage, this is the task, this is the toil.[117]

In effect, Spinoza preserves here the French distinction between *le peuple* apprehended conceptually, that retains its sovereignty, and *le peuple* understood as whimsical multitude. He addresses the conundrum by implying that wise individuals will prove able to persuade and control the multitude, even with cunning and less rational methods if necessary, as did the Hebrew prophets in ancient times. At the same time, he carefully maintains the distinction between being persuaded to act and preserving one's freedom of judgment.

For we have shown that in a democracy (which comes closest to the natural state) all the citizens undertake to act, but not to reason and to judge by decisions made in common. That is to say, since all men cannot think alike, they agree that a proposal supported by a majority of votes shall have the force of a decree, meanwhile retaining the authority to repeal the same when they see a better alternative. Thus the less freedom of judgment is conceded to men, the further their distance from the most natural state, and consequently the more oppressive the regime.[118]

[114] Spinoza, *Tractatus Theologico-Politicus*, 243.
[115] Israel, *Radical Enlightenment*, 259.
[116] Baruch Spinoza (1995), *The Letters*, trans. S. Shirley (Indianapolis: Hackett), 258.
[117] Spinoza, *Tractatus Theologico-Politicus*, 253.
[118] Ibid., 297.

It is now time to check how Spinoza's German contemporary, Samuel Pufendorf, considered by many one of the important contract theorists of the classical period (and a major influence on Locke's premises if not on his conclusions), addresses the questions of individuals' delegation of rights to their representative(s).[119] Obviously, Pufendorf differs on these points from both Spinoza and Hobbes, although he shares with the former the belief that the good of community (*persona moralis composita*) takes preeminence over the (perceived) good of individuals (*persona moralis simplex*) and, with the latter, the assumption that "the dominating human motive is men's desire for their own convenience (*utilitatem*)."[120]

Yet Pufendorf is particularly important to us for an entirely different set of reasons. His theory marks in several ways the key moment when basic continental assumptions about individuals' political representation, faced by the English 'challenge,' started to make room for individual rights without being entirely ready to abandon the top-down directionality of representation. Furthermore, as I will show shortly, Pufendorf makes room in his theory for compromise as a preferred method of *arbitratio* (in the classical sense), but this only before the actual first contract takes place. This proves that in continental Europe, even by the end of the seventeenth century the distinction between contract as public and all-encompassing compromise and compromise as a private arbitration was still in place, although it already started to lose its hold. This is to be expected since the German theorist tries hard to navigate between the Scylla of a transcendental community and the Charybdis of individual voluntarism, and "between the mind of God and the rational capacities of man."[121]

To begin with, the individualist vision is softened first by the presumed men's *socialitas*, men's natural sociability (as in Grotius) – his 'mentor.'[122] These 'laws of sociability,' which are natural laws, ensure the keeping of promises and agreements. Men are not only *willing* but also somehow *obliged* by the awareness to these laws to exit "the purely natural state" (which remains an entirely rational construction: "it would be a fiction if we supposed that in the beginning there existed a multitude of men without any dependence on each other").[123] Only in this fictional state do all men enjoy both freedom and equality by not being subjected to anyone else's authority. But the moral laws, says Pufendorf, "would have had a perfect force to obligate man, even if God had

[119] Lessnoff, *Social Contract*, 156–157. See also Thompson, *Ideas of Contract*, 131.
[120] Gough, *The Social Contract*, 113.
[121] T.J. Hochstrasser (2000), *Natural Law Theories in the Early Enlightenment* (Cambridge: Cambridge University Press), 6.
[122] For an updated survey of Pufendorf's main intellectual influences, see T.J. Hochstrasser (2000), "Socialitas and the History of Natural Law: Pufendorf's Defence of *De jure naturae et gentium*," in Hochstrasser, *Natural Law Theories*.
[123] Samuel Pufendorf (1991), *On the Duty of Man and Citizen According to Natural Law*, ed. James Tully, trans. Michael Silverthorne (Cambridge: Cambridge University Press), 116.

never set them forth in His revealed word."[124] By exiting the purely natural state men entered "the mixed state of nature," that is, various forms of association of which, as in Althusius, the first are patriarchal families. In this mixed state equality between men disappears because of the authority presupposed by any social relations, yet natural liberty remains intact.[125]

Yet Pufendorf does not stop at *sociabilitas,* for sociability by itself is not enough: "those who were members of scattered families may have enjoyed a somewhat more developed way of life [than those living in the fictional state of nature] but in no way comparable with civil life."[126] The reason is not strictly economic, that is, poverty ("which family ... seems capable of relieving") but security which, among other things, presupposes the fair judgment of an impartial arbitrator. This in-between stage, not fully out the state of nature and not completely in the 'civil state' either, is the stage where compromise remains a workable solution:

> In the Natural State if any one, either will not voluntarily make good what he was covenanted to do, or does another an Injury, or if upon any other account some Dispute arise; there's no Man has authority to force the naughty Person to perform his Bargain, to cause him to repair the Wrong, or to determine the Controversy; as there is in Communities, where I may have recourse for Help to the Civil Magistrate. And here, because Nature allows not that upon every Occasion we should betake our selves to violent Means, even if we are very well satisfy'd in our Consciences of the Justice of our Cause; therefore we are first to try, whether the Matter may not be composed after a milder Way, either by an amicable Reasoning of the Point in Question between the Parties themselves, or by a free and unconditional Compromise, or Reference of the Debate to Arbitrators. And these Refereers are to manage the Matter with an equal regard to both Sides, and in giving their Award, they are to have an Eye only to the Merits of the Cause, setting aside all Animosity and Affection.[127]

Pufendorf goes on to stress the importance of an impartial arbitration, based upon reliable documents, witnesses, and "evidence that admits of no doubt." Obviously, such a classical compromise would be impossible in the "pure" state of nature, where no *compromissore* would have had the authority to

---

[124] *Elementorum*, II, Bk. II, Obs. IV, s. 3, 241, quoted in Thompson, *Ideas of Contract*, 137. For the same idea of obligation, see also Robert von Friedburg and Michael Seidler, "The Holy Roman Empire and the German Nation," in Lloyd, Burgess, and Hodson, *European Political Thought*, 169.

[125] Thompson, *Ideas of Contract*, 137.

[126] Pufendorf, *On the Duty of Man*, 118.

[127] Ibid., 172–173. Interestingly, in Michael Silverthorne's translation, there is no direct mention of compromise, although the sense is the same: "But as nature does not allow one to plunge into war on the slightest provocation, even when one is fully convinced of the justice of his cause, an attempt must be made to settle the matter by gentler means, namely, by friendly discussion between the parties and an absolute (not conditional) mutual promise or by appeal to the decision of arbitrators," 118.

perform such a judgment. But compromise is not always a workable solution, so men have no option but to leave even this mixed state of nature and enter the civil state. Without going into the subtleties and the challenges involved by Pufendorf's two-steps-plus-a-decree contract, suffice it to observe that in his account the 'first' contract between individuals has as a result a *"persona moralis composita,"* a corporation with a legal (i.e., contractual) personality. "Anyone who dissents remains outside the future state."[128] It is this newly created corporation that, *as a whole*, determines through '*decretum*' which form of government will be established (monarchy, aristocracy, or democracy). At this point the corporation functions as a *direct democratic* assembly, because *everyone* is free to express his own opinion. As Gough emphasizes, this *decretum* intercalated between the two contracts "involves the idea that the whole body of people as united by the social contract forms for the time being a kind of democratic assembly."[129] Once again, as in the case of Grotius (and the French writers), the options are clear: either total transfer of authority or direct political involvement. The middle, lukewarm way of representation has at least at this stage no appeal. Finally comes the contract of submission itself between *populus* collectively on the one hand and distributively (*singuli*) on the other and the sovereign, be this one person or an assembly of men. Only then does a state properly speaking come into being. At this point, the will of the sovereign ought to be "taken as the will of all and everyone."[130] That this emphasis on both individuals and community is not an accident is proved by the frequency and the insistence with which Pufendorf repeats the same idea in different places and from different perspectives. The state, for example, is "conceived as one person [*persona*], and distinguished from all particular men by a unique name; and it has its own special rights and property, which *no one man, no multitude of men, not even all men together may appropriate* apart from him who holds the sovereign power or to whom the government of the state has been committed."[131] Furthermore, civil authority maintains the classical top-down directionality. "This account of the origin of the states does not imply that civil authority [*imperium civile*] is not rightly said to be of God," for it is God who through reason compels men to follow the dictates of natural law.[132]

As many commentators have observed, this attempt to reconcile the individualistic vision with the organic is rather inconsistent and almost impossible to maintain. We shall see in the next chapter that the English theorists of the contract have much clearer options.

---

[128] Ibid., 136.
[129] Gough, *The Social Contract*, 116.
[130] Pufendorf, *On the Duty of Man*, 136.
[131] Ibid., 137; emphasis added.
[132] Ibid., 138.

7.3. FRENCH CONTRACTUALISM AFTER HOBBES AND LOCKE

The Edict of Toleration at Nantes, 1598, and the accession of the King of Navarre (even with his conversion to Catholicism) entirely changed the Huguenot perspective on the right to rebel. Writers such as Hotman or Duplessis-Mornay wrote now in favor of the hereditary right of kings to succession according to the Salic Law.[133] Allied with the Gallican Parlements, the Huguenots directed their attacks against the Jesuits and the supporters of papal supremacy over the king, and for decades to come the idea of a contract theory was entirely abandoned in favor of "a veritable chorus of praise for royalism."[134] As Pierre Bayle would remark soon in his *Dictionnaire historique et critique*, the Huguenots' doctrines proved to be "*vrais oiseaux de passage qui vont en un pays pendant l'été, en un autre pendant l'hiver*"[135] ("true migratory birds that go into one country during the summer, into another during the winter").

This attitude started to change once more in the years preceding the Revocation of the Edict of Toleration in 1685, when the wave of persecution intensified again. However, in a desperate attempt to change the king's heart, the first reaction was an even more passionate declaration of fidelity on the part of French Protestants. Thus, barely two months before the Revocation, Elie Merlat, a refugee pastor in Lausanne, published a *Traité du pouvoir absolu des souveraines* that rivaled (and sometimes surpassed) the absolutism of Hobbes, from whom in effect he quoted at great length. According to Merlat, in the beginning men were equal by nature with no domination over them except those resulting from the natural difference between parents and children and between natural gifts. "If this state of innocence could have endured without the introduction of sin, there would have been no need for rulers and subjects, since every individual would have resorted to reason for the law and to his will for the magistrate."[136] But he differs from Hobbes in asserting that even after the Fall man remains a sociable animal who does not necessarily love only himself. There was no need of a contract in order to bring about sovereign powers. God created such powers as a way of protecting men from their own sinfulness. For what is of interest to us, though, these 'details' make all the difference. Even if Merlat concludes, like Hobbes, that sovereigns "have no law which binds them with respect to their subjects" and the force of the law "is not strictly in its justice but in the authority of the legislator," he also admits that in matters of conscience passive disobedience is required, since consciences

---

[133] For Hotman, see *Brutum fulmen papae Sixti V adversus Hernicum sereniss or De jure successionis regiae in regno Francorum*. For Duplessis-Mornay, see *Mémoire contre la maison de Lorraine*, quoted in Guy Howard Dodge (1972), *The Political Theory of the Huguenots of the Dispersion – With Special Reference to the Thought and Influence of Pierre Jurieu* (New York: Octagon Books), 4.

[134] Dodge, *Political Theory*, 5.

[135] Quoted in ibid., 4.

[136] Ibid., 8.

belong only to God.[137] Under these circumstances, the resilience of insisting on the independence of the *forum internum* is truly impressive. What for Hobbes is a natural arbitrary power, for Merlat is God's punishment for men's sins: "*les péchés des homes autorisent les principes d'Hobbes*"[138] ("the sins of men authorize the principles of Hobbes").

It would be a mistake to discard such theological emphasis as mere archaic remnants in otherwise modern secular theories. Besides remaining captive to an evolutionary perspective that is still questionable, such an interpretation fails to acknowledge the importance attached by these authors to these 'details': the *forum internum* is jealously kept apart from the *forum externum*. Furthermore, it fails to realize a deeper difference in some basic assumptions about the relationships between individuals, communities, and politics that such a theological vision presupposes. It is not a mere 'detail' if one assumes that individuals have allegiances that go beyond their own self-interest or if one assumes the preeminence of reason or of will. The difference between the *forum internum* and the *forum externum* and between politics based on reason and politics based on wills is not to be taken lightly, for from it follows an entire host of assumptions about sovereignty, representation, rights, and so forth.

If the Huguenot refugees ... placed great emphasis upon an inviolable something in man, calling conscience or faith that which to the more secularly minded has been named reason, it was only because of their conviction that this inviolable something in man, whether divine or natural, is a part of the pattern of the universe. Therefore, to violate conscience, faith, or reason in man is nothing less than to attack the universal law of life, to bring about the very destruction of being itself.[139]

Pierre Jurieu can help illuminate this point further, and Dodge's work, completed in 1938–1939 (before World War II), and which made many of Jurieu's works unavailable, remains an invaluable asset.[140] The most active defender of the Calvinist cause, surnamed the "Goliath of Protestants" or the "French Burnet," did not embrace many of Merlat's ideas – quite the opposite – yet he shared with this supporter of the absolute monarchy the conviction that man's conscience belongs to God and no secular sovereign has or should have power over it. But he went further, stipulating that passive disobedience is not always enough. When the king's commands are contrary to religion and conscience, active disobedience is required. "*Les rois n'ont aucun povoir sur nos biens & nos vies, lorsqu'ils veulent empiéter sur les droits de la conscience qui seule appartient a Dieu. Nos biens & nos vies sont attachez à nos consciences.*"[141] ("The kings have no power over our goods & lives, when they want to encroach upon the rights of conscience that only pertain to God. Our goods & lives are

---

[137] *Traité du pouvoir absolu*, 166–167, quoted in ibid., 9.
[138] *Traité du pouvoir absolu*, 23–59, quoted in ibid., 10.
[139] Ibid., 237.
[140] Ibid.
[141] *Avis à tous le allies* (1705), 18–23, quoted in ibid., 29.

attached to our consciences.") However, despite what can be seen as a shrewd move to attach earthly goods to conscience, Jurieu agrees that in the end "property is less dear than liberty, life, and religion" – a distinction that, among other things (as Dodge observes), differentiates him from his contemporary Locke, to whom he was (and sometimes still is) often compared.[142]

Unlike Locke, Jurieu does not devote much discussion to the state of nature. In his *Lettres pastorales*, especially the sixteenth and seventeenth centuries, he is content to observe that in the beginning men lived in a state of nature, free and independent from each other except, as in Merlat's description, for the natural dependence ordained by God between members of the same family. Property was held in common, but once again the coming of sin prompted the division of property and the establishment of government whose role is primarily a moral one. The passage from the state of nature to societies or *peuples* is rather abrupt, as seen especially in his *Examen d'un libelle contre la religion* (1691). Addressing the accusations made by his rival, Pierre Bayle, Jurieu finds that the best defense remains the attack. The (supposedly) unknown author of the *Libelle*, he argues, cannot claim that kings have their authority directly (*"immediatement"*) from God. He will first have to disprove the following theses, which in turn would undermine his own argument:

1) *Que tous les homes sont nés libres & naturellement libres, comme naturelemment tous les biens sont indivisés. 2) Que les homes pouvoient vivre sans maître & sans partage de biens, sans violer les loix de la nature. 3) Que la seule necessité de la conservation de la Paix les a obligés à se faire des maîtres, & à partager les biens. 4) Que les peuples s'étant fait des Souveraines pour leur conservation n'ont pû leur donner un pouvoir sans bornes puisqu'eux mêmes ne l'avoient pas, & n'ont pû leur donner un pouvoir destructif de la Société, puisque cela répugne à la nature.*[143]

1) That all men are born free & naturally free, as naturally all goods are undivided. 2) That men could live without master & without dividing goods, without violating the laws of nature. 3) That only the necessity of preserving Peace forced them to create masters and split the goods. 4) That the peoples creating Sovereigns for their own preservation couldn't give them a power without limits since they themselves lacked it & couldn't give a power to destroy Society, since this is repugnant to nature.)

As one can see, the transition from 'step three,' the necessity of preserving peace forced 'men' ("them") to create masters, to 'step four,' where one talks already about 'peoples,' does not seem to require further explanation. Before and after this paragraph, Jurieu would talk only about *les droit des peuples* (the rights of peoples) without mentioning or even alluding once to anything close to the rights of the individual. As Dodge observes, despite being accused of 'foreign' (i.e., British) influences, "with Jurieu, the rights which are to be guaranteed are the rights of the people or the nation, and not yet strictly the rights

[142] Ibid., 45.
[143] *Examen d'un libelle contre la religion, contre l'État et contre la révolution* (1691), available at http://visualiseur.bnf.fr/CadresFenetre?O=NUMM-82285&I=221&M=chemindefer, 93–94 (220–221).

of the individuals, as in Locke."[144] Once again, it is the community that sets up the kings, not the individuals, and there is no clear distinction between a social and governmental contract, although other paragraphs appear to imply it (as the case of the 'republic' of Israel, under Judges). From a medievalist perspective, there was nothing new under the sun.

As with the Conciliarists in the fifteenth century, Jurieu tends to regard the location of sovereignty in the community not as a result of the autonomy of each of the members of the body politic, but as a result of the ends for which each man lives in a society. Furthermore ... his theory of popular sovereignty was based more upon the ancient Roman maxim *Salus populi suprema lex esto* than upon the conception of individual rights. Such doctrines are quite foreign to the theorists of modern democracy, such as Locke and perhaps Rousseau.[145]

As a matter of fact, there are not many surprises in Jurieu's writings, except maybe for the fact that there are no surprises, despite almost a century separating him from the first monarchomachs and the fact that during this period of time the works of Hobbes became extremely popular. As at the end of the sixteenth century, whether the contract or mutual pact is express or tacit does not change the fact that both parties have obligations only so long as they are rational ones. "*Il est donc certain qu'il n'y a aucune relation de maître, de serviteur, de père, d'enfant, de mari, de femme, qui ne soit établi sur un pact mutuel et sur des obligations mutuelles*"[146] ("It is therefore sure that there is no relationship of master, of servant, of father, of child, of husband, of wife that is not established on a mutual pact and on mutual obligations"). But if the father goes beyond his fatherly duties and acts irrationally, say by trying to kill his child, the child has the right to defense, and so does the people when the sovereign fails to protect it, even in the cases where he is granted absolute powers. (Jurieu too, like most authors of the time, makes a difference between absolute and unlimited power.) Once again, the right to rebel is not an individual one and resistance is permitted only when the welfare of the entire community, that is, of the *universitas*, is at stake.

The preeminence of reason over will is obvious when Jurieu addresses Bayle's accusations that his principles would in the end grant the right to rebel to any displeased minority or even individual. He replies that to make such allegations is to deliberately confound natural with positive or civil laws.

Si c'est une loy positive & purement d'institution humane pourquoy nous en fait-il une loy divine, & un droit inviolable? Si c'est une loy naturelle & divine elle n'est doit point souffrir d'exception; car ce que Dieu et la nature ordonnent est vray en un comme en deux, en deux comme en trois: seulement les circonstances peuvent varier la nature des faits; mais le nombre n'y change rien.[147]

---

[144] Dodge, *Political Theory*, 63–65.
[145] Ibid., 93.
[146] Quoted in ibid., 50.
[147] *Examen d'un libelle*, 168 (295).

(If this is a positive law & purely a human institution why does he make it for us a divine law & an inviolable right? If this is a natural law & divine it should not at all suffer exceptions; because what God and nature order is true in one as it is in two, in two as it is in three: only the circumstances may vary the nature of facts; but the number changes nothing.)

The fact that men chose for the sake of peace and convenience to adopt as right judgment the judgment of a majority cannot obscure the fact that sometimes the majority can do wrong against God, nature, and reason. Otherwise, argues Jurieu, any majority can commit any crime under the pretense that it is just, despite the evidence of the contrary. Nobody could seriously and reasonably argue such things. However, the simple fact that the majority of wills might be irrational at times does not mean that any minority or person is entitled to rebel even if God, nature, and reason are on its or his side. This is a principle (*"une constitution"*) that is "absolutely necessary for the preservation of order" (*"je l'avoue absolument necessaire pour la conservation de l'ordre"*).[148] Nothing has changed since almost a century before when Pierre Charron, following the example of Socrates, refused to compromise by defending himself against false accusations. According to Jurieu also, one should suffer even an unjust death sentence not because it is equitable, because obviously it is not; nor because of the numbers of the accusers, because obviously the numbers have nothing to do with what is just or unjust; but for the sake of order, so that other people justly condemned to death cannot enjoy a pernicious example. The only two cases when rebellion is allowed are when an attack on religion may end up with the perdition of souls, or when a large part of society is threatened with immediate destruction – that is, when what is under threat is either the uniqueness of the *forum internum* or the sameness of the *forum externum*.[149]

There is no doubt that Jurieu's vigorous literary style compensates a great deal for his lack of originality and explains the popularity he enjoyed even during his lifetime. However, there is a central political issue on which this Goliath of Protestantism appears to deserve his surname – the issue of sovereignty. On this account, Jurieu's explanation further clarifies an issue that I tackled above and that for authors such as J.W. Allen appeared paradoxical: why do all these authors insist that though the Prince is an agent and delegate of a sovereign people, he is also an agent and a delegate of God?[150] Not surprisingly, the metaphor used by Jurieu is theological and would have made perfect sense to his contemporaries: "Just as men do not cease to be images of God because they have been begotten by other men, so kings are the images of the Divine, even though they owe their immediate origin to the people."[151] The distinction between immediate

---

[148] Ibid., 171 (298).
[149] Ibid., 172–175 (299–304).
[150] Allen, *A History of Political Thought*, 317.
[151] Dodge, *Political Theory*, 47.

and intermediate authority is used by Jurieu to explain his seemingly ambivalent position toward sovereignty in the case of both religious and civil societies. It is not a descending authority, nor an ascending one, but a circular movement:

> *C'est une autorité qui monte & dont le movement est circulaire. Elle ne descend pas, car elle ne vient pas immédiatement de Dieu sur les Synodes, des Synodes sur les pasteurs & des Pasteurs sur le Peuple, mais elle vient de Dieu immédiatement sur le Peuple & du Peuple elle monte aux Synodes & aux Evêques, c'est la maniére dont roule l'autorité des Sociétez confédérées.*[152]

(It is an authority that ascends & whose movement is circular. It does not descend, for it does not come immediately from God onto the Synods, from the Synods onto the pastor & from the pastors onto the People, but it comes from God directly onto the People & from the people it ascends to Synods & to Bishops, this is the manner in which authority rolls in confederated Societies.)

The wording might be misleading if one disregards the distinction between immediate and intermediate authority. God gives (immediate, descending) authority to the people directly, while the bishops gain their godly authority only in an intermediate, ascending manner. On the secular side, one has an immediate transfer of authority from God to the people, and then from the people to the magistrates who select either a king or a council to govern them. The primary causation is God, the secondary causation is the people. Only then does authority descend once more upon minor magistrates and from them onto the people. It is a top-down, bottom-up, and again top-down circular movement that illuminates many apparent confusions, not only in terms of where the site of sovereignty is located but also of who has the right to revolt and as a result of what type of violation. The fact that the people has its sovereignty directly from God does not excuse a lack of respect, honor, and obedience toward the superior magistrate(s), even when the latter violate their trust, so long as the violation does not threaten the welfare of the whole.

Thus, people should not be reminded too often about their rights, for such a continuous remembrance might water the seeds of sedition in the thousand heads of the 'beast.' But on the other hand, kings should not be constantly flattered about their powers and independence either, because this might have catastrophic results for the people. As a matter of fact, Jurieu, like many of his predecessors, refuses to trace precise limits on the rights of the people or the sovereign. Once again, there is no clear-cut recipe for such situations and all depends on the reasonableness of the matter at hand.[153] Since authority is not created through a voluntary transfer of individual rights, it remains essentially disputable.

Jurieu was by no means alone among the French exiles that took sides with the English revolution by using a more or less refined version of a contract

---

[152] *Traité de la puissance de l'Église*, 106–107, quoted in ibid., 89.
[153] *Examen d'un libelle*, esp. 4–5 and 70–75.

theory in support of his arguments. Among the most prominent figures were Jacques Abbadie, Antoine Coulan, and the grandson of Duplessis-Mornay, La Combe de Vrigny.[154] But despite their differences (however important in many respects), in what is of interest to us they all shared with Jurieu the same approach: they defended the rights of the British Parliament from a position that shared with its British counterpart only its form, not its basic assumptions.

---

[154] For Jacques Abadie, see his *Défense de la nation britannique où les droits de Dieu, de la nature et de la societé sont clairement établis au sujet de la Révolution d'Angleterre contre l'Auteur de l'Avis important aux Réfugiés* (1693); for Antoine Coulan, see the *Défense des réfugiés* (1691); for La Combe de Vrigny, see *Défense du parlement d'Angleterre dans la cause de Jacques II où il est traité de la puissance des rois et du droit des peoples* (1692).

8

The British Contract as Com-promise

The true and Original Notion of Civil Society and Government, is, that is a Compromise made by such a Body of Men, by which they resign up the Right of demanding Reparations....

Gilbert Burnet

In analyzing modernity, the contemporary French thinker Chantal Delsol makes the distinction between what she calls a society 'of roles' and one 'of functions.'

A role is conferred in advance, often inscribed in the destiny of the individual, and inalienable. A function is chosen by the individual, is exterior to him, and he appears interchangeable in that function. A society of roles is hierarchical and differentiated. A society of functions tends toward equality and homogeneity.[1]

The distinction between *roles* and *functions* is paralleled, in Delsol's interpretation, by the one between *person* and *individuals*. If roles are unique, so are the persons who are able to play them. Roles "remain highly personalized, whether they are obscure or highly visible." Functions, on the other hand, are interchangeable, as are the individuals who exercise them. "Functions have no obligations because they can always be carried out by someone else."[2] The function of a parent, for example, can be fulfilled by any social worker, yet the role of the father is highly personalized and unique. In the light of the previous chapters it should be quite clear by now that while France remained for a longer period of time a society of roles which "saw inequality everywhere, even where it did not exist," England moved faster toward the model

---

[1] Chantal Delsol (2003), *Icarus Fallen: The Search for Meaning in an Uncertain World*, trans. by Robin Dick (Wilmington: ISI Books), 139.

[2] Ibid., 142–143.

of a society of functions, one that "sees equality everywhere, even where it does not exist."[3]

From a theoretical perspective, as we have seen in the previous chapter, the corporatist vision in which each person was called on to play his role was translated in the different versions of continental contract theory by a refusal to equate irreplaceable persons with interchangeable individuals. The contract was designed between the people carefully conceptualized as a whole and its representatives (King, Estates, magistrates, etc.). What mattered first and foremost in such theories was the common good of *le peuple* and more specifically its most reasonable part. The wiser part *was* the people, in the same way that the brain (i.e., the conscience) or the heart (i.e., the soul) is said to *be* the person. An irrational contract was automatically void, for the requirement of rationality cannot be discarded nor replaced by sheer will. As a matter of fact, the perspective of a mere combination of wills was frightening for almost all French authors of the time, who referred the conception to the crowd, the "thousand-headed beast." Not surprisingly then, contract theories never became truly popular in seventeenth-century France.

From this perspective as well the story was quite different across the Channel, both in practical and theoretical terms. We have already seen how because of its historical peculiarities – of which the partial homogenization of local allegiances, the increasing role of a national Parliament, and disputed elections coupled with the increasing political enfranchisement played probably the most important roles – England was the first country to witness at an unprecedented scale the development of what I labeled 'centrifugal individualism.' Starting with the sixteenth century and increasingly during the seventeenth, *every* Englishman was considered and (at least to a certain extent) felt *equally* represented by *his* representatives, his King or the King in Parliament. Their consent was his consent, as was made clear, for example, by Sir Thomas Smith or Richard Hooker. As a result, the directionality of representation changed. The individual, more specifically the individual's will, became the rather undisputed source of any political authority. England, as Kahn put it, evolved into "a society of discrete individuals" based upon "the new fiction of the autonomous political subject – a subject not bound by traditional notions of status and hierarchies."[4]

Yet by accepting that *he* is equally represented as many others by *his* representative(s), this Englishman tacitly accepted his loss of uniqueness. He was no longer a person, but an individual. He no longer performed a role, but was content with a function. Once the costume became the person, the emphasis switched from rationality to the will of the majority. By 1566, in his *De republica anglorum*, Sir Thomas Smith reported as an established principle

---

[3] Delsol, *Icarus Fallen*, 144.
[4] Victoria Kahn (2004), *Wayward Contracts: The Crisis of Political Obligation, 1640–1674* (Princeton: Princeton University Press), 13.

not requiring further explanation that in both houses "as the more number doth agree, so it is agreed on, or dashed."[5] "No other kingdom in Europe achieved anything quite like for another two centuries."[6] Even the neo-Stoic movement in England, although deeply influenced by French authors, mainly Montaigne and Charron, veered "sharply from the path it had taken in the rest of the Europe and eventually became a refuge for malcontents and cynics in the Jacobean court, and a target of suspicion ... rather than a basis for their monarchist political theory," as it did across the Channel.[7] By the time of the English revolution, a modern vocabulary was already in place in which 'will' and 'interest' played a central role. Looking back to the late 1640s, the Presbyterian Charles Herle remarked in 1655, "the word *Interest* is a word of late much come into use among us" (*Wisdomes Tripos*, 169).[8]

At this point, it is worth remembering once more that such distinctions were not as clear-cut as they may sound in an academic presentation. Modern as they were, vocabularies were still intermingled and meanings disputed. It was, in Kahn's words, a "struggle over language and over representation."[9] We have seen, for example, that even Englishmen were not willing to give up the language of 'the whole political body,' even though much of the time they understood by it a collection of discrete individuals united by their own wills. In the same way, British aristocrats seemed often times as concerned by the 'many-headed beast' as were their French counterparts – from whom indeed it appears they borrowed the expression, through the translations of Montaigne by Florio in 1603 or Du Bartas by Sylvester.[10] Even Levellers and Republicans such as Milton in different ways expressed contempt for the uneducated and vulgar multitude.

Obviously, the struggle over the people was a double-edged one. "Nowadays there is no vulgar, but all statesmen," commented Francis Bacon ironically, who did not love "the word 'people.'"[11] And although the word 'people' did not include women, children, and the poor, it is indisputable that seventeenth-century England witnessed an incredible increase in political inclusiveness.[12] By

[5] Sir Thomas Smith (1906), *De republica anglorum*, ed. Leonard Alston (Cambridge: Cambridge University Press), 55.

[6] Michael Davis (2003), *Actual Social Contract and Political Obligation: A Philosopher's History through Locke* (Lewiston, N.Y.: Edwin Mellen Press), 105.

[7] Lisa Ferraro Parmelle (1994), "Neostocism and Absolutism in Late Elizabethan England," in *Politics, Ideology and the Law in Early Modern Europe: Essays in Honor of J.H.M. Salmon*, ed. Adrianna E. Bakos (Rochester, N.Y.: University of Rochester Press), 13.

[8] Quoted in Richard Tuck (1993), *Philosophy and Government 1572–1651* (Cambridge: Cambridge University Press), 223.

[9] Kahn, *Wayward Contracts*, 1.

[10] See an excellent review of this subject in Christopher Hill (1975), *Change and Continuity in Seventeenth-Century England* (Cambridge, Mass.: Harvard University Press), esp. 181–204.

[11] C.D. Bowen (1963), *Francis Bacon*, 144, quoted in Hill, *Change and Continuity*, 192.

[12] For a somewhat different perspective, see *The Collected Essays of Christopher Hill*, vol. 3: *People and Ideas in 17th Century England* (1985), (Amherst: University of Massachusetts

the time of the debates of the Grand Remonstrance in 1641, "men of property were more prepared ... than at any time since 1536 to connive at, if not possible to foster, a popular revolt."[13] "To many in both parliament and country by 1641, the people were no longer merely to be governed, but they were to act in partnership with their representatives in the House."[14] In October 1647, Laurence Clarkson asked abruptly: "Who are the oppressors but the nobility and gentry? And who are the oppressed, is not the yeoman, the farmer, the tradesman and the labourer? ... Have you not chosen oppressors to redeem you from oppression?"[15] Frightened by the possible implications of such inclusiveness, Sir Edward Dering forgot the populism of his own actions only six months earlier and protested against the Grand Remonstrance, "this descension from a Parliament to a people." "I did not dream that we should remonstrate downward, tell stories to the people, and talk of the King as of a third person." "I neither look for cure of our complaints for the common people, nor to the desire to be cured by them."[16]

The same display of similarities and differences across the Channel can be found in the case of contract theories. The influence of the French monarchomachs and other towering figures (especially but not only Grotius and Althusius) is difficult to deny. But so are the differences. In order to sort them out amid such a vast amount of material, both from primary and secondary sources, I will appeal once more to the 'tunnel vision' strategy employed in the previous chapter. I will focus again almost exclusively on the two aspects revealing for the connection between contract theory and a particular understanding (and usage) of compromise: (a) the assumption (or lack thereof) of the equality of all the individuals entering the contract as the precondition of any compromise; (b) the existence (or not) of a moment in which individuals delegate their (political) rights into the hands of a person or group, thus creating not only an 'artificial' arbitrator, but also, by the same token, the premises of a distinct, 'professional' political sphere. This separation of politics from 'lay' individuals, as we shall see, raises disturbing questions about the proper role and status of what the first contractualists labeled as civil society.

As I have shown before, by the seventeenth century contractarianism was already a well-established practice in England. However, such a disposition

---

Press), esp. ch. 12. Although I do not dispute Hill's distinction between 'people' and 'the poor,' the very fact that he accepts that in the definition of 'people' came to be accepted yeomen, artisans, and merchants proves my point.

[13] Hill, *Change and Continuity*, 203.

[14] Derek Hirst (1975), *The Representative of the People? Voters and Voting in England under the Early Stuarts* (Cambridge: Cambridge University Press), 193.

[15] L. Clarkson (1647), *A Generall Charge or Impeachment of High Treason in the Name of Justice Equity, against the Communality of England*, 18, quoted in *The Collected Essays of Christopher Hill*, 264.

[16] John Rushworth, *Historical Collections*, 1659–1701, iv, 425–428; see also Sir E. Dering (1642), *A Collection of Speeches*, 108–109, 118, quoted respectively in Hirst, *The Representative of the People?*, 187, and in Hill, *Change and Continuity*, 193.

would not have been possible in the absence of a wide array of more theoretical literature. After all, as Quentin Skinner argues, "what is possible to do in politics is generally limited by what is possible to legitimize. What you can hope to legitimize, however, depends on what courses of action you can plausibly range under existing normative principles."[17] The theoretical struggles of seventeenth-century Britain are not therefore to be dismissed beforehand. The remainder of the chapter is thus devoted to this literature. But even restricted to an analysis of the two issues mentioned above – equality and delegation – there still remains too much ground to cover. Under these circumstances, selection is unavoidable and yet disputable. The criterion of the selection used is relevance. To check the impact of contractualist thinking on seventeenth century England I will start obliquely, discussing in the first two parts two rival theories, namely patriarchalism and republicanism, in order to see how their supporters discussed contractualism. If one can show that during that time contractualist thinking was the pivot around which all justifications gravitated, one can prove the centrality of contract for the British *Weltanshauung*. The reminder of the chapter will try to demonstrate that for the seventeenth century Englishman, from Hobbes to Burnet, contract was assimilated with compromise, which explains the British positive outlook on both contract and compromise.

8.1. PATRIARCHALISM AND CONTRACTUALISM

As Gordon Schochet persuasively argues, patriarchalist and contractualist theories in seventeenth-century England were not historically successive, as one might think, but rather complementary, the former trying to address the challenges of the latter. Since the appeal to origins was largely accepted in the Stuart period, both theories aimed at developing what Schochet calls 'genetic political assumptions.' Before the emergence of a contract theory there was no real need for its patriarchal counterpart. What is of interest to us is that the patriarchalist criticism of contract theories confirms the individualist and equalitarian perspective on contract. By 1606, in the *Convocation Book* meant (unsuccessfully) to add an official body of political principles to Anglican doctrines, the common understanding of the contractualist premises is plain:

If any man therefore affirm that men at first, without all good education or civility, ran up and down in woods, and fields, as wild creatures, resting themselves in caves and dens, *acknowledging no superiority one over another*, until they were taught by experience the necessity of government; and that therefore they chose some amongst themselves to order and rule the rest, *giving them power and authority so to do*; and that consequently all civil power, jurisdiction and authority, was first derived from the people, and *disordered multitude*; or either is originally still in them, or else is deduced

---

[17] Quentin Skinner (1998), *Liberty before Liberalism* (Cambridge: Cambridge University Press), 105.

by their consents naturally from them; and is not God's ordinance originally *descending* from Him, and depending upon Him, *he doth greatly err.*[18]

We deal here with equal individuals ("acknowledging no superiority one over another") unable to decide anything precisely because of this equality. The only solution therefore to avoid endless violence is the creation of a government by handing each person's power and authority to "some" who will become both judges and enforcers of the laws. This passage, like many others, makes plain that by the beginning of the seventeenth century the switch of the directionality of authority from descending to ascending brought forward by the British versions of contract theory was already obvious to its critical contemporaries.

Robert Filmer is probably the most famous exponent of patriarchalism able to raise an entire set of criticisms pertaining to the nature of 'representative bodies' and to 'the manner of the people passing their consent': contractualists, he argued, never bother to clarify if this consent is "express or tacit, collective or representative, absolute or conditioned, free or enforced, revocable or irrevocable" – such questions are rather conveniently ignored.[19] Yet probably the most astute of Filmer's criticisms concerns the difficulty of claiming that the 'whole people' is nothing but a collection of discrete individuals. "The whole people is a thing so uncertain and changeable that it alters every moment, so that it is necessary to ask every infant so soon as it is born its consent to government, if you will ever have the consent of the whole people."[20] His observations about the discrepancies between theoretical claims and practices are relevant even (and particularly) today, when participation in the electoral process is reduced to record-low numbers.

Literally, and in the largest sense, the word people signifies the whole multitude of mankind; but figuratively and synecdochically, *it* notes many time the major part of a multitude, or sometimes the better, or the richer, or the wiser, or some other part; and oftentimes a very small part of the people, if there be no apparent opposite party, hath the name of the people by presumption.[21]

Once one gives up the conceptualized notion of people as a whole in favor of the more 'realistic' one that claims the people is a collection of individuals, the problems are almost insurmountable. The same set of difficulties is

---

[18] *Convocation Book*, ch. 2, pp. 2–3, emphasis added, quoted in Gordon J. Schochet (1975), *Patriarchalism in Political Thought: The Authoritarian Family and Political Speculation and Attitudes Especially in Seventeenth-Century England* (New York: Basic Books), 92–93. Refused by James, the book was first published in 1690 by William Sancroft, the nonjuring Archbishop of Canterbury.

[19] Sir Robert Filmer (1696), *Observations upon Aristotles Politiques Touching Forms of Government*, in *Observations concerning the original and various forms of government, as described, viz. lst. Upon Aristotles politiques. 2d. Mr. Hobb's* ... (London), 146

[20] Ibid., 121.

[21] Ibid., 226, quoted in Schochet, *Patriarchalism*, 124.

encountered at the level of any representative assembly. "It is further observable in assemblies, that it is not the whole assembly, but the major part only of the assembly that hath the government." If one seriously considers the claim that an assembly, say Parliament, displays a unity of will because of the wills of a majority, one is also forced to accept that "the same assembly may make, at one sitting, several forms of commonwealth, for in several debates and votes the same number of men, or the self-same men do not ordinarily agree in their votes; and the least disagreement either in the persons of the men, or in their numbers, alters the form of government." If government takes its authority from the combined wills of a majority, then government lasts only as long as that specific majority lasts. "For in the very instant, as it were in the twinkling of an eye, while their vote lasteth, the government must begin and end."[22] Therefore, "it is a false and improper speech to say that a whole multitude, Senate, Council, or any Multitude whatsoever doth govern where the major party only rules; because many of the multitude that is so assembled, are so far from having any part in the government, that they themselves are governed against and contrary to their wills."[23]

If one really believes that every man was born free by nature and governed only by consent, it follows that one can never equate the will of the majority with the wills of the whole people. Here, Filmer mounts a direct attack on Bodin's notion of sovereignty. When discussing the Popular Estate, when "all the people or the greater part thereof hath the sovereignty," Bodin offered the example of "threescore thousand citizens": if forty thousand of them have the sovereignty and twenty thousand do not, it is still to be called a popular Estate. "But," argues Filmer, "I must tell him, though fifty nine thousand, nine hundred, ninety nine of them govern, yet it is no popular Estate; for if but one man be excluded, the same reason that excludes that one man, may exclude many hundreds, and many thousands, yea, and the major part itself." Once the principle is accepted, nobody can be excluded from his right to government through consent, regardless if part of the minority or majority. To accept that people willingly accede to delegating their powers to a majority, argues Filmer, is absurd as long as *it is natural to use it themselves* in laws that concern them. "And to suppose the people so unnatural, as at the first to have all consented to give away their right to a major part, (*as if they had liberty given them only to give it away and not to use it themselves*) is not only improbable, but impossible."[24] Since even in a trial by jury each of the twelve jurors retains his negative voice against the majority, "how much more ought the natural freedom of each man be preserved, by allowing him his negative voice, which is but a continuing him in that estate, wherein, it is confessed, nature at first placed him"?[25]

---

[22] Ibid., 110.
[23] Ibid., 111.
[24] Ibid., 120–121.
[25] Ibid., 121.

As one can see, Filmer was determined, as was James I before him, to bring the fight to the contractualists, playing their own professed premises against their ultimate consequences. When it comes to the question of representation "of the people" the same strategy is applied. The presumed "Representors" of the people are in fact, he argues, "representors of Provinces, Cities, and Burroughs-Towns," but even they are not chosen by the whole people and not even by the major part of it. Even so, all these representatives can never meet all at one time, "but still they must be imagined to be the people." And again, even so, these representatives have to choose their own representatives ("to represent the representors") in order to work the laws in committees. In such smaller assemblies there is also a Speaker who can easily persuade the others to follow his lead. How could one claim, then, to have a popular government? Since there is no question of ruling and being ruled in turn, as Aristotle had it, how could one talk about the sovereignty of the people?[26] "If it be true, that men are by nature free-born, and not to be governed without their own consent, and that self-preservation is to be regarded in the first place, it is not lawful for any government but self-government to be in the world, it were sin the people to desire, or attempt to consent to any other government."

To pretend that a major part, or the silent consent of any part, may be interpreted to bind the whole people, is both unreasonable and unnatural; it is against all reason for men to bind others, where it is against nature for men to bind themselves. *Men that boast so much of natural freedom, are not willing to consider how contradictory and destructive the power of the major part is to the natural liberty of the whole people.*[27]

In the end, however, such observations, no matter how astute, amounted to little. When it came to proposing its own theory, patriarchalism itself was open to even more devastating criticisms. Not surprisingly, then, it failed on all counts to prevent the success of contractualism.

A normative social or political theory is regarded as acceptable by a given culture or historical period not so much because of its 'truth' as because of its persuasive force. Successful persuasion is largely the result of the doctrine's ability to 'fit into' a culture and to incorporate and rely upon the principles that are widely accepted or taken for granted. In a culture that was beginning to make fundamental *distinction* between polit- ical and social authority, a theory such as patriarchalism that presupposed their identity was bound to become outmoded, irrelevant, and therefore unacceptable.[28]

One may dispute the argument but not its conclusions. By the end of the seventeenth century and the beginning of the eighteenth, contractualism domi- nated the theoretical field. Even family relationships came to be accepted as essentially contractual. In 1705 Bishop William Fleetwood pushed the contract theory even further when he wrote that "there is no Relation in the World,

---

[26] Ibid., 142–143.
[27] Ibid., 143–145; emphasis added.
[28] Schochet, *Patriarchalism*, 57; emphasis added.

either Natural, or Civil and agreed upon, but there is a reciprocal duty obliging each Party."

For every relation being built and depending upon a Contract, either suppos'd in Nature and reason, or actually agreed upon and made betwixt the Parties related, upon what terms they found it convenient; it must need be, that each Party is oblig'd to perform his part of that Contract upon which the Relation stands: For Justice and Reason know no difference of Parties or Relations; with them (as with their everlasting Fountain) there is no respect of Persons: They only have regard to what the agreement is, and how it is perform'd.[29]

In contract, the parties have, so to speak, no face. Their identity is indifferent. The only thing that matters is "the contract upon which the relation stands." There are no longer 'persons,' as Delsol put it, but only faceless individuals performing their functions according to the contract. Contract became the basis of all relationships, "either Natural or Civil and agreed upon." But if this was the case, how did contractualism resonate with the republican movement quite active in England, especially in the second half of the seventeenth century?

8.2. REPUBLICANISM AND CONTRACTUALISM

Consider the following paragraph by Donald W. Hanson that nicely resumes the general accepted opinion about the change brought forward by the success of contractualist thinking.

Contract thinking depicts men as essentially equal, discrete, and autonomous units of will, whose consent is the only legitimate source of obligation. This broad conception involved the repudiation not only of the basic assumption of a static and graded social order, but also the whole style of a traditional political order: ancestral piety and reverence for the past, the personal and familial nature of obligation and loyalty, and the fragmentary and local character of organization and interests.[30]

This is the contractualism said to be one of the keystones of the nascent liberal movement. How can this vision accommodate republicanism? If republicanism emphasizes personal virtue and direct involvement in public life, liberty, and personal responsibility, displays contempt for any form of selfishness, claiming the supremacy of public good over private interest, or that reason ought to dominate will, how can such republicanism possibly fit into the contractarian frame of mind? The answer depends on the definitions we are using. There are several forms of contractualism, as there are several forms

[29] William Fleetwood, (1705) *The Relative Duties of Parents and Children: Husbands and Wives, Masters and Servants, Consider'd in Sixteen Sermons: with Three More Upon the Case of Self-murther* (London: Charles Harper), 86, 88–89, 394, quoted in ibid., 83–84.
[30] Donald W. Hanson (1970), *From Kingdom to Commonwealth: The Development of Civic Consciousness in English Political Thought* (Cambridge: Harvard University Press), 318.

of liberalism and republicanism. Some of them are incompatible but others are not. Since no such academic distinctions (nor labels) were ever used during the seventeenth century it is to be expected that some conceptually shady areas could manage to accommodate both intellectual tendencies. Not surprisingly, more and more scholars have started to question a clear-cut dichotomy of liberalism and republicanism.[31] The language of contract is essential on this point. Because of its widespread use in seventeenth century England and the variety of meanings it was able to acquire in various discourses, it "emerged as a central term in the struggle over political legitimation and obligation" both in 'liberal' and 'republican' discourses.[32]

In the previous chapter I have tried to show that French contractualism, although similar in form to the English version, was based upon fundamentally different assumptions. The fact that the contract was between the whole and the King (and ultimately between the whole people and God) did not change the classical understanding of representation. If the people provided its representatives (King, Estates, or Parlements) with its authority, such authority was still *descending* upon the representatives, since the whole was always above the parts. As a result, there was no question of individual representation and no delegation of personal authority. To use Delsol's distinction, French contractualism still worked with persons, not individuals, and therefore was theoretically at least more compatible with republicanism. Paradoxically for a country that beheaded a king and replaced another, the story again was rather different across the Channel.

The problems of definition are even more complicated in the cases of liberalism and republicanism. Liberalism emerged as a political label only during the nineteenth century and "no one in or before the Puritan Revolution called himself or herself a republican. 'Republican' and 'republicanism' were terms of abuse and caricature."[33] Consequently, there have been many scholarly debates about the proper definition of the two terms. In the case of republicanism, two main understandings emerged in the footsteps of Skinner and Pocock, respectively. One emphasizes republicanism as a program to replace hereditary monarchy ('constitutional republicanism'), the other as a language of ideas about political action and civic virtue ('civic republicanism').[34] Both have received serious refinements in recent years, but as far as our concerns go it is not the kingless form of government that is of interest. In this, I side with Worden

---

[31] See, e.g., Isaac Kramnick, Jeffrey Isaac, Johnathan Scott, or Quentin Skinner.

[32] Kahn, *Wayward Contracts*, 22.

[33] Blair Worden (2002), "Republicanism, Regicide and Republic: The English Experience," in *Republicanism: A Shared European Heritage*, vol. 1, ed. Martin Van Gelderen and Quentin Skinner (Cambridge: Cambridge University Press), 307.

[34] For a discussion of these two trends, see, e.g., Andrew Hadfield (2006), "Republicanism in Sixteenth- and Seventeenth-Century Britain," in *British Political Thought in History, Literature and Theory, 1500–1800*, ed. David Armitage (Cambridge: Cambridge University Press), 111–128; and Worden, "Republicanism, Regicide and Republic," 307–327.

when he asserts that constitutional arrangements were secondary to the republican thinking of the time, at least in the first half of the century, and in any case are less revealing for us today.

In pre-civil-war England, the principle of monarchy enjoyed the hold that democracy enjoys today. We hear many complaints about the functioning of democracy, about the gap between practice and ideal, but the ideal itself is virtually exempt from criticism. In pre-civil-war England it was the abuse of monarchy, not the principle, that attracted complaint.[35]

From this perspective, as we have seen, England was no different from France during the Fronde. What is thus of interest to us is how (or if) the language of virtue, the emphasis on reason, and the understanding of political action (self-government) as a requirement (or obligation) of liberty were able to accommodate the language of contract and of natural rights during seventeenth-century Britain. From this perspective, an author such as James Harrington is less interesting than, say, Algernon Sidney. As Scott argues persuasively, among his fellow republicans "Harrington was the exception." While Sidney focused on virtues, Harrington focused on self-interest. (Consider the example of the two girls dividing a pie.) While others following prudence claimed that "no certain form [of government] can be prescribed at all times," Harrington, following Hobbes ("I firmly believe that Mr. Hobbes – – will in the future ages be accounted the best writer at this day in the world"), claimed that a constitution well crafted could supply the imperfections of its citizens once and for all, making it the core of his new science.[36] (Consider Harrington's famous example of the cats and kittens so well *tight* as their only possible motions were to act as automata, in this case as cooks.) I think Scott is right in arguing "that the substance (as opposed to form) of classical republicanism lay in certain moral political assumptions and practices. Neither in these terms, nor linguistically, was Harrington's thought straightforwardly republican."[37]

Giving the scope of our inquiry, Algernon Sidney is a much more interesting figure. One of Thomas Jefferson's favorite authors[38] aside John Locke, Sidney's life and martyrdom were in themselves an embodiment of the republican values he professed in writing. And yet, he was from the beginning difficult to fit in a neat box. All attempts to qualify him as a democrat, a liberal, a philosopher, or a constitutionalist had to elude aspects that apparently at least contradict such labels.[39] He was a contractarian but shared with Filmer, against

---

[35] Worden, "Republicanism, Regicide and Republic," 311.

[36] James Harrington (1977), *Political Works*, ed. J.G.A. Pocock (Cambridge), 423.

[37] Jonathan Scott (2002), "Classical Republicanism in Seventeenth Century England and the Netherlands," in Van Gelderen and Skinner, *Republicanism*, 65.

[38] "I have lately undertaken to read Algernon Sidney on government.... As often as I have read it, and fumbled it over, it now excites fresh admiration [i.e., wonder] that this work has excited so little interest in the literary world." Letter of September 17, 1823, in Lester J. Cappon, ed. (1971), *The Adams-Jefferson Letters* (New York: Simon & Schuster), 598.

[39] See Martyn P. Thompson (1987), *Ideas of Contract in English Political Thought in the Age of John Locke* (New York and London: Garland Publishing), 197; or Thomas G. West (1996),

whom he wrote his *Discourses Concerning Government*, some of the same basic assumptions. Though praised by Locke (who ranked him with Hooker, Pufendorf, Paxton, and himself as recommended authors for the student of "the Original of Societies, and the rise and extent of political power"), he differs from him in significant aspects.[40] And yet he differs also from Grotius or Pufendorf, presumably the two contract theorists who influenced him most.[41] According to Thompson, his version of contract was not entirely 'philosophical' nor entirely 'constitutional' but 'integrated,' making use (as did Filmer, whom he refuted) of both types of arguments.

There is truth in all these observations. The reason, I think, is to be found in this seemingly peculiar mélange of republicanism and liberalism. If Sidney's contract theory appears closer to the continental versions than to the British ones it is because these versions, as we have seen, may easier accommodate the principles of republicanism than (for lack of a better word) 'liberal contractarianism.' Unlike these 'liberal' versions, there is no mention of any state of nature and he considers Hobbes's *bellum omnia contra omnes* "an epidemical madness" possible only "if God so abandon the world to suffer them to fall into such misery."[42] According to Sidney, men are by nature equally free, but this liberty is a "*rational* liberty." They follow reason, not passions, and therefore are drawn by their very nature into societies, beginning with families. "The truth is, men are hereunto led by *reason which is his nature*. Everyone sees that they cannot well live asunder, nor many together, without some rule to which all must submit."[43]

Although liberty is "a gift from God and nature" and he defines it as "solely ... the independency upon the will of another," Sidney also agrees that it cannot be unlimited.[44] First, man is under obligation to God, "the creature having nothing, and being nothing but what the creator makes him, must owe all to him." Yet since God made man free, "man therefore must be naturally free." The second obedience, in typical classical fashion, is due to parents "who are the instruments of our generations" – but this obedience too is not much of an impediment since it is not a political obligation and "when they die we are their heirs, we enjoy the same rights, and devolve the same to our posterity."[45] Political freedom is thus ensured, at least for the head of the family. But there is yet another restriction, one that is or should be self-imposed in the light of

---

introduction to *Discourses Concerning Government*, by Algernon Sidney, ed. Thomas G. West (Indianapolis: Liberty Fund).

[40] *The Educational Writings of John Locke*, ed. J. Axtel, 400, quoted in Thompson, *Ideas of Contract*, 197.

[41] See Thompson, *Ideas of Contract*, or West's introduction to Sidney, *Discourses Concerning Government*.

[42] Sidney, *Discourses Concerning Government*, 84.

[43] Ibid., 189.

[44] Ibid., 51.

[45] Ibid., 431.

reason. "The public interest and the concernments of private men ... cannot be preserved by one who is transported by his own passions or follies, a slave to his lusts and his vices."[46] The one that is incapable of self-control or virtue is, as in Aristotle, "a slave by nature."

Several consequences follow from these premises. To begin with, the scope of the government is twofold: not just to ensure the safety of the individual but also to encourage virtue and the common good. "Liberty without restraint [is] inconsistent with any government *and* the good which man naturally desires for himself, children and friends."[47] On the one hand, "publick safety" ought "to be provided, liberty and propriety secured."[48] Yet on the other hand, its aim is also to ensure that "justice is administered, virtue encouraged, vice suppressed, and the true interest of the nation advanced."[49] The emphasis on virtue and public interest does not preclude man's personal freedom. "I am not afraid to say that a man is the judge of his own concernments." A man can do whatever he pleases with his own house, land, or estate. "No one is or can be deprived of this *privilege*, unless by his own consent, *and* for the good of that society into which he enters. This *right* therefore must necessarily belong to every man in all cases, *except only such as related to the good of the community, for whose sake he has divested himself of it.*"[50]

In this one paragraph one can observe at work Sidney's to and fro between republicanism and liberalism, between positive and negative liberty. Undoubtedly this can be confusing. Noticing the widespread usage of the language of rights by English republicans, Skinner, for examples, concludes, "one cannot therefore distinguish neo-roman from contractarian accounts of civil liberty by reference to their supposedly contrasting treatment of rights."[51] As a matter of fact, as the above quoted paragraph proves, one can. If public good requires it, the *right* to do what you please may became a revocable *privilege*. According to natural law, the *reason* why men are willing to accept restrictions on their natural liberty is because man's good is not possible independent from the good of all and the only *reasonable* condition for this acceptance is that everyone is willing to consent to the same restrictions. Therefore, the ends of the government are as natural as man's nature.

> This submission is a restraint of liberty, but could be of no effect as to the good intended; unless it were general; nor general, unless it were natural. When all born unto the same freedom, some will not resign that which is their own, unless others do the like: This general consent of all to resign such a part of their liberty as seems to be for the good

---

[46] Ibid., 395.
[47] Ibid., 189.
[48] Ibid., 379.
[49] Ibid.
[50] Ibid., 460; emphasis added.
[51] Skinner, *Liberty before Liberalism*, 19, note 58.

of all, is the voice of nature, and the act of men (according to natural reason) seeking their own good.[52]

There are, claims Sidney, two ways of ensuring that these ends of the government are met. One is by securing the rule of law, because only laws, applicable to everyone, can prevent corruptibility from creeping into governmental decisions. "For this reason the law is established, which no passion can disturb. 'Tis void of desire, fear, lust and anger. 'Tis *mens sine affectu* [mind without passion], written reason, retaining some measure of the divine perfection.... 'Tis deaf, inexorable, inflexible."[53] Yet despite the fact that law "is reason" (and if otherwise it shouldn't be obeyed), law in itself is not enough: first, because even if reason is universal and natural, the contexts vary from one society to another, therefore these laws should adapt to a particular set of conditions; second, because even in a particular society, conditions are prone to change and someone has to take these changes into account. Therefore, virtuous and prudent men should *double* laws and the legislative process in order to ensure adaptability. These men are the magistrates (according to Sidney, kings are nothing but superior magistrates). They are best equipped for the prudence that no abstract law can provide. Yet in order to select the best persons for the job (on this point Sydney does not discriminate between men and women – Queen Elizabeth, unlike Henry the Fifth, was as good a ruler – "she knew she did not reign for herself, but for her people"),[54] one needs people educated or virtuous enough to recognize excellence wherever they see it. It is the same vicious circle (or virtuous, depending on how one choses to look at it) that characterized classical thought. Consent, therefore, is not in itself enough to ensure the legitimacy of the ruler(s). Leaders had to deserve their position.

The question baffled many commentators because of the difficulties it raises.[55] How can one reconcile merit (based upon virtue and reason) with consent (based upon sheer will)? And yet, as Sidney himself confessed, "the question is not, whether it be a paradox or a received opinion ... but whether it is true or not; for many paradoxes are true, and the most gross errors have often been more common."[56] For a republican such as Sidney everyone has a personal responsibility in protecting his freedom and the freedom of all. His much-discussed insistence on the right to rebellion or his warlike statements are to be understood in this context. Since self-preservation is not the chief good of men, it follows that a just war is preferable to a shameful peace. People who care for nothing beyond stage-plays and bread are of course not seditious.[57] "Where there are no men, or where those men have no courage,

[52] Sidney, *Discourses Concerning Government*, 189.
[53] Ibid., 345.
[54] Ibid., 484.
[55] See, e.g., West's introduction to ibid.
[56] Ibid., 100.
[57] Ibid., 165.

there can be no war."[58] The claim that "civil war is a disease … but tyranny is the death of the state" is nothing but a call for personal involvement.[59] In time of crisis "every man is a magistrate."[60] What contract theory offered for such a republican view was just a provisional solution under the circumstances of an increasing number of people ("as if by way of compromise," according to Guy Coquille) that made direct participation impractical. When times require it, such a provision no longer holds.

Consequently, political representation was for Sidney what democracy was later on for Churchill, "the worst form of government, except for all those other forms that have been tried from time to time."[61] "The question is not," he says, "whether the parliament be implacable or infallible" (because, he accepts, it is not) "but whether an assembly of nobility, with a house of commons composed of those who are best esteemed by their neighbors … are more or less subject to error and corruption" than the king.[62] The organic theory is presented here with a twist. Following Aristotle he agrees that, theoretically speaking, one 'head' (i.e., a monarch) can be better equipped than a hundred. But this will never happen in 'real life.' And besides, one has to make a distinction between the 'natural' head and the 'figurative' one. Since people create figurative heads, there can be many (i.e., the parliament), not necessarily one. The only way of establishing a 'head' as a 'head' is if it performs its function for the entire body (Ch. III, S. 39). Power, any power, is arbitrary – the power of a king as well as the power of a parliament. Therefore, the possibility of corruption is always present, given the frailty of human nature. But "'tis better to depend upon those who are under the possibility of being again corrupted, than upon one who applies himself to corrupt them, because he cannot otherwise accomplish his designs." By all means, parliamentary representation is not an ideal situation. "It were to be wished that our security be more certain; but this being under God, the best anchor we have, *it deserves to be preserved with all care, till one more unquestionable strength be framed by the consent of the nation.*"[63]

Because the question of the Parliament, unlike that of personal involvement and responsibility, was not central to Sidney's thinking, it is no surprise that the related topics of 'representation' and 'equality' do not constitute a major concern. Although the members of the Parliament (Lords and Commoners) ought to be *selected* based upon their merits, the issue of *election* is never fully developed. From this perspective, Sidney follows the classic Weltanschauung: he is still teleological; it is not the process that counts, but the end product. An individual might err. The people as a whole, it appears, cannot go astray without suffering terrible consequences. Elected by individuals from boroughs,

---

[58] Ibid., 164.
[59] Ibid., 458.
[60] Ibid., 446.
[61] From a House of Commons speech on November 11, 1947.
[62] Sidney, *Discourses Concerning Government*, 449.
[63] Ibid., 480; emphasis added.

shires, and the like, the MPs are to be considered representatives (or deputies) of the whole nation, not of every single individual. The 'principal' that delegates this authority is 'the people' as whole, repeats Sidney over and over. 'Power' remains not with the individuals, but with the entire nation, as in the continental versions of the contract theory. In a statement that bears close resemblance to a later one by Burke, the 'deputies' have to take into consideration not only the desires of their own electorate, but the good of the country as a whole. Yet, because the very matter of representation was secondary at best for someone preoccupied more with direct involvement, even the issue of the imperative mandate versus a trustee mandate is relegated to a couple of lines: it simply does not matter (Ch. III, S. 44). Individuals elect magistrates (i.e., heads), but these magistrates (kings or MPs or both) ought to represent the 'public good.'

Considering all of the above, it is of little surprise that the second issue crucial to our inquiry, the issue of equality (central at least for explaining the British embrace of compromise) is also peculiar in the case of Algernon Sidney. Following Aristotle, he claimed that "tho [*sic*] … all are equally free, all are not equally endowed with those virtues that render liberty safe, prosperous, and happy."

That equality which is just among equals, is just only among equals; but such as are base, ignorant, vicious, slothful, or cowardly, are not equal in natural or acquired virtues, to the generous, wise, valiant, and industrious; nor equally useful to the societies in which they live: they cannot therefore have an equal part in the government of them; they cannot equally provide for the common good.[64]

It is the responsibility of the people to select the best few to govern them, as it is also their responsibility to remain watchful about the performance of those in power. "If the multitude therefore do institute, the multitude may abrogate; and they themselves, or those who succeed in the same right, can only be fit judges of the performance of the end of the institution."[65] As in the classical version of compromise, Sidney agrees that when a dispute arises between private equals, say Caius and Seius, the matter "must be referred to a judge [*compromissarius*] superior to both; not because 'tis not fit that a man should be judge in his own case, but because they have both an equal right, and any of them owes any subjection to the other." In the political realm, however, things are different. There is no question of equality between the people and the magistrates. Although the magistrates are (or should be) superior in virtues compared with other individuals, the people ('the nation,' as he phrases it) remains superior to all magistrates. Magistrates are but servants.

[I]f there be a contest between me and my servant concerning my service, I only am to decide it: He must serve in my own way or be gone if I think fit, tho he serve me never so well; … I cannot therefore stand in need of a judge, unless the contest be with one that

---

[64] Ibid., 101.
[65] Ibid., 54.

lives upon an equal foot with me. *No man can be my judge, unless he be my superior; and he cannot be my superior, who is not so by my consent, nor to any other purpose that I consent to.* This cannot be the case of a nation, which can have no equal within itself.... The strength of the nation is not in the magistrate, but the strength of the magistrate is in the nation. The wisdom, industry and valor of a prince may add to the glory and greatness of a nation, but the foundation and substance will always be in itself. If the magistrate and people were upon equal terms, as Caius and Seius, receiving equal and mutual advantages from each other, no man could be judge of their differences, but such as they should set up for this end.[66]

In the final instance, the nation (i.e., the people as a whole) has the right to act upon the magistrates as a master upon his servant. Since there is no possible equality between the master (the nation) and its servants (the magistrates), no compromise is possible either. But if in this republican version of the contract theory there is no place for compromise, what about the liberal one much more popular during the seventeenth century and thereafter?

8.3. THE ADVENT OF THE 'NEW' COMPROMISE IN POLITICS

Claiming to have something new to say about either Hobbes or Locke might raise some eyebrows, and for good reason: no authors of the seventeenth century have been more discussed, commented upon, interpreted, and reinterpreted than these two. Even a review of the literature on either would be futile. There are literally thousands of commentaries. However, if one wants to understand the British versions of the contract theory one cannot avoid considering, even if only briefly, those proposed by Hobbes and Locke. If seventeenth-century Englishmen understood contract theory as a generalized compromise – as I argue – here is where one must look for a proof. Not only did the two present the most theoretically articulated versions of the social contract, but their impact upon their contemporaries was undeniable as well, despite some claims to the contrary. The fact that, for example, Hobbes was attacked from so many sides even during his lifetime, even by friends, is nothing but proof of this impact. Descartes, with whom he was "acquainted and mutually respected each other,"[67] wrote about Hobbes that "I found him much more capable in moral philosophy than in metaphysics and physics. Nevertheless, I could not in any way approve his principles.... They are very bad and very dangerous in that *he supposes all men to be wicked, or gives them reason to be.* His whole aim is to write in favor of the monarchy, but one could do this more advantageous and solidly by adopting maxims which are more virtuous and solid."[68]

[66] Ibid., 461; emphasis added.
[67] Excerpts from *Hobbes' Prose Autobiography*, quoted in Thomas Hobbes (1994), *Leviathan – with selected variants from the Latin edition of 1668*, edited with introduction and notes by Edwin Curley (Indianapolis and Cambridge: Hackett Publishing), lxvii.
[68] Descartes (1996), *Oeuvres*, ed. Charles Adam and Paul Tannery (Paris: Vrin), IV, 67, quoted in ibid. lxviii; emphasis added; see also Hugo Grotius's criticisms.

Here, Descartes implies something worthy of consideration: If one supposes men to be wicked, they may very well willingly comply with the diagnosis. In other words, it may very well become a self-fulfilling prophecy.

Hobbes himself was very much aware of the disputes he provoked and the publicity they brought, as both his Verse and Prose Autobiographies demonstrate:

> My book de Corpore through this liberty
> I wrote, which proved a constant war to me.
> The clergy at Leviathan repines,
> And both of them opposed were by divines.
> For whilst I did inveigh 'gainst papal pride,
> These, though prohibited were not denied
> T'appear in print: gainst my Leviathan
> They rail, which made it read by many a man
> And did confirm't the more; tis hoped by me,
> That it will last to all eternity.[69]

Yet if Hobbes himself was convinced that his Leviathan "will last to all eternity," his adversaries begged to differ at least as far as the quality of this eternity was concerned. Royalists and Whigs, Catholics and Anglicans – all took position for and against some of Hobbes's tenets, but used them as a reference nevertheless.[70] A case in point would be Lord Cavendish, his protector, who consulted with Hobbes upon the question of hereditary monarchy in the context of the heated debate surrounding the possible succession of the Duke of York to the throne. Hobbes's position was clear and in accordance to the one professed in *Leviathan*: as long as the King in Possession wants to disinherit his diseased Heir, he may do so, "but is not obliged thereunto." "Who shall force him for I suppose the sound King living cannot be lawfully deposed by any person or persons that are his Subjects; because the King dying is *ipso facto* dissolved; and then the people is a Multitude of lawlesse men relapsed into a condition of war of every man against every man Which by making a King they intended to avoid."[71]

Cavendish, however, took from Hobbes only what was convenient to support his position. In a speech meant to support the Bill "for preventing the

---

[69] *Hobbes' Verse Autobiography* – quoted in Hobbes, *Leviathan*, lx.

[70] See, e.g., Edward Clarendon (1676), *A Brief View and Survey of the Dangerous and Pernicious Errors to Church and State in Mr. Hobbes's Book, Entitled Leviathan*; George Lawson (1657), *An Examination of the Political Part of Mr. Hobbs his Leviathan*; Robert Filmer (1652), *Observations Concerning the Originall of Givernment, upon Mr. Hobbs Leviathan, Mr. Milton against Salamasius, H. Grotius De Jure Belli*; Seth Ward (1654), *Vindiciae Academiarum ... Together with an Appendix concerning what M. Hobbs, and M. Dell have published on this Argument*, etc.

[71] Thomas Hobbes (2005), *The Hereditary Manuscript*, in *A Dialogue between a Philosopher and a Student, of the Common Laws of England*, ed. Alan Cromartie; and Thomas Hobbes, *Questions Relative to Hereditary Right*, ed. Quentin Skinner (Oxford: Clarendon Press), 178.

Duke of Yorke, or any Papist, from succeeding to the Crowne," he invoked Hobbes's authority:

For admit, according to Mr. Hobbes, that Monarchical Government is form'd by an Agreement of a Society of Men, to devolve all their power and interest upon one Man, and to make him Judge of all Differences that shall arise among them; 'tis plain, that this can be for no other end, than the Security and protection of those that enter into such a Contract.[72]

As Skinner observes, these are indeed Hobbesian premises if one substitutes "a society of men" with "the individual members of a multitude," but Cavendish draws conclusions therefrom opposite to those of *Leviathan* that "would have left Hobbes horrified." "[H]e was quixotic enough to believe that Hobbes's authority could be recruited in support of the Whig cause. If Hobbes had not died a year earlier, this would surely have been enough to kill him off."[73] What kind of people, asked Cavendish, "can be suppos'd to have been so void of sense, and so servilely inclin'd, as to give up their Lives and Liberties to the unbounded disposal of one man, without imposing the least condition upon him"? "'Tis hard therefore to counceive, that Absolute Monarchy could ever have been constituted by consent of any Society of Men."[74]

Cavendish is a good example for understanding why Hobbes's absolutism is, after all, at best of secondary impact. What fascinated not only his contemporaries but later generations of scholars were Hobbes's premises, not his conclusions. Although his claim to have inaugurated modern political philosophy might have been an overstatement, it is difficult to deny his contribution to a different way of understanding both politics and political philosophy.[75] If nowadays Hobbes is mostly discussed in a liberal context and almost never as an exponent of absolutism it is because of his liberal premises and his understanding of representation.[76] This very observation, in turn, may raise some eyebrows about the possible uncompromising 'absolutism' of some basic liberal assumptions.

In a context in which all the certitudes of antiquity and medieval times came to be questioned and neither grace nor nature could be taken for granted, he was the one trying to secure politics on a foundation stronger than any opinion.

---

[72] Cavendish (1681), 2, quoted in ibid., 175.
[73] Ibid., 175–176.
[74] Cavendish (1681), 2, quoted in ibid., 175–176.
[75] Joseph Cropsey, for example, who was no supporter of Hobbes's ideas, acknowledged that his work "is the first modern system in which the political philosophy is ample and accessible." Joseph Cropsey (1964), "Hobbes and the Transition to Modernity" in *Ancients and Moderns*, ed. Joseph Cropsey (New York: Basic Books), 213. For other comments about the modern impact of Hobbes, see, e.g., Hannah Arendt, Lucien Jaume, and Leo Strauss.
[76] Just two examples from many: Pierre Manent (1994), *An Intellectual History of Liberalism*, trans. Rebecca Balisnki with a foreword by Jerrold Siegel (Princeton: Princeton University Press); Mark E. Button (2008), *Contract, Culture, and Citizenship: Transformative Liberalism from Hobbes to Rawls* (University Park: Pennsylvania University Press).

Opinions are by definition disputable, and the major challenge of modernity is how to reconcile pluralism of opinions and values with the requirements of political legitimacy. Who is to be the arbitrator (i.e., the *compromissarius*)? But this is precisely the challenge that compromise is supposed to address. So what was the novelty of Hobbes's position? Why did Devine claim that Hobbes was the first to offer a theoretical basis for political compromise and that "contemporary defenses of compromise as the key to democratic politics are in the Hobbesian tradition"?[77]

Beginning, as did the ancients, from his observation of the conflict, both of opinions and interests, among men, Hobbes takes a radically different approach to the reconciliation of such conflict. When men come into disagreement as to what is right or good, a "common measure" must be found in order to settle their differences. Contrary to the ancients, Hobbes rejects right reason as the common measure. In claiming to decide any controversy by right reason, men really mean deciding according to their own reason. So it becomes necessary for the solution of any such conflict that an arbiter be agreed upon, and that his reason be stipulated to be right reason. If the arbiter is not accepted as judge by all parties, the conflict will not end. The substitution of an arbiter for the use of right reason extends to disputes about goodness or truth as much as to conflict of interests.[78]

While I fundamentally agree with Devine's interpretation, I think that a few more qualifications will only strengthen the argument. To begin with, we have seen that although Hobbes still acknowledges the existence of a *forum internum* to be differentiated from *forum externum*, he was definitely working inside the new developed centrifugal individualism, in which the *persona* (the masque) becomes the *person* (L, I, 16). It does no longer reveal the inside, but for Hobbes this does not matter, for *forum internum* has no relevance when it comes to acting. *Forum externum* (the costume, as Charon had it) was the individual. As we have seen before, the acting will ought to remain deaf to any cries coming from the inner conscience. To follow the dictates of reason is unreasonable. Thus, if one is represented, one is represented without a rest, for "every man [has] given the sovereignty to him that *beareth their person*" (L, II, 18; my emphasis).

Furthermore, in terms of the equality of the parties involved in dispute – the prerequisite, as we have seen, of any successful compromise – Hobbes is definitely an equalitarian. It is no longer the 'heads of the families' that are equal, as in previous versions of the contract theory, but every single man (and, presumably, woman).[79] Equality becomes with Hobbes a matter of principles.

<hr/>

[77] Francis Edward Devine (1972), "Hobbes: The Theoretical Basis of Political Compromise," *Polity* 5, no. 1: 57–76. Much of the following discussion is indebted to Devine's commentary. However, it is interesting that Devine fails to consider the historical usage of compromise and chooses to focus solely on the theoretical argument.

[78] Ibid., 59–60.

[79] For some interesting discussion of Hobbes's position concerning women and contract theory, see, e.g., Jean Hampton (1986), *Hobbes and the Social Contract Tradition* (Cambridge:

Men are not equal just in terms of their natural freedom but different in terms of virtue (as, for example, with Sidney); they are made by nature "equal in the faculties of body and mind." "Though there be found one man sometimes manifestly stronger in body or quicker of mind than another, yet when is reckoned together the difference between man and man is not so considerable that one man can thereupon claim to himself any benefit which another may not pretend as well as he" (L, I, xiii).[80]

The fact that virtue does not and cannot make a difference in Hobbes's theory should not come as a surprise, considering that from the beginning he posits that he is not interested in "this or that particular man," but in the abstract man, the generic individual (L, Introduction, 4). "Besides, I speak not of the men, but (in the abstract) of the seat of power" (L, Letter Dedicatory). Since "virtue generally, in all sort of subjects, is somewhat that is valued for eminence, and consisteth in comparison" it begets inequality, "for if all things were equal in all men, nothing would be prized" (L, I. viii, 1). But it is precisely this "competition of riches, honour, command, or other power" (since all virtues are nothing but power, L, I, 10) that "inclineth to contention, enmity, and war" (L, I, 11). The causes of these differences are to be found in passions (L, I, viii, 14–16). Yet although the 'objects' of passion differ among individuals, the passions "are the same in all man," it is on this generic equality that one should focus (L, Introduction, 3).

Equality for Hobbes is therefore both the problem and part of the solution. "From this equality of ability ariseth equality of hope in the attaining of our ends. And therefore, if any two men desire the same thing, which nevertheless they cannot both enjoy, they become enemies" (L, I, xiii, 3). The vicious circle of the war of every man against every man has started. Everyone suspects everyone and is this anticipation of violence that begets insecurity and finally open war. Men are equal because they are all equally untrustworthy. Yet this equality is also part of the solution. Hobbes's abstract man might be selfish but not stupid. He understands that "the situation is absurd, or at best a logical contradiction."[81] In "this war of every man against every man ... nothing can be unjust. The notions of right and wrong, justice and injustice, have there no place. Where there is no common power, there is no law; where no law, no injustice" (L, I, xiii, 13). Justice and right, therefore, ought to be installed, not for their own sake, but to avoid death (or at least to appease the fear of death). It is a rational choice.[82] But how is this rational choice to be implemented?

Cambridge University Press); Jean Hampton (1993), "Feminist Contractarianism," in *A Mind of One's Own*, ed. Louis Antony and Charlotte Witt (Boulder: Westview Press); or Carole Pateman (1989), *The Sexual Contract* (Stanford, Calif.: Stanford University Press).
[80] This quotation and the following ones are from Hobbes, *Leviathan*.
[81] Manent, *An Intellectual History*, 24.
[82] See, e.g, David Gauthier (1986), *Morals by Agreement* (Oxford: Oxford University Press), or David Gauthier (1990), *Moral Dealing: Contract, Ethics, and Reason* (Ithaca, N.Y.: Cornell University Press).

Since different men are differently ruled by various passions, each will arrive at different notions of right and wrong. And since they are equal, who is to be the arbitrator?

Here is where the new compromise comes into play. Reason, instrumental reason in the service of individual wills, reason "born up from necessity," comes up with an intelligent solution – the new form of compromise.[83] In the absence of any other common ground except the fear of death, every man *promises* to every other man "*to lay down this right to all things, and be contended with so much liberty against other men, as he would allow other men against himself*" (L, I, xiv, 5; emphasis in the original). That Hobbes understands this covenant or contract as a mutual promise (a com-promise) is not in doubt, since he spends quite some time clarifying the meaning of 'promise' as contract. When both parts "contract now to perform thereafter ... he that is to perform in time to come, being trusted, his performance is called *keeping of promise, or faith*" (L, I, xiv, 11; emphasis in the original).

Signs of contract are either express or by inference. Express are words spoken with understanding of what they signify; and such words are either of the time present or past ..., or of the future ..., which words of the future are called PROMISE.... In contracts the right passeth, not only where the words are of the time present or past, but also where they are of the future, because all contract is mutual translation, or change of right; and therefore he that promiseth only (because he hath already received the benefit for which he promiseth) is to be understood as if he intended the right should pass; for unless he had been content to have his words so understood, the other would not have performed his part first. And for that cause, in buying and selling, and other acts of contract, *a promise is equivalent to a covenant*, and therefore obligatory. (L, I, xiv, 13, 16; emphasis added)

"Before the time of civil society, or in the interruption thereof of war," because "there is nothing [that] can strengthen the covenant of peace agreed on," the only solution remains "to swear by the God he feareth; which swearing, or OATH, is a form of speech, added to a promise, by which he that promiseth signifieth that unless he perform, he renounceth the mercy of God (L, I, xiv, 31). But "covenants without the sword are but words, and of no strength to secure a man of all" (L, II, xvii, 2) and "mutual promises where there is no security of performance on either side (as when there is no civil power erected over the parties promising)" – "such promises are no covenants" (L, I, xv, 5). "And therefore, to promise that which is known to be impossible, is no covenant" (L, I, xiv, 25). Since God has no sword, "it appears ... that the oath adds nothing to the obligation" but eventually a blasphemy (L, I, xiv, 33). Something or someone more trustful has to be artificially constructed, a power that everyone will reckon with.

"The only way to erect ... a common power" out of this untrustworthy multitude, the only way to reconcile, as Lucien Jaume put it, The One and the

---

[83] Manent, *An Intellectual History*, 25.

Multiple in political terms, "is to confer all their power and strength upon one man, or upon one assembly of men, that may reduce all their wills, by plurality of voices, upon one will" (L, II, xvii, 13).[84] This is "the generation" not only "of that great Leviathan, or rather (to speak more reverently) of that *Mortal God*," but also of the Sovereign who becomes the overall *Compromissarius* (L, II, xvii, 13, 14). Unless men accept this new compromise, and "covenant mutually to stand to the sentence of another, they are far from peace as ever. This other to whose sentence they submit is called ARBITRATOR. And therefore it is of the law of nature *that they that are at controversy, submit their right to the judgment of an arbitrator*" (L, I, xv, 30; emphasis in the original).

Although this new compromise bears some resemblance to the classical, it is also radically different. It takes place not between two parties but between every man and everyone else. Such generalization of compromise does not involve any danger, since as we have seen all men are equal by nature and the superiority of the new *compromissarius* is undisputable since it is the very result of the compromise. If before the contract no one could be trusted to keep his promise, now this Arbitrator forces everyone to keep it thanks to his sovereign power. His authority is not confined to a particular disagreement, for "it is not enough for the security, which men desire should last all the time of their life, that they be governed and directed by one judgment for a limited time" (L, II, xvii, 5). He can use it anytime and as he sees fit for the peace and the security of the commonwealth. Furthermore, this authority and power to reinforce the contract is the result (not the pre-condition) of the new compromise. His merits and even his form (one individual or many) are secondary at best. One or many, it is still *one person*. "For by this authority, given him by every particular man in the commonwealth, he hath the use of so much power and strength conferred on him that by terror thereof he is enabled to conform the wills of them all to peace at home and mutual aid against their enemies abroad" (L, II, xvii, 13).

The unity of this Sovereign or Arbitrator (or *compromissarius*) – a unity stressed repeatedly by Hobbes, especially in chapter 16 – is ensured by virtue of representation. Since men are equally abstract, there are no smaller communities to elect each their own *compromissarius*. The unity of the *compromissarius* is essential for Hobbes's theory. "To *personate* is to *act*, or *represent*, himself or another; and he that acteth another is said to bear his person, or act in his name" (L, I, xvi, 3). Because he represents each individual he makes One out of a Multitude. What before *preceded* the contract, namely the people conceptualized as a whole, now becomes the *result* of the contract. Only through representation can a multitude become one political entity – a commonwealth.

---

[84] Lucien Jaume (1986), *Hobbes et l'état représentatif moderne* (Paris: Presses Universitaires de France), esp. the concluding chapter.

A multitude of men are made one person, when they are by one man, or one person, represented so that it be done with the consent of *every one* of that multitude in particular. For it is the unity of the representer, not the unity of the represented, that maketh that person one. And it is the representer that beareth the person, and but one person, and unity cannot otherwise be understood in multitude. (L, I, xvi, 13)

But this is exactly what the Sovereign does – it bears the person of every single individual entering the contract. His actions are therefore their actions. His decisions, whatever they might be, are their decisions. They have nothing to complain about. Since they "decide" every law, they have nothing left to decide but how to run their lives in the domains not regulated by laws. "It is not Wisdom but Authority that makes a Law" or, as he put it in the *Leviathan*, "*Authoritas, non Veritas, facit Legem*" (Authority, not Truth, makes Law).[85] "Therefore, the sovereign's will becomes the determiner of good and evil for each individual subject. This is not because the sovereign possesses any special knowledge of good and evil, but because he, and he alone, possesses under the social contract the right to will in such matters."[86] In order to preserve the compromise and to avoid futile disputes, there are no other *compromissores*, other judges or arbiters. From this perspective, at least, "Hobbes' sovereign is unquestionable an uncompromising figure."[87] It is paradoxically this uncompromising position that is needed to justify compromise as the only acceptable political practice for avoiding open conflict.

Hobbes' view of the good as a matter of will resting on desire provides the necessary support for compromise. If, instead of opposing conflicting opinions as to the truth for mutual correction through reason, men are merely opposing conflicting sets of desire for a workable reconciliation, then compromise is clearly a morally acceptable solution to disagreement. The transition from Hobbes' authoritative arbiter to compromise as the solution to disputes requires merely a different view as to what men will sacrifice to avoid open physical conflict.[88]

Yet the implications, as Devine implies, do not stop here. Once individuals accept the idea of being represented by a sovereign authority *as individuals* they also accept the idea of an individual delegation of their political rights. The extent to which and the conditions upon these delegated rights are only of secondary importance. For all that matters, law making and decision-making processes concerning the good of the commonwealth are no longer their preoccupation, nor their duty. As long as the sovereign (or the arbitrator) does not interfere with their private good, there is nothing to be concerned about. From different perspectives, both Pierre Manent and Lucien Jaume arrive at the same conclusion:[89] Hobbes's theory posits an unprecedented distance between

---

[85] Hobbes, "A Dialogue," in *A Dialogue between a Philosopher and a Student*, 10.
[86] Devine, "Hobbes," 64.
[87] Ibid., 68.
[88] Ibid., 69.
[89] One may, rightfully I think, speculate on why French scholars (consider also Pierre Rossenvallon or George Castoriadis) seem more aware of the tensions between political representations of

political life and the individual's life. If for the ancients, following in the footsteps of Aristotle, participation in the life of the polis was the condition of personal fulfillment, while for medieval man the fulfillment of his role in society represented at the same time the fulfillment of his political duty as a member of a political body, no such requirements or "duties" are to be found in the new version of political representation. There is "*une division du travail entre <la politique> et <la vie>*"[90] ("a division of work between <politics> and <life>"). There are people looking upon their own lives and there are professional '*compromissores*' that will take care of the dirty job of politics, as T.V. Smith later claimed. But this "*division du travail*," while solving some problems, creates others as well. "The *distinction* between civil society and the state *and* their *union* through the idea of representation," argues Manent, "sets off a natural oscillation between two extreme possibilities: the 'withering away' of the state on the one hand, the absorption *of* civil society by the state on the other."[91]

Yet Hobbes had no particular interest in 'civil society.' Unless doubled by the establishment of a sovereign, his social contract (a term that in effect he never uses) amounts to little if any: absent the sovereign or the arbitrator, people cannot be trusted to keep their promises. Therefore, the two distinct 'movements,' that is, the compromise of everyone with everyone and the approval of a sovereign empowered with each individual's rights, are in effect conflated into a single one. So, despite the fact that Hobbes emphasizes the unity of the newly created body politic, he never discusses it as an independent reality (whenever for various reasons the sovereign disappears, people return to the state of nature and therefore of war of everyone against everyone). Thus, Locke is the author one should turn to in order to better understand the nascent 'civil society.'[92]

Once again, to discuss or even to review all the complexities of Locke's theory would be an impossible enterprise. Even a detailed comparison between Hobbes and Locke is beyond the scope of these pages. What I am looking for is simply to what extent his version of the social contract differs from Hobbes's as far as the basic assumptions of a modern compromise are concerned. Since many scholars claim that the latter marks a radical departure from the former it is of interest to see if *from this perspective* the claim is sustainable. I will argue that it is not. Despite their differences (some remarkable), both authors share the same basic assumptions about compromise as the very basis of political legitimacy and about the new understanding of political representation.

individuals and so-called popular sovereignty, but for the time being this is outside the scope of this enterprise. For now, I will only say that it is possible that the French Revolution posed, for reasons I only alluded to, a more striking contrast between these two sets of concepts than the English Revolution had done a century earlier.

[90] Jaume, *Hobbes et l'état*, 227.

[91] Manent, *An Intellectual History*, 27.

[92] I am fully aware that for many authors, 'civil society' was nothing but a different term for 'political society.' For the sake of convenience, however, I will not discuss now the various historical usages of the expression.

This is far from denying that, in the long run, the differences between the two and especially their interpretation by succeeding generations of scholars have not had a serious impact on both politics and political philosophy. What I am trying to suggest once again is only that despite serious and fundamental changes (both theoretical and practical), some basic and often ignored assumptions did manage, once accepted, to survive without being seriously challenged to this day.

That Locke was familiar with Hobbes's work despite never mentioning him by name is beyond doubt.[93] The two shared, as did so many Englishmen of that time, the conviction that "promises, covenants, and oaths … are the bonds of human society."[94] According to Locke, even "conjugal society is made by a voluntary compact between man and woman" (ST, 78).[95] As did Hobbes, he repeatedly uses promise as an equivalent of contract, compact, consent, and the like (ST, 14, 116, 122, 184, 194–195). Yet there are also major differences in the understanding of their domain of effectiveness. For Hobbes, one cannot make a compact with God, nor can the sovereign be part of the contract. For Locke, however, since "grants, promises, and oaths are bonds that hold the Almighty how much even more so in the case of princes"? (ST, 195). For Hobbes, promises, even made under constraint or out of fear, were as binding as any contract. For Locke, "promises extorted by force, without right" cannot be considered consent. "To say I gave my promise … when I put my hand in my pocket and deliver my purse myself to a thief who demands it with a pistol at my breast" does not "excuse the force and passes the right" (ST, 186). Furthermore, if for Hobbes promises made in the state of nature are but words, for Locke they are perfectly possible and binding, "for it is not every compact that puts an end to the state of Nature between men, but only this one of agreeing together mutually to enter into one community, and make one body politic."

[Other] promises and compacts men may make with one another, and yet still be in the state of Nature. The promises and bargains for truck, etc., between the two men in Soldania, in or between a Swiss and an Indian, in the woods of America, are binding to them, though they are perfectly in a state of Nature in reference to one another for truth, and keeping faith belongs to men as men, and not as members of society. (ST, 14)

All these differences are of course easy to explain considering the different assumptions the two authors have about the condition of man in the state of nature and about the nature and functions of the social contract. But they have

---

[93] In a letter dated February 12, 1673, for example, a friend of Hobbes, John Aubrey, tried to persuade Locke in his capacity of advisor to the Lord Chancellor (Earl of Shaftesbury) to intervene for licensing the publication of "A Dialogue between a Philosopher and a Student, of the Common Laws of England," highly recommending the manuscript. For more details, see Hobbes, *A Dialogue between a Philosopher and a Student*, xvii–xviii.

[94] John Locke (1685), *Works*, vol. 5, *A Letter Concerning Toleration*, published online by the Liberty Fund: http://files.libertyfund.org/files/764/Locke_0128–05_EBk_v4.pdf.

[95] The following quotations from *The Second Treatise on Civil Government* will use the abbreviation ST, followed by the paragraph number.

no impact as far as the new understanding of compromise is concerned. For both Hobbes and Locke, men are by nature equal and free. Although Locke (like Sidney) accepts that this equality does not extend "to all sorts of equality" and there are inequalities based on age, birth, virtue, merit, or even mere convention, such inequalities are of no concern because they are not "political" (ST, 54). They do not (and, unlike for Sidney) should not transfer into political authority – at least not after corruption poisoned the golden age.[96] They are different kinds of authority in the same way in which political and paternal powers are "so perfectly distinct and separate, and built upon so different foundations, and given to so different ends" (ST, 71). The state of nature is "a state also of equality, wherein all the power and jurisdiction is reciprocal, no one having more than another" (ST, 4, 54).

Indeed, unlike Hobbes, Locke asserts, "though this be a state of liberty, yet it is not a state of license.... The state of Nature has a law of Nature to govern it, which obliges every one, and reason, which is that law, teaches all mankind who will but consult it, that being all equal and independent, no one ought to harm another in his life, health, liberty or possessions" (ST, 6). For Hobbes, as we have seen, neither reason nor truth make the law – authority makes it. For Locke the laws of nature are the laws of reason and, if this was not enough, have the authority of God to back them up. Men in the state of nature have not only the ability or power to recognize these laws, but also the power to execute just punishment in case of transgression. (As for Hobbes, "the law of Nature would, as all other laws that concern men in this world, be in vain if there were nobody that in the state of Nature had a power to execute that law," ST, 7.) It is precisely this double political power – to distinguish between right and wrong and to execute proper punishment – that makes possible mutual promises even in the state of nature.

And yet, despite all these significant differences, a Hobbesian moment is unavoidable, considering the basic premises.[97] If everyone is equally entitled as everyone else to judge the right and the wrong (i.e., to interpret the law of Nature) who is to be the arbitrator and where is his superior authority to come from? It is the same question that obsessed Hobbes and that modern compromise came to address: "Who shall be judge?" (ST, 20); that is, *Who shall be Compromissarius?* "Men living together according to reason *without a common superior on earth, with authority to judge between them, is properly the state of Nature.* But force, or a declared design of force upon the person of another, *where there is no common superior on earth* to appeal to for relief, *is*

---

[96] Following Hooker, Locke agrees that in an uncertain "golden age" (?!), before corruption spread throughout the world, such distinctions of merit could have translated into political authority, but this was only because "the golden age ... had more virtue, and consequently better governors, as well as less vicious subjects" (ST, 111). Yet this is no longer the case. As in other instances of the ST one can see how Locke's theory combines new and old ideas without always paying attention to their inherent incompatibilities.

[97] I borrowed this expression from Pierre Manent.

the state of war" (ST, 19; emphasis added). As one can easily see, despite the difference emphasized between the state of nature and the state of war, the distinction is ultimately based upon a very shaky foundation. Any misinterpretation of reason, any force or threat of force, will blow the peaceful state of nature into pieces.

The solution, as for Hobbes, is of course the transformation of the Multitude in One body politic through a contract entered voluntarily by every single individual, a mutual consent or promise – that is, a com-promise – able to erect through a willing transfer of individual rights (or powers to judge and to redress wrongs) a common superior arbitrator acknowledged as such by all the participants in the compromise (ST 15, 21–22, 87–89, 95–99, 131–132, etc.). "Those who are united into one body, and have a common established law and judicature to appeal to, with authority to decide controversies between them and punish offenders *are in civil society one with another*" (ST, 87; emphasis added). This political body is sometimes referred to simply as 'society,' but also as 'people,' 'commonwealth,' 'community,' and even 'political society.'

But what is the difference between a promise made "in the woods of America" and one that creates a civil society? It cannot be the number of people involved in the contract, argues John Simmons, and it cannot be what Locke claims it to be – namely the want of a common arbitrator – because "common judges with authority may be present even in a state of nature." "Reference only to a part of that agreement, the creation of a common judge with authority, will not suffice."[98] Simmons goes into a lengthy analysis of what Locke really intended to say to conclude that it is that "each person in the state of nature lacks the one distinctive sort of moral obligation that transaction creates – what we normally refer to as 'political obligation.'"[99] Interesting as this is, I think that the analysis misses the point. If one understands by the social contract the generalized compromise that I claim it to be, then Locke said exactly what he intended to say.

In the state of nature two or a few individuals can enter a mutual agreement because keeping promises "belongs to men as men," not as "members of a society." If, say, disputes arise, they may even agree upon a common arbitrator, as in the classic version of the compromise (as Pufendorf also has it). However, this type of agreement is not a proper social contract because it lacks the essential ingredients of the modern compromise. It is not generalized to a large number of people and it involves just a momentary disagreement, not all matters pertaining to public life. Furthermore, it depends upon the acknowledged authority of the arbitrator, which in the state of nature, considering the natural equality of everyone with everyone, can always be questionable. The

---

[98] John Simmons (1999), "Locke's State of Nature," in *The Social Contract Theorists: Critical Essays on Hobbes, Locke, and Rousseau*, ed. Christopher W. Morris (New York and Oxford: Rowman & Littlefield), 102.

[99] Ibid., 106.

classical compromise, therefore, is not safe for three main reasons, as Locke explains further on:

Firstly, there wants an established, settled, known law, *received and allowed by common consent* to be *the standard of right and wrong*, and the common measure to decide *all controversies between them*. For though the law of Nature be plain and intelligible to all rational creatures, yet men, being *biased by their own interest*, as well as ignorant for want of study of it, are not apt to allow of it as law binding to them in the application of it to their particular case.

Secondly, in the state of Nature there wants a known and *indifferent judge, with authority to determine all differences* according to the established law. For everyone in that state being both judge and executioner of the law of Nature, men being partial to themselves, passion and revenge is very apt to carry them too far....

Thirdly, in the state of Nature there often *wants power to back and support the sentence* when right, and to give it due execution. (ST, 124; emphasis added)

One can see why classical compromise will not do and why it is necessary to advance to the next level, where the authority of the *compromissarius* is undisputable because it is created by the consent of the parties, and involved in all disputations of all individuals. It is not only a matter of arbitration; it is also a matter of imposing the right punishment. In the classical compromise, after the arbitration of the *compromissarius* the parties were forced to accept the judgment and the penalty (*poena*) of an already existing system of law. There is no such thing in the state of nature, where legislative and executive powers are combined in every single individual. It is, as many commentators have observed, Locke's merit to try to separate these two powers, thus creating the premises for the modern political systems.[100] Yet this separation raises another question: Who is to be the sovereign? If in Hobbes the sovereign has both the legislative and the executive power, the problem is solved. Not so in Locke. One may be tempted to answer that it is the legislative.[101] After all, after the creation of civil societies, "the first and fundamental positive law of all commonwealths is the establishing of the legislative power, as the first and fundamental law which is to govern even the legislative" (ST, 134). The legislative, he emphasizes repeatedly, is "the supreme power." However, Locke never claims it is also the sovereign.

To understand why is it so, one has to be familiar with Locke's usage of the concept of sovereignty. In the usually ignored First Treatise, in which he discusses and rejects *Patriarcha*, he mentions "sovereignty" (Adam's sovereignty, patriarchs' sovereignty, kings' sovereignty) almost in excess, only to refute the claim of sovereignty every single time. By contrast, in the Second Treatise the very word is mentioned only a few times, mostly in connection with paternal

---

[100] Of course, Locke mentions also the federative power. But since he agrees that it cannot be easily separated from the executive and it is not essential for the sake of this argument, I will leave it aside, at least for the moment.

[101] Pierre Manent, for example, observes that there is no real separation of powers in Locke, not at least in the modern sense of checks and balances, considering the absolute superiority of the legislative.

authority (ST, 61, 69, 83, 108, 115). Here again he rejects the claim that a father possesses a "sovereign" power over his children or a husband over his wife. The only time when sovereignty is accepted without qualifications is when he talks about God's power over his creatures, and man's duty to obey his laws, "for men being all the workmanship of one omnipotent and infinitely wise Maker; all the servants of one sovereign Master, sent into the world by His order and about His business" (ST, 6).

Sovereignty, thus, for Locke (as for Hobbes) is absolute power, power without limitations whatsoever. The legislative cannot claim it, despite being the supreme power of the commonwealth, for it is a restricted power: first, because each individual does not give up his legislative power entirely when entering into a civil society, but only "so far forth as the preservation of himself and the rest of that society shall require" (ST, 129); second, because (a) it cannot be arbitrary, (b) its laws "ought to be designed for no other end ultimately but the good of the people," (c) it cannot raise taxes or affect individual properties without the consent of the people given to their deputies, and (d) it cannot transfer its powers to anybody else (ST, ch. 11). Needless to say, the executive power, despite being granted completely by each individual, is in its own way even more restricted by the legislative (ST, ch. 12–14). Any infringement of these limitations, either by internal or external powers, equates with dissolution of government and the return of power in the hands of the commonwealth (ST, ch. 19). The dissolution of government does not equate with the dissolution of society. There is no return to anarchy. The community retains the power to erect a new government – this is one of the main novelties brought forward by Locke (at least in comparison with Hobbes), and this is the reason why so many commentators have seen in Locke's theory a major step forward. So perhaps after all, civil society is the ultimate locus of sovereignty insofar as it only trusts its powers in the hands of the government. If so, then the theory of a modern compromise would fall apart.

If the commonwealth is indeed an "*independent* community which the Latins signified by the word *civitas*" (ST, 133) and can resist without major difficulties the dissolution of the power it erected, we are back after a long detour to the classical/continental versions of contract theory where the corporate body has supremacy over its representatives and political representation remains top-down. The individualist, voluntarist features of Locke's theory would be at best secondary. Apparently, the only way to dismember such a community is by its being "mangled into pieces" by a foreign conquest (ST, 211). But this is highly counterintuitive, as many scholars have already observed. "Given Locke's individualist version of the social contract, therefore, the dissolution of society posed a profound dilemma, which, understandably enough, he never deliberately confronted, or attempted to resolve."[102]

---

[102] Julian H. Franklin (1994), "Locke on the Dissolution of Society," in Bakos, *Politics, Ideology and the Law*, 176.

This dilemma may be restated as follows: if the dissolution of the government does not translate into a dissolution of 'the people,' then the community enjoys a higher status than the individual; we are back at the medieval, corporatist vision of society, so Locke's liberal status comes under question, but the right of 'the people' (as a conceptualized community) to erect a new government whenever it sees fit is preserved intact. If, on the other hand, the dissolution of the government entails the dissolution of the community as well, then the rights of the individuals for the sake of which the body politic has been brought into being through contract are preserved (recuperated) intact, being returned in the hands of the trustors, and Locke's liberal stance is unquestionable. Yet then we are back in the state of nature where each and every single individual regains the right to rebel whenever she or he feels like it without any superior able to judge if she or he is right or wrong, for everything is reducible to a matter of individual will.

Clearly, this is not what Locke had in mind – hence his shyness in confronting the problem. So is his commonwealth a 'corporate body,' as his language of unity appears to suggest and Julian Franklin straightforwardly asserts, or is it rather a collection of individuals?[103] If we are to compare Hobbes and Locke on this issue, it seems that Hobbes is much more individualistic than Locke. While in both cases each individual has to consent to the social contract, for the former this consent of every single member is assumed to include the choice of the sovereign as well. "I authorize and give up my right of governing myself to this man, or to this assembly of men, on this condition, that thou give up thy right to him, and authorize all his actions in like manner" (L, II, xvii, 13). The majority rule, which is nothing but the arithmetical counting of wills, intervenes only in the case of a sovereign composed of many. "[I]f the representative consists of many men, the voice of the greater number must be considered as the voice of them all. For if the lesser number pronounce (for example) in the affirmative, and the greater in the negative, there will be negatives more than enough to destroy the affirmatives" (L, I, xvi, 15).

In Locke's theory, however, majority rule intervenes as soon as civil society is instituted. "[E]very man, by consenting with others to make one body politic under one government, puts himself under an obligation to everyone of that society to submit to the determination *of* the majority" (ST, 97). He agrees with the idea of a government, but not with the particular form that this government (monarchy, aristocracy, democracy, one or many, etc.) ought to have. This is for the majority to decide, "or else this original compact, whereby he with others incorporates into one society, would signify nothing, and be no compact if he be left free and under no other ties than he was in before in the state of Nature" (ST, 97). One may say that once Locke's man agrees with the idea of a political community, he no longer has control over the details. Supposedly then, the presumption of a self-dependent,

---

[103] Ibid., 175.

corporatist body situated between individuals qua individuals and government has some solid basis.

Still, for all we know, considering the ambiguity of his language, he strongly suggests that since the legislative is "the soul that gives form, life, and unity to the commonwealth," when it is altered "dissolution and death follows," "every one [being] at the disposure of his own will" (ST, 212). Also, when the executive power takes over the legislative, all is reducible to anarchy "and the people become a confused multitude without order or connexion" (ST, 219). As Julian Franklin argues, "in all these passages, as well as others less dramatic, the dissolution of society seems to follow directly upon the dissolution of government."[104] For what is of interest to us it means that despite all the striking differences, the basic assumptions of Hobbes and Locke are similar. Once representation is understood bottom-up, as representation of individuals, the handling of individual rights, be it partial or total, temporary or definitive, the result is the same: there is no middle way between full anarchy and a full separation between a government of professional representatives and lay individuals. The acclaimed birth of the civil society as a midway between politics and the individuals was a stillbirth. Without a government able to secure (as in the state of nature) the proper functions of both legislative and executive powers, such a society ceases to exist. If this conclusion is right, then the implications of this modern compromise are even more important than I have suggested so far.

It can be argued that despite the evidence indicating an understanding of the contract theory as a mutual promise or a generalized compromise, we are still in the realm of speculation. As a matter of fact, however, we are not, for we find compromise used as equivalent to a social contract. Born in 1643 in Edinburgh, Scotland, Gilbert Burnet is today a rather forgotten figure, despite acquiring quite a reputation during his lifetime, especially for his *History of the Reformation of the Church in England*. This reputation was further enhanced by the posthumous publication of *A History of my Own Times* (1724).[105] He took part in all the controversies of the day, taking position against the policies of James II, thereby placing himself in the Whig camp. Like many authors of the time, he used a combination of natural law arguments with constitutionalist ones. Tim Harris observed recently that he "might have been a Scot, but there was nothing particularly Scottish about his line of argument."[106] On the contrary, by making appeal to a contract theory that integrated both philosophical and constitutional arguments (as did Sidney) he was in many ways more typical for his time than the Englishmen Hobbes or Locke.[107] Since we

[104] Ibid., 179.
[105] For more biographical details, see T.E.S. Clark and H.C. Foxcroft (1907), *A Life of Gilbert Burnet, Bishop of Salisbury* (Cambridge: Cambridge University Press).
[106] Tim Harris (2006), "In Search of a British History of Political Thought," in Armitage, *British Political Thought*, 104.
[107] See Thompson, *Ideas of Contract*, 262.

are interested more in the general apprehension of compromise and contract during that time and less on the philosophical articulation of concepts, Burnet is therefore more revealing than his today more famous contemporaries, with whom he shares some basic assumptions.

It is difficult to ascertain to what extent either Hobbes or Locke influenced Burnet. The writings of the former were available and most likely he was familiar at least with some of them, as were most of the people in his circle. Locke's writings, however, were published mostly after Burnet's literary debut (the *History of the Reformation* was published in 1679, while Locke's *Letter on Toleration* appeared only ten years later in 1689). The text of Burnet's I am more interested in, *An Inquiry Into the Measures of Submission to the Supream Authority*, was published in a collection of papers in 1688, while Locke's *Two Treaties* appeared only in 1690.[108] When one leaves aside the constitutional arguments (from Magna Carta to the laws passed under Charles I) and focuses on the 'natural rights' side of his argument, Burnet's similarity to Hobbes and Locke is quite amazing. For all three, men are naturally born free and equal ("it is certain that the Law of Nature has put no difference nor subordination among Men, except it be that of Children to Parents, or of Wives to their Husbands"). "[T]his liberty must be supposed entire, unless so far as it is limited by Contracts, Provisions and Laws."[109]

This is a point repeatedly stressed by Burnet: since liberty is natural it does not have to prove itself. The law of nature has preeminence over positive laws. "The degrees of Civil Authority are to be taken either from express Laws, from immemorial Customs, or from particular Oaths." "In all Disputes between Power and Liberty, Power must always be proved, but Liberty proves it self [*sic*]; for one being founded *only* upon Positive Law, and the other upon Law of Nature."[110] If liberty is natural, power over others is an artificial construction. It has to be not only *approved* by all affected by its exercise but also *erected* through everyone's contribution. Not surprisingly, self-preservation is the first duty of the free man. "It is no less certain, that as the Light of Nature has planted in all Men a Natural principle of the Love of Life, and of desire to preserve it; so the common Principles of all religions agree in this, that God sending us in this World, we are bound to preserve that Being, which he has given us, by all just and lawful ways."[111] The distinction between 'just' and 'lawful' is not accidental. As for Locke, one has to make appeal to "the Rules and Forms" *if* one has time. But if the danger to one's life or property is imminent,

---

[108] However, I would not go so far as to speculate about a possible influence of Burnet upon Locke, since clearly the two *Treatises* were written quite a few years apart.

[109] Gilbert Burnet (1688), "An Inquiry Into the Measures of Submission to the Supream Authority: And of the Grounds upon which it may be lawful or necessary for Subjects to defend their Religion, Lives, and Liberties," in *A collection of papers relating to the present juncture of affairs in England*, 2.

[110] Ibid., 4.

[111] Ibid., 3.

one is justified "both to recover what is our Own, with just Damages, and also to put such unjust Persons out of a Capacity of doing the like injuries any more, either to our selves, or to any others."[112] For Burnet as for Locke, property is the material embodiment of freedom; this is the first liberty to be protected *à tout prix*. If, therefore, either the king or his officers attempt to raise taxes or affect the individual's property in any ways without consent, they are "to be considered as private Persons who came to invade and disturb us."[113] The conclusion does not need to be spelled out loud.

Such an invasion of property rights without consent and in disregard of the laws of the land equates with overstepping the executive's boundaries and an attack on the legislative power. Unlike Hobbes but like Locke, Burnet makes a clear distinction between the executive and the legislative, with the legislative being the supreme power and the executive just a "trust" conferred by the legislative. "The Supream Authority must still be supposed to be lodged within those who have the Legislative Power reserved to them, but not with those who have only the Executive; which is plainly a Trust, when it is separated from the Legislative Power."[114] While the king enjoys full executive power, "the Legislative Power is lodged between Him and the Two Houses of the Parliament."[115] "So then, the not resisting the King, can only be applied to the Executive Power, that so upon no pretence of ill Administrations in the Execution of the Law, it should be lawful to resist him; but this cannot with any reason be extended with an Invasion of the Legislative Power, or to a total Subversion of the Government."[116]

Here again one has to confront the challenge posed by the dissolution of the government. Is such dissolution to be equated with dissolution of the civil society (nation, community, etc.) or not? Like Locke, Burnet refuses to confront the challenge head on, speaking only about the need to reassemble "a Legal and Free Parliament." But since "that is left to every Englishman's Judgment and Sense" and the subversion of the government equates with "a Destruction of the Nation," one can safely conclude that, once again, the only way of preserving a commonwealth as a commonwealth relies upon the proper function of its government.[117] Burnet solves Locke's separation of powers, which he embraces, with a Hobbesian conflation of Civil Society and Government. Although he uses both terms, it is quite clear that for him, as for Hobbes, everyone should agree to form both a civil society and a government to protect it at the same time. He sometimes even combines the two, talking about Civil Authority and about Civil Government. Without the creation *ab nihilo* of a

---

[112] Ibid.
[113] Ibid., 7.
[114] Ibid., 2.
[115] Ibid., 7.
[116] Ibid., 9.
[117] Ibid., 14, 13.

commonly accepted *compromissarius*, no modern politics would be possible. Here is the proof:

The true and Original Notion of Civil Society *and* Government, is, that *is a Compromise* made by such a Body of Men, by which they resign up the Right of demanding Reparations, either in the way of Justice against one another, or in the way of War, against their Neighbours; to such a single Person, or to such a Body of Men as they think fit to trust with this. And in the management of this Civil Society, great distinction is to be made, between the Power of making Laws for the Conduct of it, and the Power of executing those Laws.[118]

All the paradoxes and the tensions we are confronting today between individuals, civil society, and political communities, between sovereignty, powers, and representation, are bundled in this one paragraph.

---

[118] Ibid., 2.

9

Conclusions

Compromising the Art of Compromise –
The One-Dimensional Man

> The life of mind has quietly moved out of the way, making room for the terrible and pathetic encounter of the fanatic and the zombie.
>
> Alain Finkielkraut, *The Defeat of the Mind*

Nearing the end of this lengthy journey, we are better equipped to appreciate how illuminating the concept of compromise proves to be for politics, although not necessarily for the same reasons that we had in mind when we began. The most challenging aspect of the concept, the one that has puzzled the few scholars who bothered to consider it seriously, remains its built-in ambiguity. On the one hand, compromise appears as a perfectly suitable approach to politics in a pluralistic society, hence the widely accepted definition of politics as "the art of compromise." On the other one, despite several attempts to clear its bad reputation, it seems that in moral terms compromise is bound to remain for most people at least a suspicious concept, insofar as it appears to endanger something precious in the self. As a matter of fact even the contexts in which these different connotations occur suggest a similar difference. The positive occurrences point mostly toward some external, objective compromise ("the matter was settled by compromise," "they have reached a compromise," etc.), while the negative ones predominantly relate to the personal sphere ("he compromised himself," "I will not compromise my reputation," etc.).

We may now understand why this ambiguity is not a mere accident and why compromise is a concept worth consideration: it occupies the fragile and unsettling space not just between public and private, but also between (political) representation and self-representation. We have to seriously (re) consider the possibility that the lines of tension between commendable and condemnable compromise have their origins not outside, but *inside* the individual, thanks to the forgotten interplay between *forum internum* and *forum externum*. If, as we have seen in Chapter 2, Chiara Lepora concludes that in choosing compromise the feeling of "being (morally) compromised" is almost unavoidable and should not be taken lightly, it is because in any compromise one's *forum internum* is potentially at stake.[1] Absent this dialectic of the individual between *forum externum* and *forum internum*, the alternatives for the one-dimensional man are clear-cut: one either can never compromise or, on the contrary, one is never afraid to compromise, for there is nothing left to 'be' compromised.

Consider, for example, Finkielkraut's bleak vision. Both from a practical and a theoretical perspective, the clashes between the fanatics and the zombies are replayed, with increasing sophistication, at various levels.[2] In practice, the 'fanatics,' men of a single idea and one truth, clash with the 'zombies,' men of no convictions at all. Dogma is opposed by the dogma of relativism. Both categories come under different disguises – political, religious, ideological, or the like – and the distinction between the man of one truth and the man of no truth at all tends to fade. The line of division between the fanatics and the zombies does not run, as we are tempted to believe, between camps but *through the heart of each*. No domain of public life, no country, no political party appears immune to the threat of fanatic *or* the zombie. Considering the present context, this might not be an unfortunate accident, but an unavoidable situation, as Chantal Delsol seems to suggest.

Our era remains paralyzed in a formidable either-or situation: Once the subject latches onto one truth, dedicates himself to it, and follows its ways, he sooner or later risks becoming its unconditional accomplice and henchman, destroying anything that stands in its way. But if he 'frees' himself from certainty (from meaning, from truth), he locks himself into a shallow and narcissistic existence – one that paradoxically leaves him vulnerable to any new passing dogmatism.[3]

Not surprisingly then, the two extremes end up with radically different attitudes toward compromise. As Avishai Margalit put it from a slightly different perspective, once one embraces the economic, value-free picture of politics everything is potentially subject to compromise. If, on the contrary, one embraces a religious, value-laden view of politics, nothing can ever become subject to compromise.[4] Apparently Delsol is right – we are in an either-or situation in which neither scenario offers rosy prospects, for neither the obstinate refusal to compromise, nor its counterpart – its elevation at the rank of a political virtue – are coming without their own dangers. Apparently it is

---

[1] Chiara Lepora (2012), "On Compromise and Being Compromised," *Journal of Political Philosophy* 20, no. 1: 1–22.
[2] Alain Finkielkraut (1995) [1987], *The Defeat of the Mind*, translation and introduction by Judith Friedlander (New York: Columbia University Press).
[3] Chantal Delsol (2006) [2000], *The Unlearned Lessons of the Twentieth Century: An Essay on Late Modernity*, trans. Robin Dick (Wilmington: ISI Books), 98.
[4] Avishai Margalit (2009), *On Compromise and Rotten Compromises* (Princeton: Princeton University Press).

impossible to avoid "both the Scylla of rigidity and the Charybdis of nihilism in foundations."[5]

It is hoped that by the end of this intellectual journey, we can reassess such theoretical and practical disputes in a new light. The aim of this chapter is not therefore just to review the main findings of this genealogical incursion, but also to show the way they relate, however eclectically, with some important authors and recurrent themes in political thought, while suggesting avenues of further research.

9.1. COMPROMISE AND THE TWO-DIMENSIONAL MAN

For if a man strikes many coins from one mould, they all resemble one another, but the supreme King of Kings, the Holy One, blessed be he, fashioned every man in the stamp of the first man, and yet not one of them resembles his fellow. Therefore every single person is obliged to say: the world was created for my sake. (Sanhedrin, IV, 51, quoted by Chantal Delsol)

The quest for the elusive meaning of compromise began with a review of the major points of contention about the usefulness of political compromise. A handful of conclusions emerged from Chapter 2. First, as John Morley observed at the end of the nineteenth century, the British transformation of compromise from a political method useful when rightly limited to a principle of public life risked undermining the general sense of morality which "means at the same time the depravation of the political sense itself." Second, the various attempts to delimit the positive from the negative implications of compromise, which "rightly limited it," as Morley had it – seen in the works of authors such as T.V. Smith, Martin Benjamin, or Martin P. Golding – are difficult if not altogether impossible to maintain from an objective perspective. What for some appears a benign compromise of interests is for others an unacceptable compromise of principles. Third, efforts to embrace compromise as an essential moral practice, such as the theory put forward by David Gauthier, or to claim its amorality, as did Richard Bellamy, remain open to devastating criticisms as well. Finally, the rare claims that the propensity for compromise represents a national trait lack any explanatory power absent a conceptual genealogy in specific historical settings. What emerges from all these findings is the difficulty of disambiguating the moral from the political aspects of compromise, which in turn suggests that compromise cannot be properly apprehended outside the relationship between the private and the public.

As a matter of fact, the history of the usages of compromise from Roman times up to the seventeenth century undertaken in Chapter 3 confirmed the peculiar position of compromise at the intersection of the private and public spheres. We have seen how *compromissum* started off as a private, verbal

---

[5] Paul W. Ludwig (2010), "Without Foundations: Plato's *Lysis* and Postmodern Friendship," *American Political Science Review* 104, no. 1: 135.

contract by which the parties willingly subjected themselves to the arbitration of a third party, the *compromissarius* or *compromissor*. Yet even though the practice was primarily designed to avoid the hassles of a formalized court of justice and the *compromissarius*, unlike a *judex*, was not limited in his judgment by any existing laws, it also depended on and was regulated by the public sphere, which acknowledged its validity and enforced the penalty imposed (*poena*).

As *electio*, a second meaning related to *arbitratio* that was acquired during the Middle Ages, *compromissum* revealed even more forcefully its political potential. Used mostly, albeit not exclusively, as a method of election inside the Church, *compromissum* avoided both the difficult requirement of unanimity and the doubtful election based upon the wills of "the majority and better part" ("*major et sanior pars*"). Each group or community designated its most trusted *compromissarius* and these *compromissores*, after deliberation, made the final election. The acknowledged right to designate a *compromissarius* meant also that a specific community enjoyed formal rights and a formal status as *universitas*, being assimilated with a legal *persona*. Thus, despite the large numbers involved, the existence of these *universitas* ensured the prerequisite of any *compromissum*, that is, the equality of the parties, despite the obvious inequality of the individuals composing them.

Yet the genealogy of compromise has revealed another intriguing fact. Starting with the second half of the sixteenth century and continuing throughout the seventeenth, while the French became increasingly suspicious about compromise, using it consistently with negative connotations, the British embraced it almost as a virtue in a display of topsy-turvy consistency. Obviously, then, in order to understand such a discrepancy in a time of increased intellectual exchanges across the Channel, one had to return to the (self-) apprehension of medieval man before the split in the usage of compromise occurred. What Chapter 4 revealed was the crucial importance of the forgotten dialectic of the individual between the *forum internum* and *forum externum*, formalized sometime around the twelfth century, most likely as a consequence of the Roman distinction between *lex publica* and *lex privata*.

According to the conciliar literature, each individual has two fora. The *forum internum* was considered the forum of freedom and authenticity. There was no mundane jurisdiction over this forum, where the only judges were one's conscience and God. The *forum externum*, on the other hand, defined the individual through his membership to one or more *universitates*, and thereby subjected him to the authority of that worldly community: the Church, the kingdom, the guild, the parish, and so forth. What is essential to understand was that the interplay between the public and private spheres did not occur only among individuals, or only between individuals and *universitas*, but first and foremost *inside* the individual – a vision with long lasting consequences both for the self-identification of the individual and for understanding his relationship with the public sphere. That this dialectic of the individual preceded its formalization by the Catholic Church is beyond doubt.

Troel Engberg-Pederson is among the contemporary authors who seize on the crucial importance of the way a person understands her- or himself and is in turn understood by others for her or his relationship with both ethics and politics: "If ... ancient Greek and Christian thought agree in their understanding of the person, and if it is also the case that this understanding finds expression in their doctrines in ethics and the philosophy of action, then the modern attack on the concept of the person will presumably not be an insignificant affair."[6]

If so, then the distinction between *forum internum* and *forum externum* is better suited to understanding this dialectic between private and public. As a difference clearly located *inside* the individual, it cannot be avoided but has to be confronted head-on. What Christianity had managed to do for medieval man was to make him fully aware not only of the distinction between *forum internum* and *forum externum*, but also to familiarize him to the point of normalcy with the interplay between uniqueness and sameness at work inside the two fora.

In the *forum internum* one is unique because one is unique in God's eyes and has a personal relationship with God that is under no control except that of one's conscience. In the *forum externum*, on the other hand, one is unique for fulfilling an irreplaceable function in the largest (the body of Christ, i.e., the Church) or a smaller (the people, the kingdom, the village or the city, the guild, or the like) *universitas*. Yet one is also the same as others, for in the *forum internum* one is created like everyone else after God's image and shares in the same rationality, while in the *forum externum* one shares with everyone else the quality of membership.

Hence, for classical thinkers (both before and after Christianity) man can never be apprehended as atomistic but always in relationship with others. "Anyone who cannot form a community with others, or who does not need to because he is self-sufficient is either a beast or a god."[7] The classical and medieval insistence that politics must be conducted in accordance with justice and must serve to develop virtues is better understood once one takes into consideration this dialectic at work inside the individual. Because of his *forum externum*, man is by necessity political, belonging to several *universitates*, and virtue ought to inform both of his fora – the *forum internum* as private morality, the *forum externum* as ethical conduct. In the *forum externum* politics met ethics, and the latter could not have been conceived outside its relationship with the former.

As long as the medieval person managed to strike the proper balance between the two fora, he was neither afraid of compromise, nor did he embrace it as a virtue. Compromise remained a useful tool to be used in exceptional

---

[6] Troels Engberg-Pedersen (1990), "Stoic Philosophy and the Concept of the Person," in *The Person and the Human Mind: Issues in Ancient and Modern Philosophy*, ed. Christopher Gill (Oxford: Clarendon Press), 110.
[7] Aristotle (1998), *Politics*, trans. C.D.C. Reeve (Indianapolis: Hackett Publishing), Book 1, ch. 2.

situations. The key to understanding this balanced attitude is to be found in the interplay between the two fora. One's forum internum could not have been represented and/or compromised. As we have seen in the same chapter, as far as the individual (king, magistrate, or layman) was concerned, any type of political representation could involve only the *forum externum*, never the entire person. The king, the pope, the bishop, or the magistrates were represented as occupants of their respective offices. As member of some *universitas*, say 'the people,' any individual was once again represented only insofar as his *forum externum* was concerned. In both cases, the *forum internum* remained off limits and representation preserved its descending character. If the king, Estates, or Parlements represented the people, they still represented something of a superior nature. Since the question of representing individuals never occurred, there was no danger of losing one's uniqueness by accepting the idea of being equally represented alongside with many others. Evidently, one's virtue could not be represented. As a result, there was no fear of compromising oneself, for the *forum internum* remained unaffected.

Thus, thanks to the acceptance of the two fora, the emphasis on belonging went hand in hand with the emphasis on the uniqueness of every human being. The one ensured the other. The two constitutive poles made sense only insofar as they informed each other and yet remained apart. However, the split in the usages of compromise beginning in the second half of the sixteenth century signaled that the challenge brought forward by the series of crises marking that era were differently addressed on either shore of the Channel. The balance tipped toward one pole or the other.

9.2. COMPROMISE AND THE ONE-DIMENSIONAL MAN

The only liberty is the liberty of the office.... The true liberty of the subject has no location in any private realm. (Conal Condren)

As shown in Chapter 5, in France the increased pressure on the *forum externum* as a consequence of the emergent absolutist regime made wider the gap between *forum internum* and *forum externum* to the point of severing them altogether. Both Montaigne and Charron clearly delimit the two facets of the individual, yet the sophistication of the medieval dialectic between uniqueness and sameness not only *between* but also *within* each of the two fora was lost in the process: the *forum internum* became the sole repository of authenticity and uniqueness, while the *forum externum* came to be assimilated with blind conformism. The inner self came to be apprehended as the only 'true' self, while the outer self was relegated to the role of a mere costume. Centripetal individualism was born, which in turn helps us understand the almost obsessive French fear of 'being compromised.' As Charron put it, "*each one of us plays two roles and has two personae, the one alien and in appearance only, the other our own and essential to us. It is important to know the difference* between the skin and the costume."[8] This widening gap between the two fora had a double-edged consequence: on the one hand, the individual became increasingly aware of his uniqueness and suspicious of any perceived attempt to compromise his authenticity, that is, his *forum internum*; on the other hand, fulfilling one's duty in the *forum externum* remained the only basic political requirement.

If by the seventeenth century the French used compromise consistently with negative connotations, it was because *compromissum* as *arbitratio* over the *forum internum* was a risky enterprise. All three requirements for a successful classical compromise – namely the *recognized* authority of the arbitrator to *equally represent* the interests of both parties, the willingness to *accept the risks* involved in a third party's judgment, and the basic *equality of the parties* involved in the dispute – came into question. Not accidentally, all the French usages of compromise involved, in one way or another, the same *forum internum*: "I will not compromise my conscience, my honor, my virtue, or myself" were all ways of saying "I will not accept someone else's arbitration over my *forum internum*, over what makes me first and foremost a unique individual."

As we have seen, any compromise presupposes the equality of the parties, and if the *forum internum* is apprehended solely in terms of uniqueness any arbitration is by definition suspect, creating a false equality between incomparable parties.[9] Thanks to this centripetal individualism one can also better understand the common praise of the people as a conceptual whole and the demise of the people as a "thousand-headed beast." In the former case, 'the people' was characterized essentially by its highest qualities, including reason. In the latter, "individuals, in all their divergences, leave only the lowest parts of their personalities to form a common denominator."[10]

Considering the disconnect between *forum internum* and *externum* during France's absolutist period, the later seemingly schizoid emphasis of the French revolutionaries on both individuals and direct participation and on the cohesion or wholeness of '*le peuple*,' '*la Nation*,' or '*la Republique*' starts to make sense. In this simplified picture there was no longer place for different overlapping *universitates* competing over the same *forum externum* of the individual. *L'État* absolutist was destroyed, but its legacy endured under new names and became even more jealous of what came to be perceived as contender *universitates*, as Tocqueville later observed in his *Old Regime and the Revolution*. Le Chapelier's words from 1789 have resonated throughout modern French history: "*Il n'y a plus de corporation dans l'État; il n'y a plus que l'intérêt particulier de chaque individu et l'intérêt général. Il n'est permis*

---

[8] Pierre Charron (1986) [1604], *De la sagesse*, texte revu par Barbara de Negroni (Fayard), 322; emphasis added.

[9] Georg Simmel (1950), *The Sociology of George Simmel* (New York: Free Press), 222.

[10] Ibid., 32.

à personne d'inspirer aux citoyens un intérêt intermédiaire, de les séparer de la chose publique par un esprit de corporation.[11] ("There are no longer corporations inside the State; there is only the particular interest of each individual, and the general interest. It is not allowed for anyone to inspire citizens to an intermediary interest, separating them from the public sphere by a corporatist spirit.")

If by the eighteenth century French revolutionaries were not willing to compromise, neither were they willing to accept a civil society that might function as bridge between the atomistic individual and the *universitas* of the Nation. They forgot that a bridge has a double function – it connects the two shores and yet at the same time separates them. Neither in theory nor in practice were the French prepared for something like this. Although my research did not go so far, I suspect that from this perspective the period encompassing the French revolution may offer new insights in this matter.

In England, on the other hand, as I showed in Chapter 6, thanks to an array of factors that I have tried to disentangle, the development of a different kind of individualism paralleled the peculiar understanding of representation as representation of individual wills. Here, for the first time, the idea of every individual being represented without rest in the Parliament was widely accepted, along with an insistence on the majority of wills. If in France the distance between the two fora widened to the point of estrangement, in Britain it shrank like Balzac's wild ass's skin (*le peau de chagrin*) to the point of disappearance. The two fora collapsed into each other, and the end of the sixteenth century and the whole of the seventeenth witnessed the birth of modern, one-dimensional man. If Condren is right asserting that in seventeenth-century England the distinction between the private and the public was not a matter of fact, accepted more or less consciously as such by all the participants in the public sphere, it is because the borders between the *forum internum* and *externum* became fluid. If in France centripetal individualism focused almost exclusively on the *forum internum*, in England, as we have seen, the private was equated not with a sphere of independence, but with an absence of right. If "the only liberty was the liberty of office" it was because what mattered first and foremost was the *forum externum*.[12] "The true liberty of the subject has no location in any private realm."[13] As previously discussed, Hobbes made clear both in *De cive* and *Leviathan* that at a close scrutiny *forum internum* had no relevance. What happens "*in foro externo*" is all that matters. Hence, there was no reason for fearing compromise and contracts of wills became the basis of both civil society and government.

---

[11] Quoted in Pierre Rosanvallon (2004), *Le modèle politque Français – La société civile contre le jacobinisme de 1789 à nos jours* (Paris: Editions du Seuil), 13.

[12] Conal Condren (2006), *Argument and Authority in Early Modern England: The Presupposition of Oaths and Offices* (Cambridge: Cambridge University Press), 73.

[13] Ibid., 76.

9.3. COMPROMISE AND CIVIL SOCIETY

What ... makes the idea of civil society so attractive ... is its assumed synthesis of private and public "good" and of individual and social desiderata. (Adam B. Seligman)

The assimilation of compromise with the contract that gave birth to *both* civil society and government presented the Englishmen with another conundrum: since both spheres, the civil and the political, were created as the result of individual wills, was civil society political or not? How should one maintain the distinction between the public and the private since both were artificial creations and the distinction between *forum internum* and *forum externum* was lost? We are still struggling with these questions. In a sense, the new compromise posed the same problem as the classical, Roman one. The latter, as we saw in Chapter 3, was a private verbal contract meant to *avoid* the formalized system of justice and its shortcomings, yet was acknowledged and *reinforced* by that very judicial system, that is, by the public sphere. The new compromise shared this ambiguity. It was apprehended as a *political, public* method devised to *protect* the private from the interference of the public.

Marx was partially right when he grasped that the political is personal and pointed toward "the splitting of man into public and private" as a modern political development due to the rift between the political state and civil society.[14] He also rightly observes that in medieval times "the old civil society had a directly political character." As we have seen, belonging to one or more *universitates* was a constitutive part of man's identity. Family, religion, profession, and the like "defined in this form the relationship of the single individual to the state as a whole, that is, his political relationship."[15] Yet by his failure to notice the dialectic at work inside the individual, his final analysis fails as well – as do his conclusions. The dialectic between *forum internum* and *forum externum* that informed the dialectic between uniqueness and sameness and between public and private *was* in place during the medieval times. Man was not reduced, as Marx and scholars following in his footsteps had it, only to his public dimension as member of some *universitas*. If the political character of civil society was *either* abolished *or* exulted in modern times it was because the private and the public *either* came at odds *or* collapsed.

We are now able to see the irony: once externalized, this forgotten dialectic at work inside of the individual had opposite effects. French centripetal individualism and the complete *separation* between the *forum internum* and *externum* ended in *confusion* between public and private. From now on, more often than not, Europeans will have to face both theoretically and practically the claim that the personal is political. On the other hand, British centrifugal individualism and the *collapse* of the two fora into one-dimensional man, once

---

[14] Karl Marx (2000), "On the Jewish Question," in *Selected Writings*, ed. David McLellan (Oxford: Oxford University Press), 54.

[15] Ibid., 62.

externalized, ended up with the total *estrangement* of the political from the personal, as a counterreaction to the politicization of the personal.

Not surprisingly, given the confusion, Marx's solution for the "individual withdrawn behind his private interests and whims and separated from the community" was the abolition of the state altogether, and thus the effacement of the distinction between public and private.[16] The abolition of private property, the bourgeois family, and so on became then necessary steps. In recent times, the partisans of multiculturalism and some strains of feminism have tackled the same problem from a different direction but with the same confusion between the two fora. One constitutive trait of the individual – gender, ethnicity, religion, or the like – became *the* defining one. In yet another twist, if for Marx and the multiculturalists the distinction between public and private will disappear as the result of the incorporation of the private into the public, for the supporters of an economical, 'realistic' perspective on politics, the difference should disappear by the private taking over the public. Needless to say, for the former, the willingness to compromise is close to zero, while for the latter compromise enjoys an undisputable preeminence.

Obviously, because of its built-in ambiguity, in the actual struggle over the distinction or the lack thereof between public and private, civil society is perceived by many as offering a possible solution to the contemporary crisis as an intermediary between the two. Resurrected in the 1970s, the idea of civil society proved ambiguous enough to appeal not only to liberals, but also to conservatives and neo-Marxists.[17] The "dialectic and tension between public and private, as constitutive of civil society" appeared attractive enough to mobilize the energies of many scholars.[18] Yet if, as we have tried to demonstrate, the intersection of the private with the public *begins* inside the individual, then civil society is more of a distorted projection of this lost dialectic between the two fora of the self.[19] If so, then the way we apprehend civil society is intimately connected with the ways in which we apprehend ourselves. Furthermore, it remains, historically speaking, associated with the ascending understanding of representation.

9.4. COMPROMISE AND ASCENDING REPRESENTATION

C'est le mot de représentation qui, mal compris, a brouillé toutes choses. (It is the word representation which, misapprehended, has confused everything.) (François Guizot)

The widespread feeling of frustration and disappointment experienced in democracies old and new all across the world needs, unfortunately,

---

[16] Ibid., 61–63.
[17] For a review of the literature on the genesis and revival of civil society, see, e.g., Adam B. Seligman (1992), *The Idea of Civil Society* (New York: Free Press).
[18] Ibid., 5.
[19] Intuitively, Seligman acknowledges the intimate connection between the double identity of the individual "as moral agent and as subject without whom no cogent theory of civil society is possible" (5). Yet absent the dialectic of the individual, his argument remains rather weak.

little supportive evidence, yet so far no one has tried to connect it with the uncompromising attitude toward compromise: apparently one can either 'go British' and embrace it as a basic political principle, or 'go French' and abhor it as endangering one's identity. Yet, as we have seen, neither the problem of representation nor the one of compromise can be properly grasped absent the understanding of self-representation.

The loss of confidence in politicians is repeatedly confirmed by polls and translates into record low turnovers at different levels of the electoral process.[20] It has been claimed that citizens' loss of trust in *their representatives* not only raises ethical or philosophical difficulties but also endangers the very functioning of many democratic institutions, affecting the decision-making process.[21] I argue that the problem is misstated. At least partially responsible for this situation is the modern concept of representation as representation of individuals delegating their rights and authority to an individual or a group of individuals. So deeply embedded is the assumption that this is *the only* proper way of understanding political representation that it perpetuates itself practically unchallenged in media, politics, academia, and (probably most importantly) in the ranks of the electorate itself.

Obviously, this is not the only way of handling representation. As shown in Chapter 7, in all French versions of contract theory – both Huguenot and Catholic – there is the insistence that the right to rebellion does not belong to the individual except in two circumstances: if the king or the powers to be required an abdication of faith, involving therefore the precious *forum internum*; or if the sovereign, regardless of how one defines it, endangers the people as a whole, that is, as *universitas*, endangering therefore the *forum externum* of each individual. What is remarkable is that, taking a closer look, other continental thinkers considered 'pioneers' of contractarianism (from Grotius and Althusius to Spinoza and Pufendorf) display the same distrust in individual will as the basis of contract as did their French counterparts. In one way or another they all differentiated between reason and will, public and private, *forum internum* and *forum externum*. Such contracts remained essentially "governmental," that is, between the people as a whole and its rulers. Even more interesting is that such "antiquated" contractarianism proved more suitable for revolutions – from the Glorious Revolution to the American one – than its more modern counterpart, the social contract.

---

[20] The GfK Trust Index for 2008 and 2009 found politicians the least trusted class of professionals, with a general trust level between 14 and 18%, going as low as 6% (Greece) or 10% (France). For comparison, firefighters, teachers, postal workers, and doctors enjoy levels of trust over 80%. Even lawyers appear to be more trustworthy than politicians. In the United States, the levels are somewhat higher (21%) yet they remain the lowest level of trust for any group of professionals. See GfK Custom Research press releases for 2008 and 2009.

[21] See V.A. Braithwhite and Margaret Levi, eds. (1998), *Trust and Governance* (New York: Russell Sage Foundation); C. Offe and U.K. Preuss (1991), "Democratic Institutions and Moral Resources," in *Political Theory*, ed. D. Held (Cambridge: Polity Press).

Only when the difference between the two fora was completely lost and the people came to be reduced to a collection of one-dimensional individuals willingly delegating their rights to 'their' representative(s) can one properly speak of an ascending theory of representation. If so, then Hobbes cannot be considered an author trying to salvage the medieval concept of *universitas* in the face of an increased individualistic trend, but rather as the theoretician who gave the final blow to the classical understanding of both the individual and the individual's relationship with the political sphere, changing the directionality of representation.

There are, however, two problems with this new understanding. On the one hand, as many scholars have already observed, an unprecedented distance between individuals and politics paralleled the empowerment of individuals with rights. One has rights only to hand them over to one's representative. On the other hand, the ascending theory of representation switched the emphasis from reason to will. If reason is disputable, goes the argument, will is not. If, therefore, one is to find an undisputable ground for decision making in a pluralistic society on which all authority is not potentially questionable, it is on will and not reason that one has to focus. And yet, on a closer look, the very concept of will seems at least as problematic to handle in practical situations as reason. (If the ancient Greeks lacked words for 'compromise' and 'representation,' they also lacked one for 'will.')[22] As H. Frankfurt observed, it is peculiarly characteristic for humans to have second-order desires, whereby their will is informed by reason. We do not just will, we also will to will or not to will. "Besides wanting and choosing and being moved to do this or that, men may also want to have (or not to have) certain desires and motives. They are capable of wanting to be different in their preferences and purposes, from what they are."[23]

From this perspective, as shown especially in Chapters 7 and 8, criticisms of the fiction of the representation of wills go a long way back, paralleling or even preceding the success story of the peculiar British understanding of what political representation stands for. The fact that such criticisms were most of the time muted or inaudible should not come as a surprise, considering the overwhelming acceptance of this theory not only by political philosophers, but also by politicians and the electorate itself. And yet, considering same electorate's disenchantment today with the formalized political sphere, these criticisms are worth reconsidering.

At the beginning of the nineteenth century, François Guizot already claimed that the modern concept of representation was seriously flawed. He argued that a representative government ought not to be confounded with the sovereignty of the people understood as a collection of wills. Once "reason, truth and justice" are marginalized in favor of a system based on the representation of individual wills, such an understanding would not be different in principle

---

[22] See Engberg-Pedersen, "Stoic Philosophy."

[23] H. Frankfurt (1971), "Freedom of the Will and the Concept of a Person," *Journal of Philosophy* 68, no. 7.

from an aristocratic government, for "it connects the right to govern, not with capacity, but with birth."[24] Once one declares the individual sovereign in virtue exclusively of his will, whether this individual is a king, a nobleman, or a lay citizen does not matter. "The participation in sovereignty is in each case the result of a purely material fact, independent of the worth of him who possesses it, and of the judgment of those over whom it is to be exercised."[25] The principle of the sovereignty of the people understood as a mere collection of individual wills "is then radically false; for, under the pretext of maintaining legitimate equality, it violently introduces equality where none exists, and pays no regard to legitimate inequality."[26]

Obviously, we do not *really* believe, claims Guizot, in the equality of wills as foundation for a representative government, otherwise we will not prevent children or madmen from voting, for their wills do not differ in nature from that of a full-grown man.[27] We *do believe* instead that some are better equipped than others to seek and discover justice, and to protect the general interests of a society. It is reason, not will, that we take into consideration in any election. We do not *truly* believe that the only legitimate laws for an individual are the ones of which he had willingly consented, for then "this axiom [does] not leave any standing place for organized power." For what if my will changes? "Yesterday my will was the only source of legitimacy for the law; why then should the law remain legitimate when it is no longer sanctioned by my will? Can I not will more than once? Does my will exhaust its rights by a single act?"[28] Answering that the individual 'willingly' accepted the will of the majority as his will won't do either. We do not *really* believe that a majority of wills would transform an unreasonable decision into a reasonable one, nor an evidently unjust law into a just one, for then the despotism of the majority could not be checked.[29] "What we call representation ... is not an arithmetical machine employed to collect and count individual wills."[30] Furthermore, we do not *truly* believe that we stand in relationship with 'our' representatives as a master over his servant (rather the opposite), nor do we truly believe that each and every single one of us can possibly be equally represented by the same individual or group of individuals, for this would deny the very individuality, that is, the uniqueness that we pretend to cherish so much.

So why cling to a model of representation that we don't really believe in, trying to improve something evidently misconstrued from its very basic assumptions?

---

[24] François Guizot (2002), *The History of the Origins of Representative Government in Europe*, trans. Andrew R. Scoble, introduction and notes by Aurelian Craiutu, (Indianapolis, Ind.: Liberty Fund), 60.

[25] Ibid., 57.

[26] Ibid., 60.

[27] Ibid., 293.

[28] Ibid., 288.

[29] For similar positions, see also Alexis de Tocqueville or John Stuart Mill.

[30] Guizot, *The History of the Origins*, 295–296.

In recent years, the idea of individual representation has come once more under scrutiny from a variety of angles. Castiglione and Warren, for example, point out that "from the perspective of those who are represented, what is represented are not persons as such, but some of the interests, identities, and values that persons have or hold."[31] The individual qua person cannot be represented because what is called 'the multiple self" cannot be reduced either to 'my' will, or to only one instrumental form of rationality. If one talks about the 'narrative self,' 'messy self,' 'loosely integrated self,' 'hierarchical self,' 'parallel selves,' and so forth – if, in other words, one is not sure how to present oneself – how can one possibly be re-presented by others claiming to represent many other persons equally as well?[32] Dryzek and Niemeyer propose as a solution "representing discourses not selves" as a way to enhance democratic deliberation.[33] Representatives are then to be apprehended as no longer 'my' representatives but as representatives of different types of discourse I believe in (liberal, social-democrat, and the like). As such, these representatives are not accountable to 'me,' qua individual, but to the ideas and/or the ideals they have promised to uphold while I, qua person, maintain intact the right and the responsibility to directly participate in the ongoing debate.

It goes without saying that such proposals for a drastic reinterpretation of representation raise questions of their own and I far from fully support any one of them in particular. However, I do think that these are all valuable attempts to radically change our way of conceiving and understanding it.[34] By reviewing and contrasting the classical notion of descending representation with its modern counterpart in a time when they still coexisted side by side and the victory of the latter over the former was far from clear, I hope to have offered a historical perspective on 'how we got here,' and by doing so to broaden our sense of possibilities to rethink some deeply embedded assumptions about politics. If one accepts the classical distinction between the two fora, one can 'save' both the uniqueness and the authenticity of the individual and his belonging to one or several *universitates* altogether with the possibility of being represented *but only* insofar as his *forum externum* is concerned.

What today appears obsolete might tomorrow be the key to survival and thriving. Evolution does not follow a linear path in biological or the political realm. The fact that the dinosaurs were so successful for such a long period of time did not guarantee their survival when times changed. It appears that

---

[31] Dario Castiglione and Mark E. Warren, "Rethinking Representation: Eight Theoretical Issues," presented at the Conference on Rethinking Democratic Representation, University of British Columbia, Vancouver (2006: 13), quoted in John Dryzek and Simon Niemeyer (2008), "Discursive Representation," *American Political Science Review* 102, no. 4, 483.

[32] See Joan McCarthy (2007), *Dennett and Ricoeur on the Narrative Self* (New York: Humanity Books); Jon Elster, ed. (1986), *The Multiple Self* (Cambridge: Cambridge University Press); Jennifer Rosner, ed. (2007), *The Messy Self* (Boulder and London: Paradigm Publishers).

[33] Dryzek and Niemeyer, "Discursive Representation," 481–493.

[34] See also David Laycock, ed. (2004), *Representation and Democratic Theory* (Vancouver and Toronto: UBC Press).

times are now changing in politics as well. And sometimes in such periods the winner loses all.

From this perspective, the American case offers a unique chance of analyzing the practical effects of intertwining the ascending and the descending understandings of 'the people' in relationship with the willingness to compromise. I suspect that the heated debates between the supporters of 'virtual' versus 'actual' representation that preceded the Independence War, as well as the clashes between the Federalists and Anti-Federalists or later between the North and the South, can be better grasped using this approach. However, the space of this final chapter can only allow for so much. This would be an entirely new project that has to be postponed.

9.5. RENDER UNTO COMPROMISE ...

We are ambivalent in valuing compromise precisely because we are in the grip of two imprecise, powerful and irreconcilable pictures both of politics and morality. (Avishai Margalit)

The willingness or unwillingness to compromise was – and to a certain extent still remains – closely associated with certain understandings of contractarianism, representation, and self-representation. It would be, however, simplistic and inaccurate to claim that the understanding of the people as a whole is always doubled by a refusal to compromise. As we have seen, during the Middle Ages this was not the case. One can be equal in one respect, and unequal in another. As long as the compromise involved only the aspects in which the parties were equal it did not involve any 'compromising.' Compromise is not an option only when both the representatives and the represented perceive – justified or not – their identity as a group, that is, the values or principles that defines 'them,' as being threatened. Only then, the first prerequisite of any compromise, namely equality, is no longer possible, for the distance between 'us' and 'them' is unsurpassable.

One can now understand why, despite their professed admiration for the Founding Fathers, the Tea Party members and supporters' claimed values echo rather the Anti-Federalist and Confederate positions – state rights (because the contract is understood as being between states) and small central government. Their veneration of President Reagan – who famously said in 1981 that "All of us need to be reminded that the Federal Government did not create the States; the States created the Federal Government" – helps us better understand their uncompromising stance. For reasons that cannot be fairly analyzed in the space of these concluding remarks, Tea Party supporters feel their identity under threat.

In addition, the alienation from 'their' representatives of the Occupy Wall Street demonstrators can be at least in part the consequence of an internalized notion of social contract among otherwise autonomous and equal individuals. The lack of a unifying program or even a clear list of demands is not an accident, but a logical consequence. As long as one keeps thinking that one is fully represented, no politician can possible satisfy the wishes of such a wide variety of individuals identifying themselves in such variety of manners. Their feelings of frustration are real. Their foundations are not.

If these preliminary conclusions are right, today's crisis of *representation* is more of a crisis of *self-representation*.

So what do these findings amount to as far as compromise as a political practice is involved? In Chapter 3 I reviewed some of the most important discussions on compromise, revealing their weaknesses and pointing toward the absence of a genealogy of the concept as possible explanation. Now that this history has at least in part been recuperated, the moment of truth has arrived: Are we better equipped to assess the generally accepted claim that politics is the art of compromise? The short answer is "Yes, if by this art one understands the ability to properly handle compromise." In other words, to render unto compromise the things that are compromise's, and unto politics the things that are politics's. The longer answer, however, requires a more direct question: Can we or can we not disentangle the positive and negative connotations of compromise not only in theory but in practice as well?

To begin with, it is clear that as much as we would like to distinguish between personal and political compromise, any analysis must take both aspects into consideration. Avishai Margalit's recent discussion of 'rotten compromise' captures well, albeit unintentionally, the impossibility of keeping them apart. "I am interested first and foremost in political compromise: compromise between groups and states rather than compromise between individuals.... I shall present individuals making compromises that strongly reflect on them personally, but in these cases the compromise under review is going to be a political compromise, on behalf of a collective."[35] This proves easier to claim than to deliver. For indeed, only a few paragraphs later, after distinguishing between the economic and the religious picture of politics, Margalit goes on to admit: "It is not just politics that is in the grip of the two pictures...; this holds true for morality itself.... We are ambivalent in valuing compromise precisely because we are in the grip of two imprecise, powerful and *irreconcilable* pictures *both* of politics *and* morality."[36]

We know now why it is so: while the two pictures are irreconcilable *today*, this was not always the case. It is because the *dialectic* of the two fora at work *inside* the individual has been lost and replaced with the outside *dichotomy* of 'either-or' that so much concerns contemporary thinkers. Simply put, the private individual has been severed from the public one. Yet, as I have tried to demonstrate, neither centripetal individualism nor its centrifugal counterpart, which developed in order to address the challenges of the sixteenth and seventeenth centuries, have traveled down through history very well. In both cases, the interplay between uniqueness and sameness at work in *both* fora has

[35] Avishai Margalit (2005), "Indecent Compromise, Decent Peace," *The Tanner Lectures on Human Values*, delivered at Stanford University, May 4–5, 1994.
[36] Ibid., 196; emphasis added.

been forgotten. It is difficult to escape what one fears most. Therefore Avishai Margalit is right, although for not exactly the right reasons.

From a somewhat more practical perspective this conclusion forces us – as John Morley put it more than a century ago – to avoid raising compromise from the level of a method of last resort to that of a principle. The fact that under the closest examination, as I have shown, many times the label of compromise is revealed to be misplaced is far from an accident – it is the symptom of a deeper contractarian perspective embedded in the Anglo-American world disposed to see contracts among individuals qua individuals even where there are none.

So far, such considerations may seem too abstract, purely theoretical, and essentially disconnected from 'the real world' of politics. It is time therefore to put them to work in concrete situations. There are plenty of practical examples of political compromises that could be discussed here using these analytics: compromises in Congress, in the Arab-Israeli conflict, among states in the European Union, or among parties in a multi-party system, and so forth. Yet such an all-encompassing review is not the aim of this enterprise and can be postponed for further studies. A few examples will demonstrate that the same approach can be used in a variety of apparently different case scenarios.

Consider probably the best known, the most-used and the most-analyzed example of a 'bad compromise' in modern times – the Munich Agreement of September 1938 between Hitler, Chamberlain, Daladier, and Mussolini.[37] It has been condemned from a variety of perspectives: it showed a lack of foresight and did not prevent the war, or was a concession to a 'bully,' a constrained bargain, a misplaced trust, and so on. But, as I showed in Chapter 2, a careful revision of all these accusations can be easily dismantled. The problem with any political decision, and especially with compromise, is that one cannot foresee all its consequences, and yet, as Max Weber put it, one has to live with them. If, argues Avishai Margalit, the same demands were to be made by Walther Rathenau on behalf of the Weimar Republic in the name of Sudeten Germans' right to self-determination, the compromise would have been considered at least acceptable, if not praiseworthy. Therefore, he concludes, the Munich agreement is "a rotten compromise, but it is rotten not because of its content, but because it was Hitler who signed it." How so? Unlike other contemporary authors who considered compromise exclusively from an 'objective' perspective, Margalit realizes rather intuitively that the person involved in a political compromise matters as much as the community or the system it stands for. Not the content of the compromise was therefore to be blamed, nor an error of political judgment, but what Hitler *both was and stood for*, which was fairly obvious by the end of the thirties: radical evil. Therefore, "compromise with Hitler was a compromise with someone who undermined morality itself."[38]

---

[37] For some modern considerations on this compromise, see the literature reviewed in Chapter 2.
[38] Margalit, "Indecent Compromise," 194.

One can now understand better why Chamberlain's agreement was a rotten compromise. By focusing solely on sameness and the assumed equality in the *forum externum* – both Hitler and Chamberlain were, after all, the leaders/representatives of two European sovereign countries and they were both supposedly acting inside a larger, conventionally accepted diplomatic system – he completely disregarded the obvious inequality that affected both fora. Chamberlain and Hitler stood as representatives of radically different political systems. Furthermore, Hitler defined himself explicitly as the representative of the entire German people, the embodiment of its *Geist*. For him, therefore, compromise was nothing but an empty word, useful only as a 'make-believe' to mislead. Chamberlain, on the other hand, was (as even Churchill, his political adversary, agreed) a basically honest human being. He did not relish the compromise, but since he viewed himself essentially as an office-holder on a mission, he chose to disregard his inner voice and assumed a 'practical' perspective on the matter on hand. As we know by now, practicality does not always pay off: Chamberlain ended up by compromising both the democratic nations he stood for and himself.

Consider another obvious case: Why are compromises almost always impossible in cases of religious and/or interethnic conflicts? Why have the Arab-Israeli or Bosnian conflict – to take just two such examples – proved extremely refractory to political compromise? To argue, as Margalit does, that they involve some religious perspective on politics, however accurate, does not take us too far. The answer is even more straightforward – these types of conflicts involve a perceived threat to one's identity. Let me repeat: to compromise means to make oneself equal to someone else and to accept an arbitration that might threaten one's identity. Compromise means the recognition of the other as equally entitled to her or his own claims. It confers legitimacy. As long as this identity is apprehended in terms of religion, ethnicity, race, or the like, obviously such requirements are impossible to meet. In both fora, it is the uniqueness that is endangered when engaging the other, not the sameness.

A core of sanguine political compromises consists of disputes that involve more than interests, narrowly conceived. Alongside interests, it also involves principles and ideas (moral, political, aesthetic, religious). What is negotiated in such serious disputes, beyond interests, is sometimes the very identity of the sides to the disputes. *By 'identity' I do not mean reputation in the eyes of others but self-identification.* A serious sanguine compromise involves not just recognition of the other but also self-recognition. This is perhaps the sense in which Marshal Pétain was accused in his trial: that when he concluded the armistice with the Nazis, he compromised the historical identity of France.[39]

Once again, Margalit proves right, but now we can better understand why. The fact that they are, in Margalit's terms, "sanguine compromises" merely serves as a magnifying glass to reveal their essence. The political leaders

---

[39] Ibid., 203; emphasis added.

involved in such disputes are not representatives of their people in the ascending sense that we take for granted. They do not represent individuals – that would make compromise almost natural. They represent 'their people' or 'their organizations' as conceptual communities defined by their ethnicity, religion, nationality, and so on. Their mandate of representation, regardless of how it was obtained (elections, designation), comes from above and it is therefore in a sense imperative, whether implicitly or explicitly. The fact that Marshal Pétain was elected by a majority or was more or less (self-) appointed to represent *La France* was as irrelevant from this perspective then as now. If such representatives compromise what they are meant to represent, they compromise both the identity of the group *as such*, that is, as the embodiment of race, ethnicity, and the like, and themselves.

But if compromise is impossible under these circumstances, how is it that French-German relationships have long since passed this phase or, to offer just one more example, that the Romanian-Hungarian tensions that exploded in Transylvania in 1990 did not amount to a 'Yugoslavisation' of Romania, as many political analysts predicted at that time? What happened in such cases that did not in others? The answer, I suspect, is to be found once again in the self-identification that occurred in the *forum externum,* which in turn affected the *forum internum*. It was not that the *universitas* has changed – the French remained French, and the Germans, Germans. Romanians did not start to identify as Hungarians, nor did the Hungarians begin to think of themselves as Romanians. The *forum externum* did change, however. It came to be apprehended as more than just the French, the German, the Romanian or the Hungarian. Once the French and the Germans started to perceive themselves as Europeans as well, as partners in the construction of the European Union, or once Hungarians and Romanians started to *aspire to identify* themselves and to be identified first and foremost as Europeans, compromise became not just necessary but possible. Their *forum externum* changed. From the European perspective one was or wanted to be an equal member in the same larger *universitas*. Self-identity was therefore no longer threatened. One might be unequal at one level, yet equal at another. And in the dimension in which one feels equal (in this case, as Europeans) one can compromise without being compromised.

Such developments indicate two things: First, that the *forum externum* is not a given but is subject to change. As we have seen, even medieval man was subject to several *universitates* – Church, guild, social class, and the like. Which was most influential in its dialectic with the *forum internum* was to some extent a matter of choice. What is important to emphasize here is that if the definable *universitas* might be a matter of choice, belonging to *some* community is not. One can choose one's belonging but not the belonging itself. Second, that all modern interpretations beginning with Hobbes that take as given that the only alternative to compromise is violence have no support in reality. In effect, whenever we are talking about political compromise, violence is not an option.

Violence does not begin where *political compromise* ends; violence only starts where *politics* ends.

Consider the case of the domestic, fiercely battled disputes over gay marriage or abortion – they are cases of compromise at least as sanguinary as those involving ethnicity, religion, and the like. Both involve problems of self-identification. The case of the political disputes over gay marriages makes the transition from the first couple of examples to the next, demonstrating that far from being abstract theory, the approach that I propose is in effect very much in use, albeit unconsciously. What changed from a few decades ago when homosexuality was taboo, to today when it is largely accepted? Why are people today more willing to accept 'civil unions' than 'gay marriages' and yet still unwilling to find a political compromise on this issue? To find the answer one must go back to the forgotten dialectic of the individual.

On the one hand, we have the supporters of gay marriages – people who identify themselves as homosexual and/or believers in human rights, including the right to choose one's partner regardless of gender. On the other, we have those (mostly religious believers) who, while agreeing on generic human rights, still argue that homosexuality is unnatural, a sin, or both. Yet despite their hard-fought disputes, both parties argue within the same classical framework: How does one define oneself first and foremost? As gay? Christian? American? An abstract human being? From the wide array of options that one has today, which is most compelling in one's *forum internum*? More precisely, which of the several *universitates* has the strongest hold on it?

Both parties agree that the rights of the human being, any human being, are unquestionable. This is a relatively new development but undeniable. The problem therefore is not here. As abstract human beings, or even as generic Americans, both camps could agree to compromise, for they are equal. The dispute therefore is not over rights but over words and thus over identification. If the wording 'gay marriage' appears more threatening than 'civil union,' it is because it threatens the identity of the believer not as a human being but as a believer. If homosexuals are not satisfied with 'civil unions' regardless of rights and insist upon the right to marriage, it is because they want *this* difference extinct. This is the conundrum that must be addressed regardless of the side one takes: What is the proper relationship between uniqueness and sameness inside and between the *forum externum* and the *forum internum*? Obviously, if there is a relationship at work between *and* within these two pairs, there is some space left to maneuver. And this is exactly the space where politics comes (or should come) into play.

In the case of abortion, however, the matter is further complicated by the presence of a third party, that is, the fetus. *It is an impossible compromise because it is a compromise turned upside-down.* If a classical compromise involved the presence of neutral third party as arbitrator, the modern one presupposes two parties arguing over a third with no say. As many commentators on compromise have already observed, this is one of the cases where people are least willing to compromise because it involves value systems. So far, so good. But once again, this would not take us very far unless we acknowledge that at the core of the dispute is more than this. It is an obvious *inequality* between the parties that makes compromise impossible. The pro-life supporters identify themselves not only as representatives of a principle, but also as representatives of someone else, that is, the fetus, while the pro-choice partisans, supporters of a principle as well, explicitly deny the humanity of the third party and (for obvious reasons) therefore cannot claim to be representatives of someone else. Since one party stands for two and one just for oneself, the equality presupposed by compromise is impossible. And yet nobody in any liberal-democratic country ever suggested seriously that the only alternative to a political compromise over abortion rights would be open violence. Needless to say, I leave aside the unfortunate examples of murder or attempted murder, for two reasons: not only do they not qualify as 'politics,' but also they are examples of pathological cases of self-identification. When in 2010 a man flew his plane into an IRS building, nobody seriously considered his action an alternative to political compromise over taxes.

Where do these conclusions leave us? Political compromise is possible and suitable in some circumstances and impossible in others. It all amounts to identification, which is essentially a political matter as much as it is a moral one, given the interplay between the two fora, *externum* and *internum*. As long as we fail to recuperate this dialectic and stubbornly work within the paradigm of the one-dimensional man, we are doomed to run not in circles but in a downward spiral, with frightening prospects.

9.6. THE FUTURE OF POLITICAL COMPROMISE

Medieval knighthood worked in this way, for example.... All members of the association were equal in matters relating to knighthood. This gave the ministerial vassal a position which had nothing to do with his duties of office, and rights which did not stem from his lord. The differences of birth between nobility, freemen, and vassals were not thereby eliminated. But these differences were 'intersected' by a new line of division which was established by the association of all those who were bound together as equals in accordance with the rights and customs of knighthood. (Georg Simmel)

To talk in the Internet era about the lessons to be learned from the Dark Ages might seem something like a bad joke. And yet, as I have tried to demonstrate, there are plenty of things to be learned once one transcends the out-of-fashion attitude. In effect, it is precisely the Internet era that makes the lesson more actual than ever before. The increasing sentiment of dissatisfaction with the formalized political sphere present throughout the world has something to do with the unconscious rethinking of civil society thanks to informal networks of socialization that in many ways mimic those established in medieval times. Both types escape state control, for different reasons to be sure. Both grew naturally, not by design but as a matter of fact. Both force us to rethink the distinction between the private and the public and the question of (self-) identification. While the formalized sphere of politics remains stuck in a seventeenth-century paradigm, a new civil society is growing because a new self-identification is developing. Simply put, a new apprehension of the self is possible right under our eyes.

Yet as long as we keep reinforcing the 'realistic' perspective according to which politics ought to embrace compromise not as a punctually useful method, but as a principle, we will feed the growing sentiment of disaffection, which most likely will be channeled, as it was in the 1930s, into worrisome, undemocratic, and violent paths. When an illiterate clown becomes a parliamentary representative in Brazil or a party called "The Best Party" that mocks formalized party rhetoric gets incredible traction in Iceland, it is sign that the so-called political realism is no longer realistic. The gap between politicians and the electorate is growing at an incredible pace and it won't be bridged by political or academic gimmicks. The problem is not outside the individual and cannot therefore be solved via some well-crafted but objective measures. The problem is inside the individual, inside each and every single one of us, and therefore it is on this subjective perception and self-perception that one should focus.

Since the understanding of political compromise is intimately related with the relationship between private and public, the apprehension of civil society becomes crucial. Cary J. Nederman is right when he asserts that Hegel's objection to various attempts to place civil society – here understood as the realm of the abstract self-centered individual – at the core of politics is "devastatingly simple": "the true child of civil society would, at the first sign of war, 'eschew military service and betake himself, with his family and [movable] property, to a safe shelter.'"[40] Since he does not (or at least not yet), it is clear that the understanding of politics mainly as a contract among abstract individuals, no matter how highly praised and accepted via various media, remains an artificial construct – and so does the understanding of politics as the art of compromise. Hence the dissatisfaction.

Not only is this child of civil society perpetually dissatisfied – no matter how much he possesses, it is never enough – but the amassing of tangibles becomes his single goal and purpose in life, to the detriment of his other social obligations, for instance, toward the state. The corporation serves the very definite function of acknowledging the intrinsic worth of the individual "as a somebody" – just because he is a member of the corporation, and not on the basis of some external and purely contingent mark of achievement. The corporation stands as a solid foundation for the individual who participates in the proceedings of civil society.[41]

---

[40] Cary J. Nederman (2009), *Lineages of European Political Thought: Explorations along the Medieval/Modern Divide from John Salisbury to Hegel* (Washington, D.C.: Catholic University of America Press), 332, quoting Shlomo Avineri (1972), *Hegel's Theory of the Modern State* (Cambridge: Cambridge University Press), 195.

[41] Ibid., 339.

Nederman goes on, asserting that the corporation, following Hegel, gives the individual "a sense that he has a voice that can be heard, that he can have some measure of direct impact on the political structure of modern society."[42] Yet his insistence on the reconstruction of corporatist civil society is, I think, too much biased in favor of the *forum externum*. It is not the *forum externum* that is missing in the contemporary man, nor his *forum internum*. It is the dialectic between the two. The one-dimensional man does not in reality exist. His two fora are still there. He still has depth, he still belongs. Trying to artificially recreate by academic fiat a corporatist civil society would be an impossible and futile task. The problem, therefore, is one of remembering and of re-apprehension of the self. It is, in other words, a subjective one.

The Internet era has created opportunities previously unimaginable for rethinking civil society and the self. At the beginning of the twentieth century, Georg Simmel noted the paradox: the modern person is so strongly individualistic, so strongly unique, precisely because she or he can choose to belong to and identify with several groups.

[T]he larger the number of groups to which an individual belongs, the more improbable is it that other persons will exhibit the same combination of group-affiliations, that these particular groups will 'intersect' once again [in a second individual].... Such multiplicity of groups implies that the ideals of collectivism and individualism are approximated to the same extent. This community provides an organizational form for his activities, and it offers in this way all the advantages of group-membership.... On the other hand, the specific qualities of the individual are preserved through a combination of groups which can be a different combination in each case.[43]

Thanks to the new social networks, the multiplication of such belongings has increased dramatically. However, a never-ending range of options proves to be both a blessing and a curse. Civil society is not necessarily strengthened by this multiplicity, first and foremost because most of these associations preserve their strictly instrumental character. (Simmel himself fails to distinguish between communities, associations, and groups.) When presented with such a wide variety of associations, the contemporary individual is also presented with a conundrum: she or he can choose to belong to any combination of these associations but cannot decide by which criteria he or she should guide the selection. Freedom of choice in the *forum externum* can become freedom of criteria. Thus, the fanatic may easily intersect with the zombie – something that in recent times we have seen more often than not.

In the seventeenth century, Aloys, a peasant from Provence, identified himself as Catholic, the son of ... from the village ..., a Provençal and a Frenchman. When it came to self-identification by membership in the *forum externum* and therefore to the extent to which he was willing to compromise *and with whom*,

---

[42] Ibid.
[43] Georg Simmel (1955), *Conflict and the Web of Group Affiliations*, trans. Kurt H. Wolff and Reinhard Bendix (London: Free Press of Glencoe), 140, 162.

most likely these different conceptual communities were ranked in this order. In the twenty-first century his descendant has a much vaster array of options as far as his *forum externum* is concerned. Not only can he still be all of the above, though probably ranked differently, but he can also perceive himself as a European enjoying EU subsidies of French farmers, a member via the Internet of Greenpeace and, say, a militant, via Facebook, in a movement for the reform of the Catholic Church. And yet none of these hypostases appears to be entirely satisfactory. He is frustrated with his political representatives, from President Nicolas Sarkozy down to the local councilwoman, Magali, he had voted for, but he does not know why he feels compromised or alienated. He gives up voting and participating in the town-council meetings, if he ever did, because he feels closer to his Internet Greenpeace buddies and his Facebook friends fighting to reform the Catholic Church. He donates money to supporters of the Provençal language, yet the website where he uses his credit card is set up in English by a Polish immigrant. He feels that he is more efficient on the Internet than in his town-council meetings. He complains over the Internet, where his web-buddies are listening in the same way that Aloys's buddies sympathized with him at the local tavern several hundred years ago.

It is difficult to say how this crisis of representation and self-representation will play out. It is entirely possible that such a multiplication of virtual belongings will forge not only a new *forum externum* but also a new understanding of the *forum internum* and of the dialectic between uniqueness and sameness at work within both. Yet there are no guarantees: the other, less rosy prospect of the individual going astray in the abyss between the fanatic and the zombie is still possible. Let us remember though: if compromise is arbitration, it presupposes a judgment as well.

Index